RE
VIVIS
CENCE

RE VIVIS CENCE

PHOTOGRAPHS
BY ANDREA BOTTO

A BRIDGE OVER GENOA

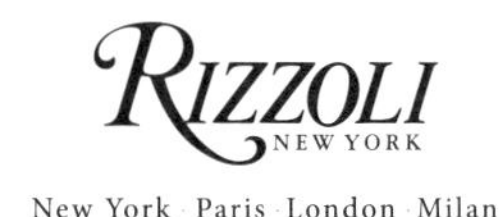

RIZZOLI
NEW YORK

New York · Paris · London · Milan

Table of Contents

A RACE
AGAINST TIME

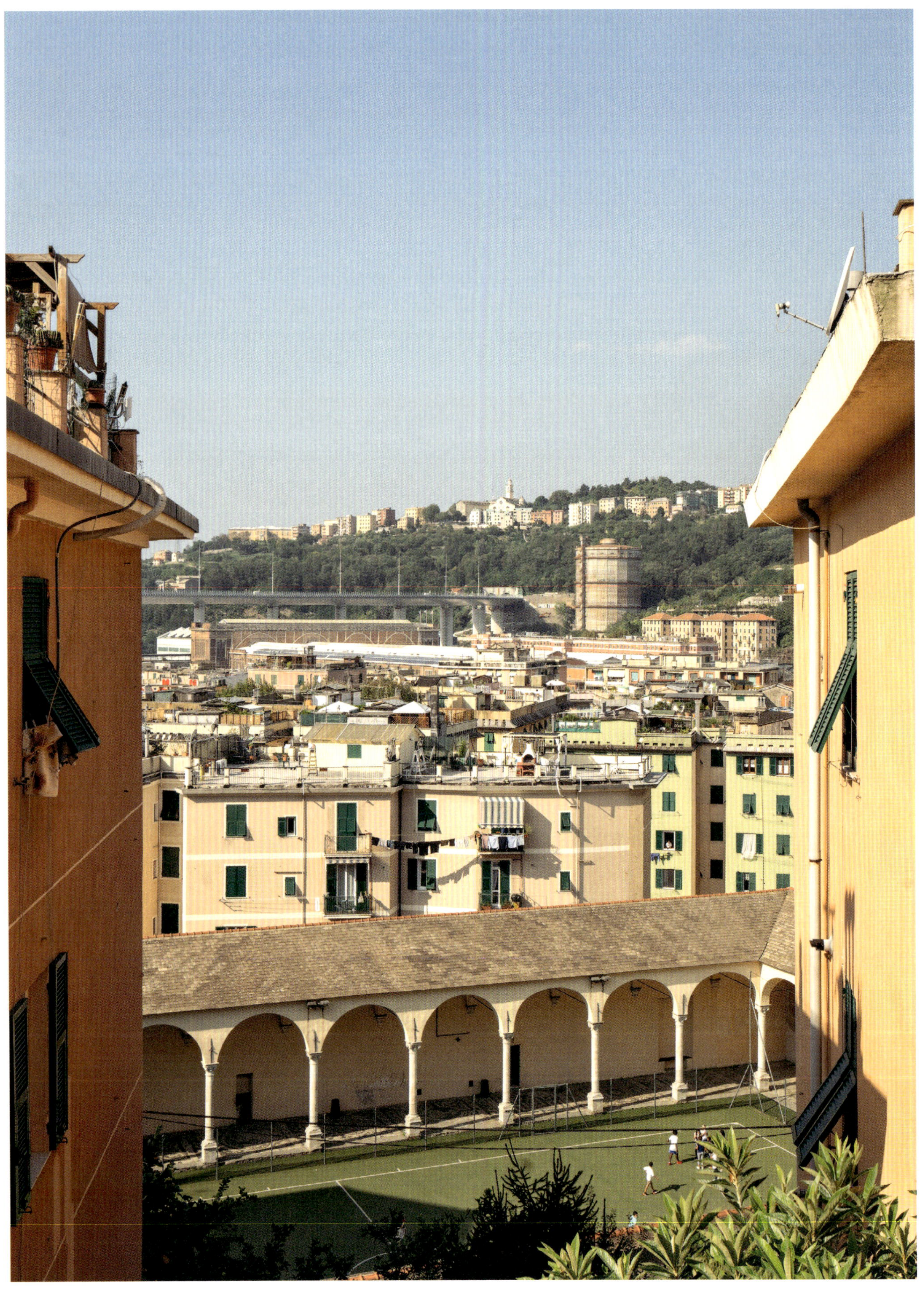

Roberto Carpaneto CHIEF EXECUTIVE OFFICER
RINA CONSULTING

For me, someone who spent their adolescent years in this part of the city, between Campasso and Certosa, the collapse of the bridge was a massive tragedy: for the victims and for the scar that was inflicted on the neighborhood, the city, and the entire country. As an engineer who has followed projects all around the world, the thought of having to make a contribution to the reconstruction of the bridge sprang to my mind immediately. Equally immediate was the feeling that the disaster could and had to become the trigger for a revival of the city, the region, our country, seeing how that event had reverberated around the world.

When we began working on the project in December 2018, I knew that the keys to success could only lie in competence and collaboration. The competence of RINA, which was necessary for this project, is rooted in the tradition of "engineering consulting," which has always brought to the fieldwork teams that are very well prepared, and especially integrated, from a technical and managerial point of view. The integration between different competencies and the speed with which that integration develops at the service of the project and our clients underpins our success all around the world.

The collaboration with the Commissioner, the structure, and with the companies charged with actually doing the work in the field, had to be the next step. RINA had to work as both a partner and a contractor, making available all the expertise and experiences of the group to the members of the team, so that the bridge could be demolished and rebuilt safely, properly, and in as little time as possible.

In this process, time was the "enemy that had to be beaten." That is why we brought into the field an integrated team, a strong one fueled by a Project Management capable of executing all the procedures and all the processes required to implement this infrastructure.

The planning of the activities, the revision of the project documentation, the authorizations, the coordination of the various phases and the many actors involved, the control over time and costs. All of this took place with a multidisciplinary work team capable of working in parallel, with no lag time, twenty-four hours a day, seven days a week. That way we squeezed the time frame, guaranteeing quality, attention, and the level of depth that were required, managing to reconcile the need to work fast with the imperative of doing everything properly and safely.

RINA added to the Project Management team the groups dedicated to the Works Management and the Coordination of Safety on the building site during the implementation phase, both for the demolition and the construction. It also added a large team of inspectors who worked in the plants scattered around the country, where the steel, that would eventually become the bridge, was taking shape. The awareness of the importance of the task to be done was always everyone's prevailing sentiment, both in the offices and on the site itself. A sentiment that we also shared with the companies that demolished and then rebuilt the bridge. This made it possible to work in an atmosphere of collaboration, based on genuine teamwork, even when dealing with the most complex situations that arose as the phases were being implemented. In addition to the expected difficulties of a project that was so complicated to manage in an emergency situation, there were the problems caused by an unexpected and violent pandemic affecting the entire world. Because of this, it was imperative that we immediately coordinate preventative measures, enhancing what had from the outset been the guiding principle of the entire building site: to safeguard the health and safety of the workers, the community, and the continuation of the work itself.

As Project Manager for the company that was responsible for coordinating the safety of the entire building site from the first day to the last, I always wanted these objectives to be maintained 100 percent. Step by step, as the project developed, we clearly perceived that even the Genoese people felt they were a part of the building process. We felt them close to us, as if they were the "fans" of our team.

They recognized that all of us were doing our best, even when we were forced to ask the citizenry to make sacrifices related to our building site's inevitably invasive operations inside the city itself. There was trust between the Genoese and the building site, and we can clearly see the result of this rise up—solid and lightweight—in the valley.

As RINA, we have succeeded in delivering the contribution that we had promised to make in the days right after the Ponte Morandi collapsed. Good thing.

ROBERTO CARPANETO

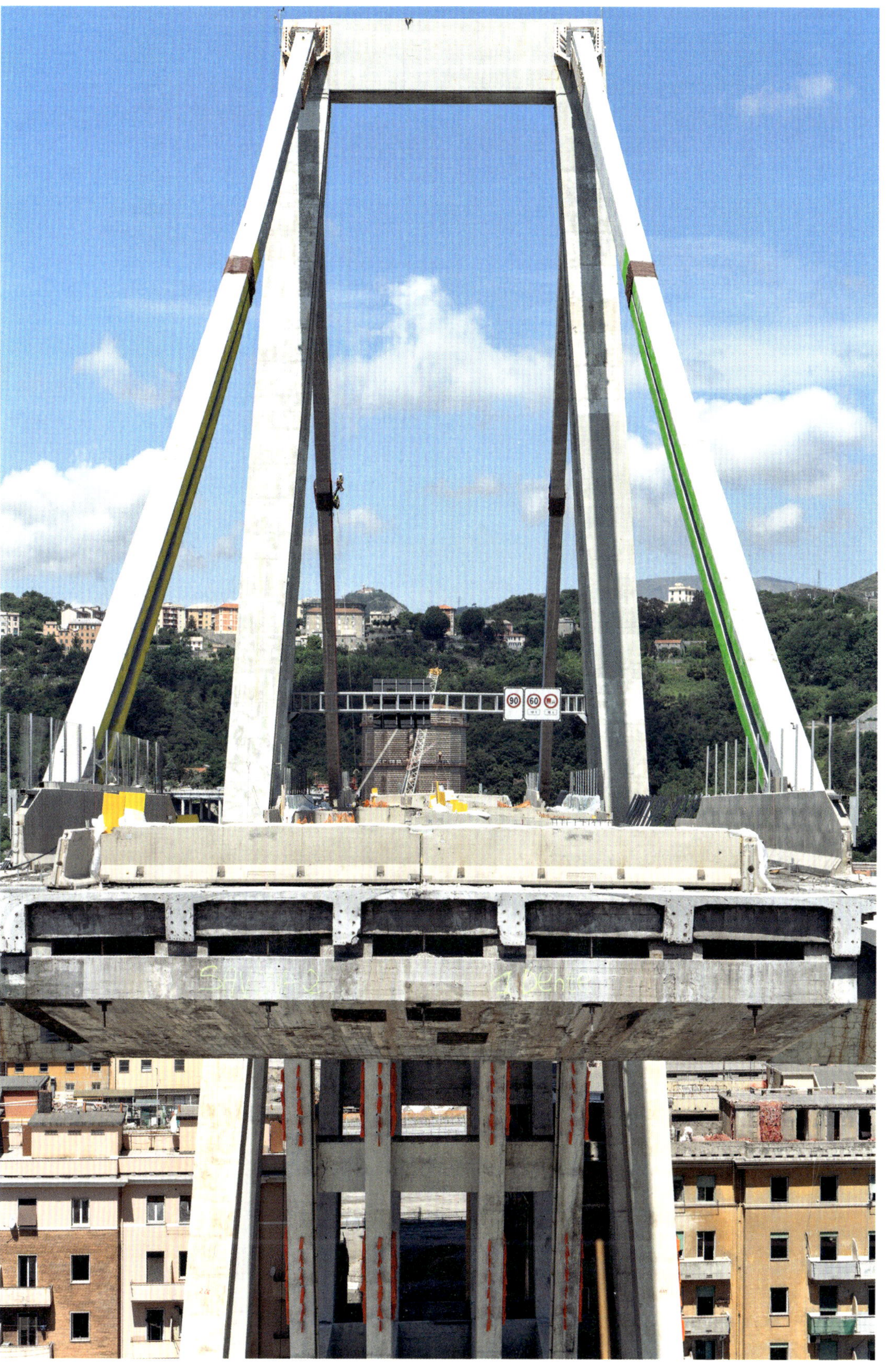

THE BRIDGE
AND THE CITY

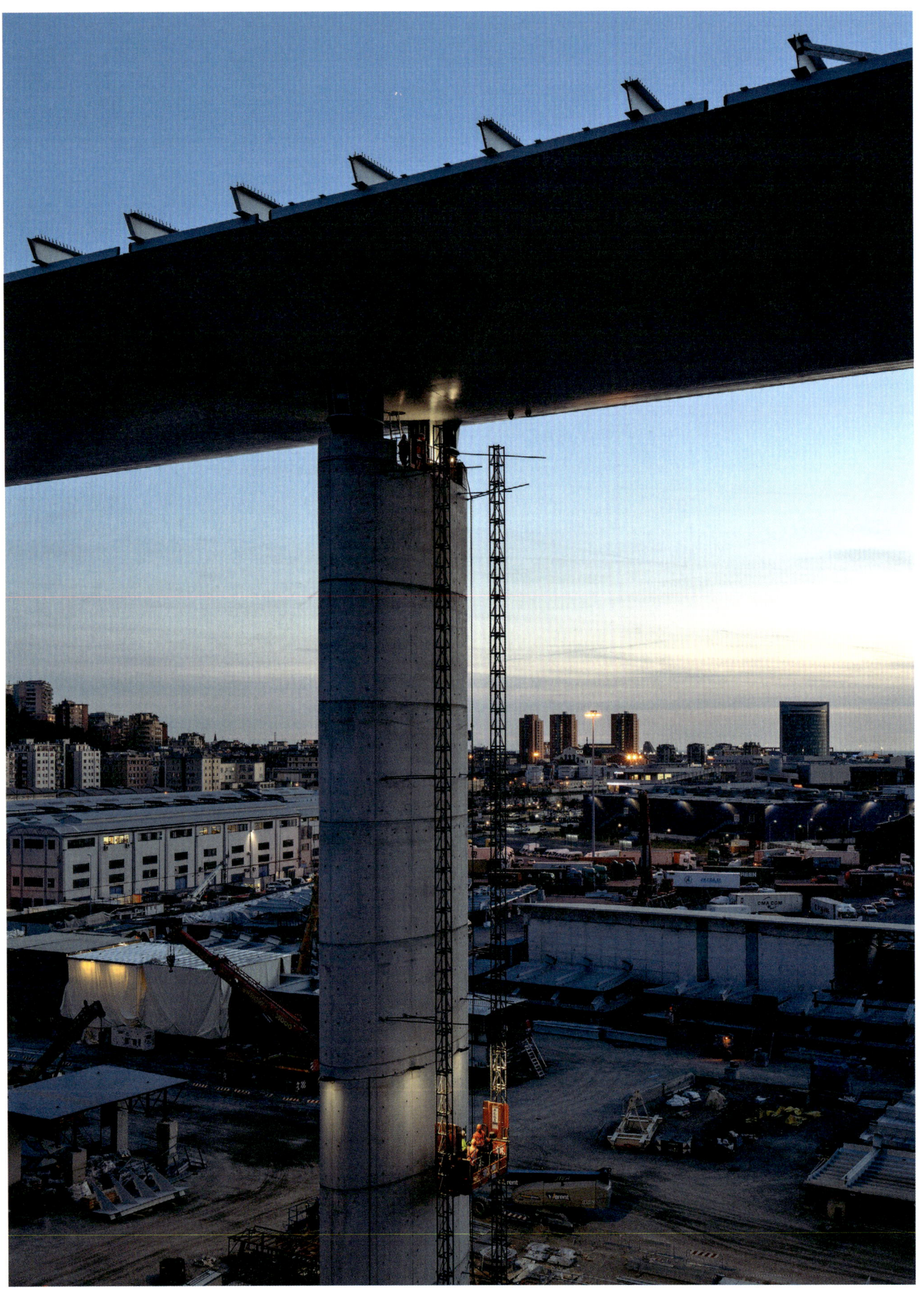

Two years after the tragedy of August 14, 2018, Genoa has its bridge once again. That rainy mid-summer's day that will forever be etched in the hearts and minds of the Genoese people, when forty-three innocent souls lost their lives, has become a milestone in the recent history of our city. Nothing will ever be the same again. However, the desire to roll up our sleeves and forge ahead has never wavered. Also and above all in the memory and the respect of those who are no longer with us.

Building a bridge in the right time frame, with the proper budget, a bridge that would be solid and sober at the same time, was the commitment we undertook from the very start, fully aware that what had happened should never happen again.

Genoa never stopped, thanks to a road system that, with extreme urgency, was immediately modified to guarantee mobility in spite of the absence of the Ponte Morandi. Today, the ribbon of road more or less one kilometer long that once again joins the two parts of the city has become much more than a highway route, born from the plan given to Genoa by the architect Renzo Piano. It has become the symbol of something greater: of the difficulties that can be overcome, of the tragedies that turn into redemption, of a country that—lest we forget, even after Covid—is capable of doing. And doing well.

I also believe that the relationship between the bridge and the city, now rediscovered, is also made up of the relationship that was created in these (almost) two years, with the building site for the demolition and the reconstruction of the new Polcevera Viaduct.

The story of the building site, told on these pages, is a great story made up of lots of smaller ones. It is the story of the demolition, first, and the reconstruction, later, of a work that is an example of ingeniousness and high technology. It is the story of the many hands, faces, lives of those who worked ceaselessly. It is the story of the intelligence and the perseverance of those who designed, planned, improved, and implemented. It is also the story of those who, from the window of their homes, saw the building site change, evolve. Of those who saw the bridge grow, day by day.

A presence that was at times cumbersome, notwithstanding the attempts to reduce to a minimum the impact of the forced cohabitation with the works underway. Nonetheless, the citizens understood and collaborated. It is an example of cohabitation that becomes a model to be exported for other works as well, projects for which it is necessary to build in a highly urbanized fabric such as the one we found ourselves working in. There are many moments in this extraordinary story that I will never forget.

The day when the detachment of the first part of the deck of the Ponte Morandi began, using a diamond wire to cut it, and, for the first time ever in the history of civil engineering, it was lowered to the ground using strand jacks, a system that had always been used to raise, but never to lower. The day of the controlled explosion of piers 10 and 11. Above all, again on that day, the moment when we told the people who had been displaced that they could finally go home, that there was no longer any risk. The day when we sailed to the barge that was still moored off the shores of the port of Genoa to see the sections of the new viaduct that were arriving.

The day we elevated the first deck, and the day when the last one was put in place and the structure was complete. Lastly, on the day of the inauguration of the new Genova San Giorgio bridge, we were all very moved. Among all these fundamental phases, well-represented in the photographs chosen for this publication, there were lots of days filled with meetings, rela-tions, encounters: everything that was needed to get here. Sometimes with great effort, at times having to face huge and small difficulties along the way. But always with the determination of getting across the line. Thanks to all those who made it possible for the dream of thousands of Genoese citizens to come true.

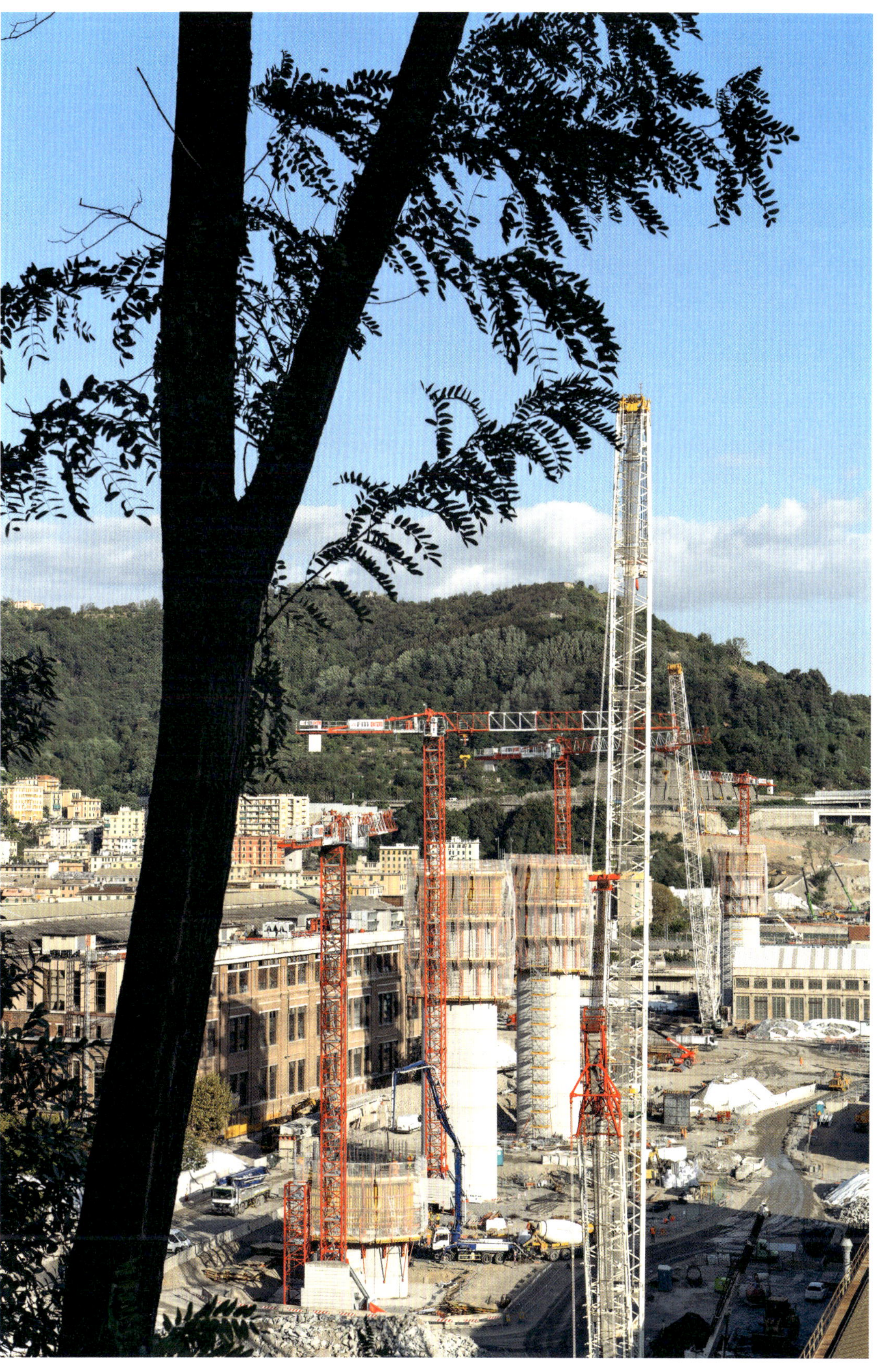

A BUILDING SITE OF RESPONSIBILITY

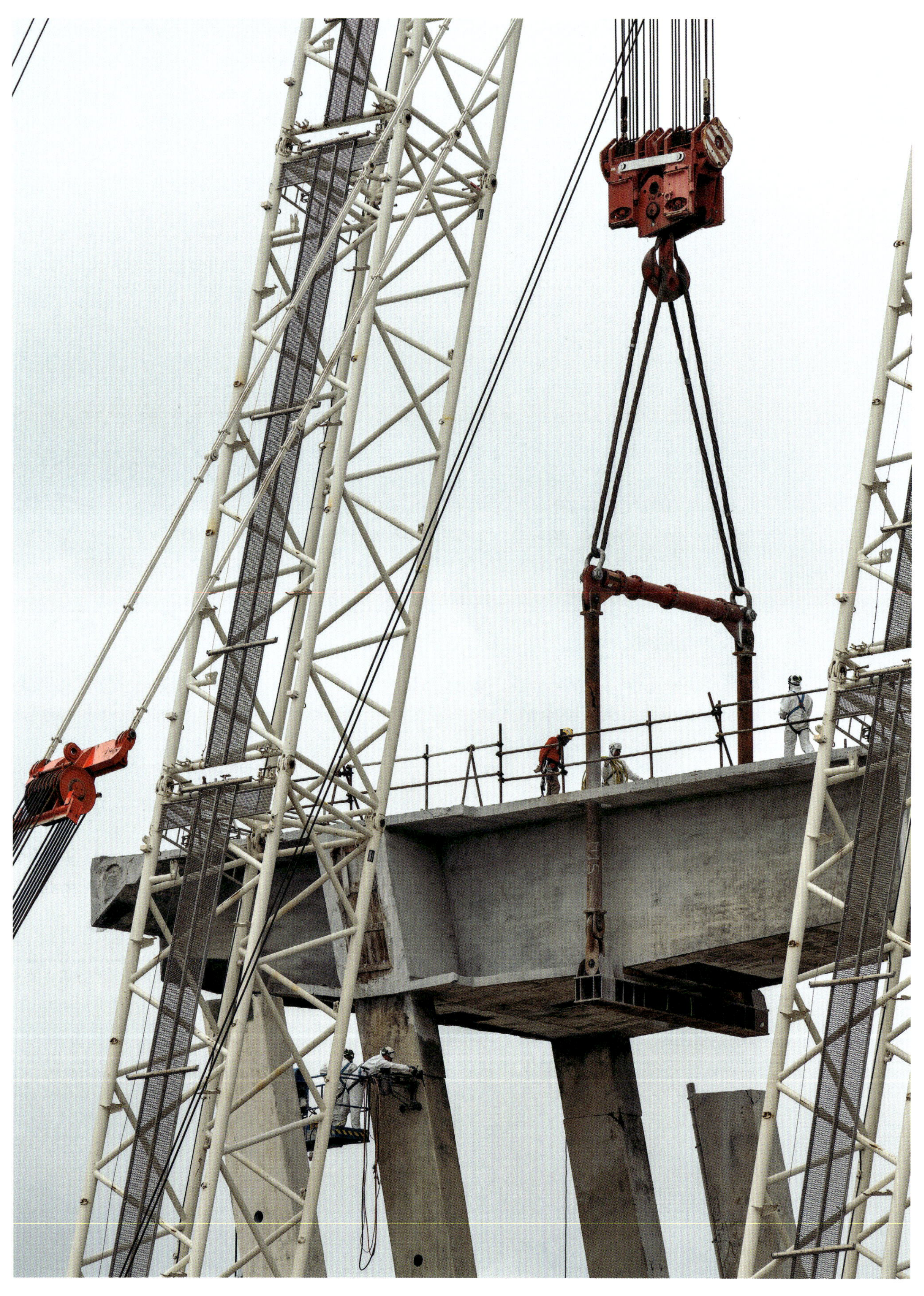

Ugo Salerno

PRESIDENT AND CHIEF EXECUTIVE
OFFICER RINA

On August 14, 2018, the first emotions I felt were ones of despair and incredulity. A huge tragedy, for the victims and also because it was the end of one of the symbols of Genoa. In truth, Ponte Morandi had always been imposing, yet silent. It was a presence that was almost taken for granted, whose tangible but also symbolic importance was fully perceived perhaps only by its absence, by the immense void left by pier 9 and the huge stays that had collapsed into the Polcevera riverbed and on the surrounding streets.

As a company, we felt the duty to collaborate, with the desire to make a significant contribution to the solution to the problem that had led to the collapse of the bridge. But ours was not just generosity spurred by emotion. We were also aware that we were capable of offering the best contribution possible to the project, from every point of view: resources, competence, skills. It was in this spirit that we joined the project: our idea was to contribute to the success of a unique work. Not because of the infrastructure in itself. The work was unique because it involved demolishing and building, at the same time, in an emergency situation and with a tight deadline, and within an urban context that had been scarred by tragedy and by the problems that had derived from it. Responsibility, commitment, and enthusiasm were the factors that allowed us to create an atmosphere of harmony and collaboration, even under circumstances that were anything but simple. There were problems, of course: technical ones that are typical of every building site, but also ones due to external elements, such as climatic extremes or the need to organize work during a pandemic. Pressure and obstacles were perhaps what supported even more the atmosphere of cooperation with the client, between the different companies, with regard to the public administration, and on down to the bodies responsible for monitoring the works. A combination of exceptional factors for one unique project.

The day of the inauguration the architect Renzo Piano described the building site for the bridge as "the most beautiful building site" he had ever worked in. I am absolutely certain this is true, but I also believe that this should be the norm. If we succeed in getting all those who work to understand the importance of their role and of the infrastructure they are building, then we will achieve a level of motivation and closeness that allows us to get results that may seem exceptional, but that simply bring to light the potential of our companies and the people who make them up. This is what occurred in the Polcevera Valley. The sense of responsibility transmitted by the Commissioner and the effective coordination, allow me to emphasize, on the part of RINA, exalted the great professionalism of the companies involved. This made it possible to overcome all the hurdles—which, trust me, were many—that could have prevented a successful outcome. On behalf of RINA I wish to thank all those who allowed us to make our contribution. This experience will remain in the heart of the over 100 colleagues who worked on the reconstruction of the bridge and all those in our company who "cheered" us on so that we could achieve these superb results.

WE HAVE BUILT
THE BRIDGE

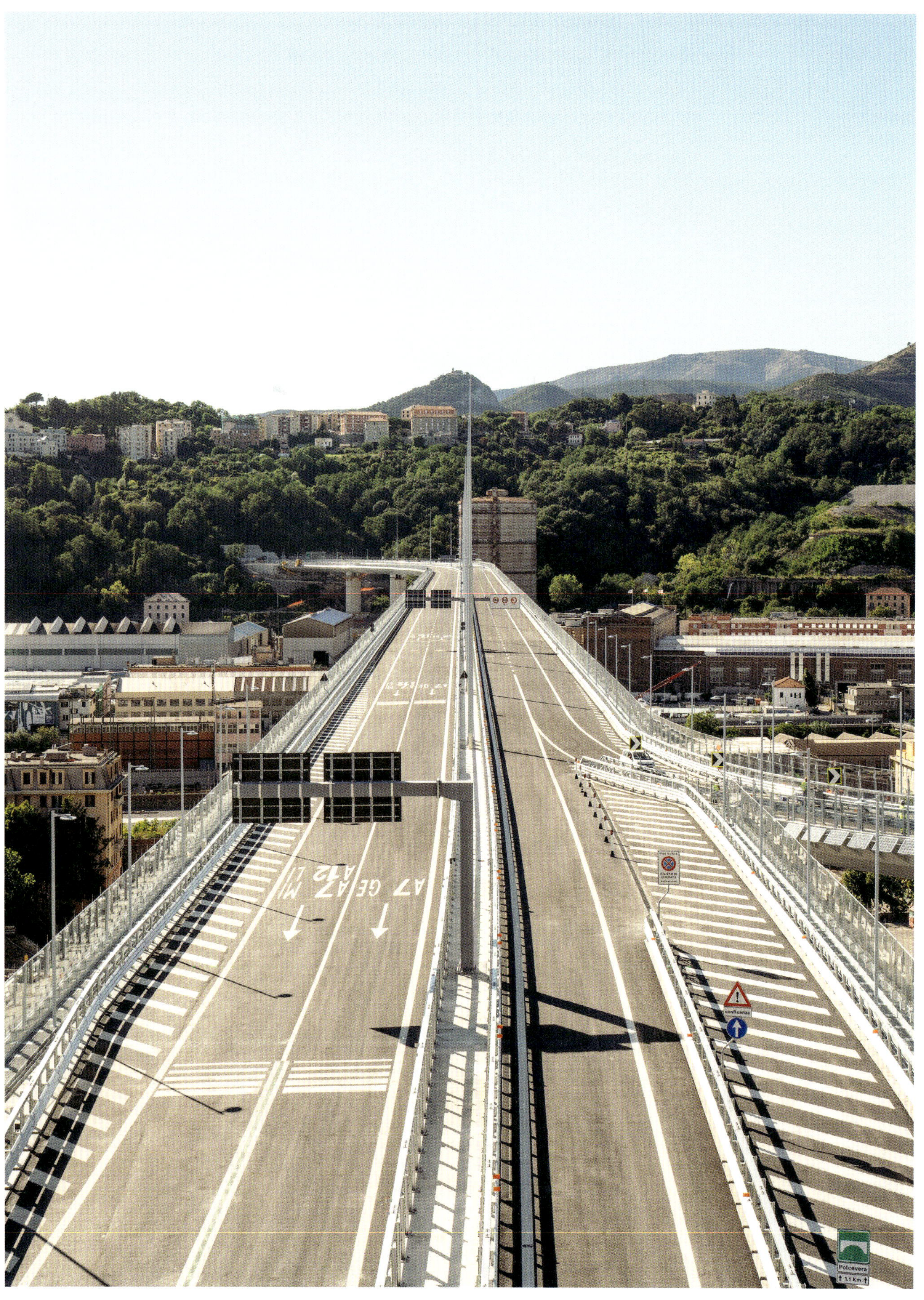

Roberto Tedeschi   GENERAL MANAGER
OF THE COMMISSIONER'S OFFICE

On August 14, 2018, I was working as Coordinator of Technical Services for the City of Genoa, and because there was a severe weather warning, I and most of my collaborators were already on duty from the early hours of the day in case we needed to deal with any emergencies that might arise.

In any case, none of us could have imagined the tragedy that would soon unfold before our eyes. When, soon after 11:30, we received the news that Ponte Morandi had collapsed, all those present felt that it concerned some superstructure or secondary element, for instance, parts of the bridge crane or the concrete barriers, but certainly not the main structure of the bridge. Unfortunately, it took only a few minutes for us to get the horrible news and then rush to the disaster site. The Head of the Local Police offered me a ride, which I took, so that I arrived at the bridge just after noon—a ride in total silence lasting less than 15 minutes—and however much we forced ourselves to imagine what could have happened, the scene before our eyes was much worse than imaginable. It was like a war scene: pier 9, the first of the three large stay systems, had collapsed on itself, pulling down to the ground over 260 meters of deck as well as the vehicles that had been traveling on it, crushing some of the industrial buildings situated below it. About thirty minutes had passed since the collapse and already at work on site was a huge emergency machine: more than fifty vehicles from all the Authorities, State and Local Administrations were endeavoring to find any survivors. Private citizens were there as well, trying to do whatever they could to help out in the rescue operations.

That was when I realized that my presence at that moment and in that place made no sense: that was the time for the rescue workers and for those who were tasked with figuring out what had happened. There would be other opportunities for me to provide my contribution.

That opportunity arose a few months later, when, in November, the Mayor of Genoa Marco Bucci, who had in the meantime been appointed Special Commissioner for the reconstruction of the Polcevera viaduct, decided to designate me as Director General of the Support Structure and gave me the job of choosing a team.

The group that was assembled was operative from the start, immediately achieving the first targets, thanks above all to two strong points that would prove to be fundamental over the course of the entire demolition and reconstruction process. On the one hand, the powers granted to the Special Commissioner by the so-called Genoa Decree Law, which gave him the mandate to act in abeyance of the Italian laws, solely complying with the European legislative framework, thereby saving a great deal of time. On the other, the freedom I was given to form my team allowed me to choose the people whom I thought I truly needed, based solely on the professional skills of each of the individual actors, confirmed by previous work experiences. Hence, the Structure began operating even before the job had been officialized. There were still no dedicated offices, but work was started immediately to prepare the paperwork that would soon be necessary to set all the procedures in motion. The working method hinged on pragmatism, the leitmotif of all the group's activity, proof of which are the dates that marked the start of the works from the last few months of 2018.

The same day that the members of the structure were nominated, November 15, 2018, the technical specifications that were needed to initiate market consultation without requiring either negotiations or a tender for the demolition of Ponte Morandi and the reconstruction of the new Polcevera bridge were approved. This procedure set the deadline for November 26, 2018, as the final date for the presentation of the applications.

A few days later, on December 5, RINA was commissioned to coordinate the project, direct the works, implement quality control, and support the Commissioner's Office within the scope of the tender. On December 14, at the end of the market consultation, which involved the contribution of an "expert commission" in support of the Commissioner, ATI was officially tasked with the demolition work (Omini – Fagioli – Ireos - IPE Progetti). Hence, it received a public contract for the work to be carried out with extreme urgency; i.e. the demolition, removal, processing, and disposal of the debris from the viaduct, with the anticipation of the contractual terms in regard to the preparation of the building site.

On the same date the PerGenova consortium was tasked with the construction of all the works. On December 15, therefore, the first areas were given over to the ATI for the demolition and the first buildings of AMIU started to be pulled down, pending the underwriting of the Agreement, later underwritten by the parties on January 18, 2019. From that day on the building site never stopped.

With just one day off, Christmas Day 2019, the building site forged ahead, round-the-clock, seven days a week both during the demolition phase and over the course of the reconstruction. Demolition and reconstruction were deeply interconnected owing to the need to speed up the timing as much as possible. They were also linked to the activities of the legal authorities, which needed to safeguard some parts of Ponte Morandi before the release from seizure, which occurred in subsequent steps and is not as yet over. All of this unfolded in an area filled with sub-services, many of which required the realization of bypasses to avoid dangerous contact points, and crowded with civil and industrial buildings, for which expropriation was necessary. In the first months of work, over 2.5 km of pipelines were moved, over 400 real estate units were purchased, four residential and nine industrial buildings were demolished. Various methods were combined for the demolition. The Gerber beams, weighing an average of 900 tons each, were lowered to the ground using strand-jacking technology, which had never been used in Italy before for the demolition of similar structures. These are hydraulic jacks that work individually or in pairs and that are able to carry up to 750 tons per jack. Moreover, they contain a variable number of wire ropes, from 1 to 50. Once the Gerber beams were removed, the next phase involved using maxi cranes to "slice" the decks in the parts localized above the piers, and bring them to the ground. The piece was harnessed, severed, completely detached from the rest, and lowered.

Within these operations each of us had the chance to see firsthand machinery of huge size and capacity at work: suffice it to say that the Terex crane used during both demolition and construction could raise a load up to 1,250 tons, and that on average present at the building site at the same time were five similar means, as well as the remaining high-capacity cranes used on a daily basis, and the earth diggers. During the busiest periods, this machinery numbered over thirty-five pieces on site. It was a colossal project that allowed the technicians who took part in it to have an immersive experience in the most avant-garde realities in the field of civil construction. It also provided an opportunity for unique professional enrichment.

In the course of my long professional experience I have never witnessed a building site for so long and so close up: you can count the days I wasn't on site on the fingers of one hand. The same goes for my closest collaborators. There are some moments that we will never forget. To go back to the demolition, for the part of the bridge that had remained on the Levante (Eastern) side of the Polcevera viaduct, we used explosives on June 28, 2019. The images went around the world, and they portrayed those seconds when the remaining structure was made to collapse in a controlled manner.

Just a few instants preceded, nonetheless, by the thorough coordination between the Structure, RINA, the companies, and the bodies commissioned to control, the Civil Protection, and the City Administration. It was a machine that had been set in motion months before so that everything would be carried out in the best way possible. And that is exactly how it went. We are very satisfied with how all the operations were conducted. A great deal of attention was focused on the theme of safety, and the specific measures adopted made it possible to meet all the objectives fully.

The reconstruction as well, which began, as we said before, while the demolition was still underway, proceeded step by step in the best way possible, from the sub-foundations to the foundations, segment after segment for the piers, all the way to the assembly of the decks and their elevation. The deck portions arrived in Genoa by sea, and were then transported to the building site with exceptional nighttime convoys. Along the way, things happened that couldn't have been predicted, but they were overcome with the help of everyone.

In March 2020, the building site activities had to necessarily be "reassessed" following the Covid-19 emergency, which nonetheless did not stop the site's operativity. Thanks to a rigid protocol, which included sanitization, distancing, protective equipment, tracing of the workers whose temperature was taken regularly, and other rules to protect the staff, the works were never interrupted, making this building site an example for all the other building sites in the country, especially when activity was resumed during phase 3 of the Covid emergency. In spite of everything, we got all the way to the end. On August 3 we inaugurated the Ponte Genova San Giorgio and the next evening the first cars crossed over it. Today, looking back. it seems incredible to think about the amount of work that was done in such a short amount of time. "Incredible" is also the adjective that can be used to describe all this work from the beginning, the experience of each one of the people who was involved in it. "Incredible" is the emotion that we feel now, like the satisfaction that we will always feel.

SOME TIME LATER, I HEADED
BACK TO THE BUILDING SITE
AREA, AND WHEN I TOOK
THE ROAD ALONG THE
POLCEVERA, I SAW,
FOR THE FIRST TIME,
THE ALMOST COMPLETE LINE
OF THE BRIDGE WITH ITS
THREE 100-METER SPANS.
A LUMP CAME TO MY THROAT,
TEARS WELLED UP IN MY EYES,
IT WAS DEEPLY MOVING TO SEE
ITS IMMENSE BEAUTY.

ANNAMARIA BONOMO
STATE ATTORNEY'S OFFICE

THE SATISFACTION STEMS FROM
THE KNOWLEDGE OF HAVING
OFFERED A MULTIFARIOUS AND
DIFFERENTIATED CONTRIBUTION
WITHIN THE CONTEXT OF
AN "ARTISANAL WORKSHOP."
NONE OF US, I BELIEVE,
HAD EVER HAD TO FACE SUCH
A RELEVANT OBJECTIVE,
DEFINED AND IMPLEMENTED
WITH PROFESSIONALITY
AND KNOW-HOW.

PIERO FLOREANI
COMMISSIONER'S OFFICE

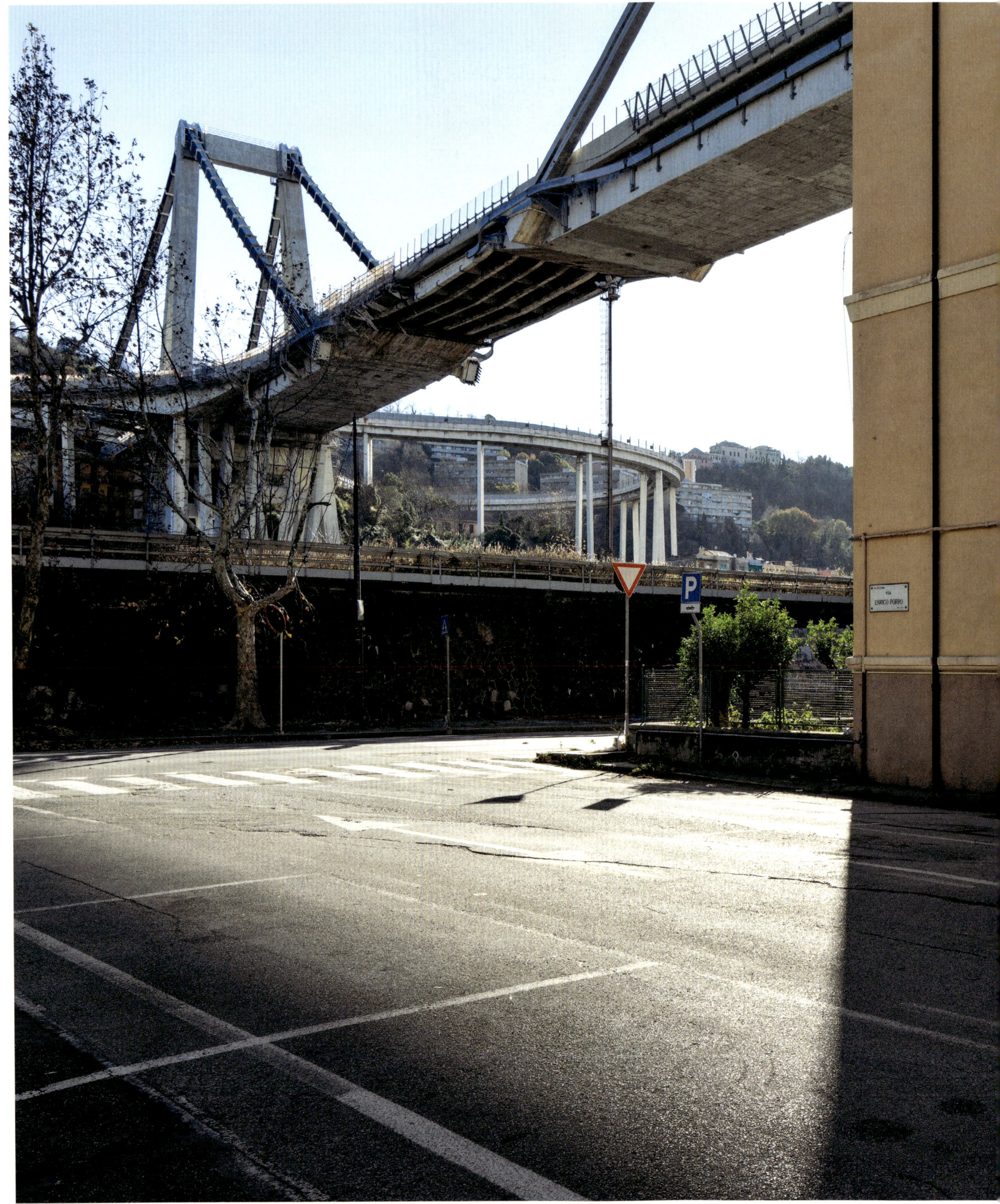
VIA
ENRICO PORRO

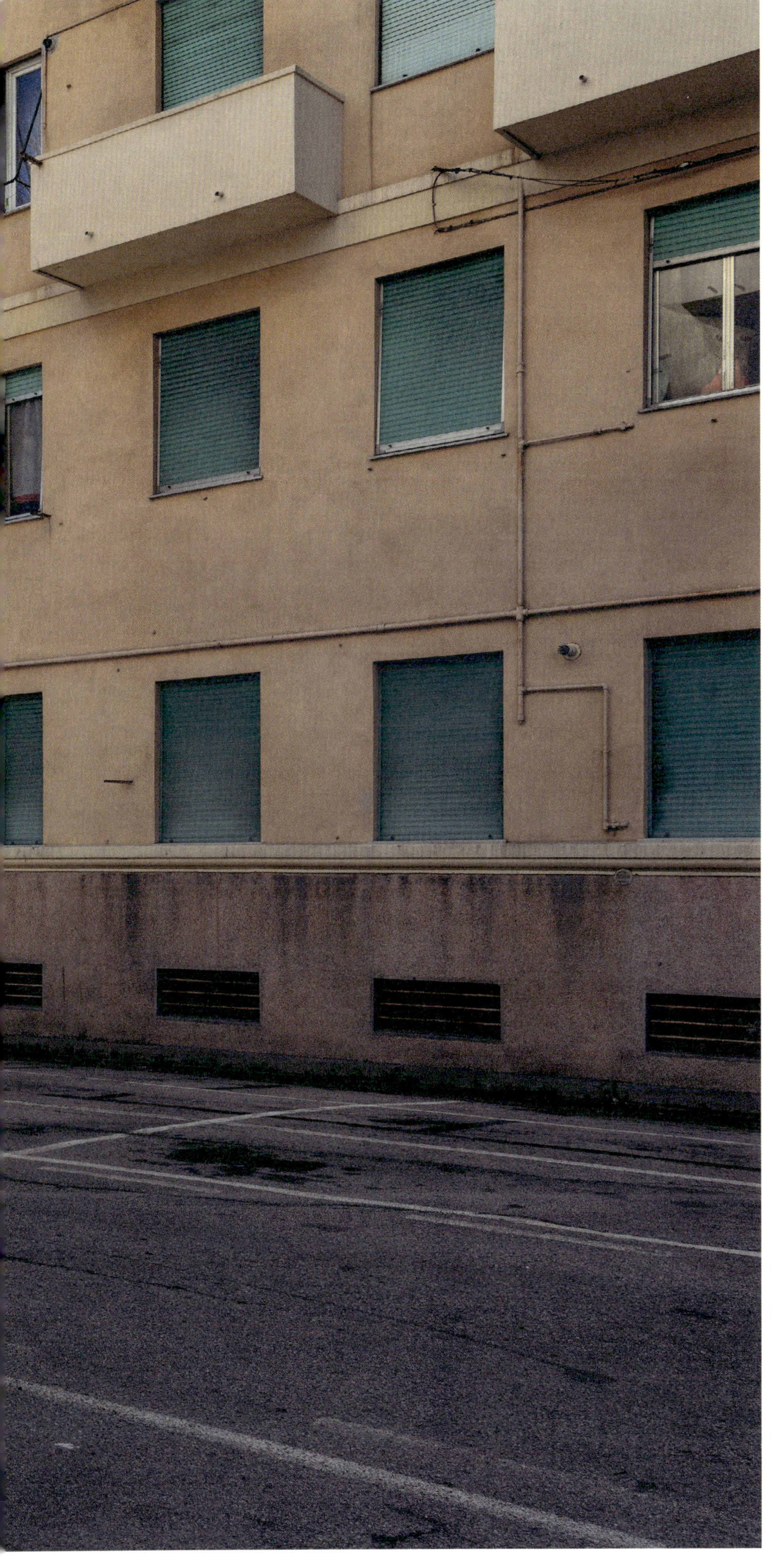

Ponte Morandi crosses the Valpolcevera torrent from west to east. While to the west of the torrent the area mostly hosted an industrial area, the portion to the east overlooked the Certosa district, a densely populated residential area. A part of this zone, after the collapse, was cordoned off as a "red zone."
Six residential buildings were evacuated between Via Fillak and Via Porro, four of which were later demolished. Though about 660 people were forced out of their homes, they soon received alternative accommodation.

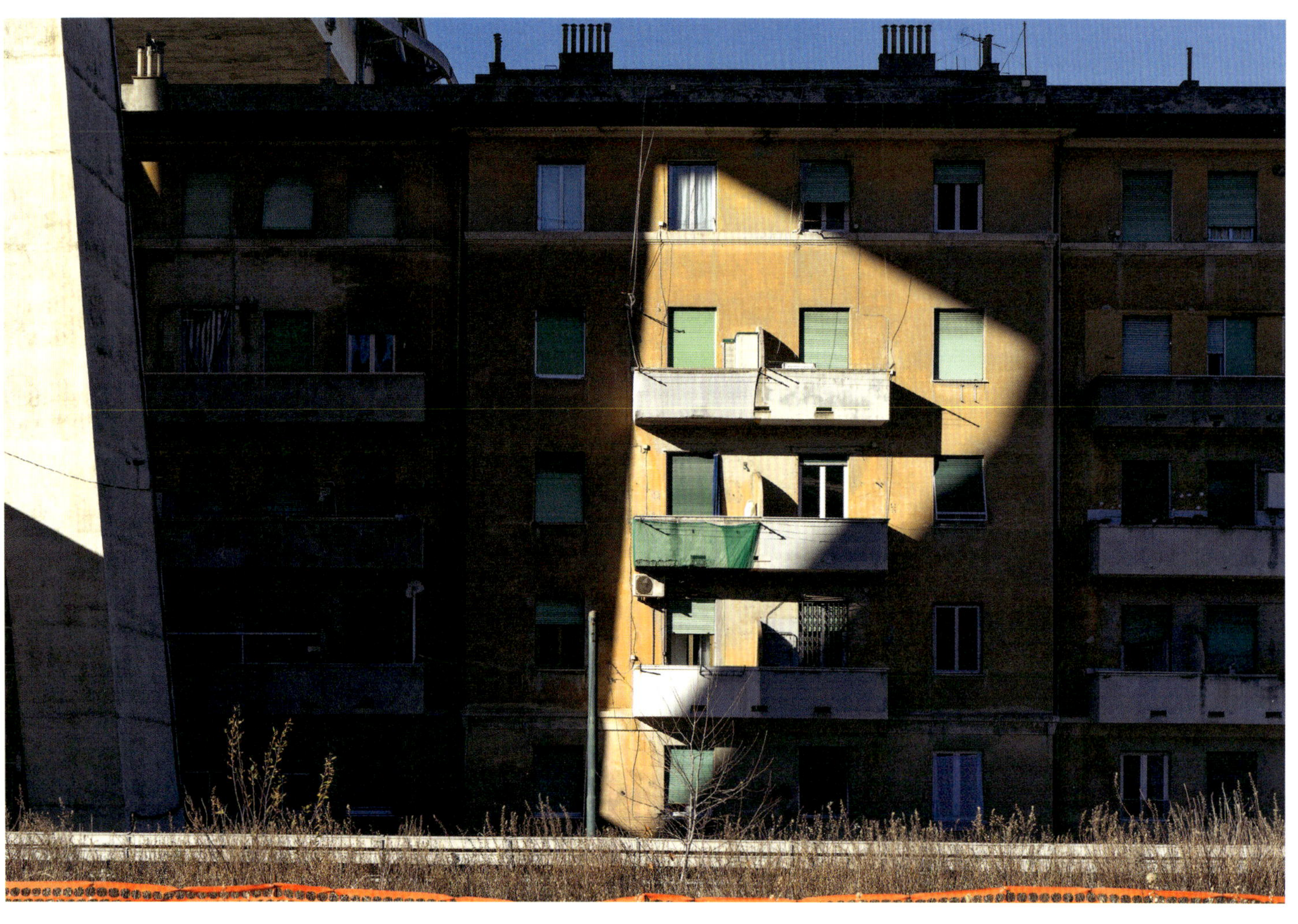

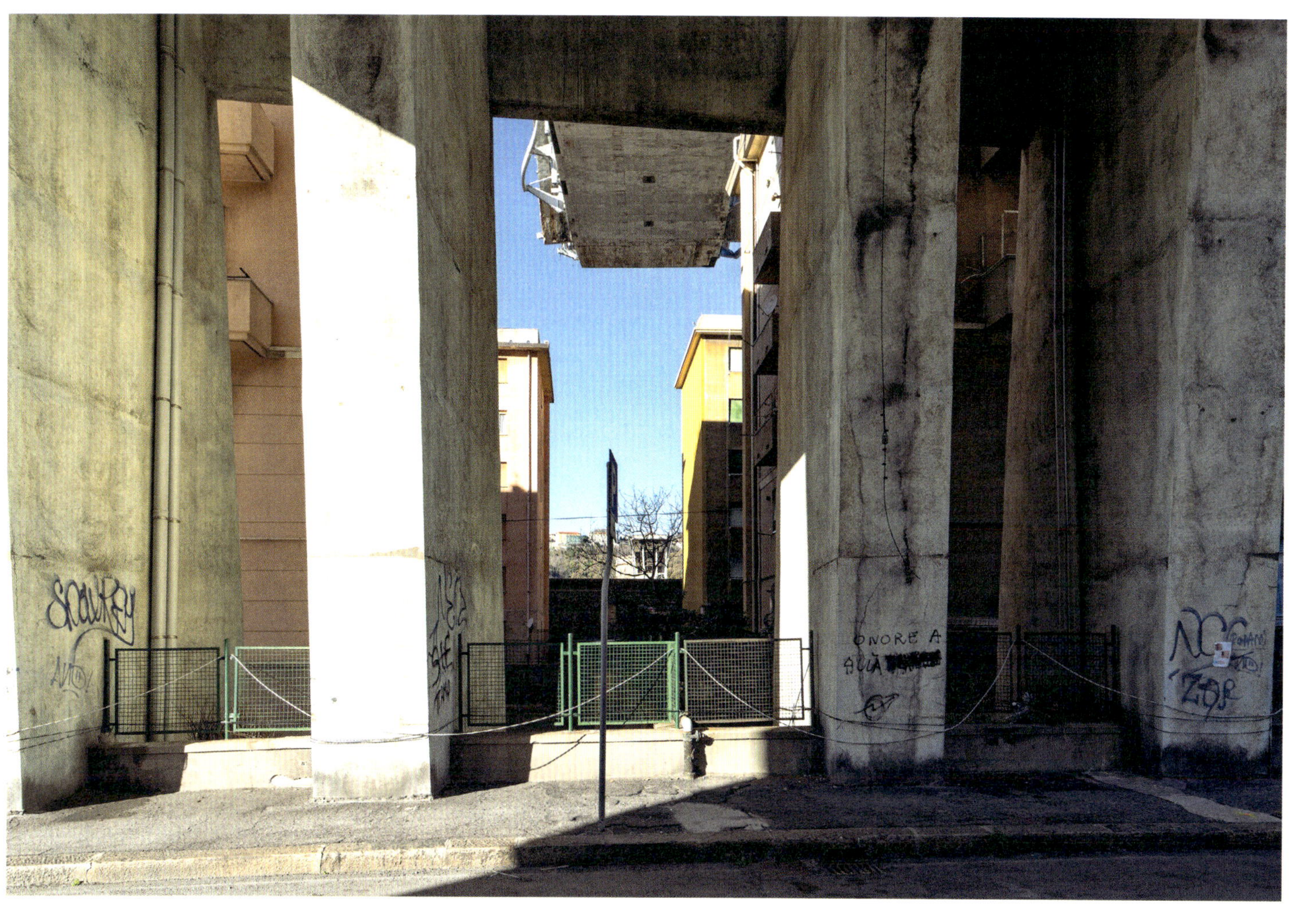

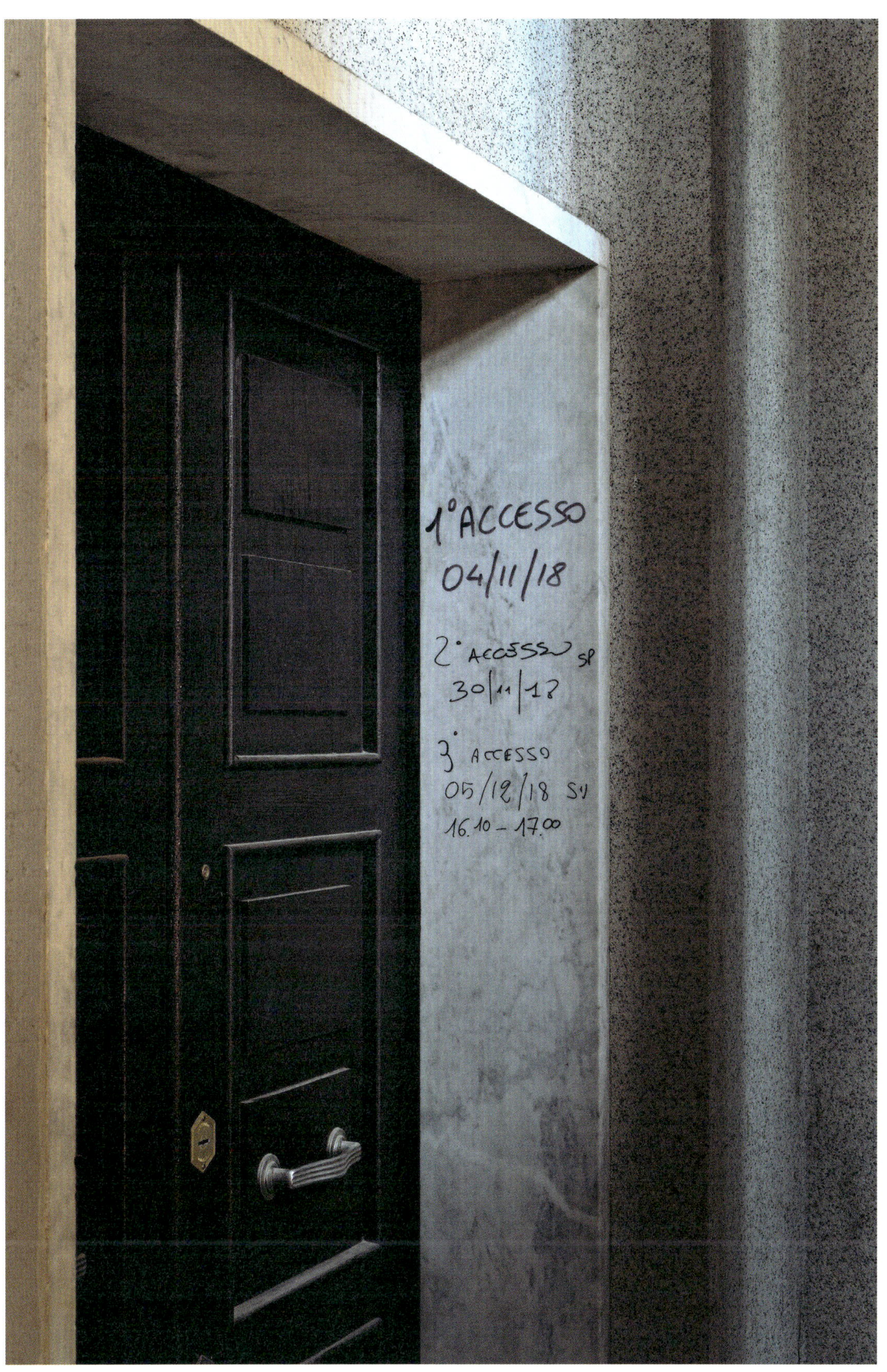

1° ACCESSO
04/11/18

2° ACCESSO SP
30/11/18

3° ACCESSO
05/12/18 SY
16.10 - 17.00

A SHIP MADE

INTERVIEW WITH **Renzo Piano**   BY **Cinzia Pica**

FROM IRON AND AIR

**Just after the tragedy of August 14, 2018, with, I imagine,
pain in your heart, your "idea for a bridge" saw the light of day.
Can you tell us how it was born?**

Even today, when I talk about the bridge, even though there are some very good reasons to be pleased with it, my gaze saddens when I think back to August 14 two years ago, while I was at CERN in Geneva, when I got the news.

A bridge is not a wall. A wall that collapses is just a wall that collapses. In the collective imaginary, bridges are unifying. A bridge that collapses, collapses three times. It left a scar of forty-three human lives lost, 260 families without a home, and a city split in two. When the idea was still that of possibly introducing a stop-gap solution by means of a temporary viaduct, I imagined a bridge crossing the Polcevera Valley step by step. I talked about it right away with the Mayor (who had not been appointed commissioner yet), and told him that it could be rebuilt in short steps. As I moved my hand over the plan I imagined 50-meter-long spans.

In those days, the idea of building a bridge in so little time seemed crazy. What do you think the winning element was?

The only way to build a solid bridge quickly, one that would be functional and long-lasting, is to do so with simultaneous construction sites, skillfully, and with careful management to support the teamwork. The right companies joined the field. Italferr for the planning. PerGenova with its two branches aimed at producing the elements of the bridge: Webuild for the reinforced cement structures, and Fincantieri Infrastructure for the steel. The building site couldn't wait for the first group to finish before the second group began. The two parts, the construction and the carpentry, went forward simultaneously, supported as regards the movement of such heavy loads by the great competency of Fagioli.

The first to enter the field and the last one to leave it was RINA, whose role was that of Project Manager and Works Director, with the delicate task of organizing everything, including the timing, thereby guaranteeing the safety and quality of the materials and the construction.

This bridge has to last a thousand years. And to be able to do that it will have to be looked after and loved. The accessibility for maintenance and the new technologies implemented by the IT will also guarantee that the bridge endures. I feel it is safe to say that in this project competence prevailed over incompetence.

And what role did the human factor play?

Not just the companies, but also and above all the individual people never stopped working. The human element was essential. I often heard the workers say: "I will never forget this building site." This doesn't happen every day. It means that there's an awareness of doing something important, and that its memory will last a lifetime.

Every time I went there to do a technical site survey, or to pay a visit to the building site for the new bridge, or when I took part in a meeting, I always noticed a glazed look in people's eyes. The veil of the tragedy that had occurred there, and the knowledge and awareness of it that have never faded.

This bridge is a rebirth after a tragedy, and the pride does not just belong to the engineers, it belongs to everyone: the welders, the workers, the manual laborers. Everyone. The pride of building such an important work unites us, it acts as a cohesive device. Even though there are different ideas, even though the color of our skin is different, even though we come from different countries, these differences vanish. And it was also an important tool for the management of the site: professionals, technicians, workers all motivated and working with passion.

This bridge has become a symbol of the city's rebirth, at times of the country as a whole, blocked by the lockdown while 100-meter spans were being raised. Who could ever have imagined it?

And I wanted a "Genoese" bridge, one that was capable of joining the right side to the left side of the Polcevera Valley in a simple, clear, strong, long-lasting, and even poetic manner.

In a famous litany Giorgio Caproni wrote "Genova di ferro e aria" (Genoa made from iron and air). Genoa's steel is truly forged by the wind. And the same can be said of the bridge. There's the steel, there's the wind, there's the beauty of the light that caresses it when it swoops down at dusk. It is a bridge that crosses the valley asking "...May I?" It is neither modesty nor humility. This bridge has its strength. The simple adjective hides the complexity. The idea of simplicity does not signify banality.

This bridge, a white ship, perhaps to some extent tries to represent the city in all its characteristics, and I hope it can also become a symbol of rebirth. But it isn't a miracle. It's just the fruit of the labor of people who worked hard and well, who would know how to do this a thousand times over, even when there wasn't a tragedy behind it. Building is a collective gesture and this bridge is even more so because the skills involved were manifold, diverse, all equally important for achieving the final result. These workers simply did their job well and this is the best possible tribute to the city.

And now that we are near the end, we can finally do what farmers do on a Sunday: lounge outside their homes and gaze at the plowed fields. We, all of us who have "built the bridge," can now admire it with respect and satisfaction.

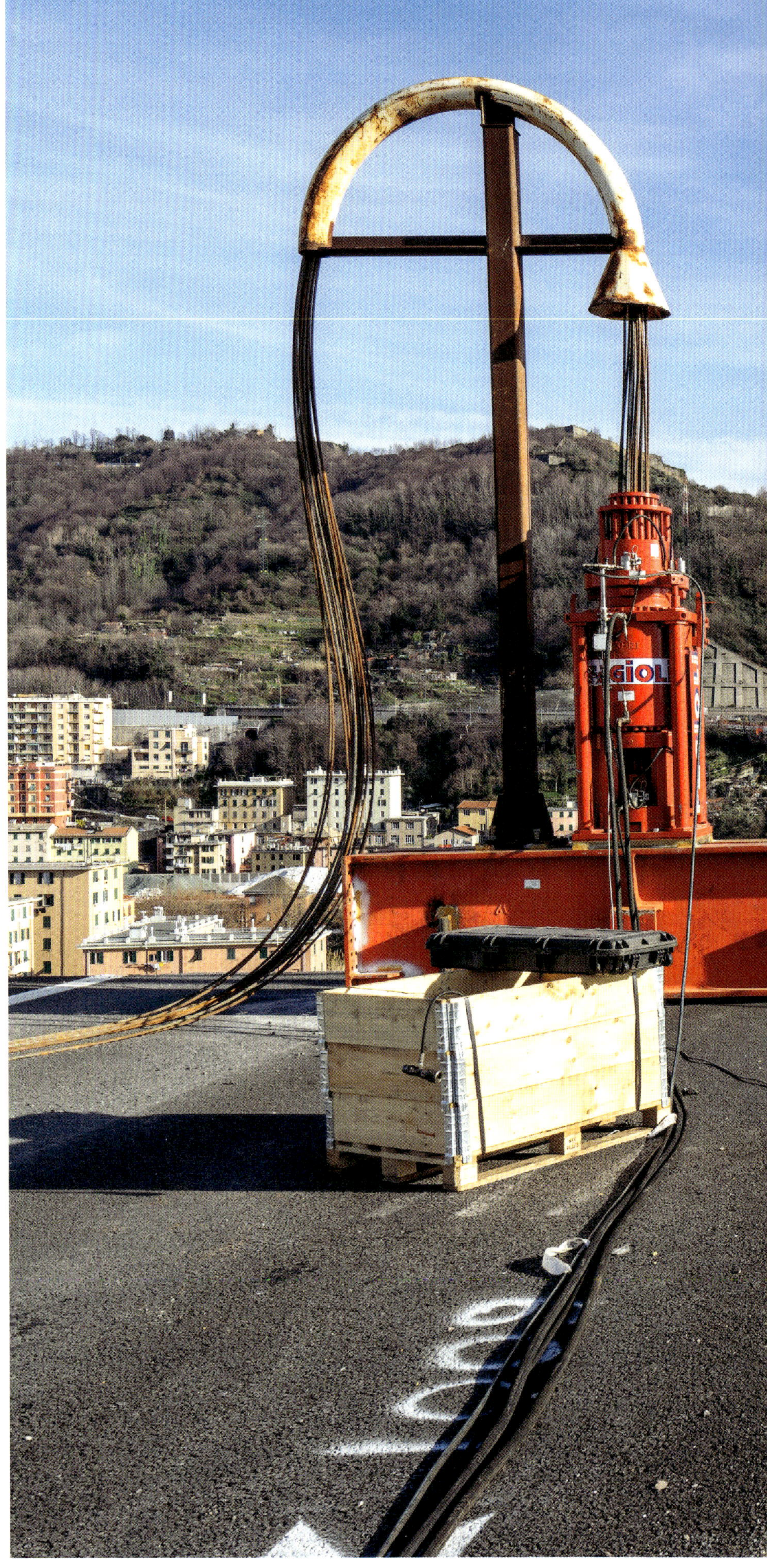

The demolition of Ponte Morandi took place partly
by mechanical dismantlement: portions of the deck
were cut and lowered to the ground using special
strand jacks. These were positioned on the deck to
the sides of the Gerber beam that had to be
brought to the ground.

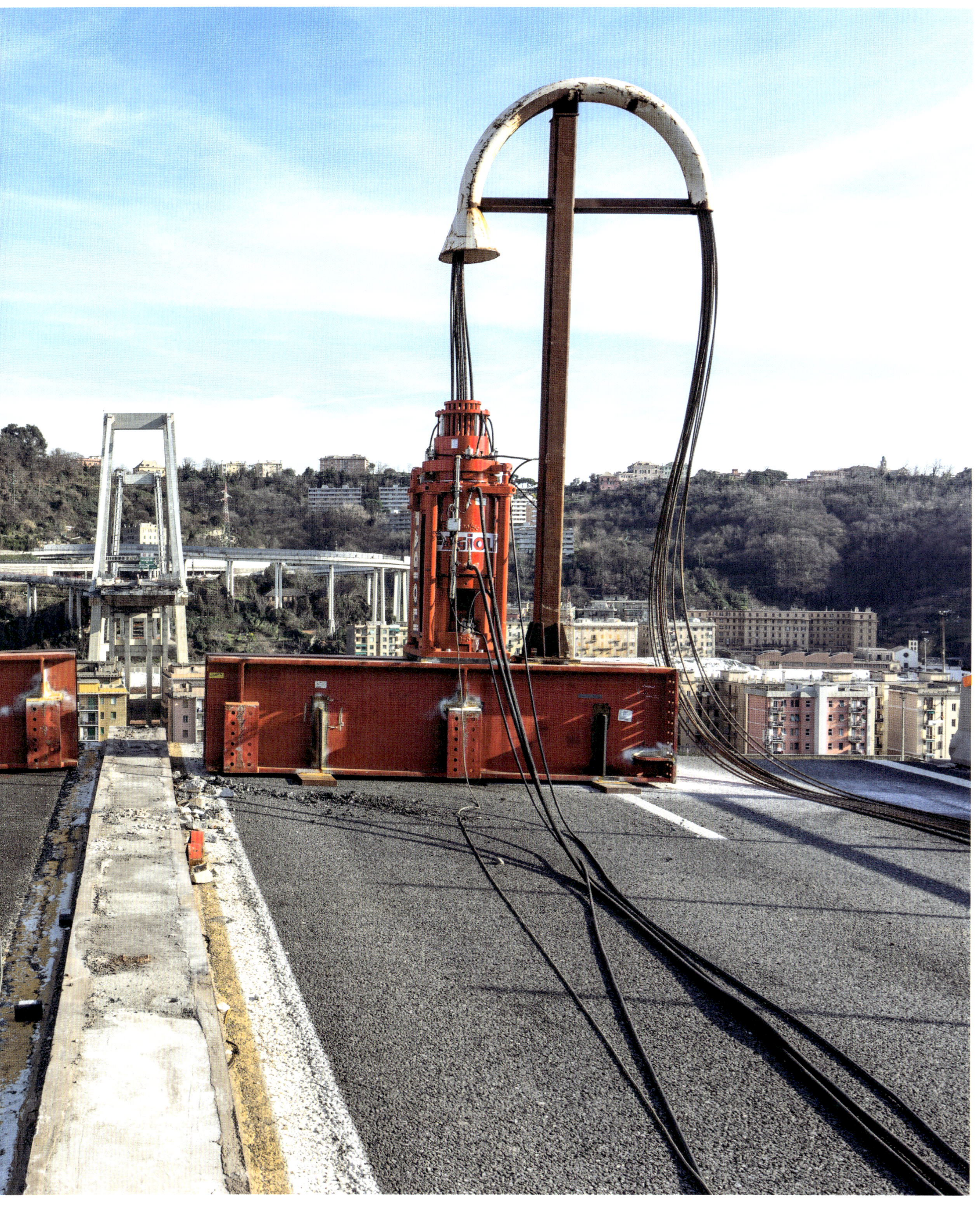

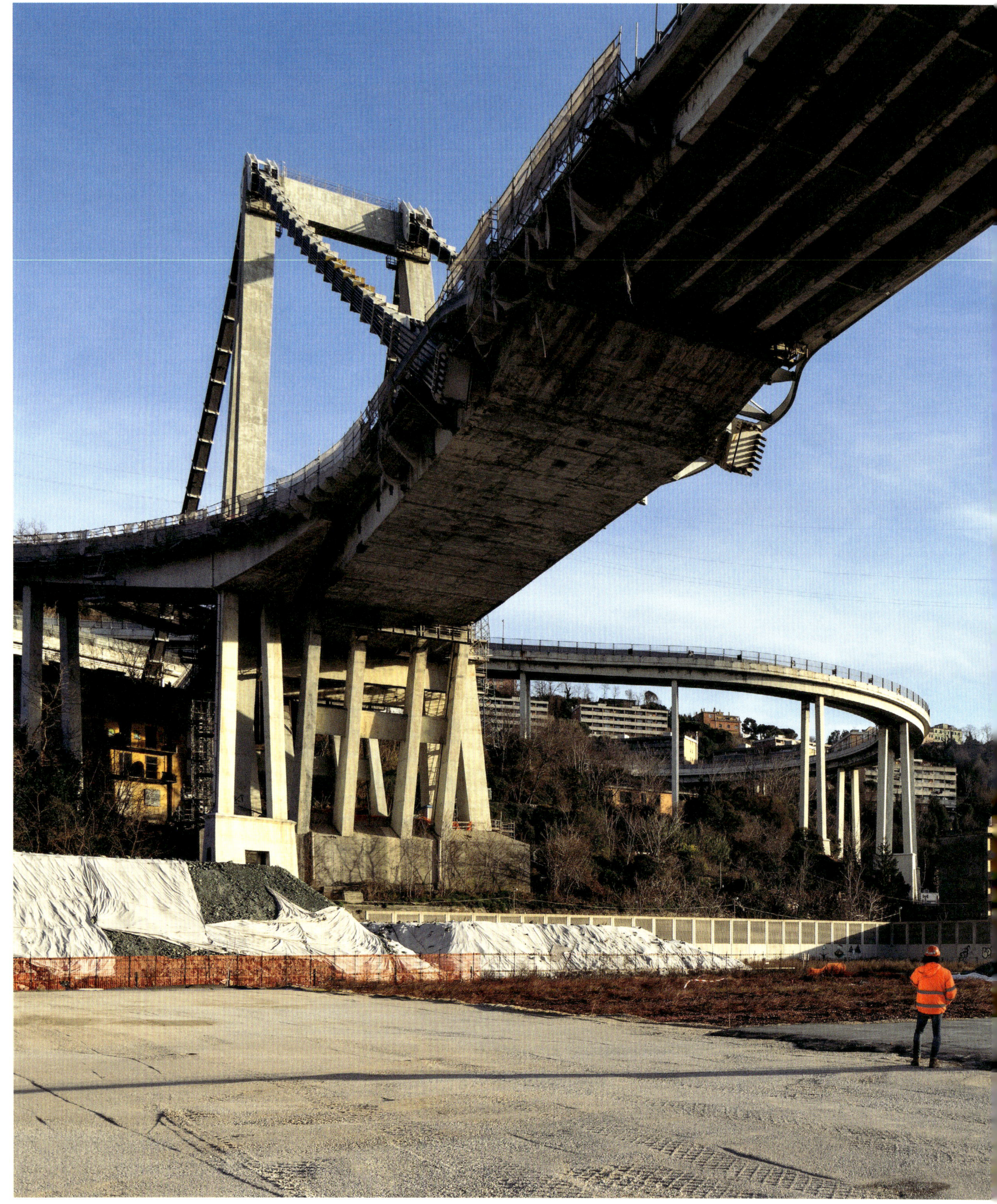

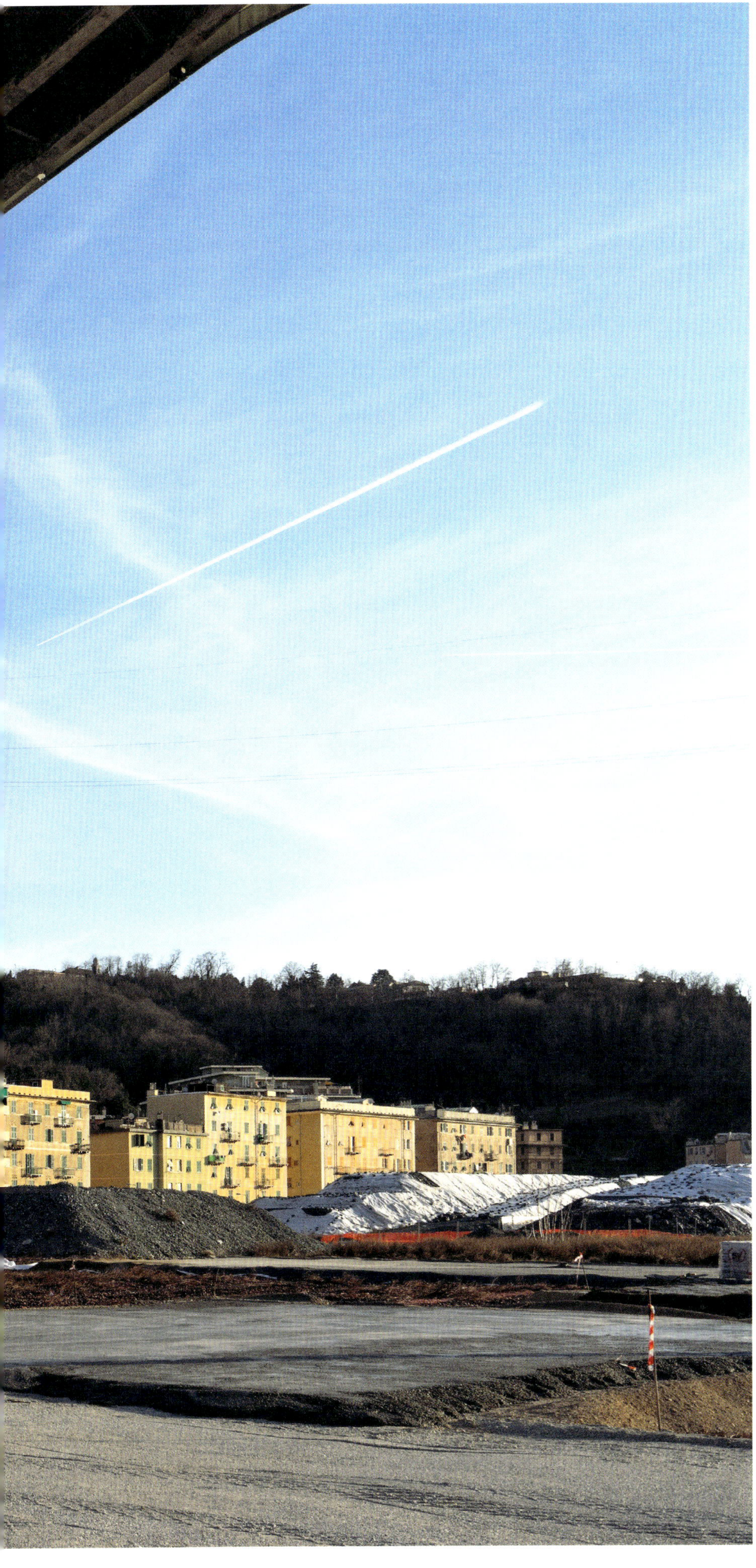

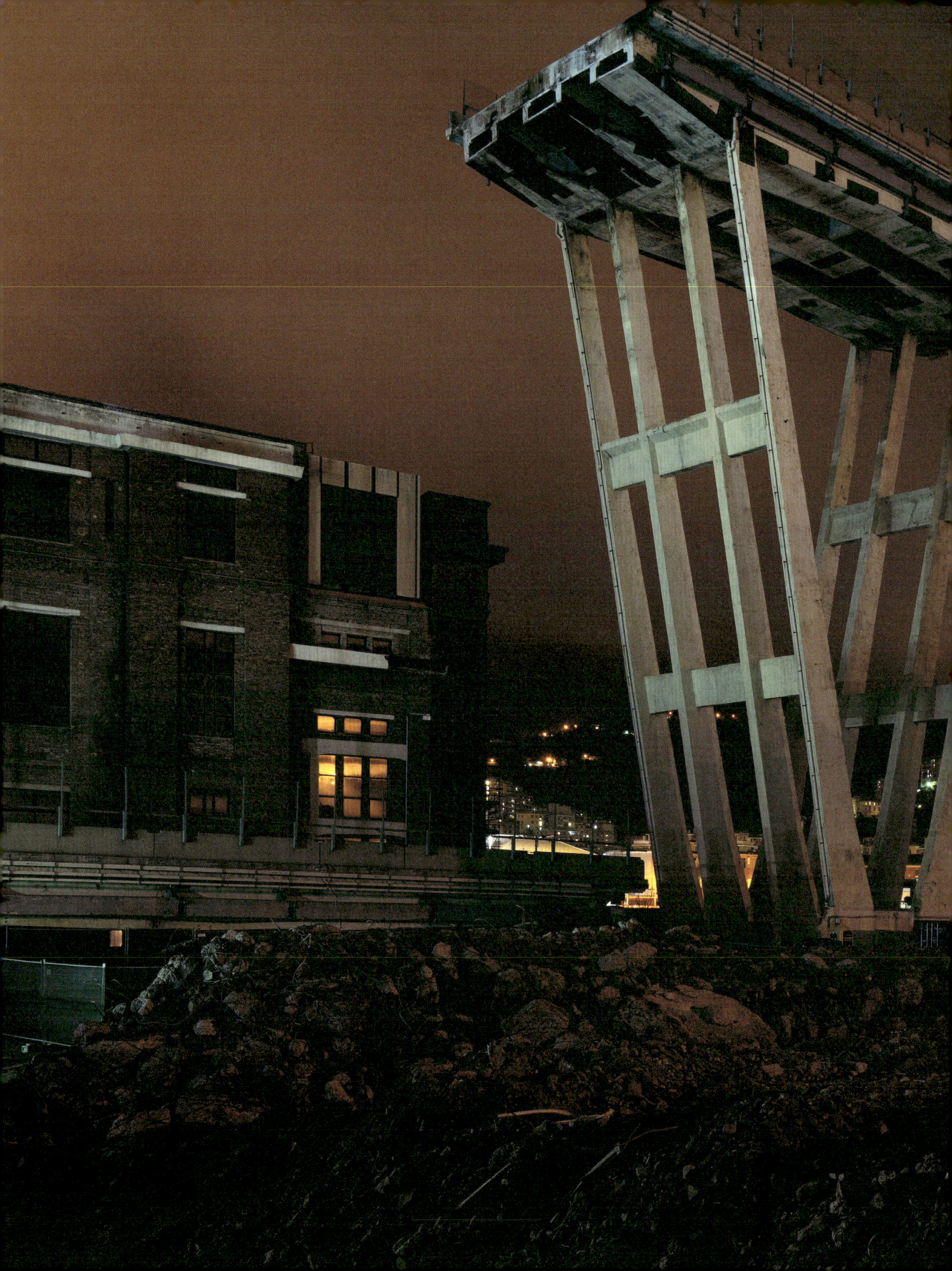

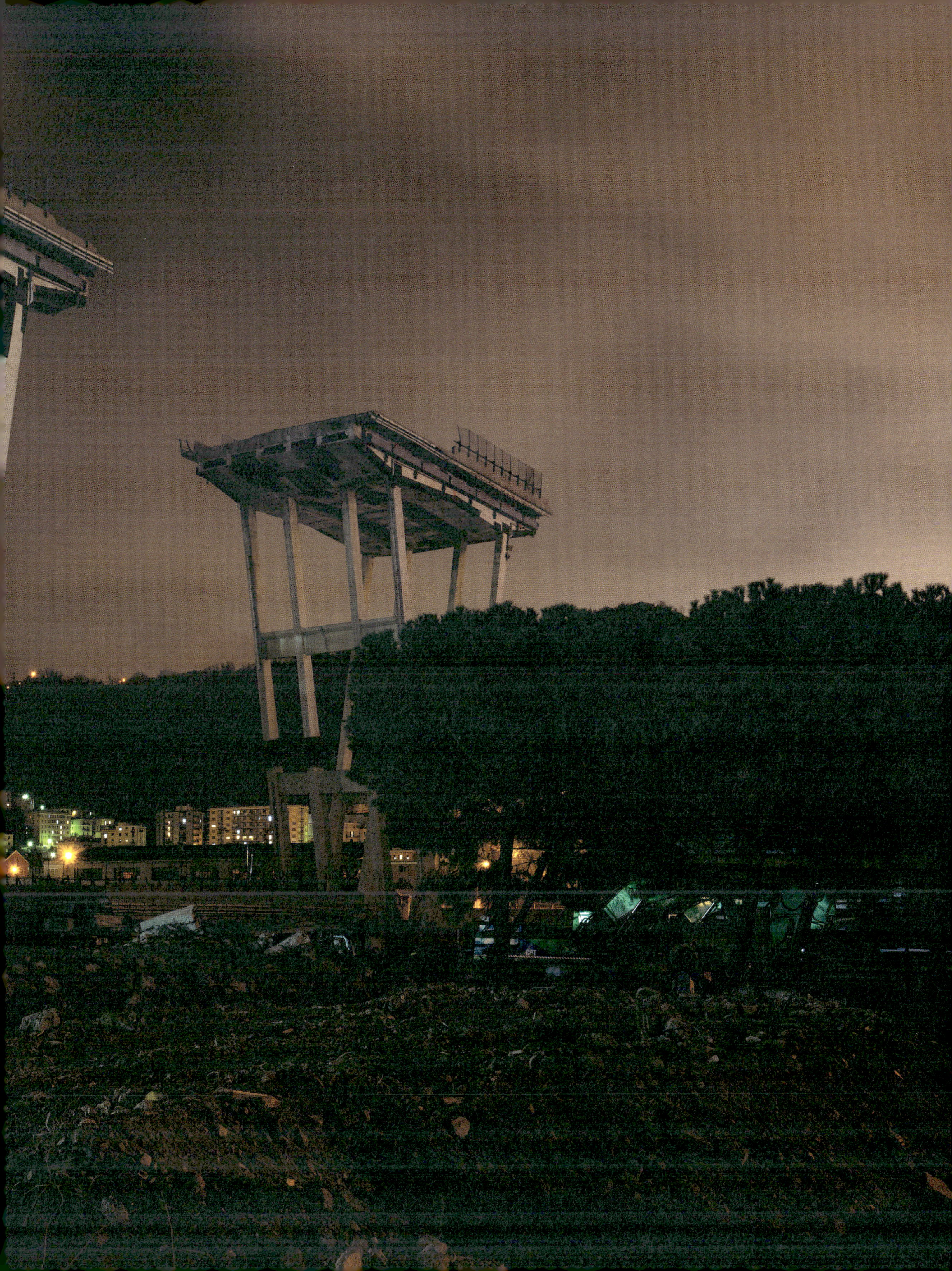

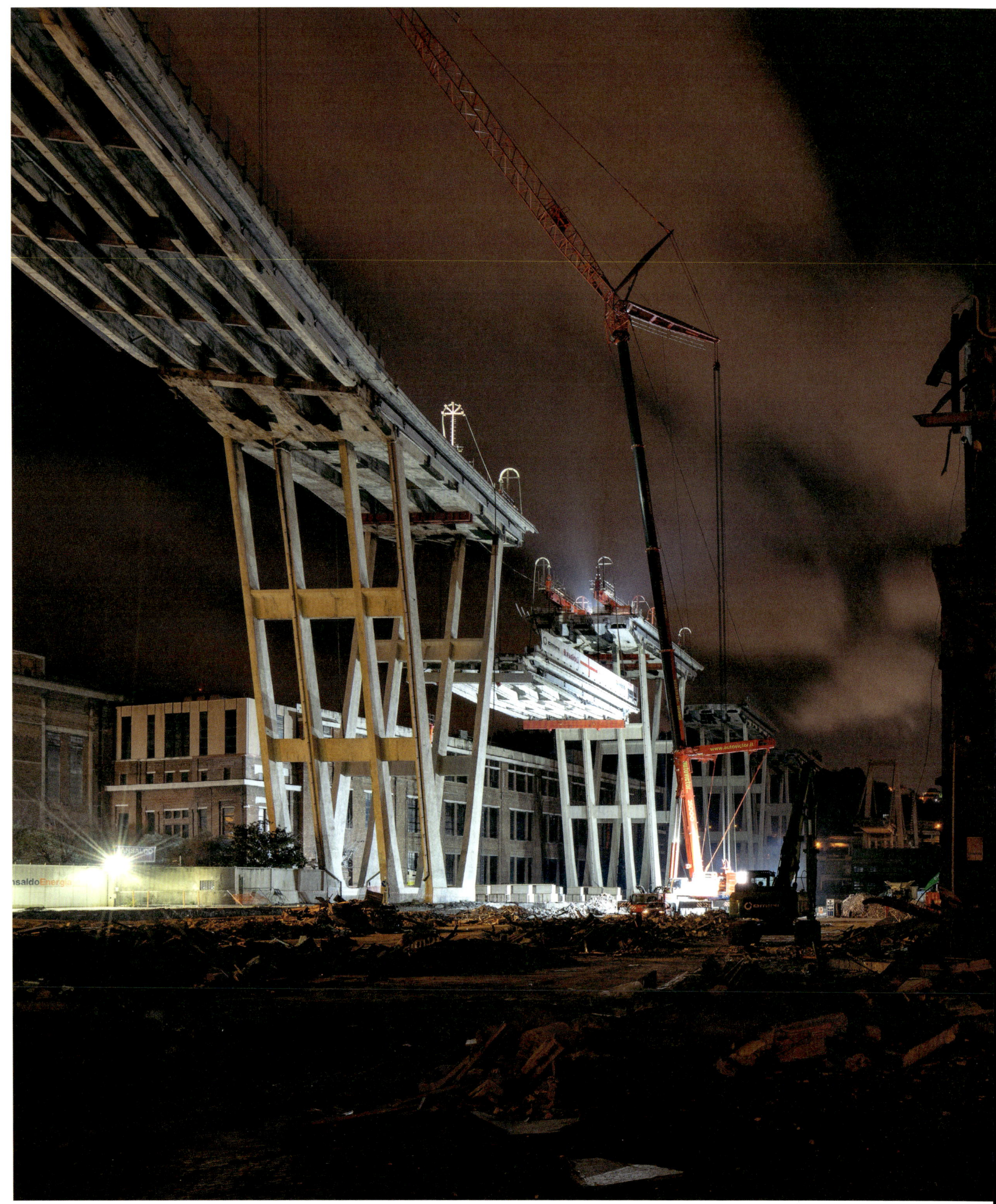

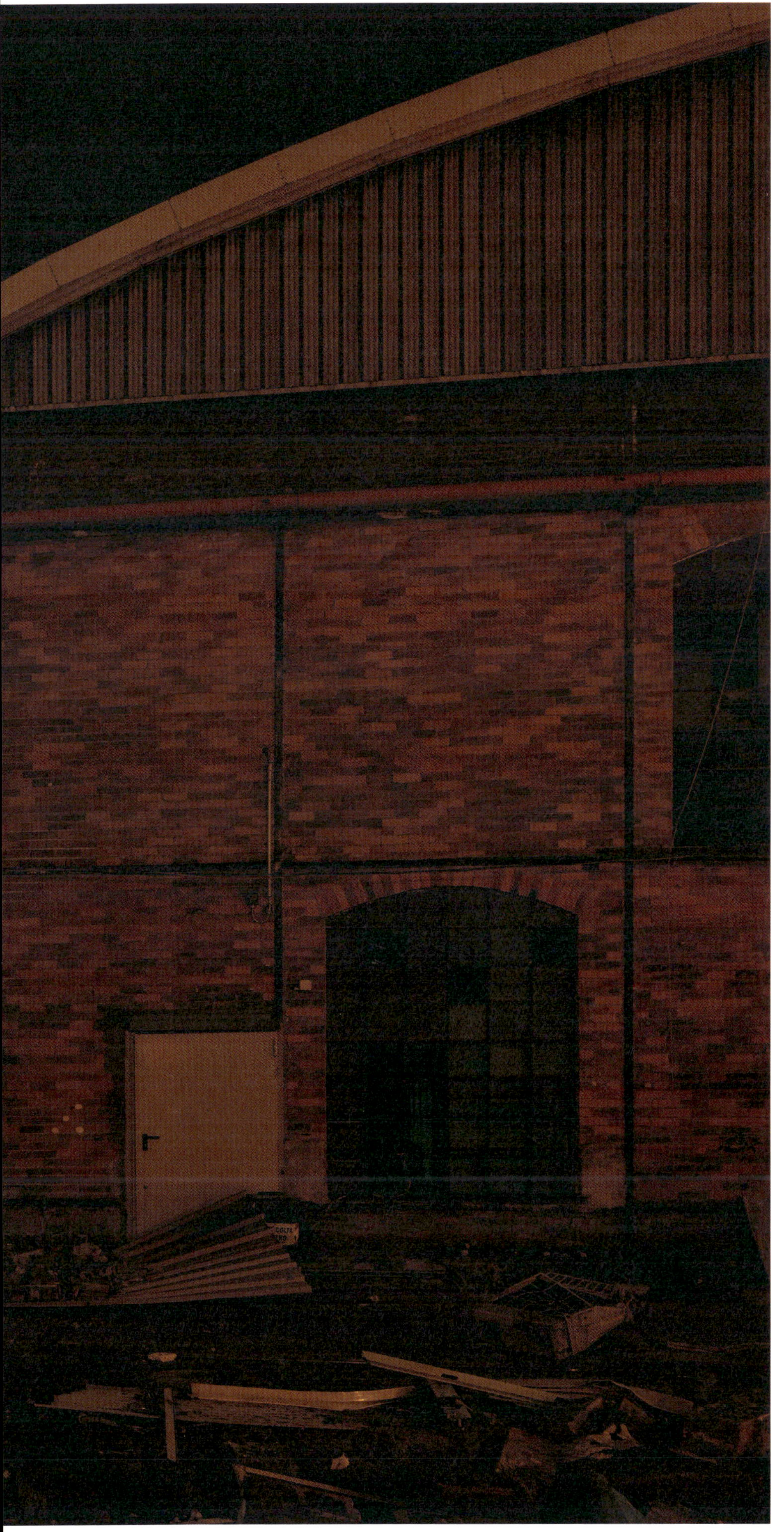

Ponte Morandi's Gerber beams were lowered
to the ground during both daytime and nighttime
operations. The building site for the demolition of
the bridge, as well as the one for its construction,
involved skilled workers who did round-the-clock
shifts, seven days a week.
The first nighttime drops were distinguished by
silence and concentration. These were very delicate
maneuvers from a technical point of view as they were
implemented on a damaged infrastructure.
The behavior of the structure was analyzed and studied
during the planning phases for the specific demolition
operations, but the awareness that there was still a
potential risk was clear to all those who participated
in or witnessed these events.

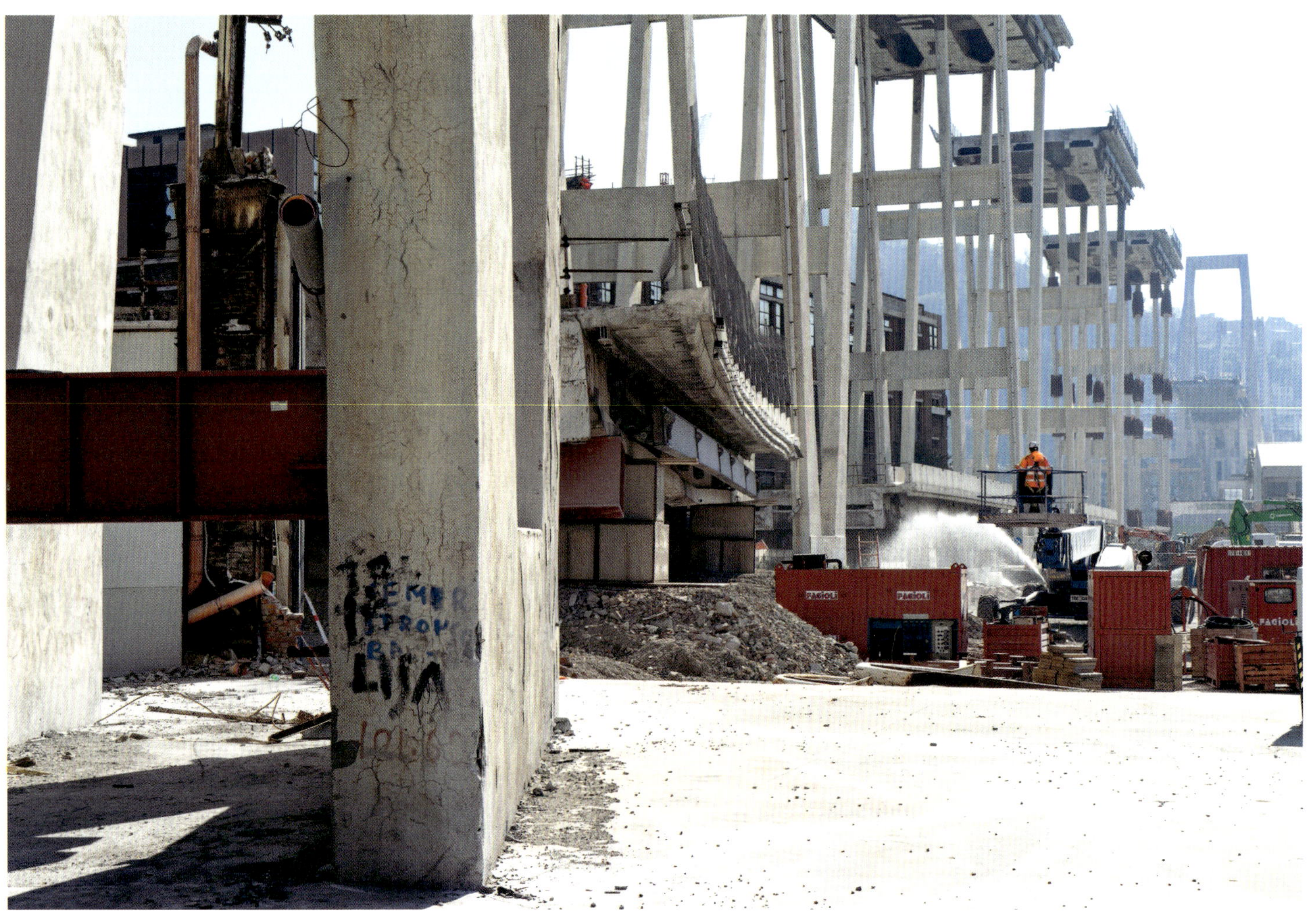

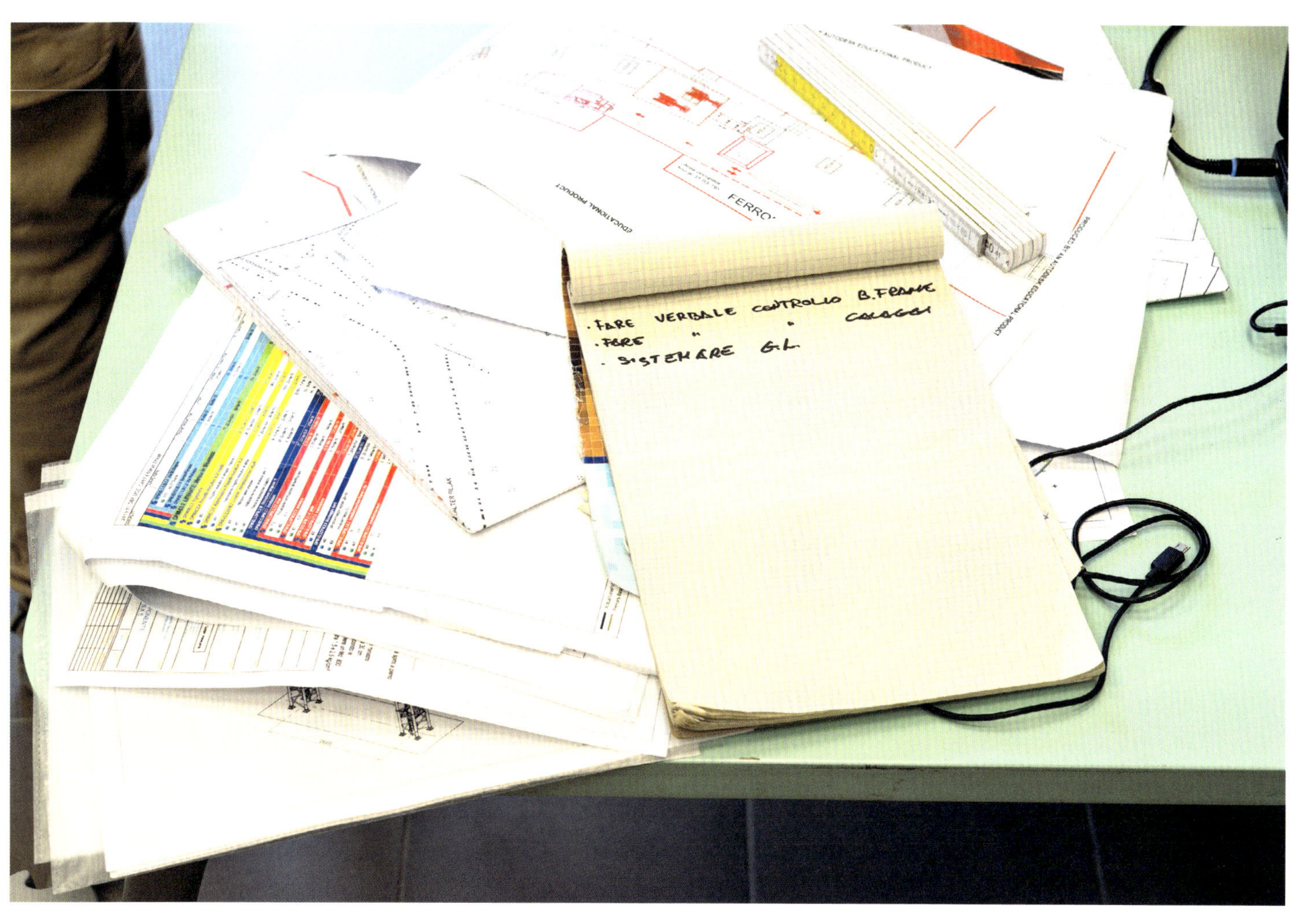
. FARE VERBALE CONTROLLO B.FRAME
. FARE   "   CORAGGI
. SISTEMARE G.L.

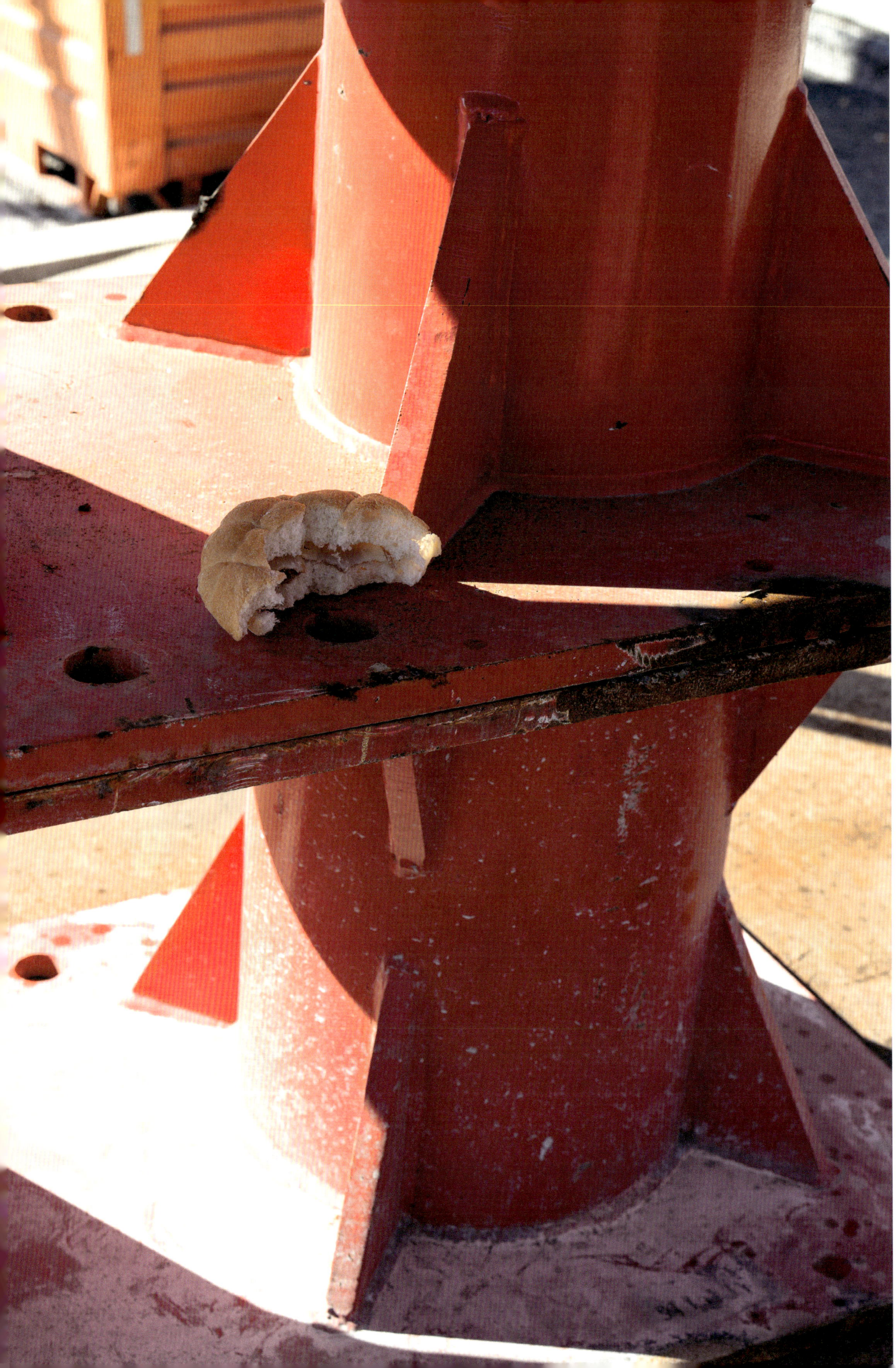

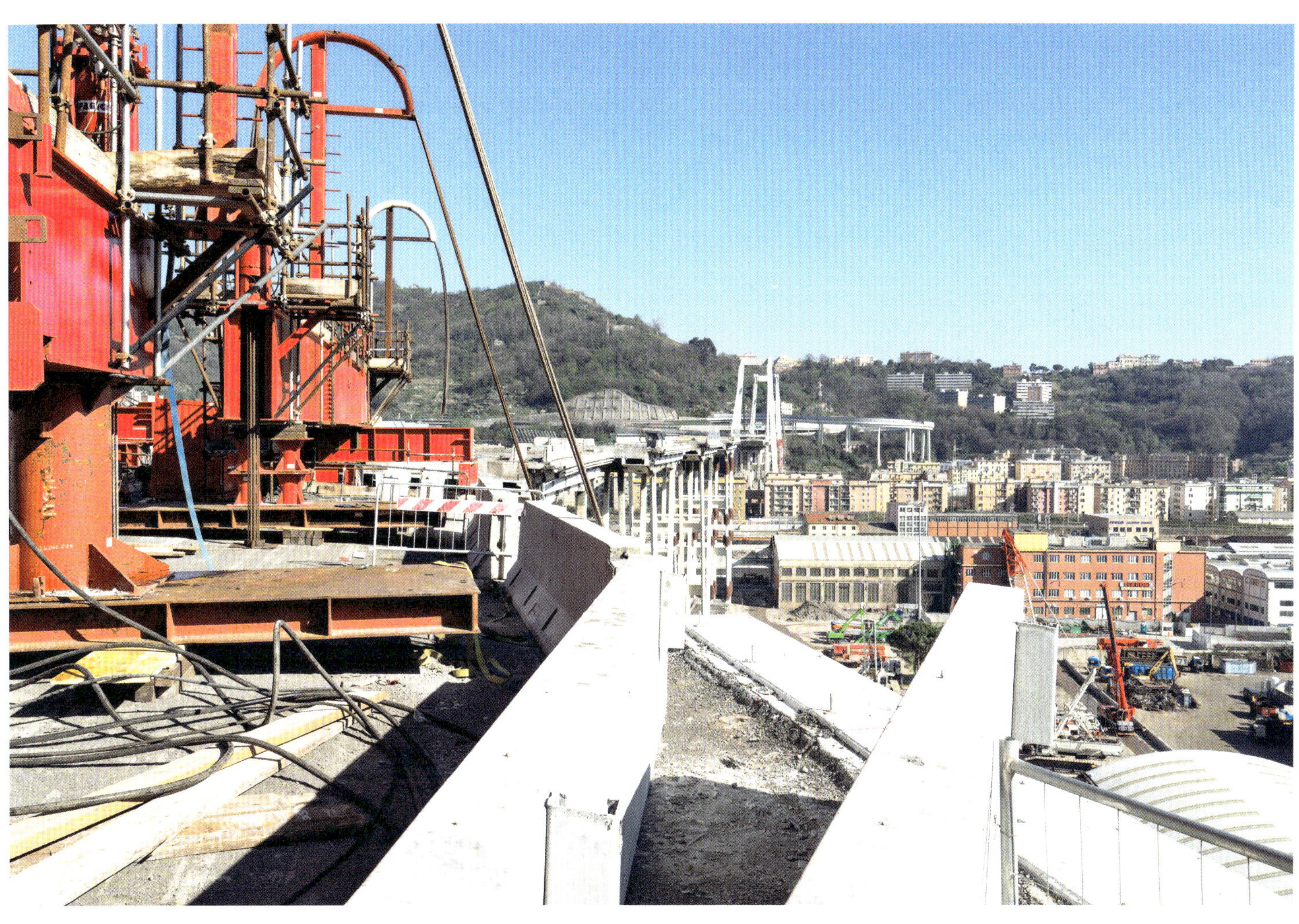

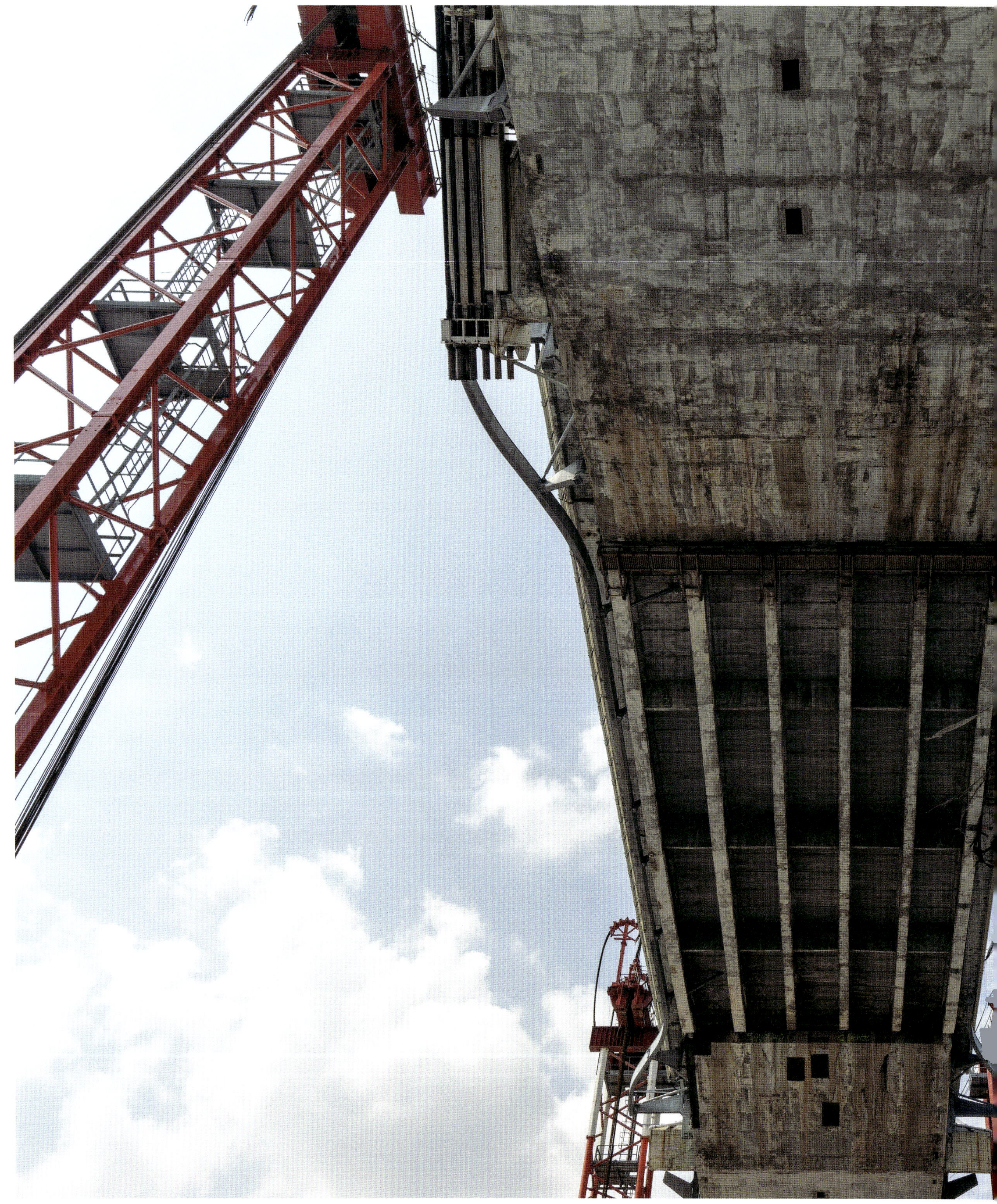

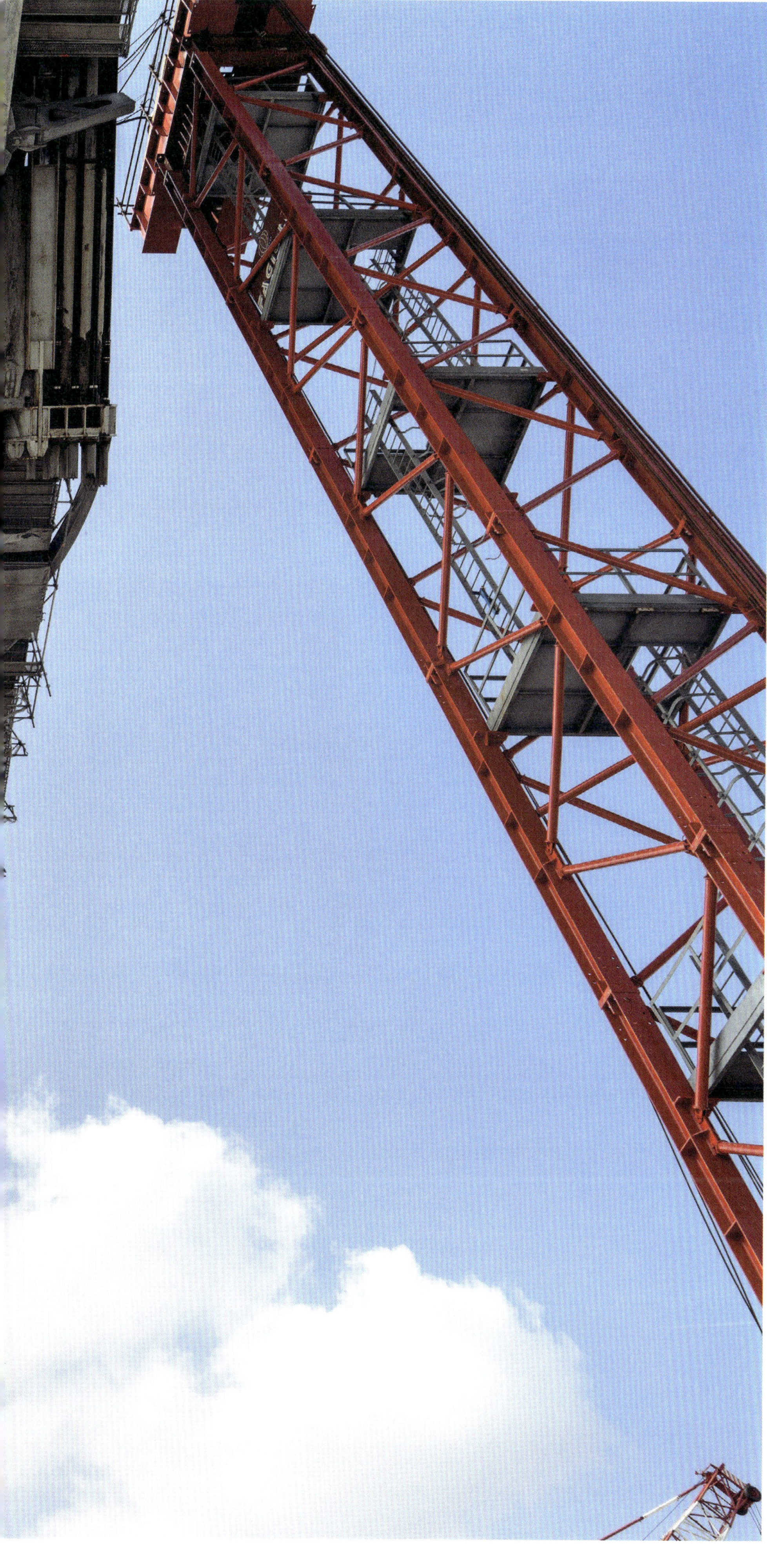

In order to work safely on piers 10 and 11 stabilization towers had to be installed. This way it was possible to proceed to lightening the structure and preparing it to be demolished by controlled explosion, without putting the building site workers at risk.

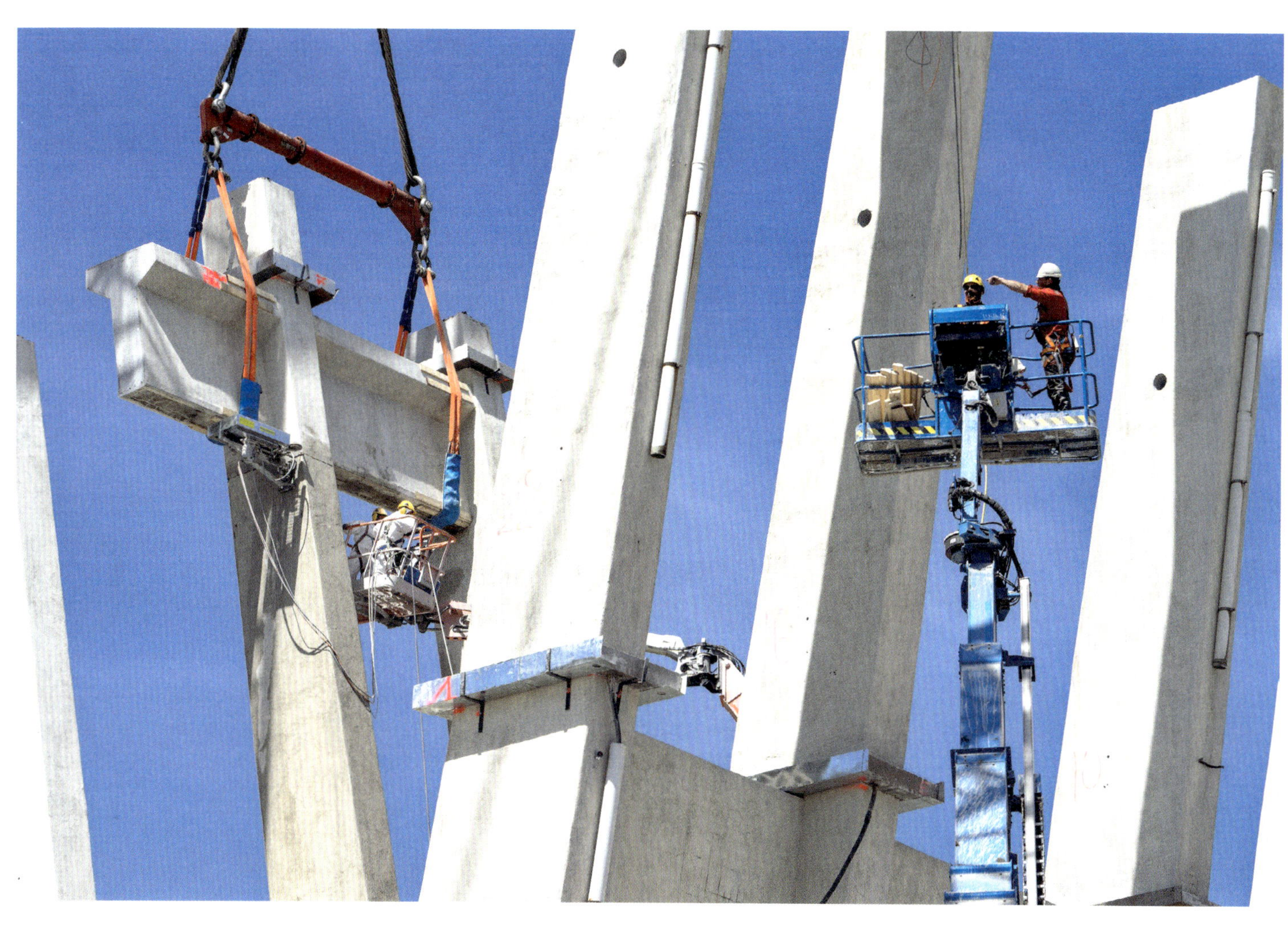

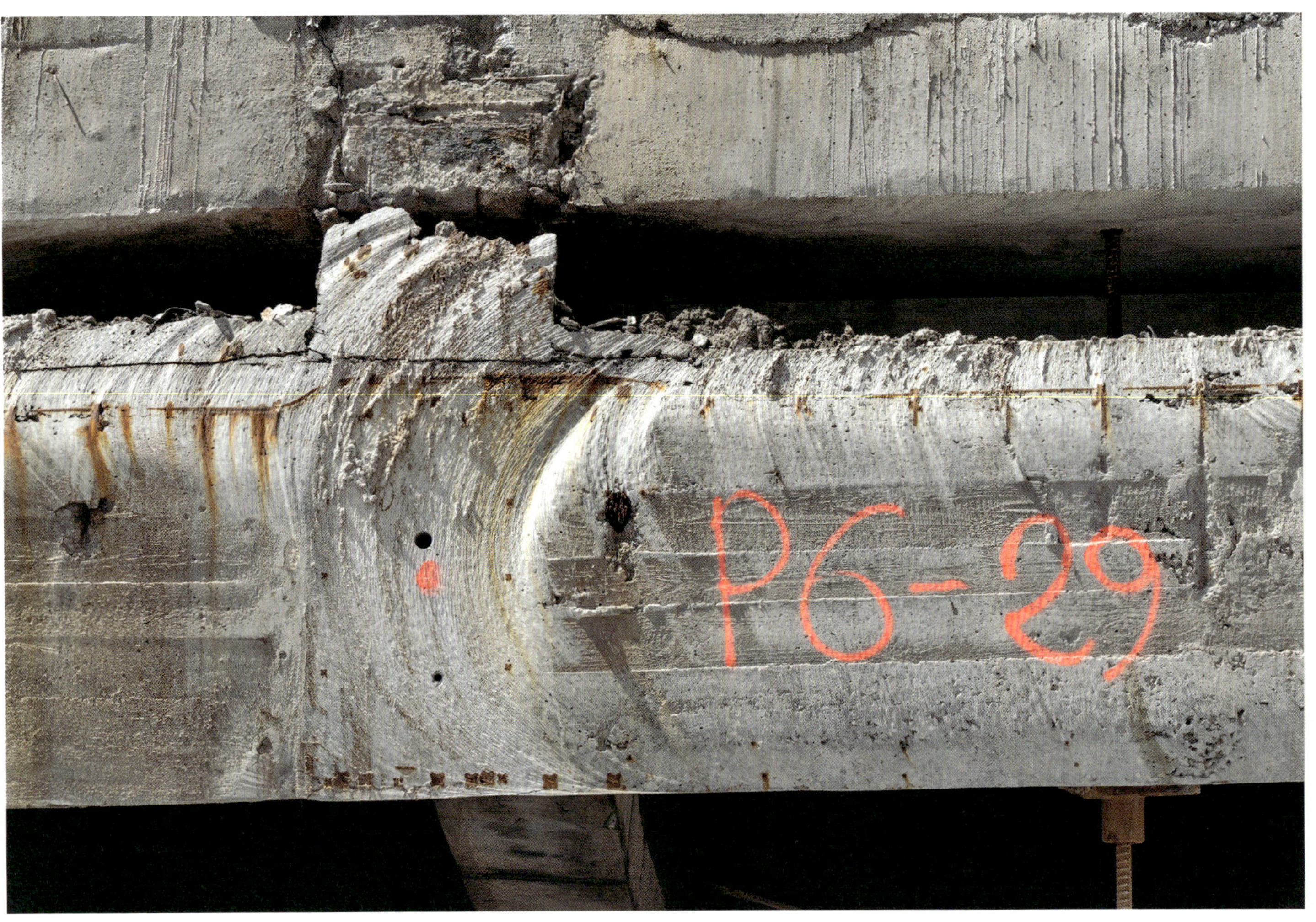

APRIL 30, 2019

Demolition by Controlled Explosion and Mitigation Measures

The demolition by controlled explosion of Ponte Morandi's piers 10 and 11 came about on June 28, 2019, in four sequential almost simultaneous phases, lasting about 6 seconds altogether, using about 500 electronic detonators, over 500 kg of dynamite, and 5,000 meters of detonating fuse.

First of all, the stays of span 11 were severed with directional explosive charges. Immediately afterwards, a wall of water was elevated, activated by explosive charges up to a height of around 90 meters. This was aimed at mitigating the spread of the dust from the crumbling of the structure. After that, the charges were detonated in the load-bearing structural elements of both spans, immediately followed by the elevation of a further quantity of water, about 40 meters in height, to the sides of both piers as a lateral barrier to prevent the dust from spreading as the debris fell.

As a further measure of mitigation for the spread of dust during the collapse phases, remotely-controlled nebulizers were activated (so-called cannon fog), with a spray between 25 and 60 meters and a load of up to 6,000 liters of water per hour.

The tanks filled with water obtained from the positioning of concrete barriers above the deck at a height of 45 meters had a width of fall equal to around 66 meters. The columns of water visible at the start of the explosion cut the dust arising from the explosion, as the tanks were made to explode at the same time as the explosion of the charges above the piers. The vibrations from the collapse were absorbed by damper suspensions, situated beneath piers 10 and 11, with particular characteristics of kinetic energy absorption caused by falling and impact on the ground. They consisted of inert materials 6-8 centimeters in size.

A separation layer was placed beneath these heaps. The layer consisted of non-woven fabric to withhold the water falling down. The non-woven fabric was also placed over the debris so that the dust was completely contained.

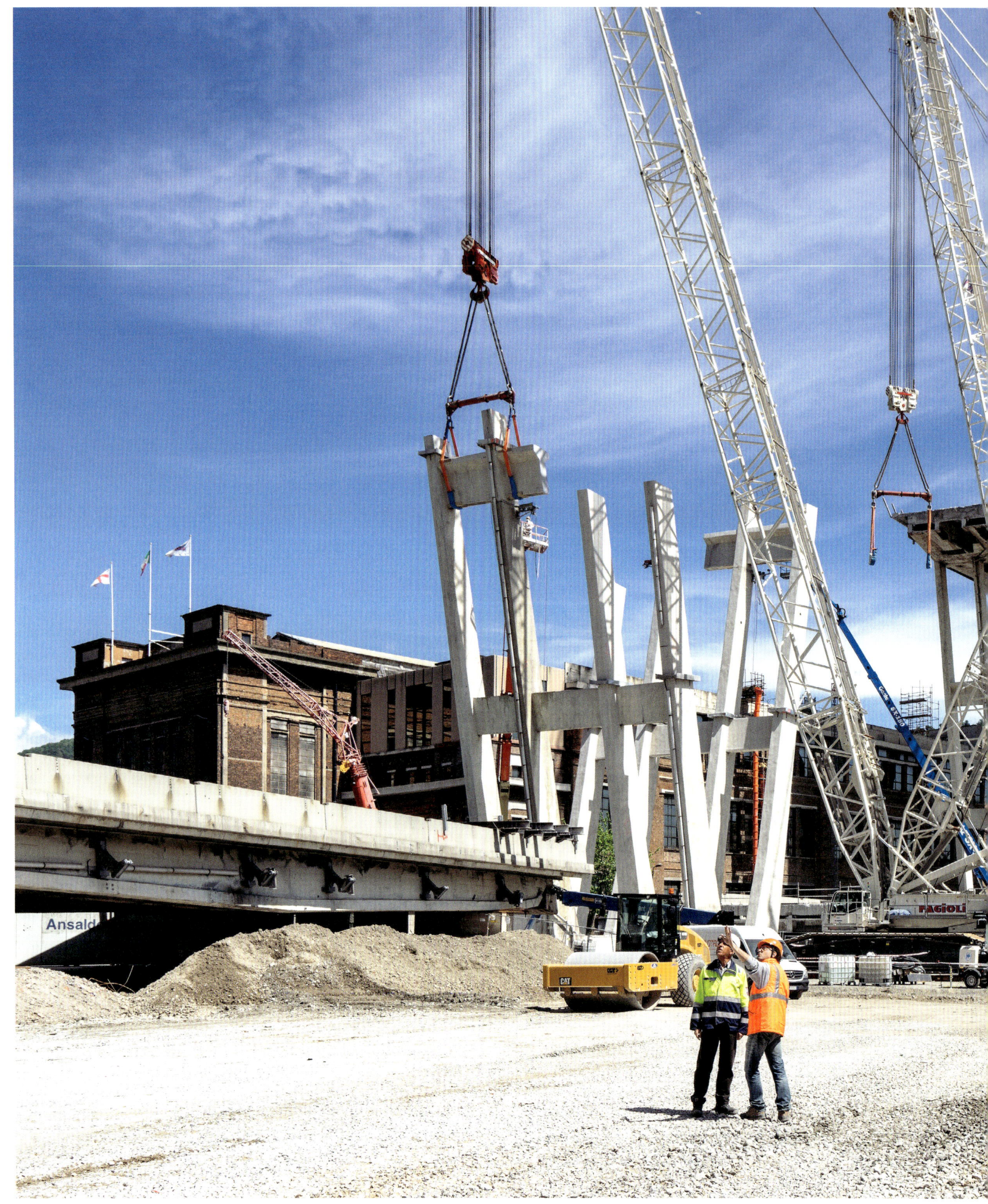

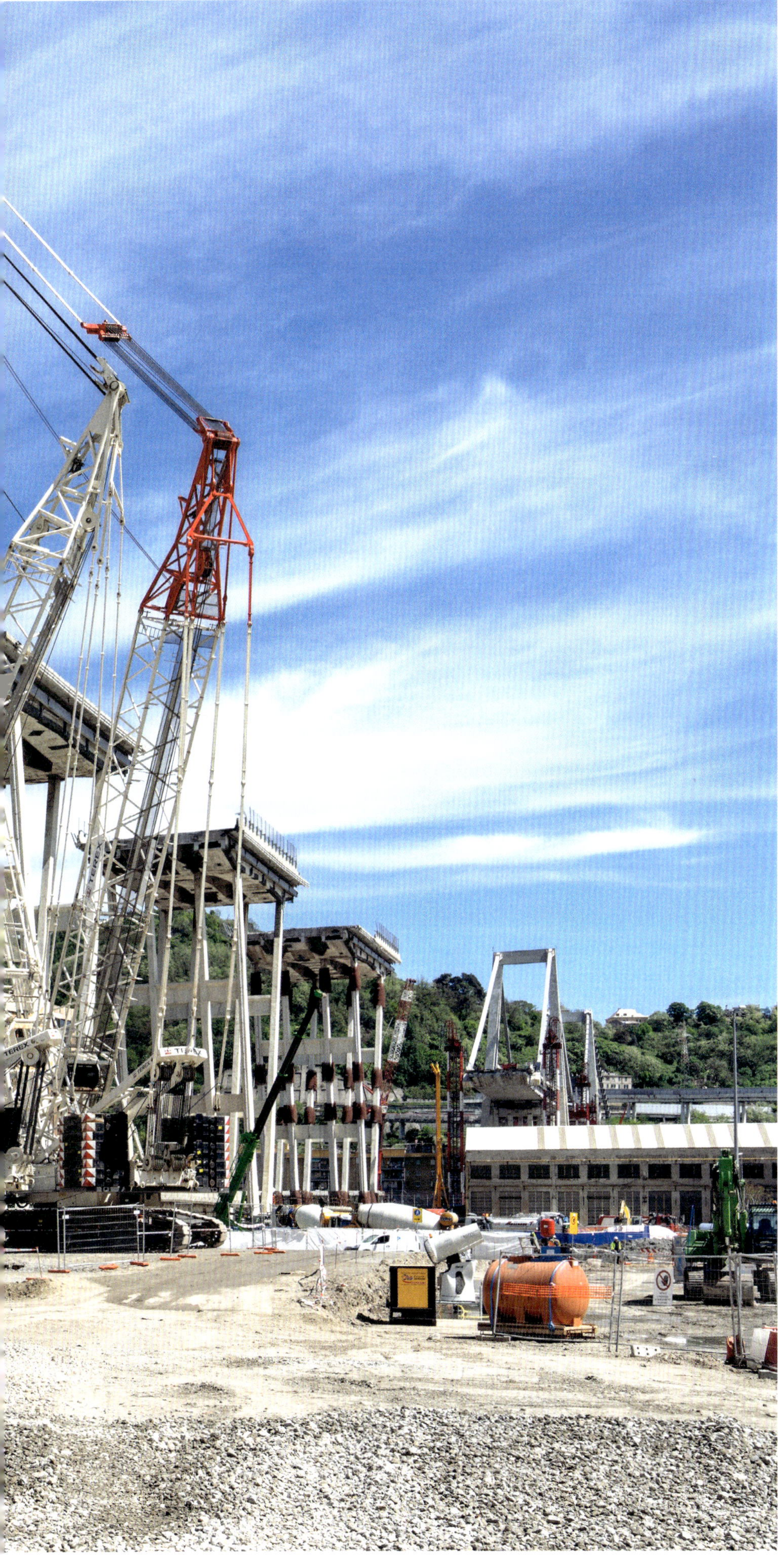

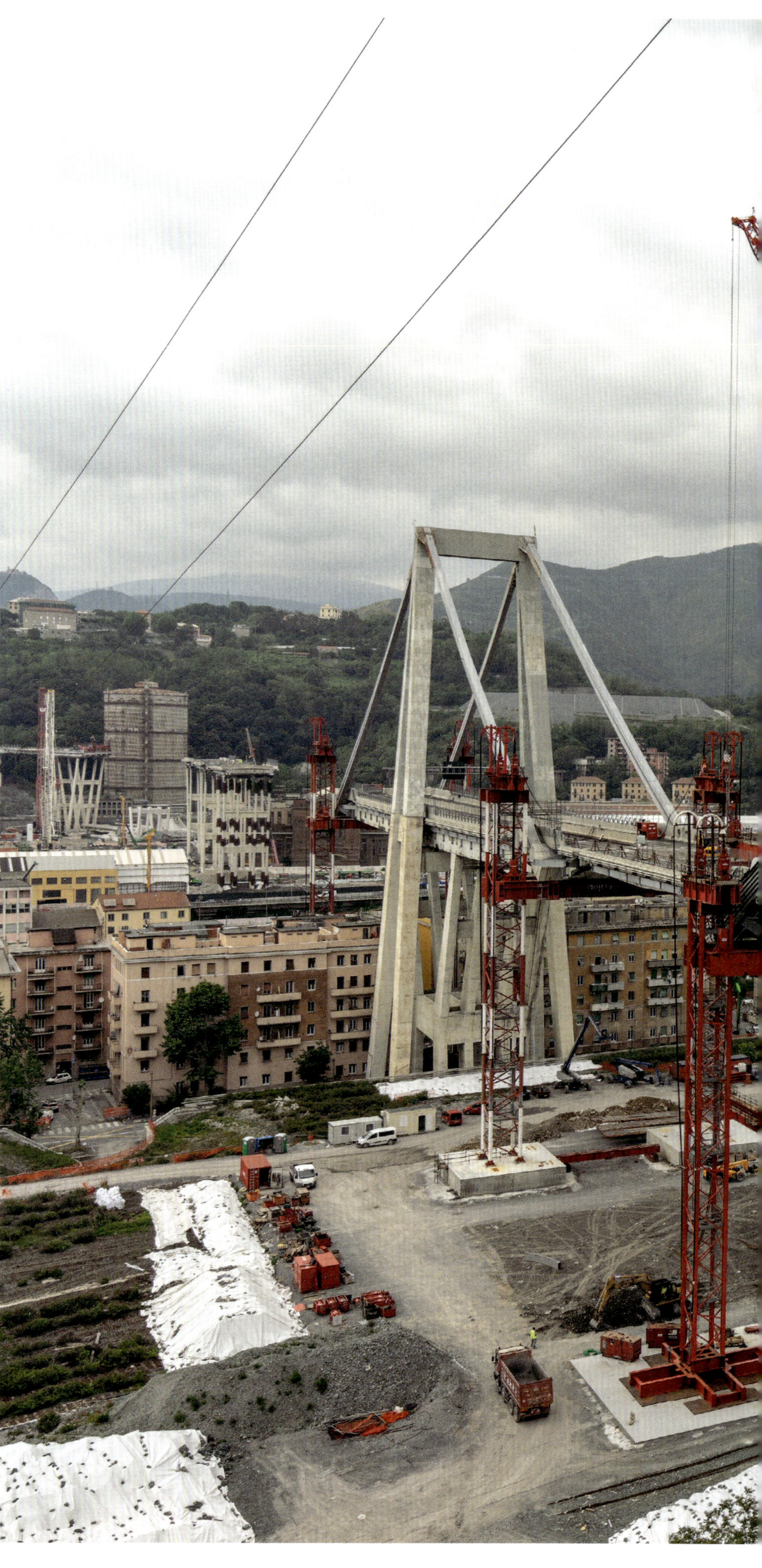

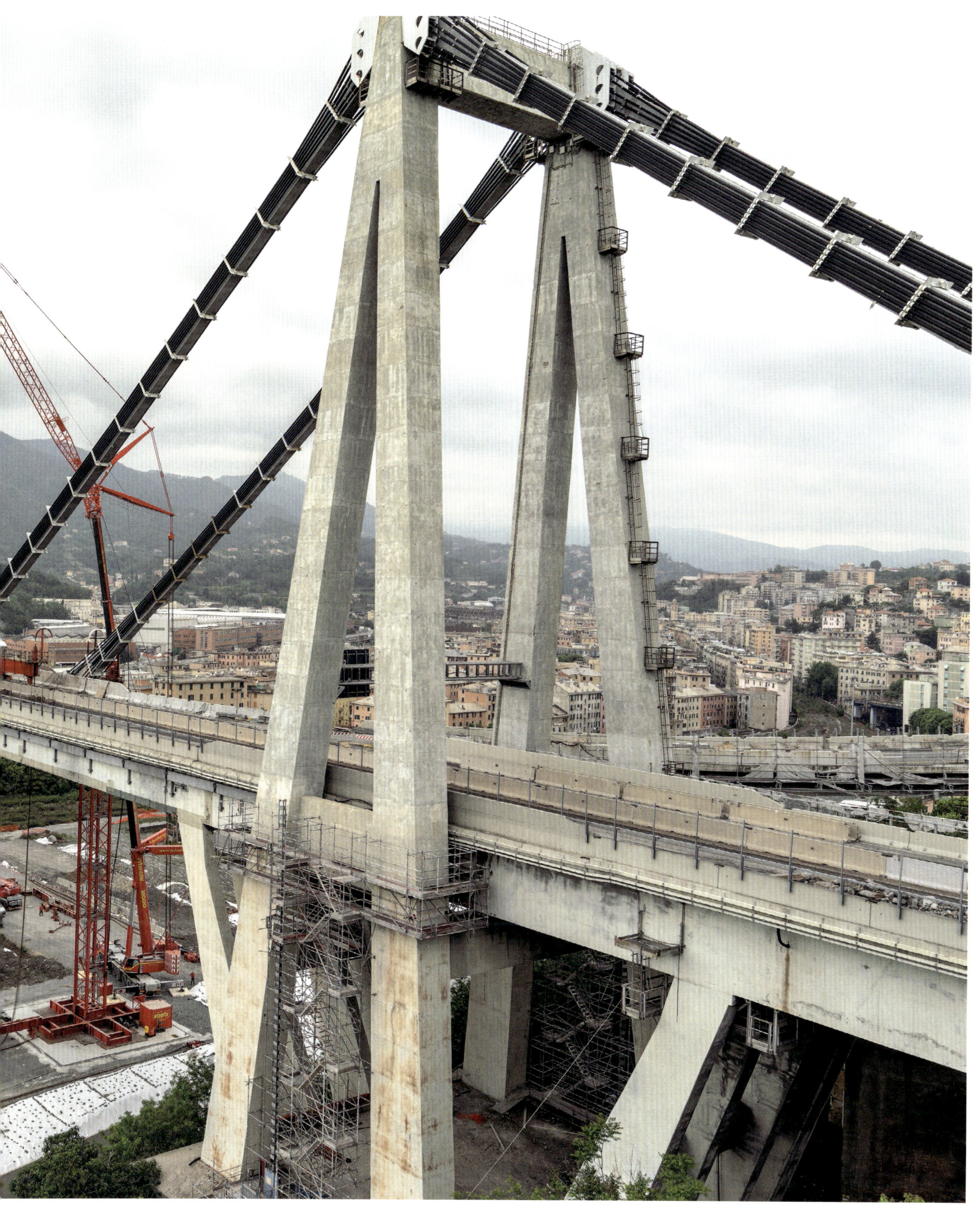

IN LIFE YOU DO LOTS OF
THINGS WITH COMMITMENT.
WITH THE UTMOST
COMMITMENT.
MOST OF THE TIME BECAUSE
IT'S WORTH IT TO YOU,
IN DIFFERENT WAYS.
PERSONAL FULFILLMENT,
CAREER, POSITION, MONEY.
FOR THE BRIDGE I BELIEVE WE
DID THE SAME, ESPECIALLY
BECAUSE IT WAS THE RIGHT
AND NECESSARY THING TO DO.

CARLO VARDANEGA
RINA

WHEN THE BUILDING SITE
OPENED, I WENT TO THE
AREA THAT HAD BEEN MADE
INACCESSIBLE, THE ONE
THAT WAS LOCATED
UNDERNEATH WHAT WAS
LEFT OF PONTE MORANDI.
GOING "DOWN THERE" WAS
A VERY MOVING EXPERIENCE:
IT ALLOWED ME TO FEEL
THE SENSE OF DRAMA,
BUT ALSO PERCEIVE THE IRON
WILL TO GO THROUGH WITH
THE RECONSTRUCTION.

CINZIA LAURA VIGNERI
COMMISSIONER'S OFFICE

Innovative techniques were used to lessen the
potential environmental effects of the explosion,
and in particular to contain the spread of the dust
deriving from the collapse of the structure and its
impact onto the ground.
The most spectacular of these techniques were the
walls of water activated by explosives situated in huge
water tanks positioned on the deck and under the spans
to be demolished. To design this "artificial rain" the
explosives were tested in a quarry, producing colored
jets of water up to 100-meters high.

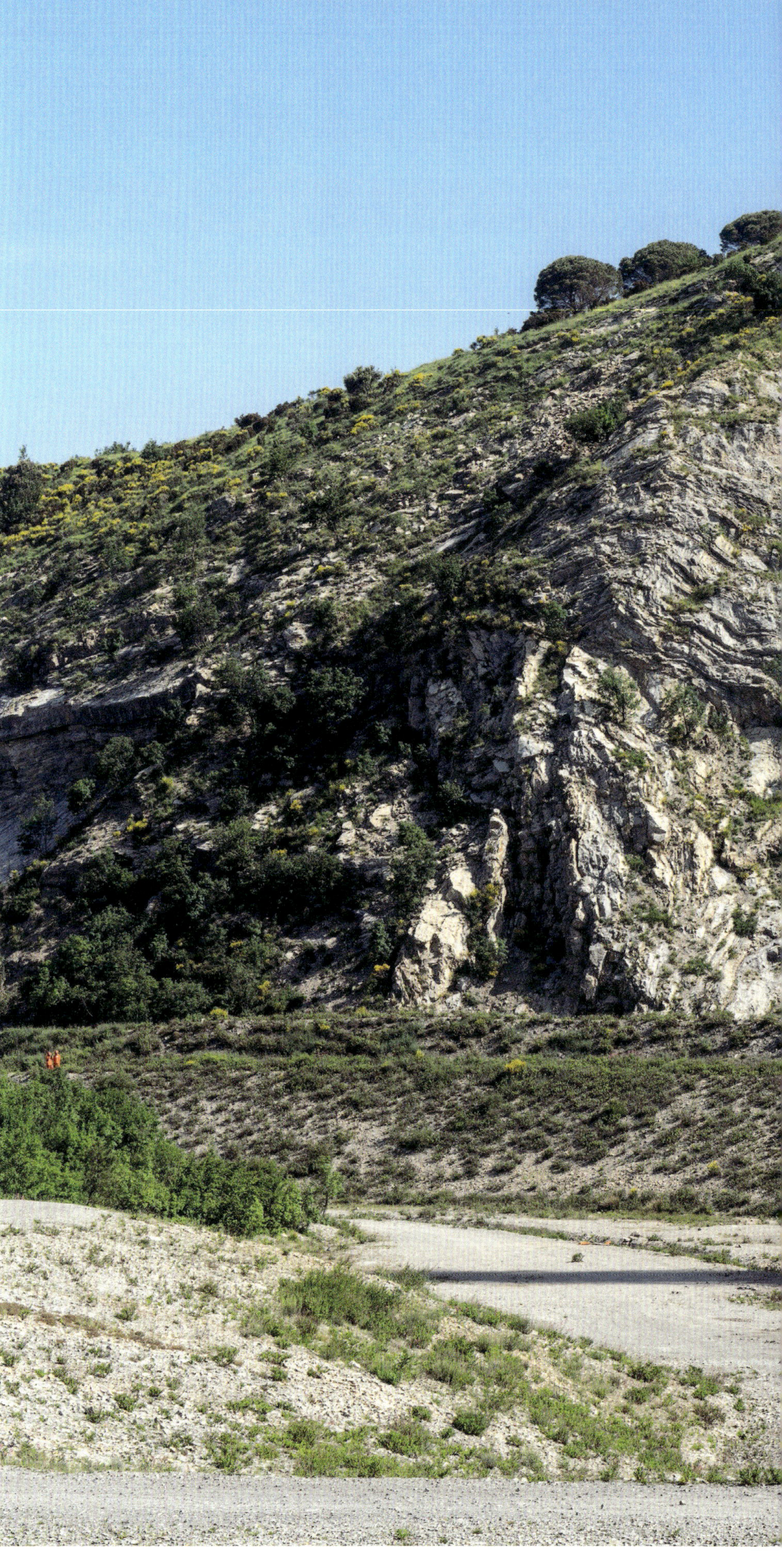

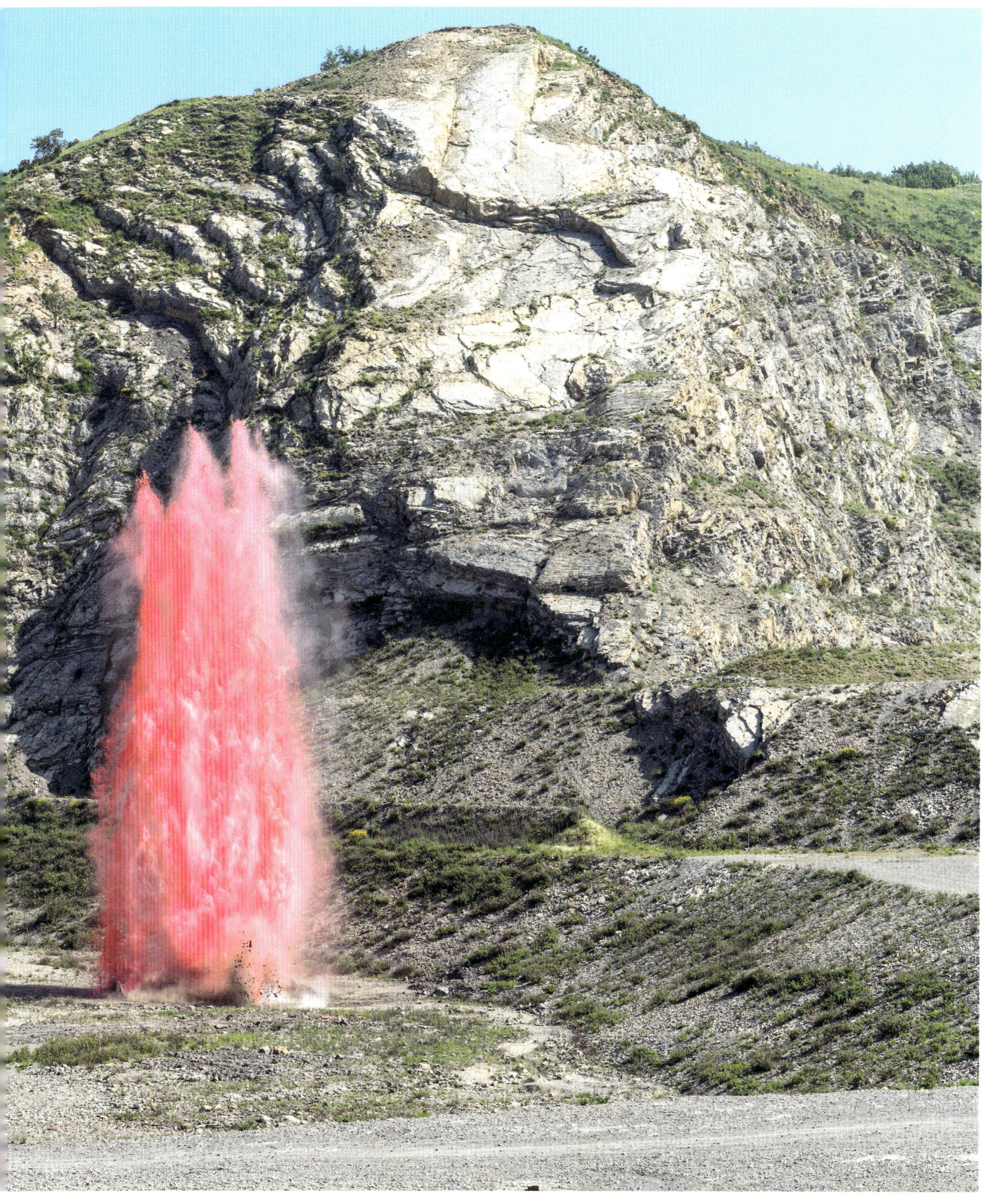

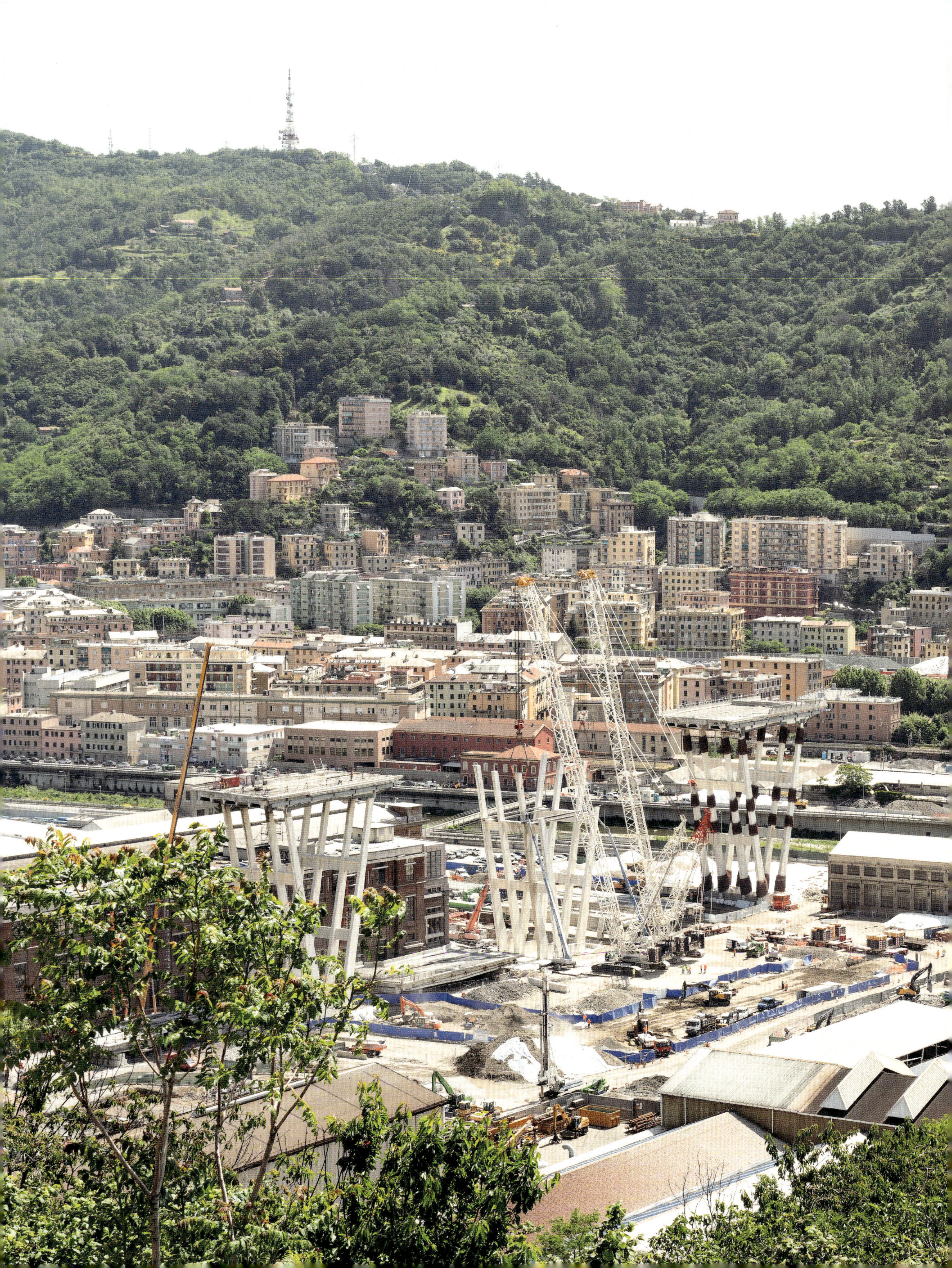

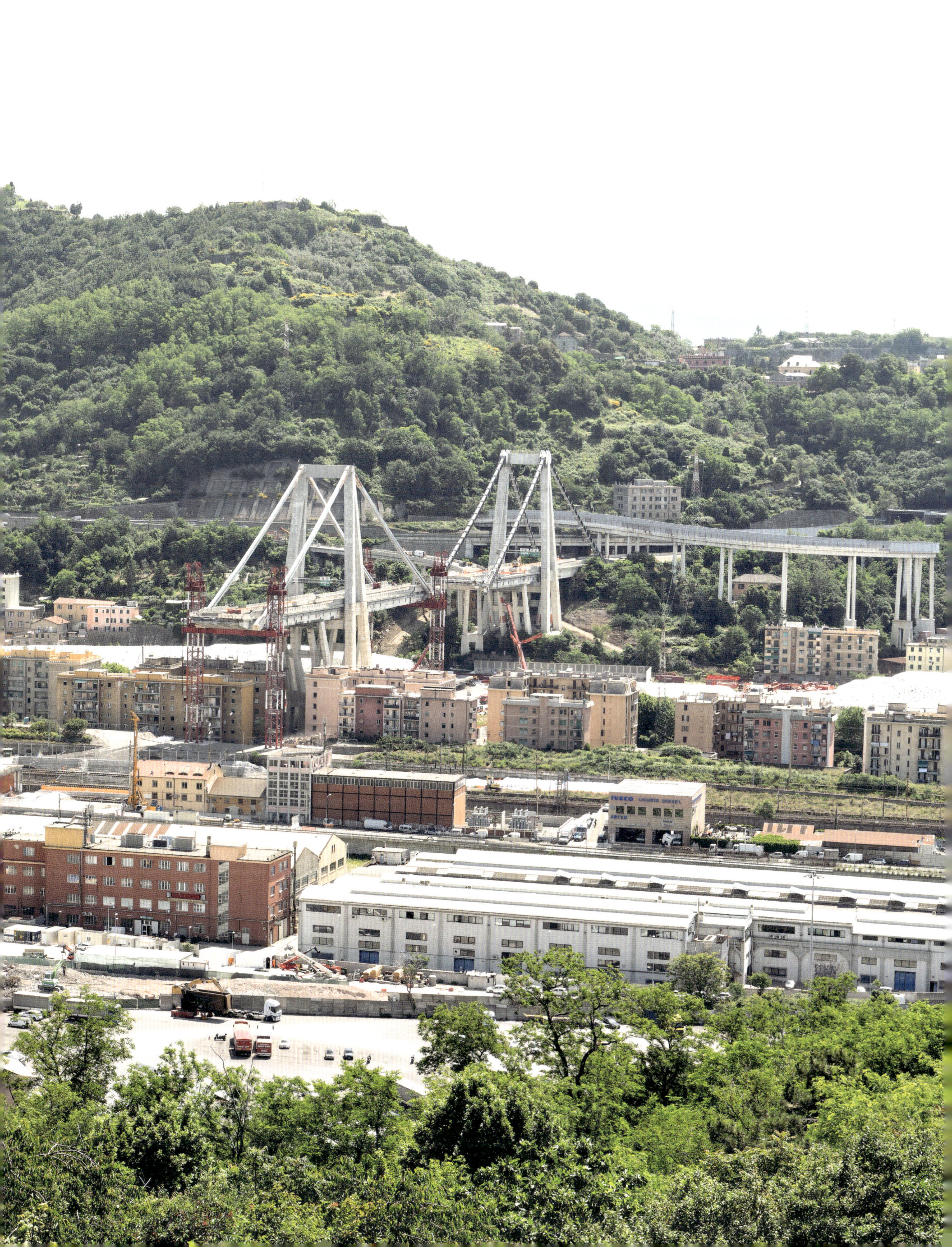

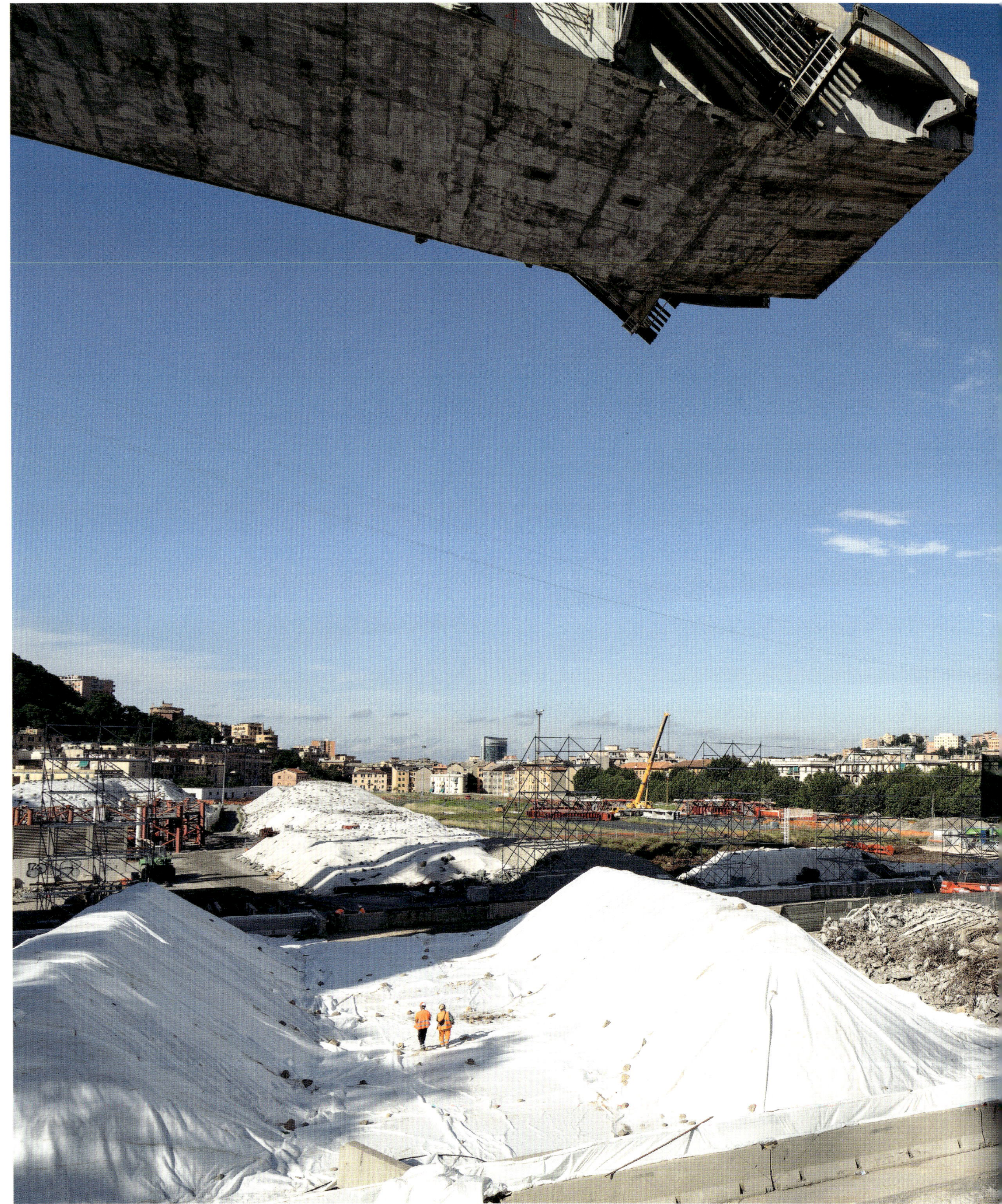

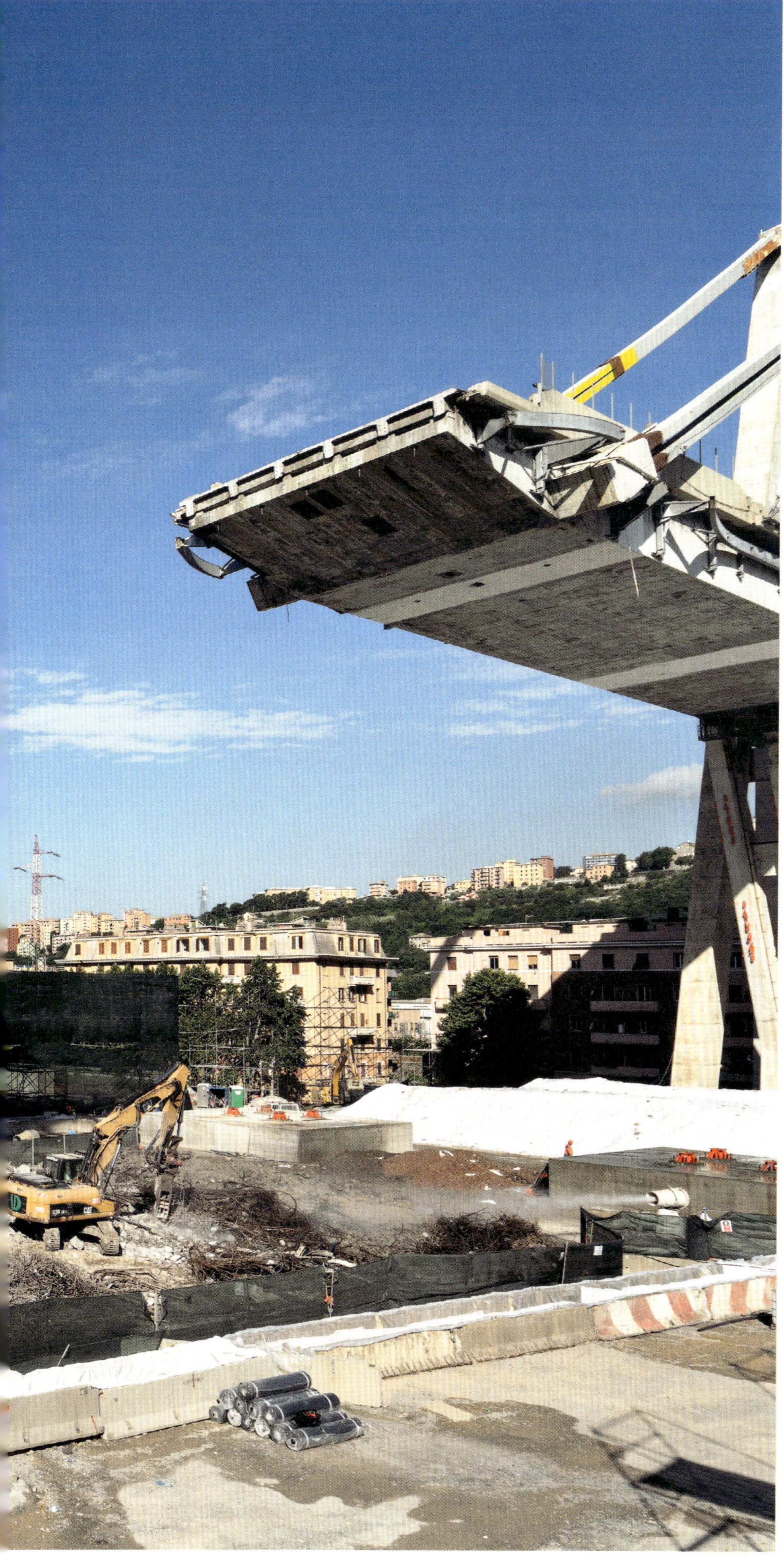

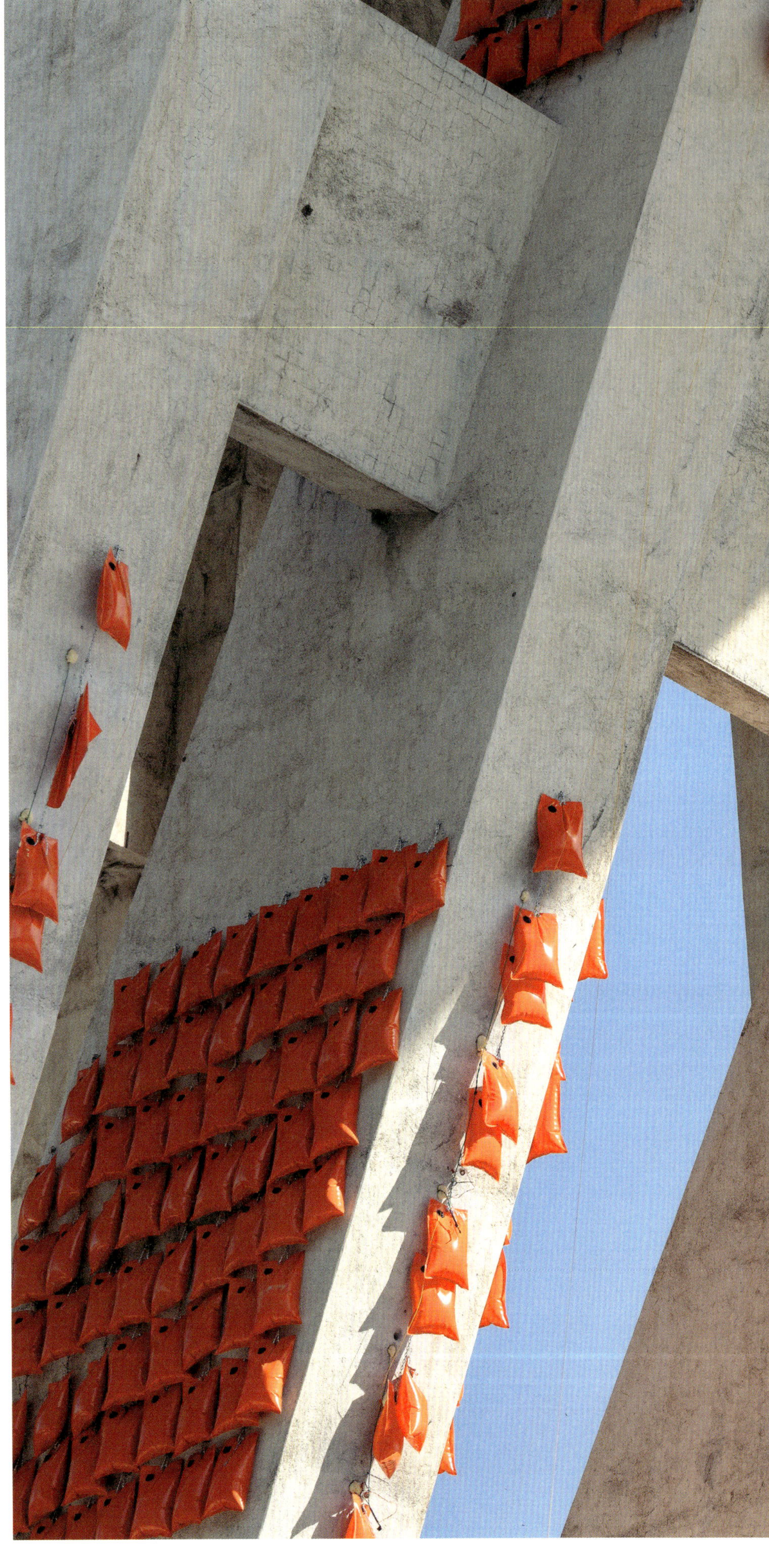

Bags filled with water had been placed in the area corresponding to where the explosives were placed to the sides of the structure in order to mitigate the spread of the dust arising from the detonation.

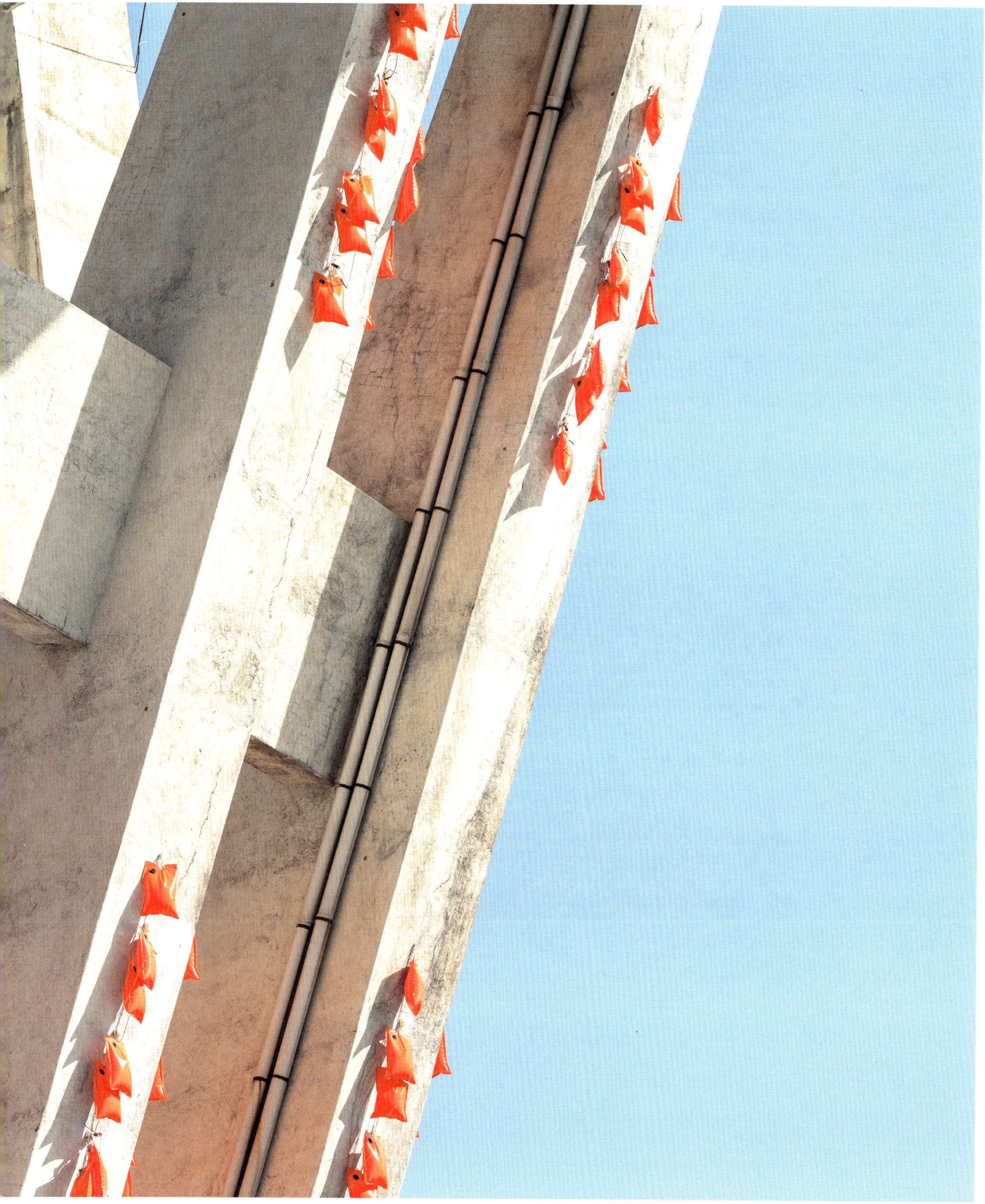

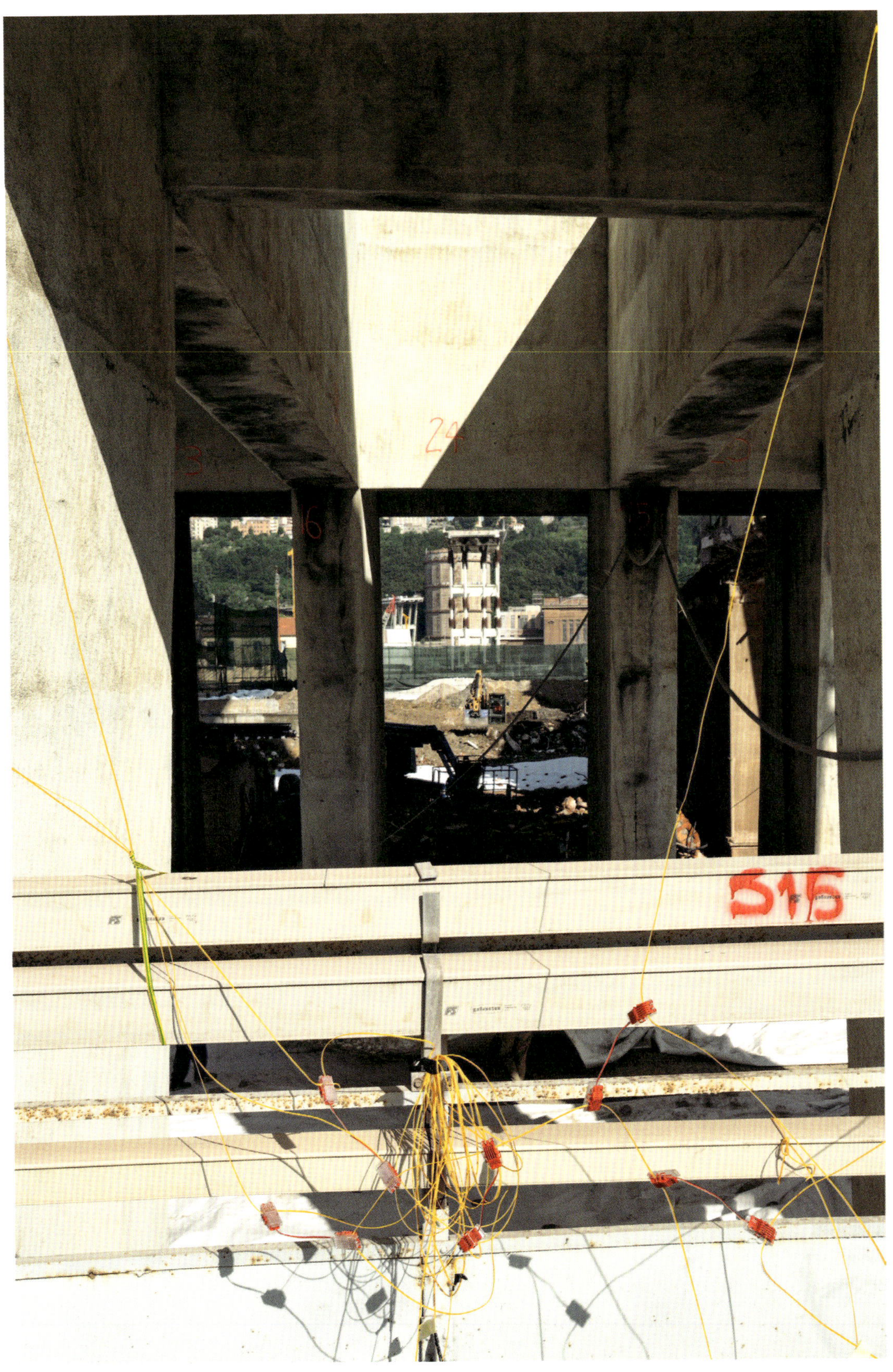

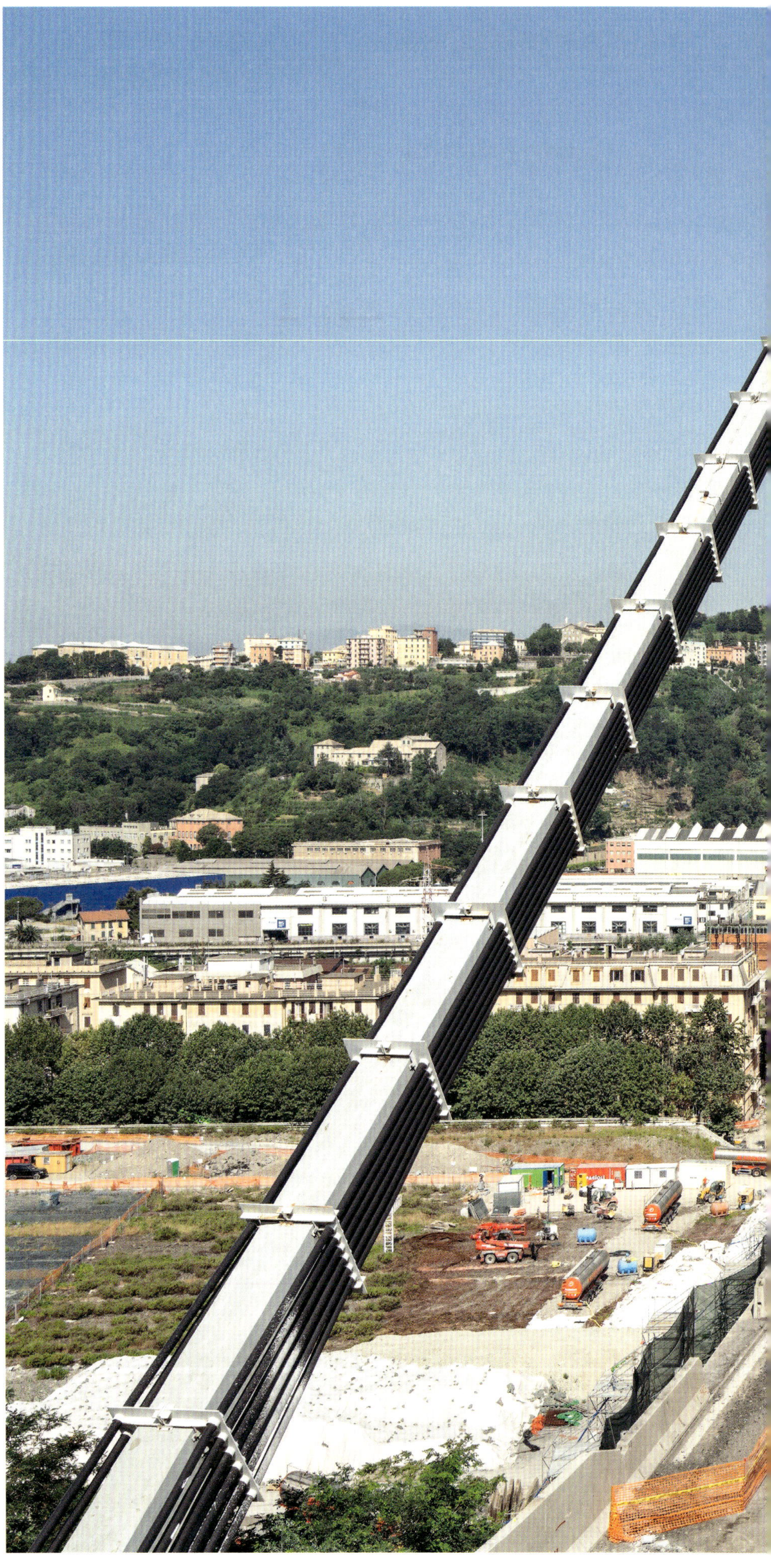

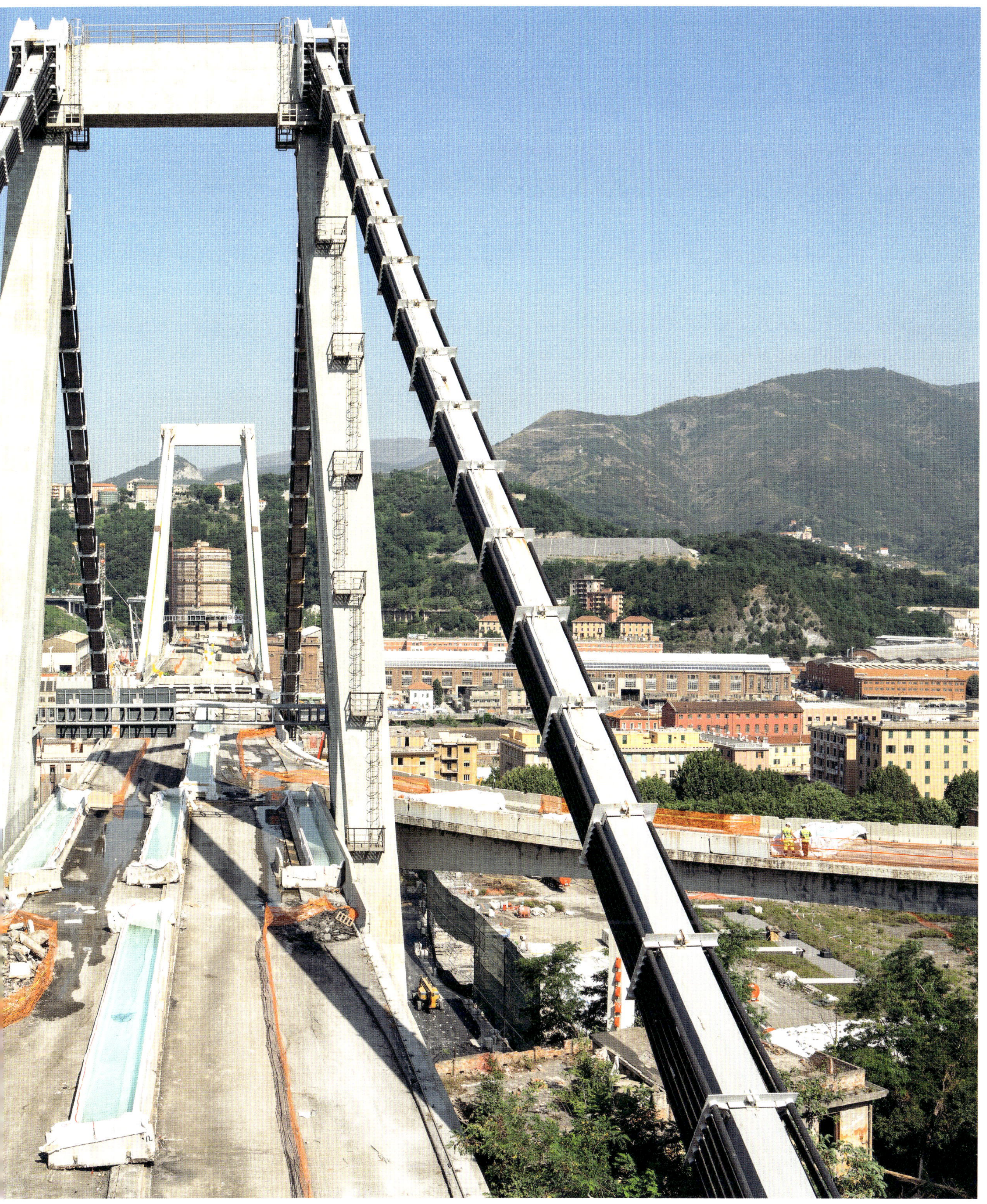

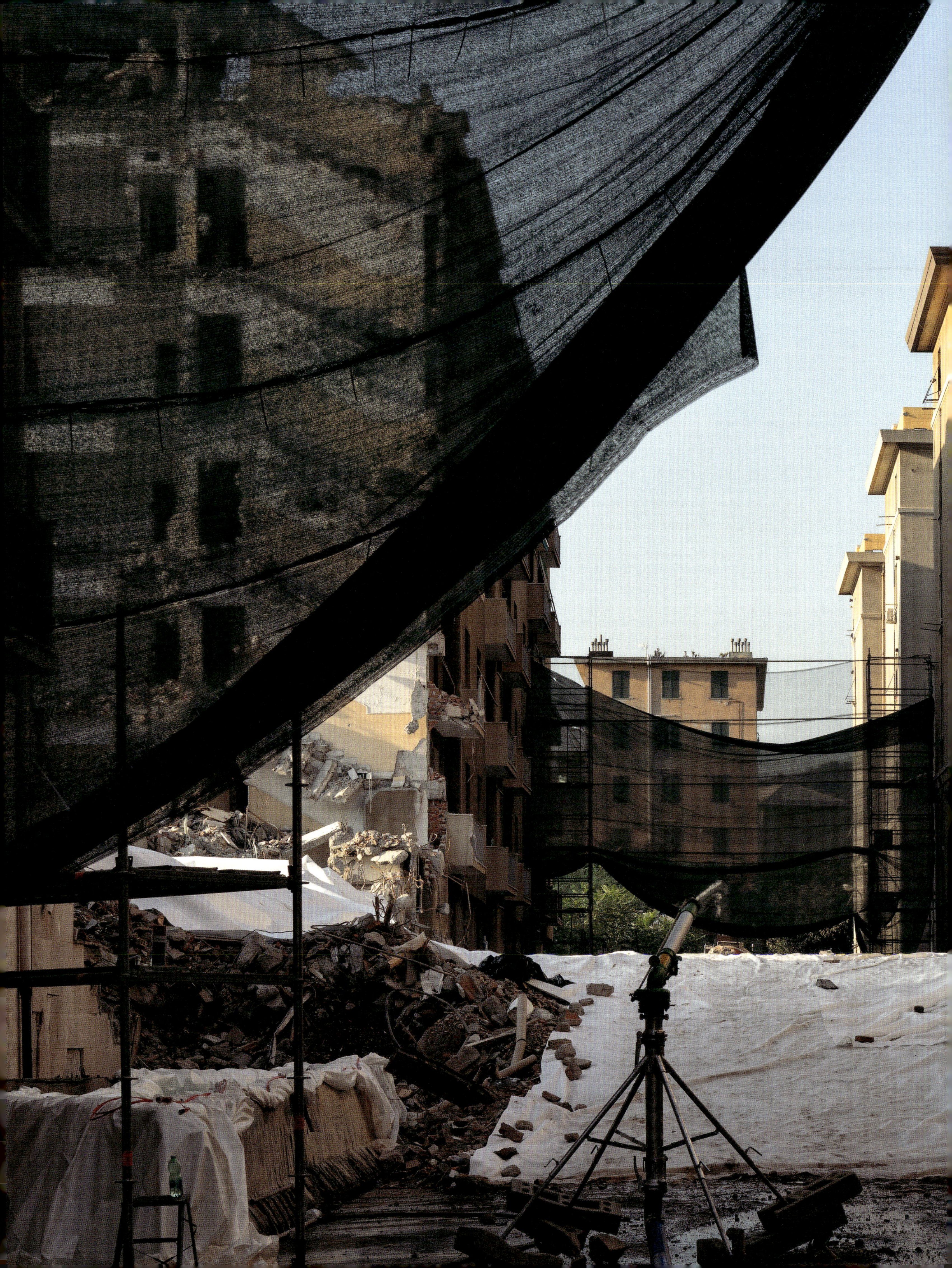

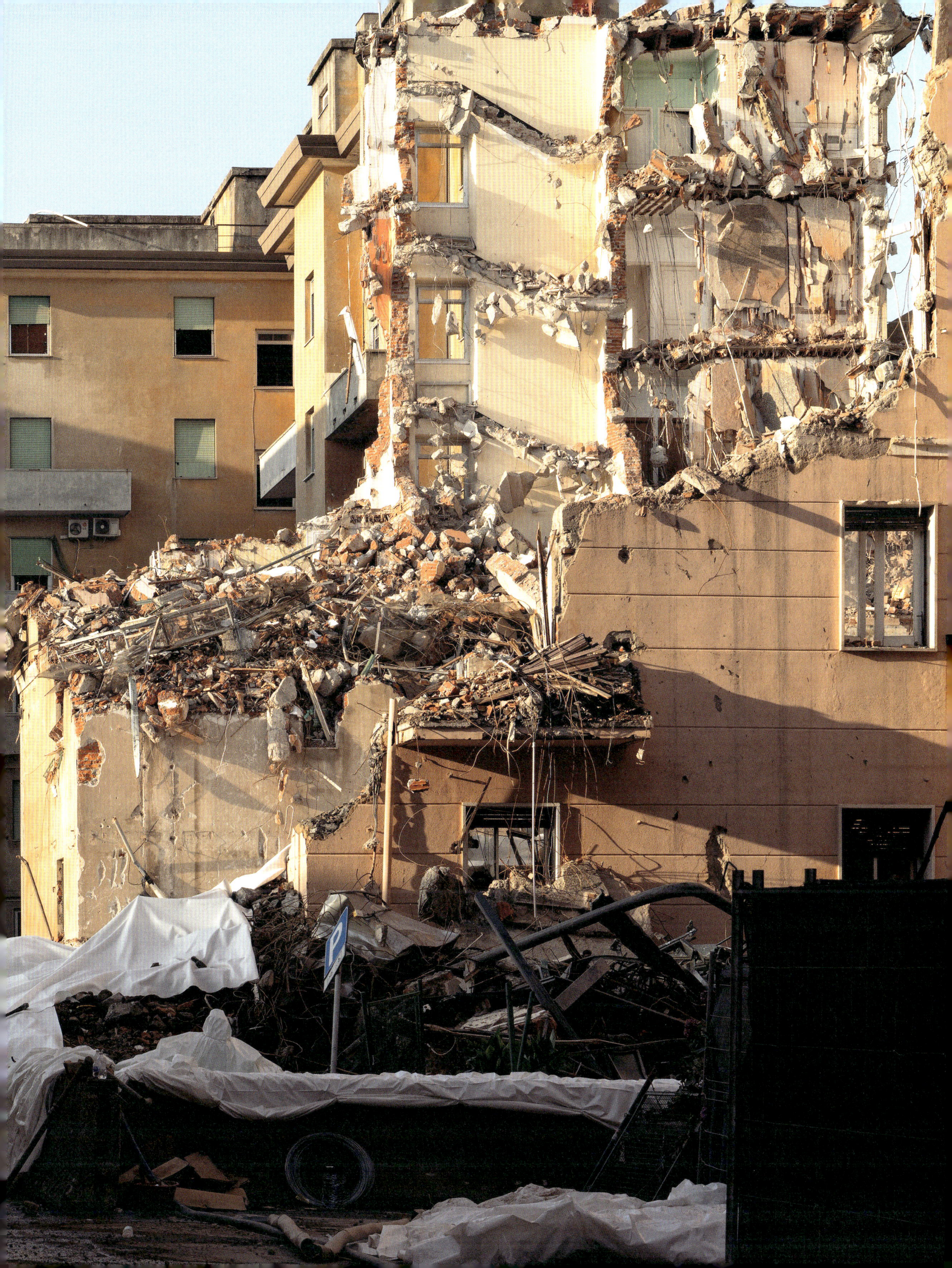

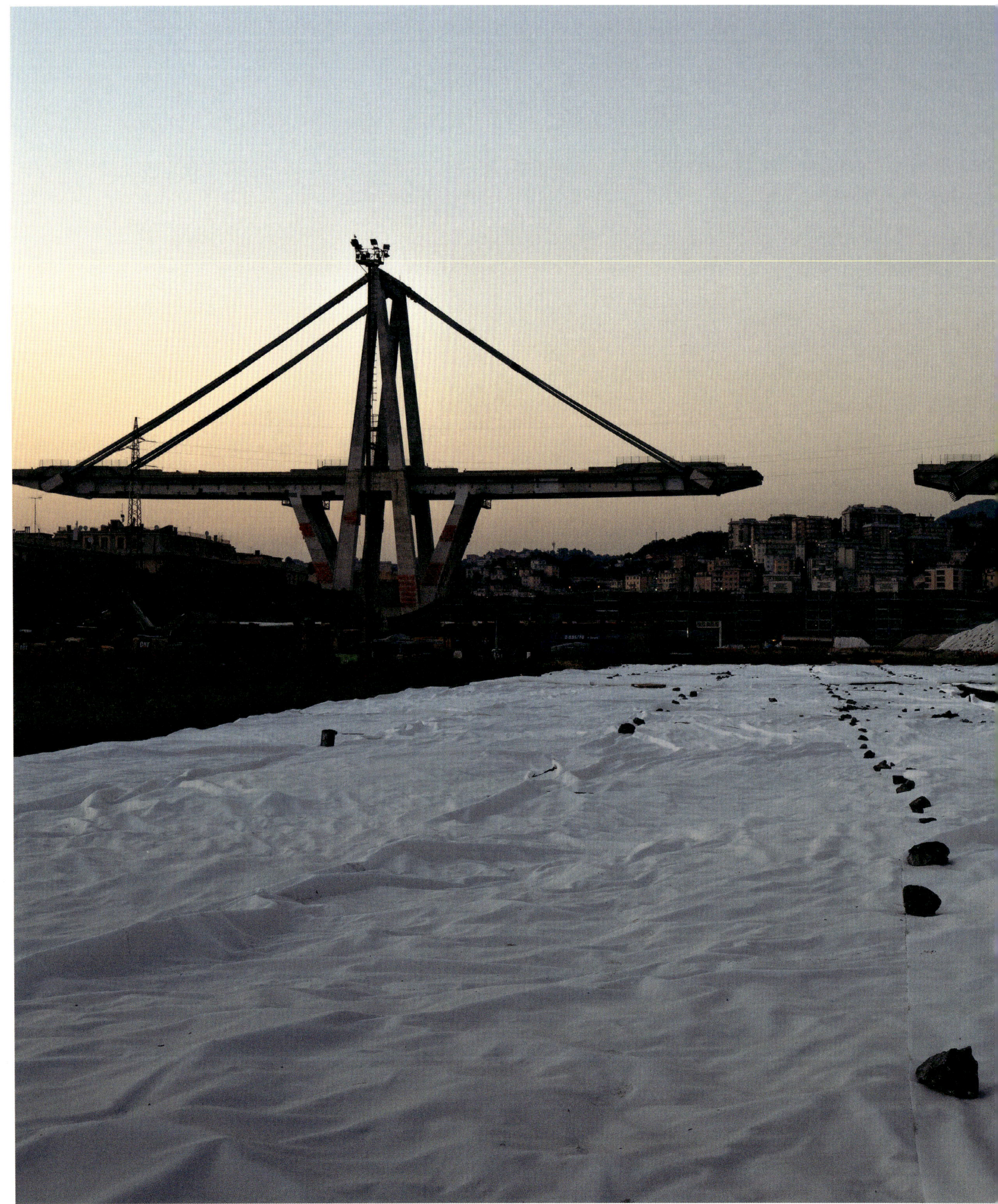

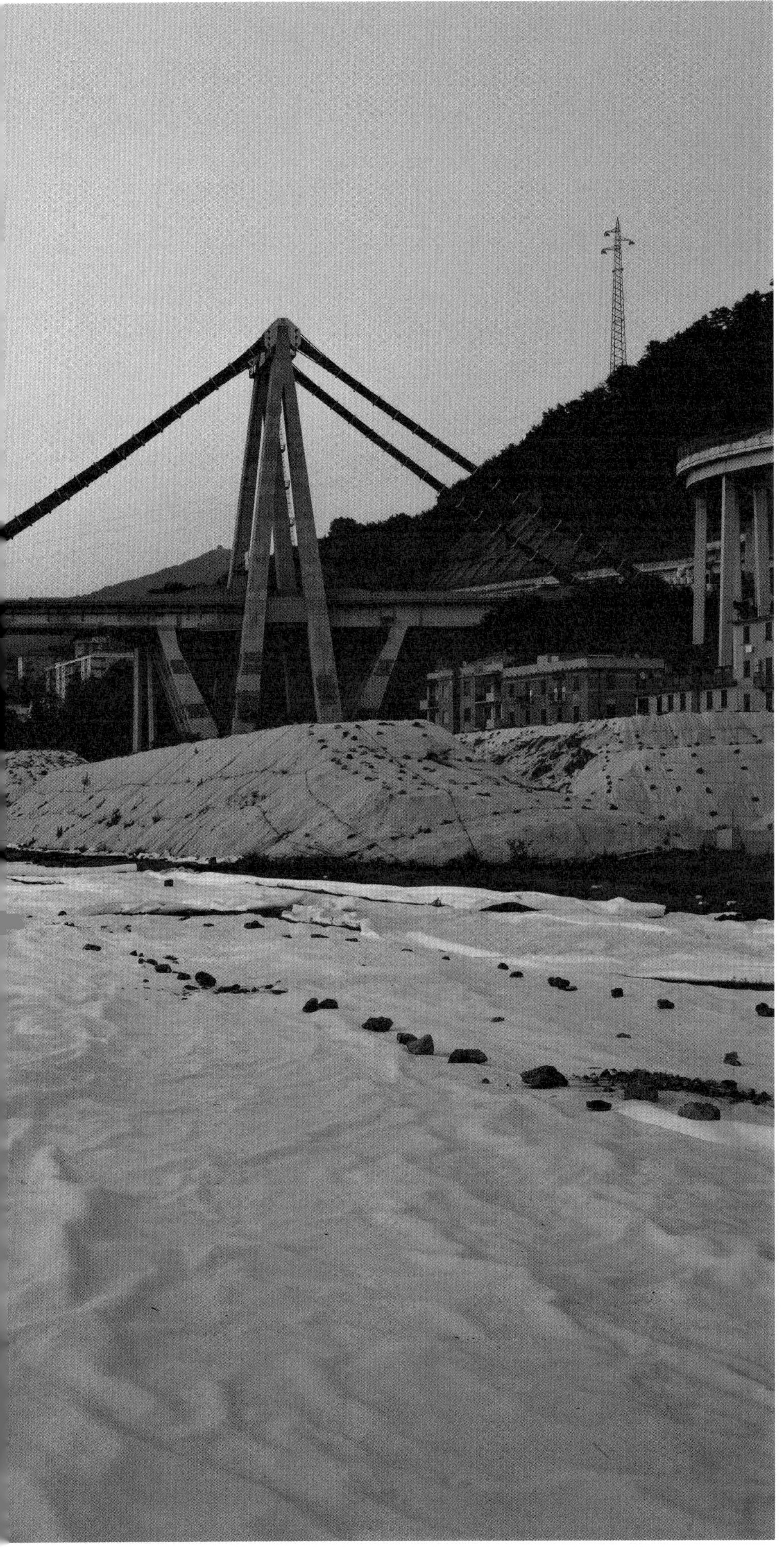

The area of the Campasso, to the south of the bridge,
was covered in non-woven fabric to withhold the water
used to trap the dust from the explosion.

THE MOST COMPLEX PROJECT
I EVER HAD TO FACE, BECAUSE
OF THE EMOTION I FELT AND
THE EXPECTATIONS THAT AN
ENTIRE CITY HAD IN THIS
RECONSTRUCTION.
IT WAS TEAMWORK THAT
WON IN THE END: INSIDE RINA,
WITH THE COMMISSIONER'S
OFFICE, WITH THE STATE
ATTORNEY GENERAL'S OFFICE,
WITH THE COMPANIES, WITH
ALL OF THE ENTITIES INVOLVED.

ANDREA TOMARCHIO
RINA

AFTER YEARS SPENT
PLANNING AND MANAGING
INTERVENTIONS,
CONTRIBUTING TO DIRECTLY
BRINGING TO LIFE A WORK
OF SUCH SIGNIFICANCE AND
SEEING IT FINISHED WAS
A TRULY UNIQUE EXPERIENCE.

UGO BALLERINI
COMMISSIONER'S OFFICE

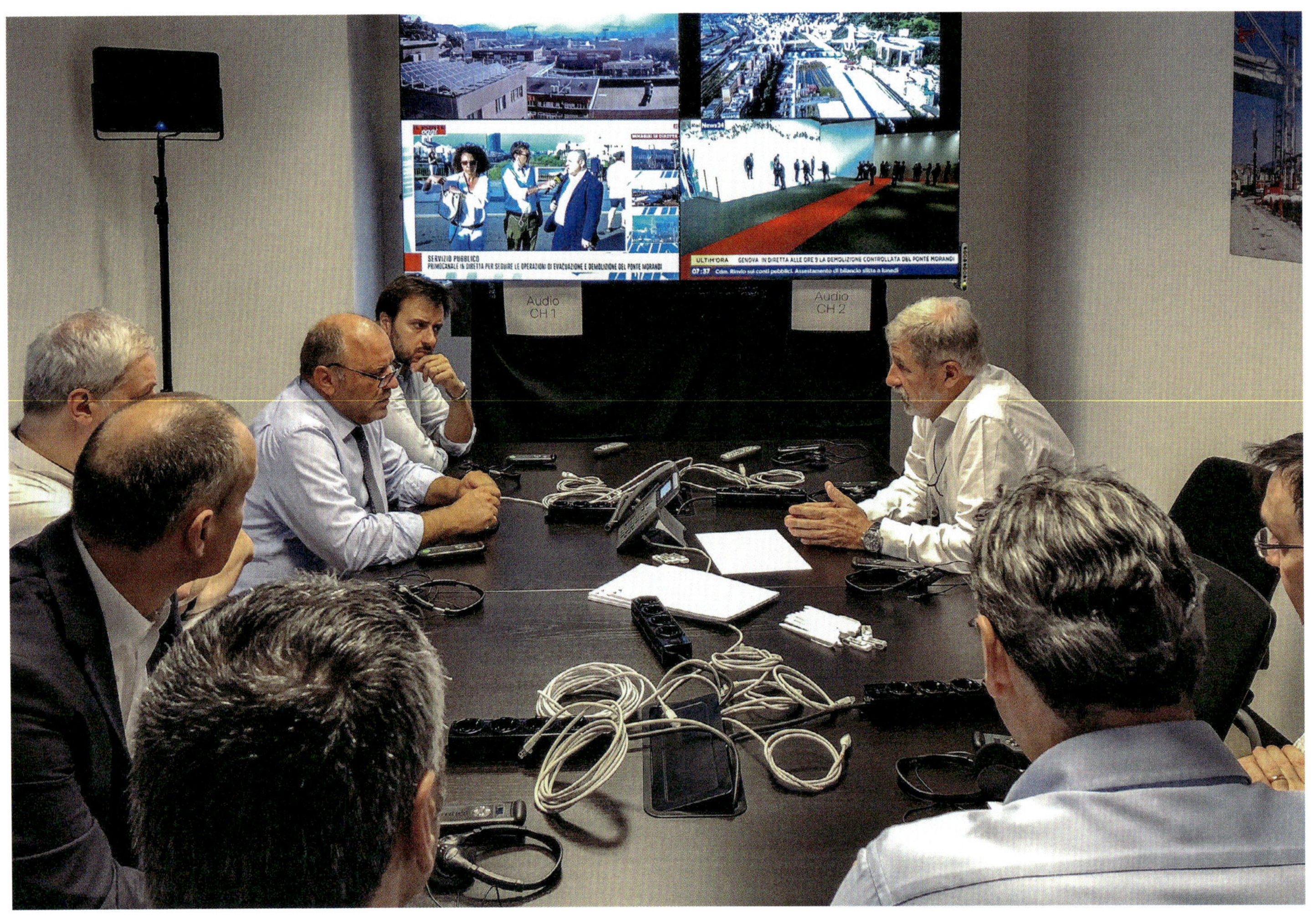

The PAC (Point of Advanced Command) set up in the RINA offices in the Campi district, 800 meters from the bridge, was the place where all the operative procedures prior to and after the explosion were carried out.

Commissioner Marco Bucci was present at the meetings of the PAC, along with the Director of his support office, Roberto Tedeschi, the Director of the Project for RINA, Roberto Carpaneto, and the Project Manager, Andrea Tomarchio.

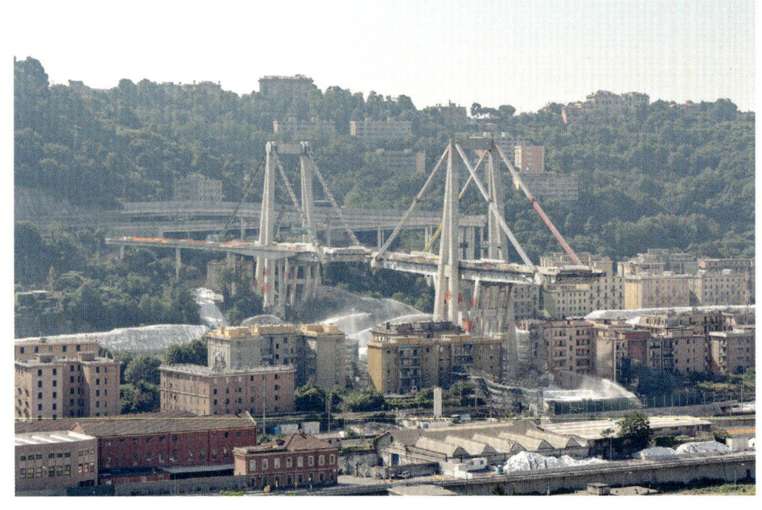 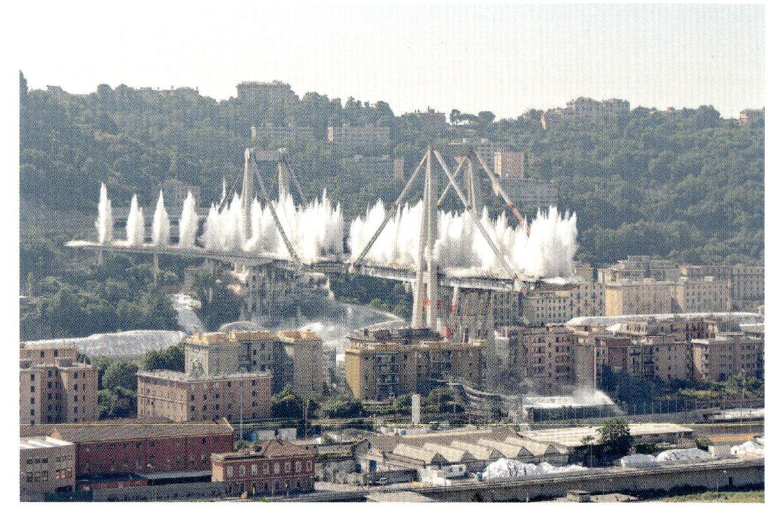

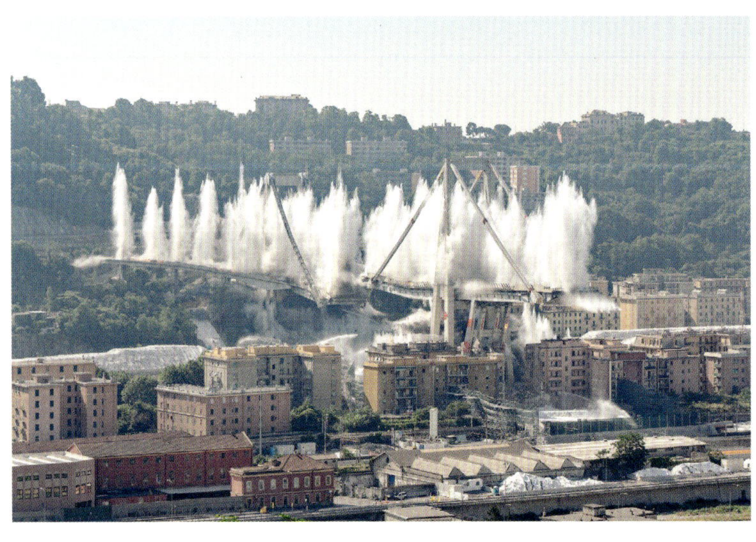 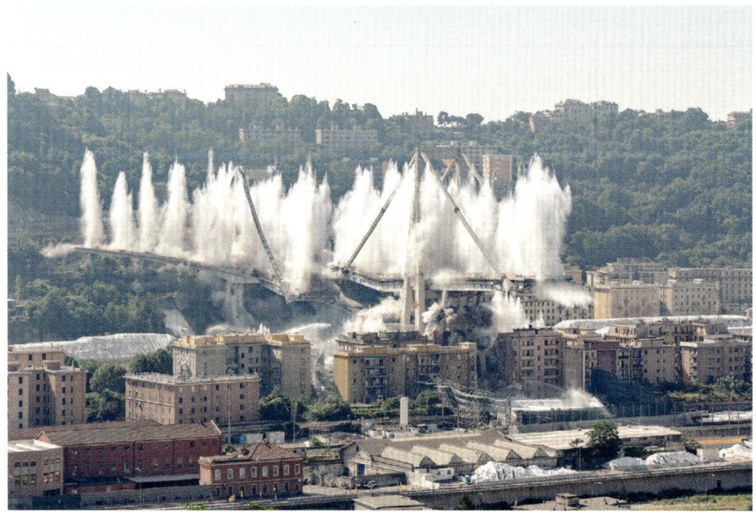

About six seconds went by between the first directional
explosion for the cutting of the stays on pier 11 and
the impact of the entire structure upon the ground.
This was done by triggering all the charges placed inside
the tanks on the deck and on the ground.

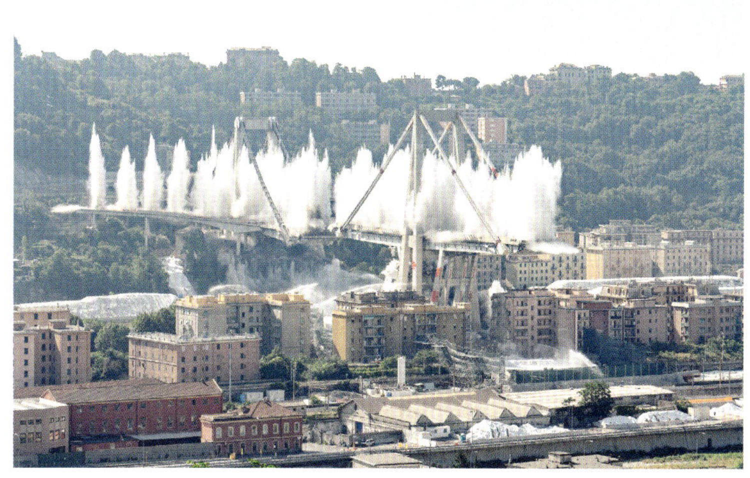

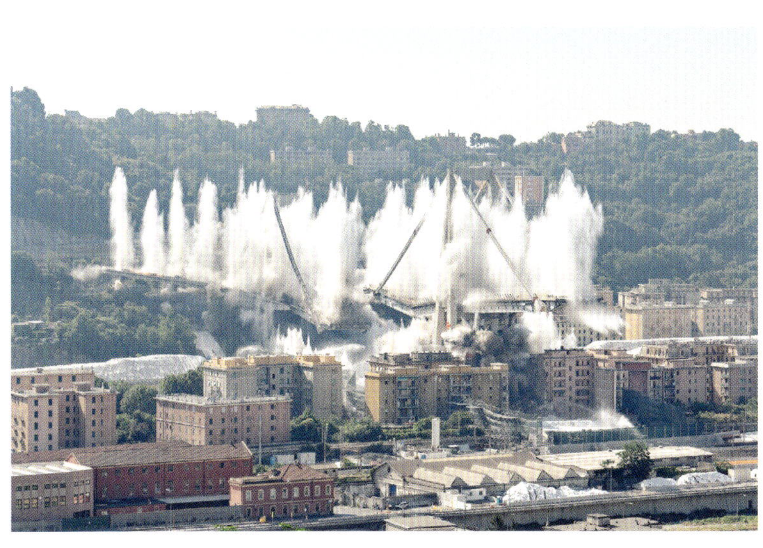

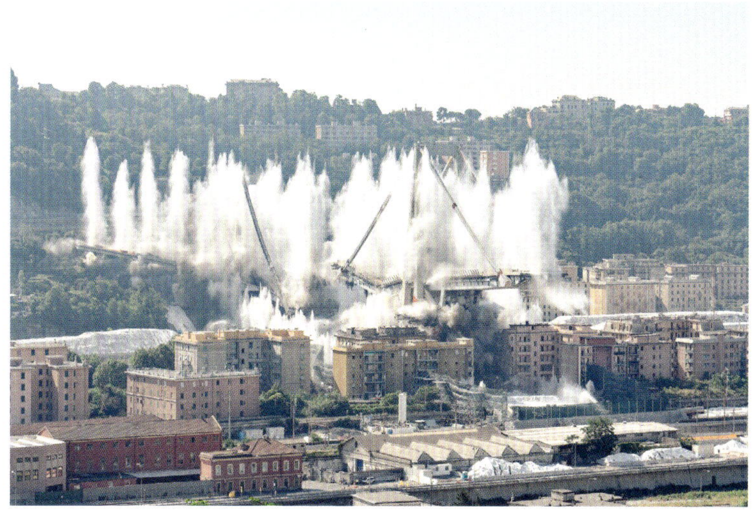

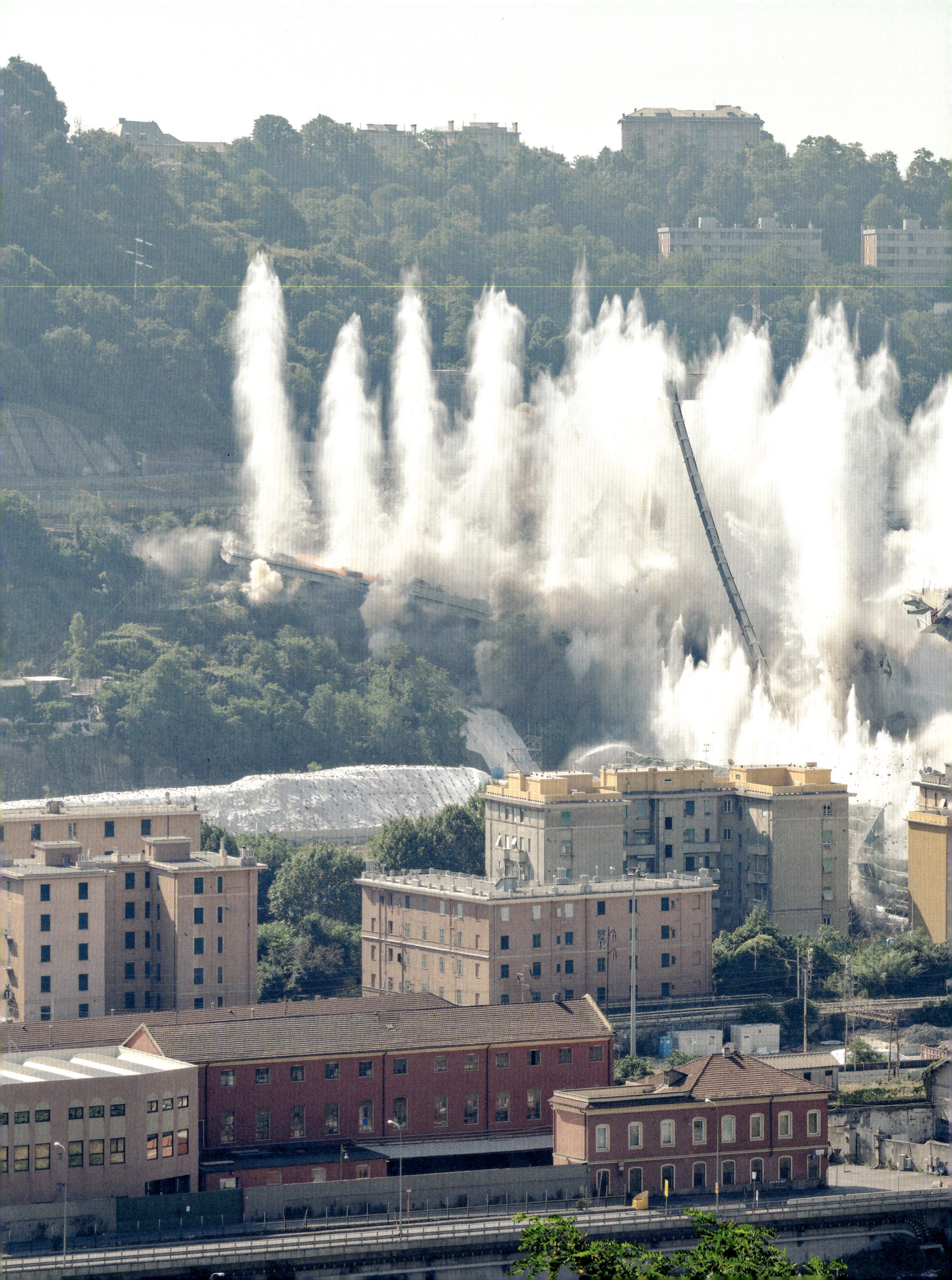

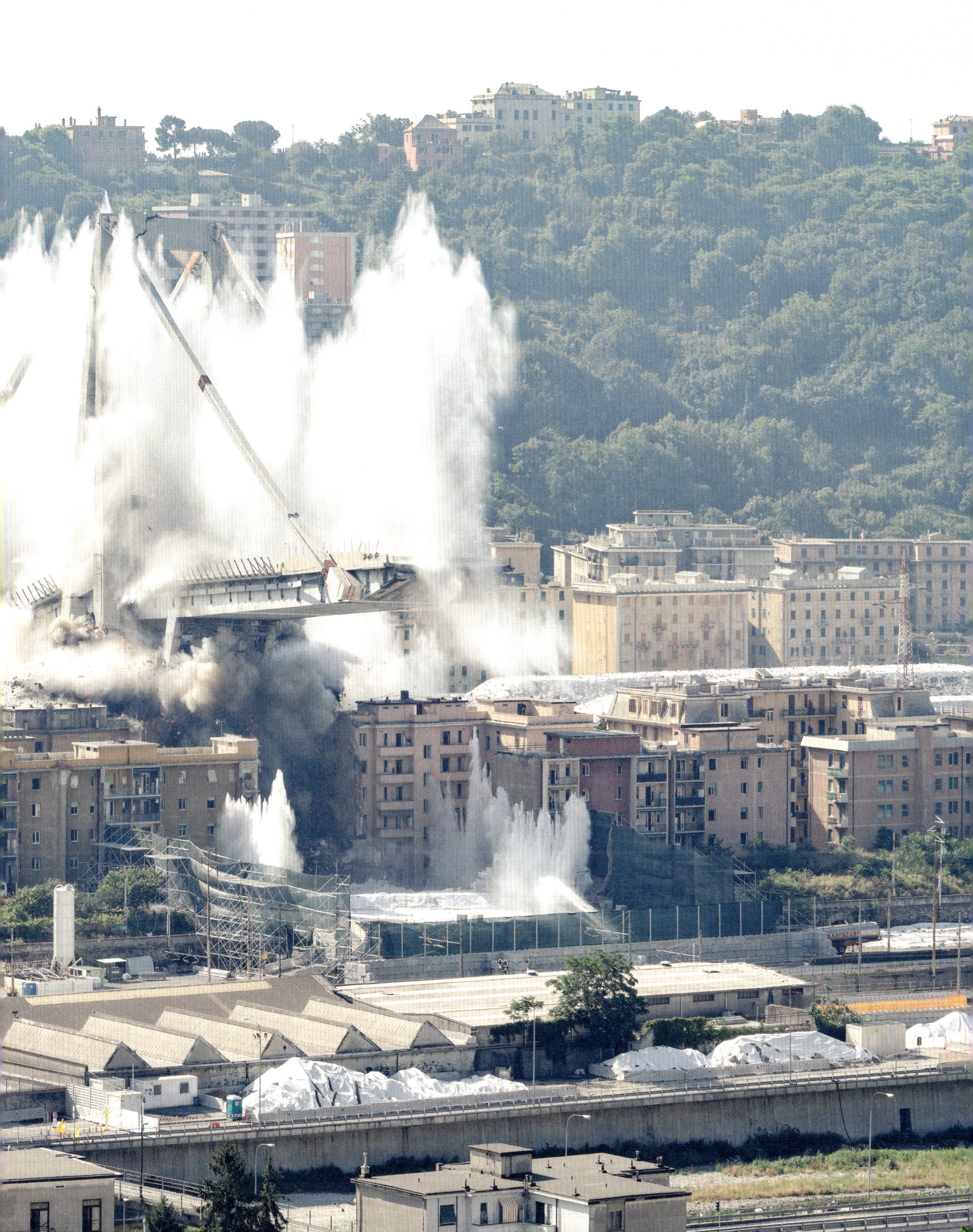

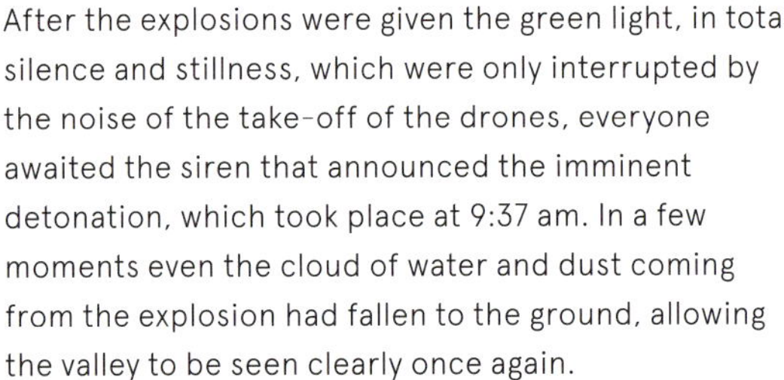

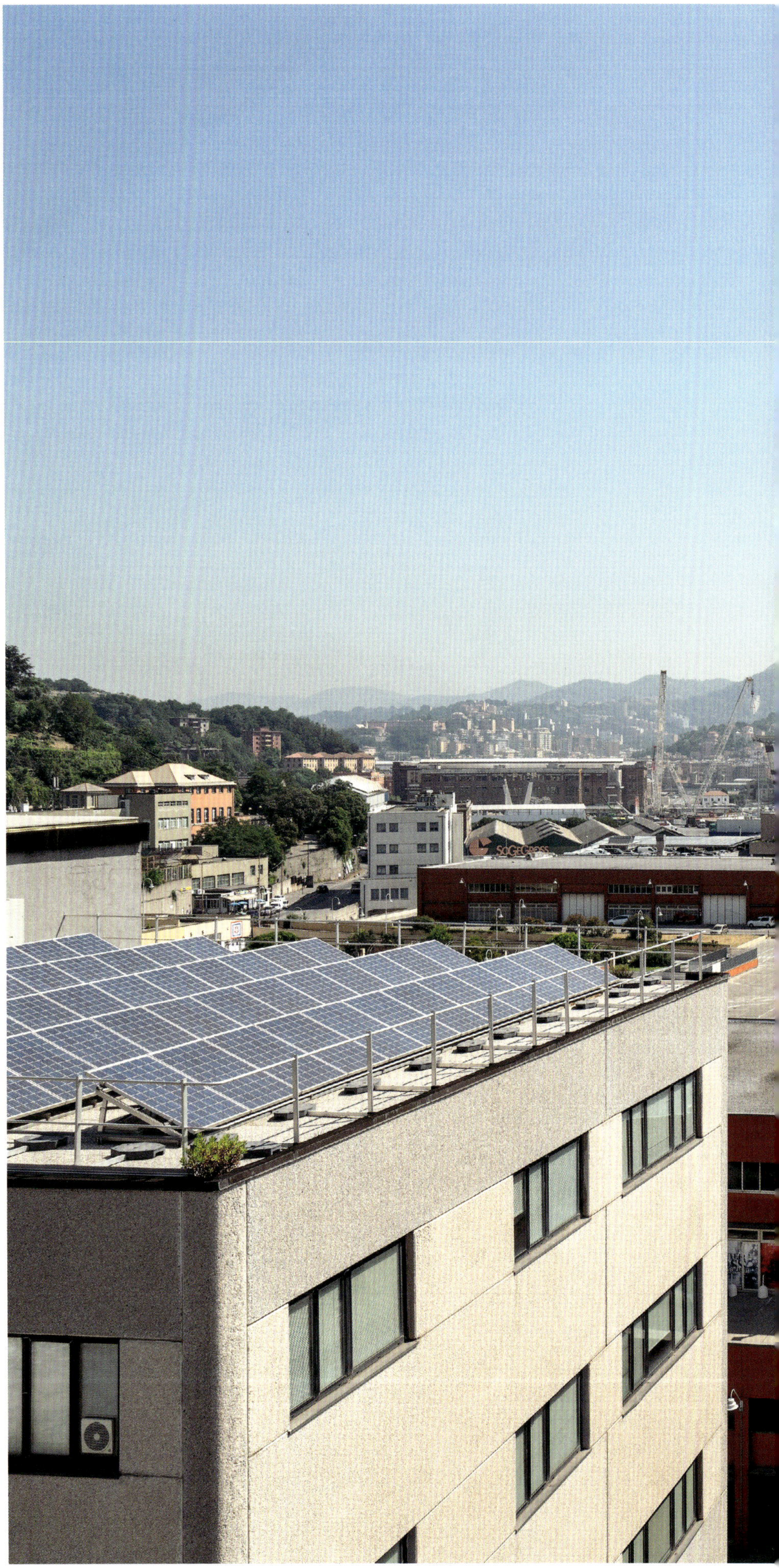

After the explosions were given the green light, in total silence and stillness, which were only interrupted by the noise of the take-off of the drones, everyone awaited the siren that announced the imminent detonation, which took place at 9:37 am. In a few moments even the cloud of water and dust coming from the explosion had fallen to the ground, allowing the valley to be seen clearly once again.

The RINA team, that of the Commissioner's Office, the demolition company, and the entities represented in the PAC witnessed the explosion from the terrace of the offices. The architect Tedeschi, Director of the Commissioner's Office, and the engineer Carpaneto, Director of the project for RINA were alone and focused in front of the monitors.

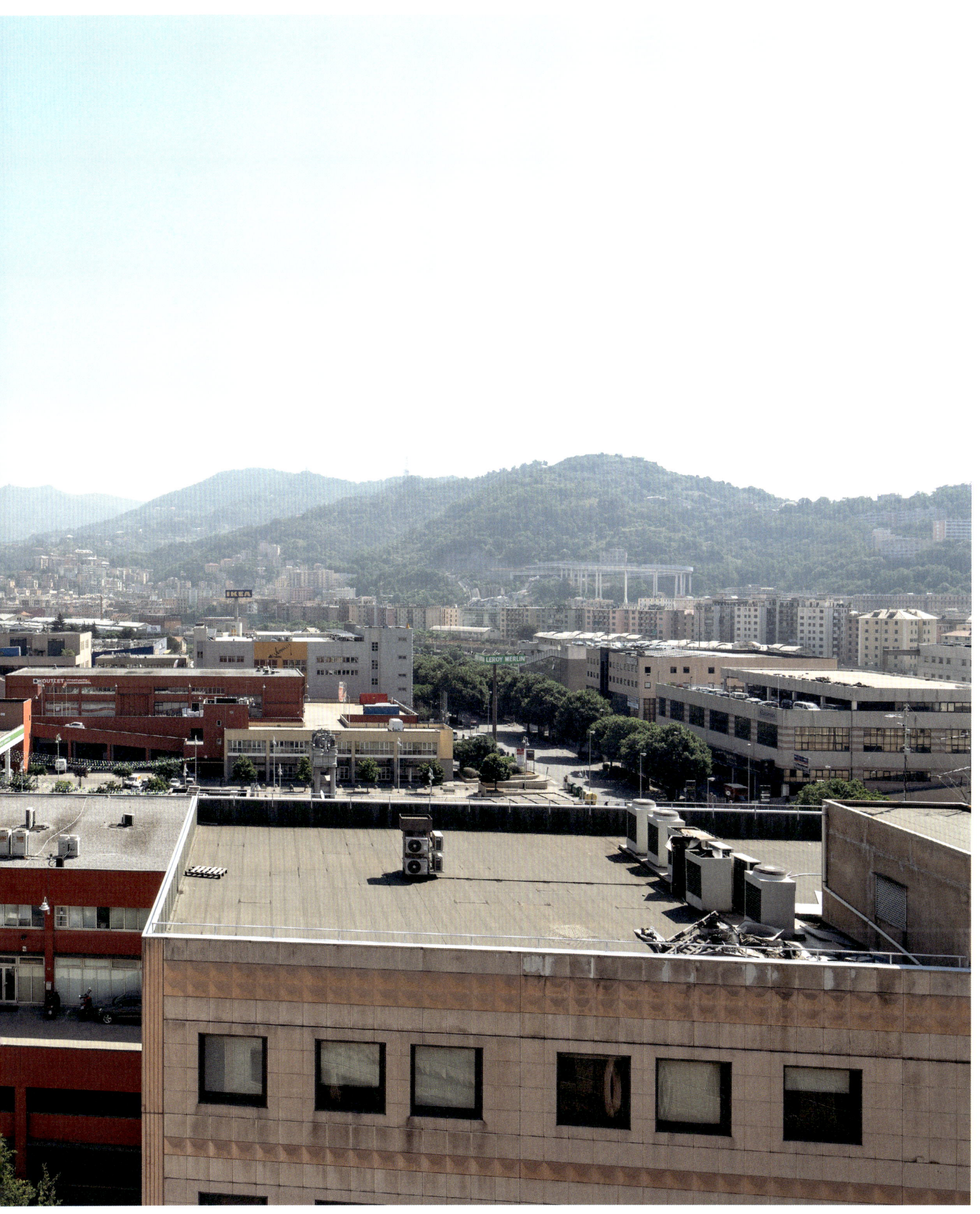

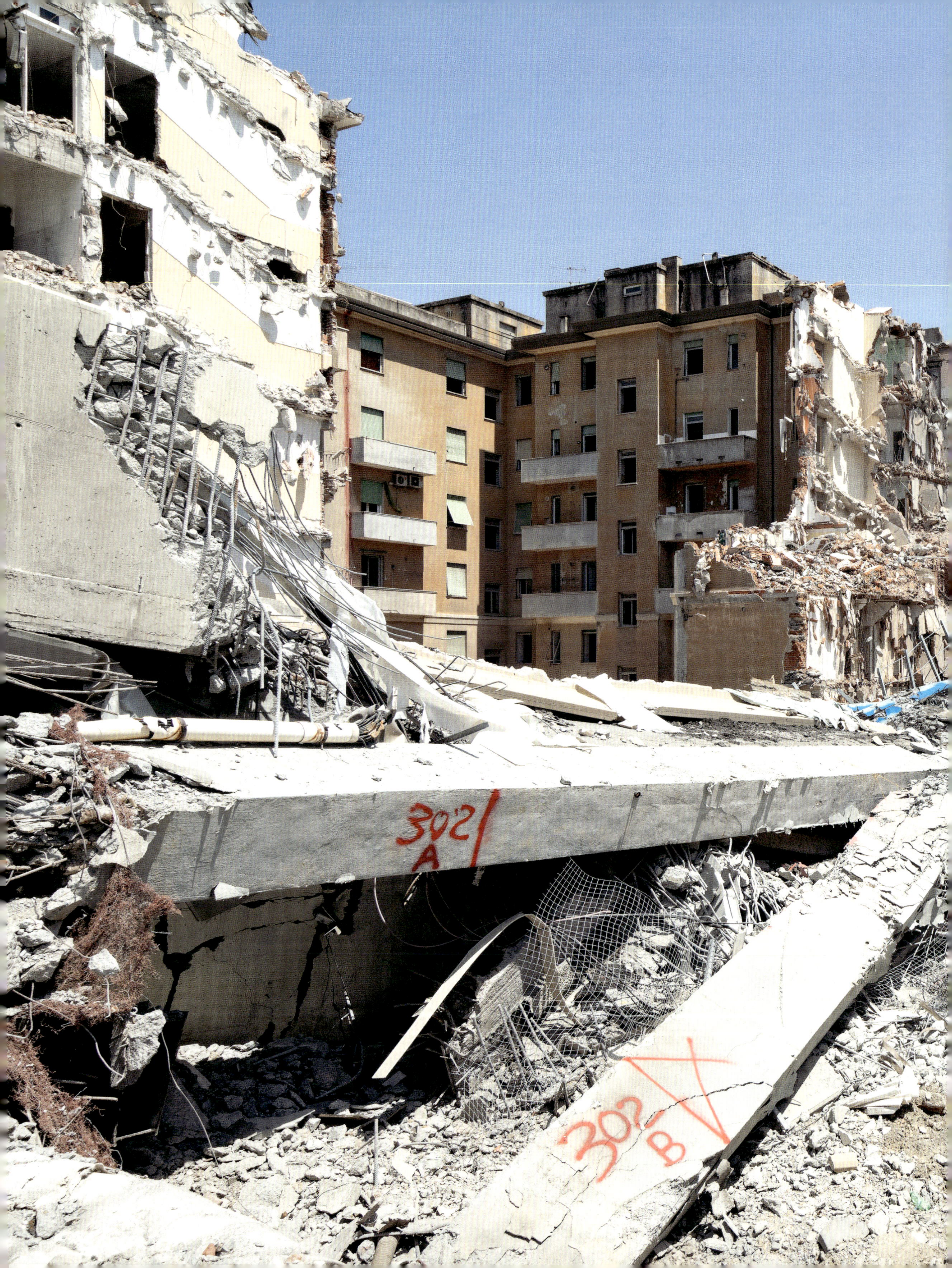
302/
A
302/
B

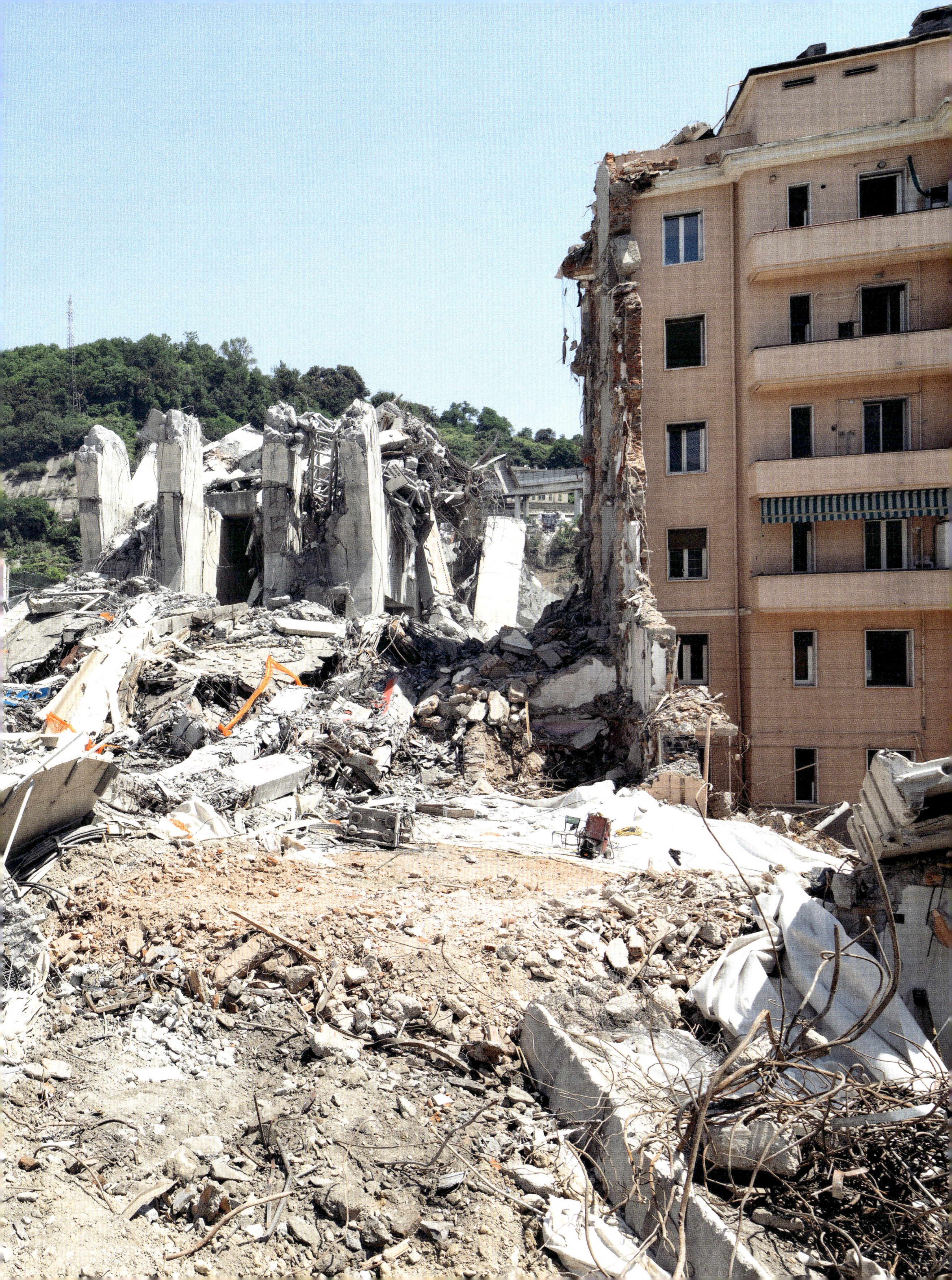

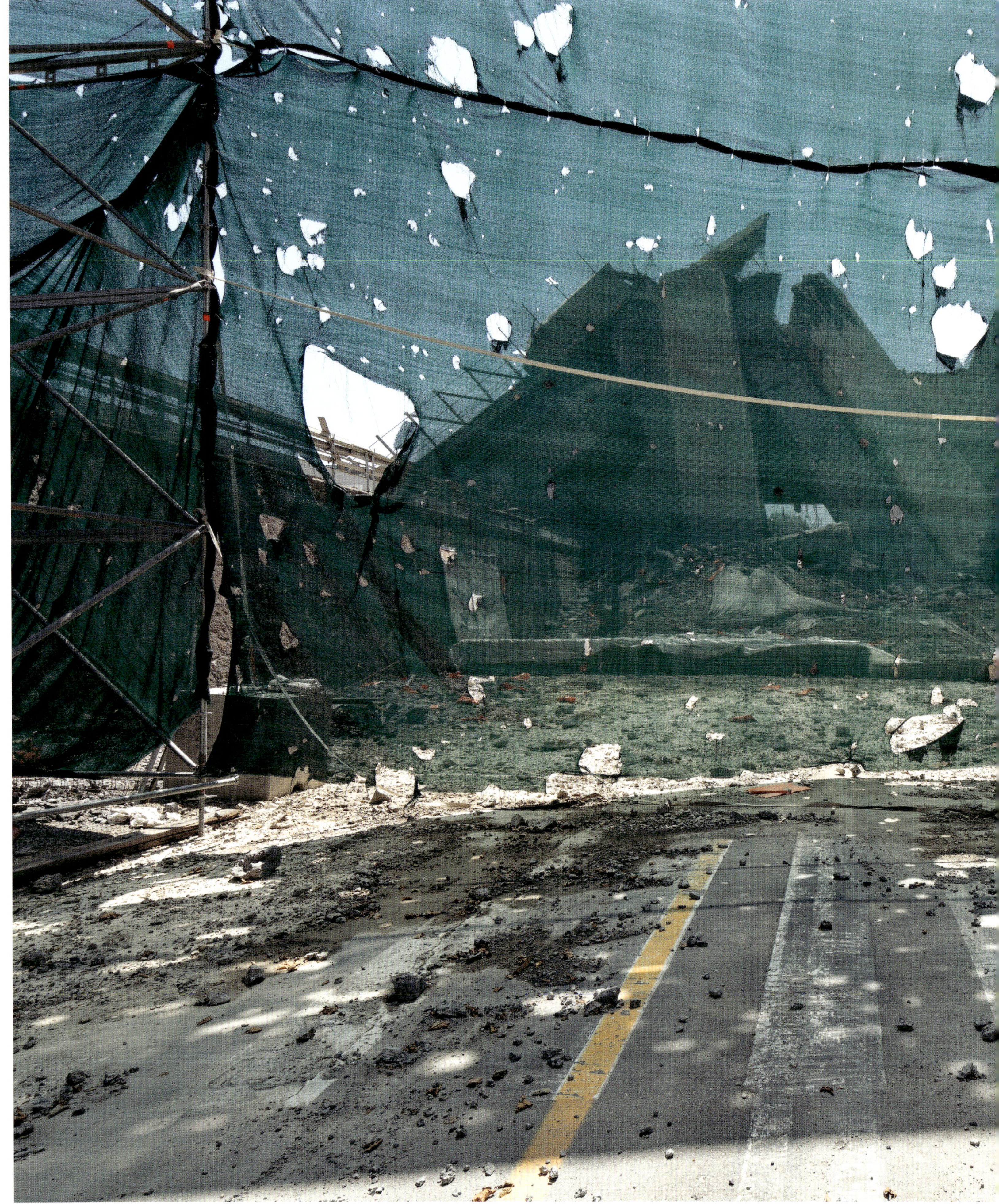

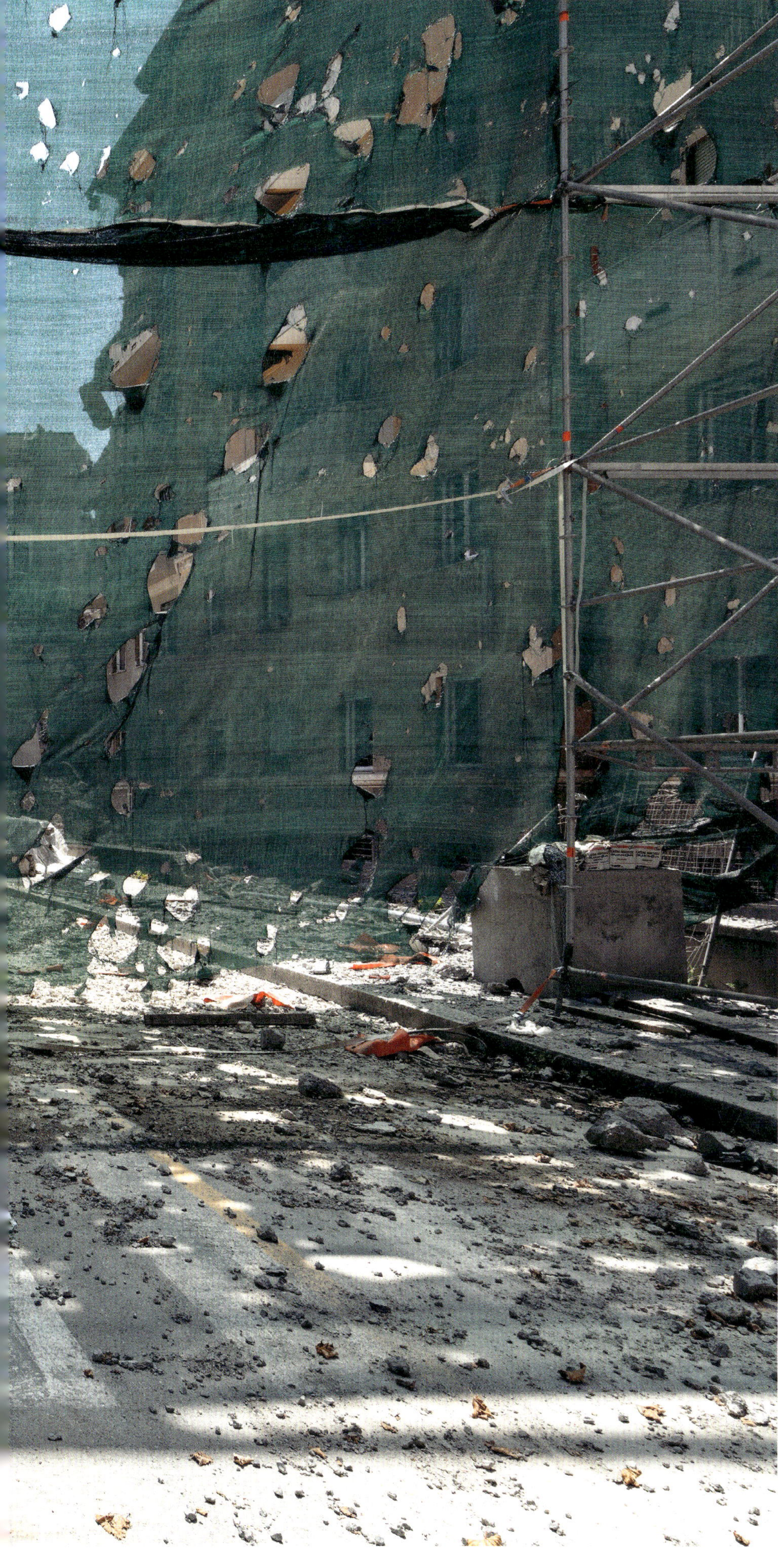

JULY 2, 2019

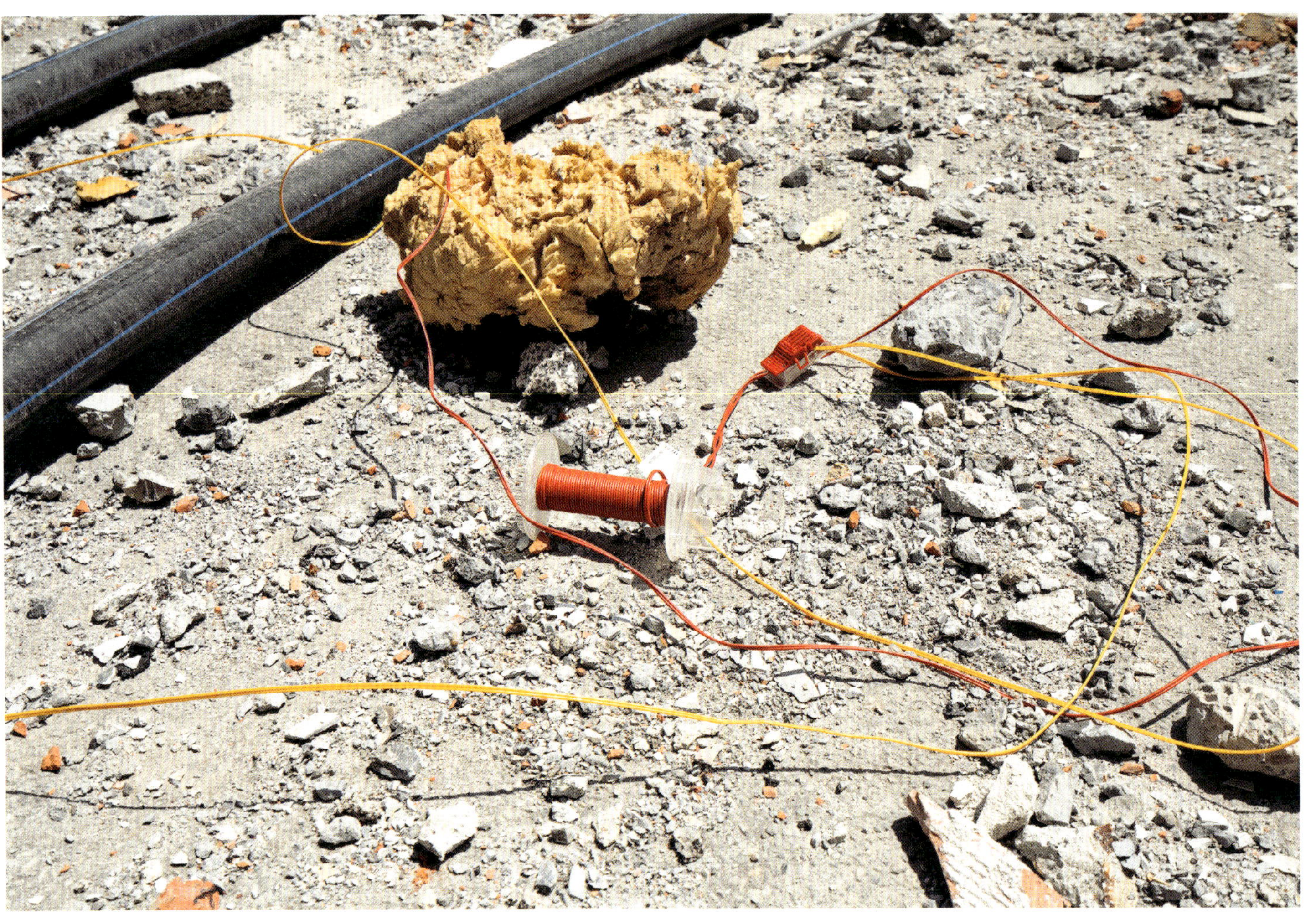

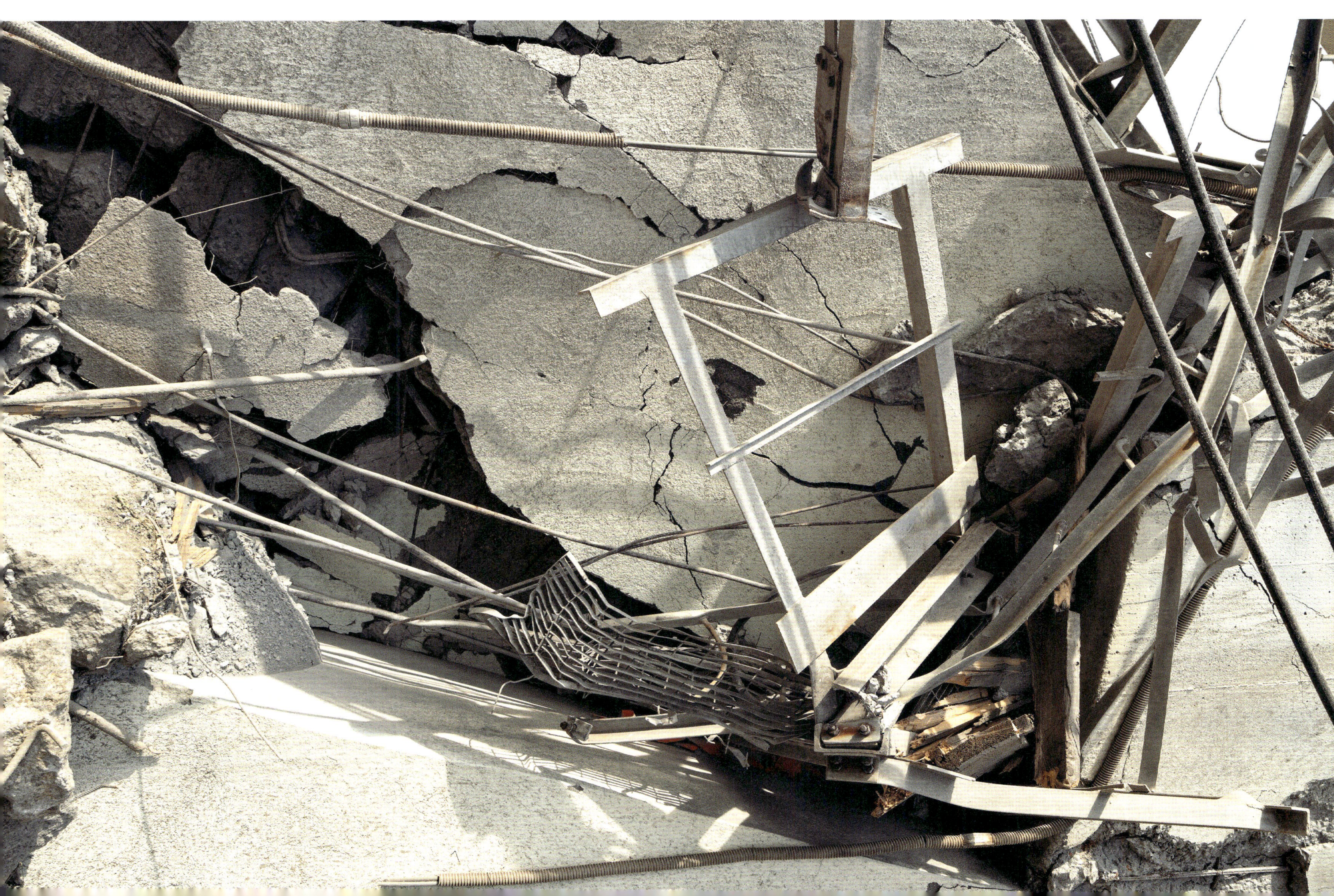
JULY 2, 2019

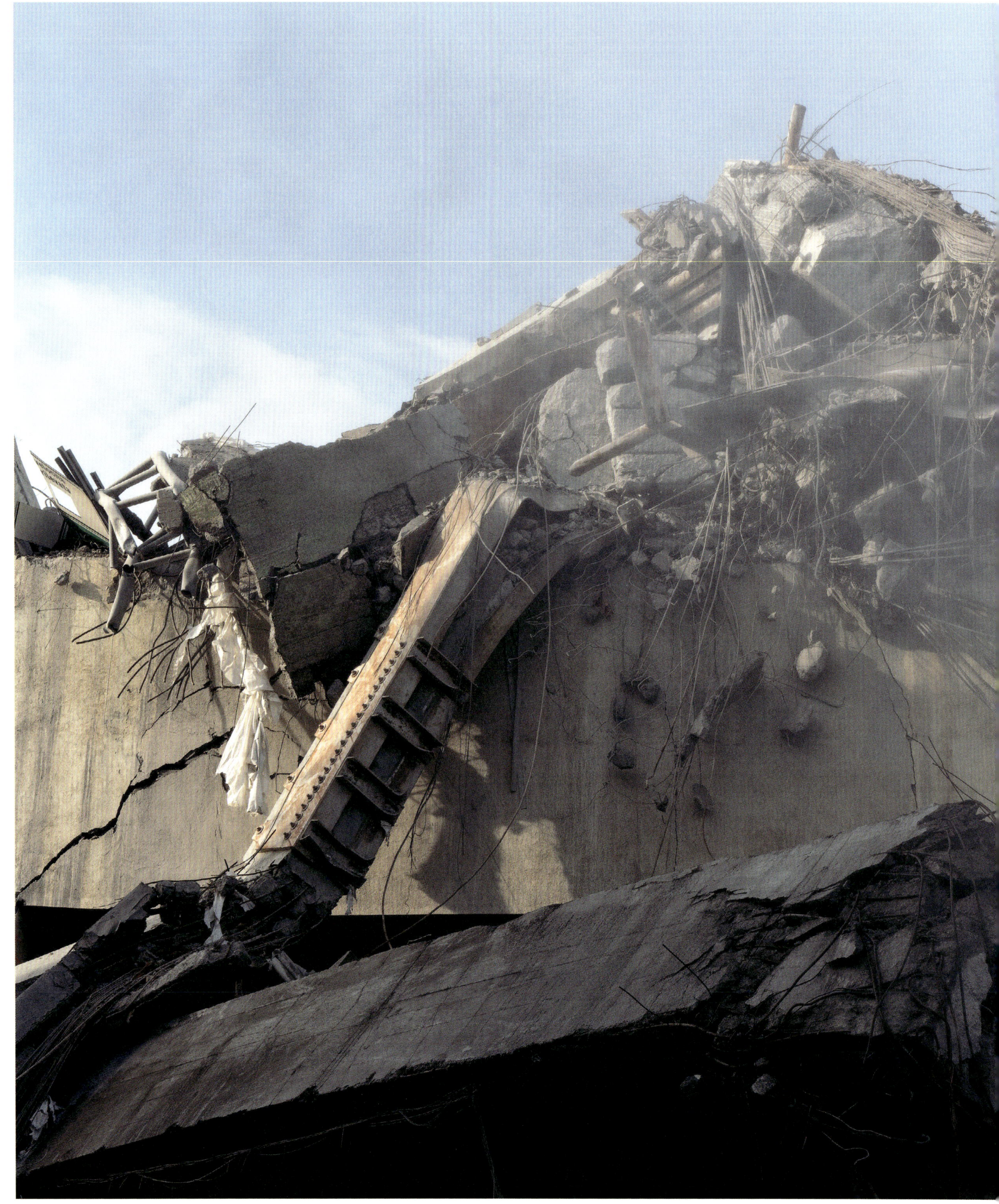

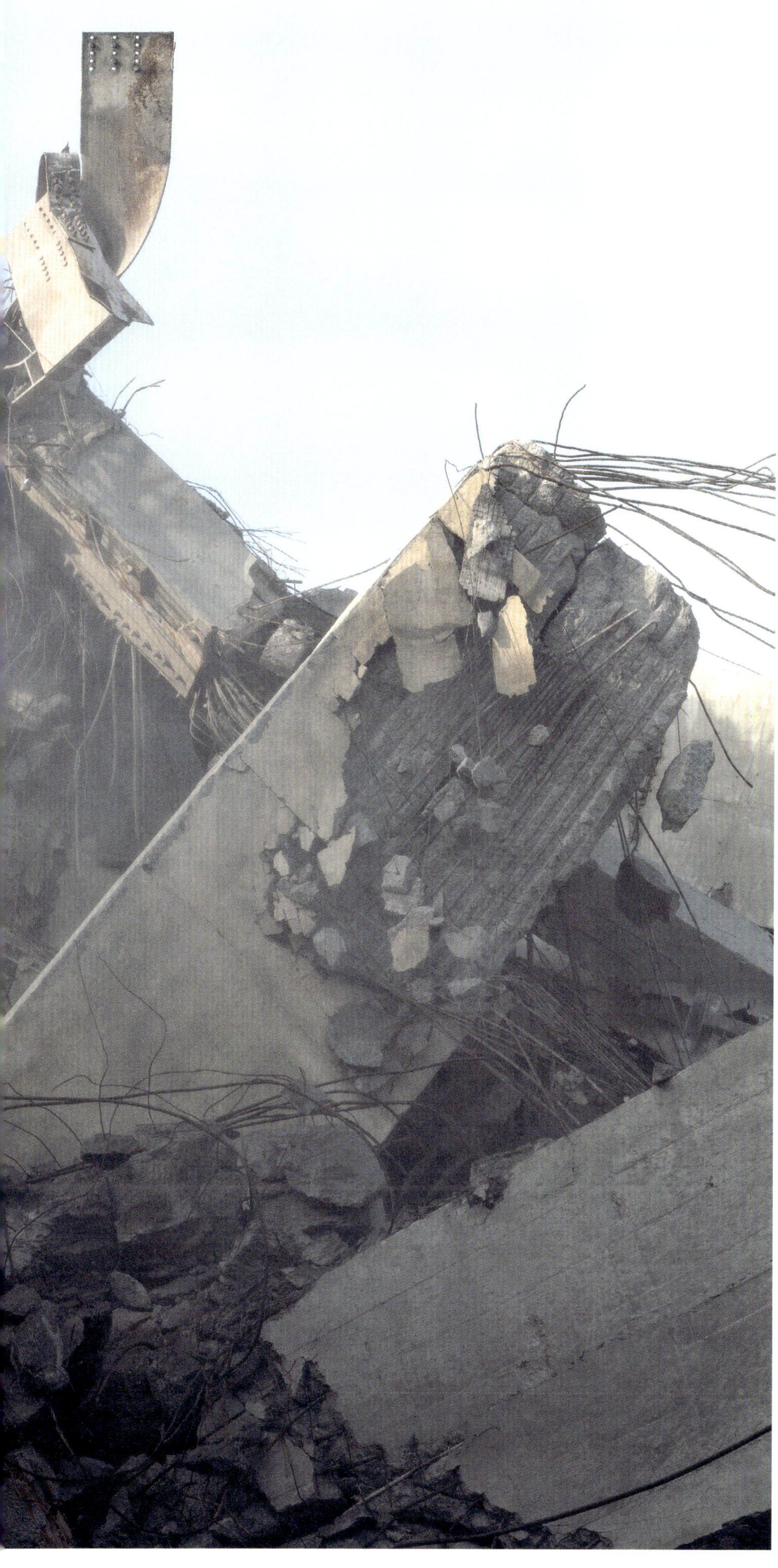

The explosion of piers 10 and 11 and the demolition
of the buildings underneath them created mountains
of debris (about 72,000 cubic meters of inert
materials) that had to be catalogued, moved,
and characterized from an environmental standpoint
so that their compatibility with the processes of
recycling or disposal could be assessed. All of these
materials were used for the reprofiling of the building
sites when the works were completed, or for other
building sites in the area.

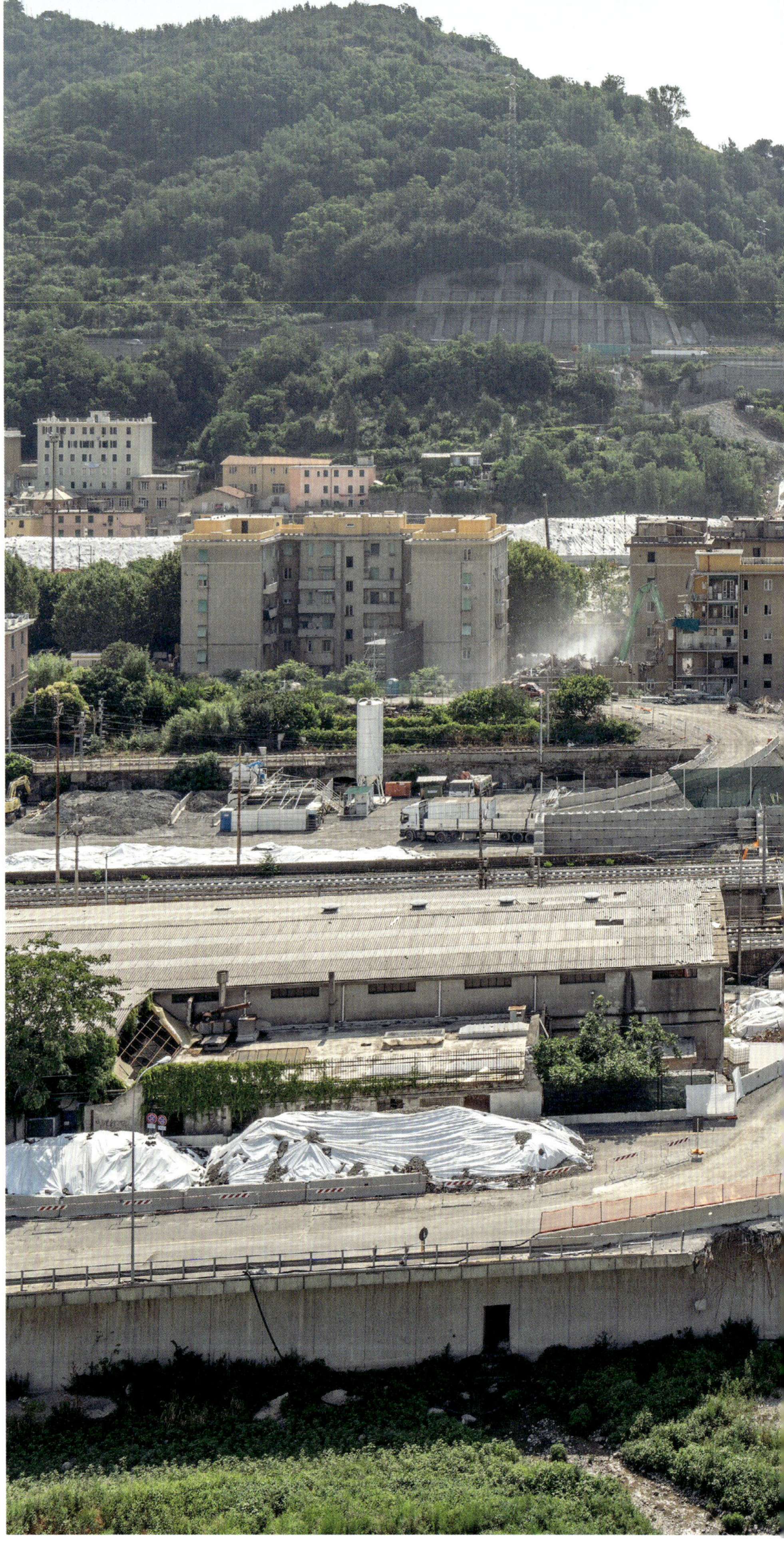

While the complex work of removing the debris of piers 10 and 11 went ahead, one sunny morning in July a work of art appeared in the valley. An anonymous graffiti artist had written the word "reviviscenza" (reviviscence) on the concrete wall bordering on the riverbed of the Polcevera torrent, which was shallow at the time, in the exact same place where almost one year before pier 9 had collapsed upon itself.

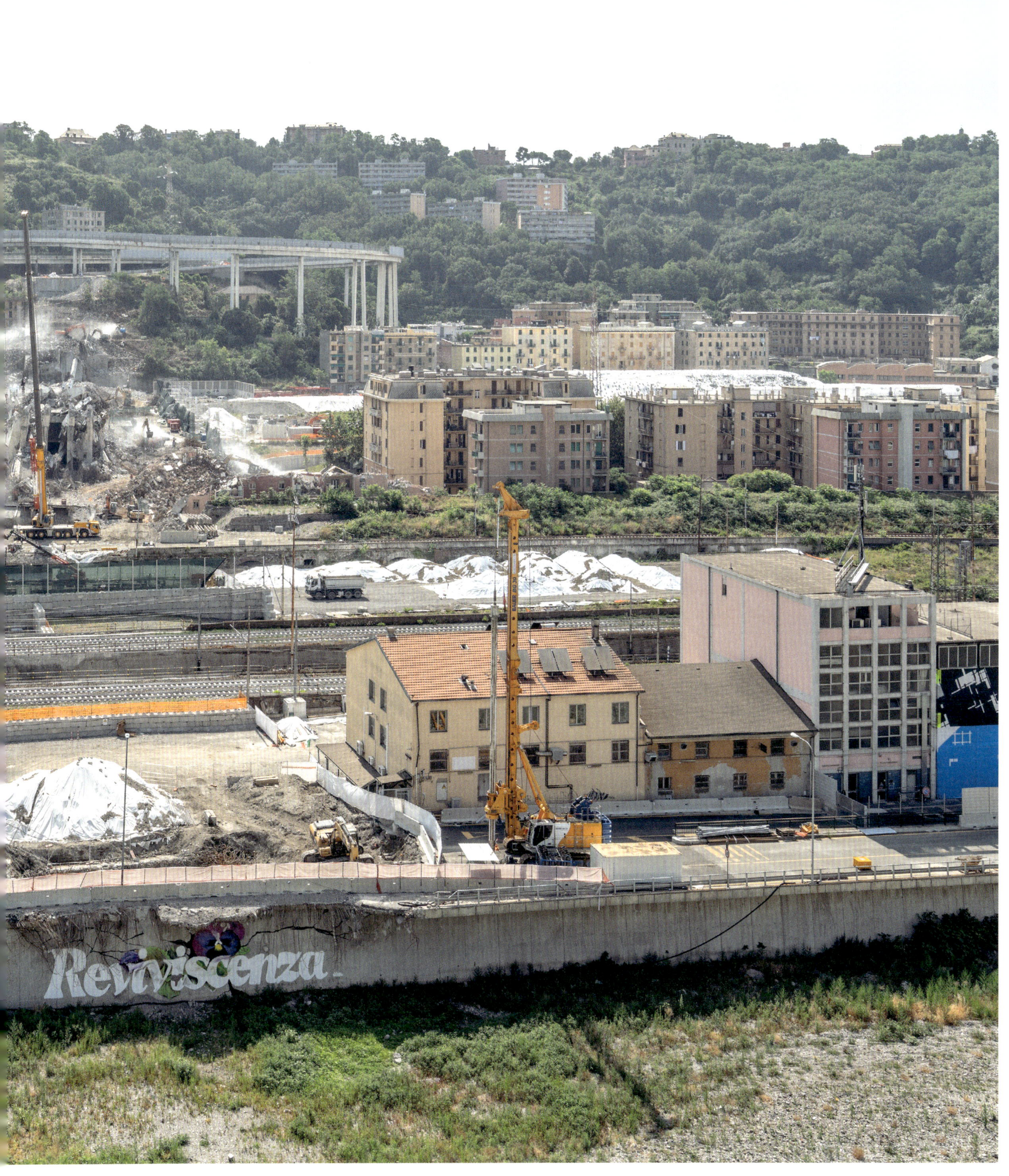
Reviviscenza.

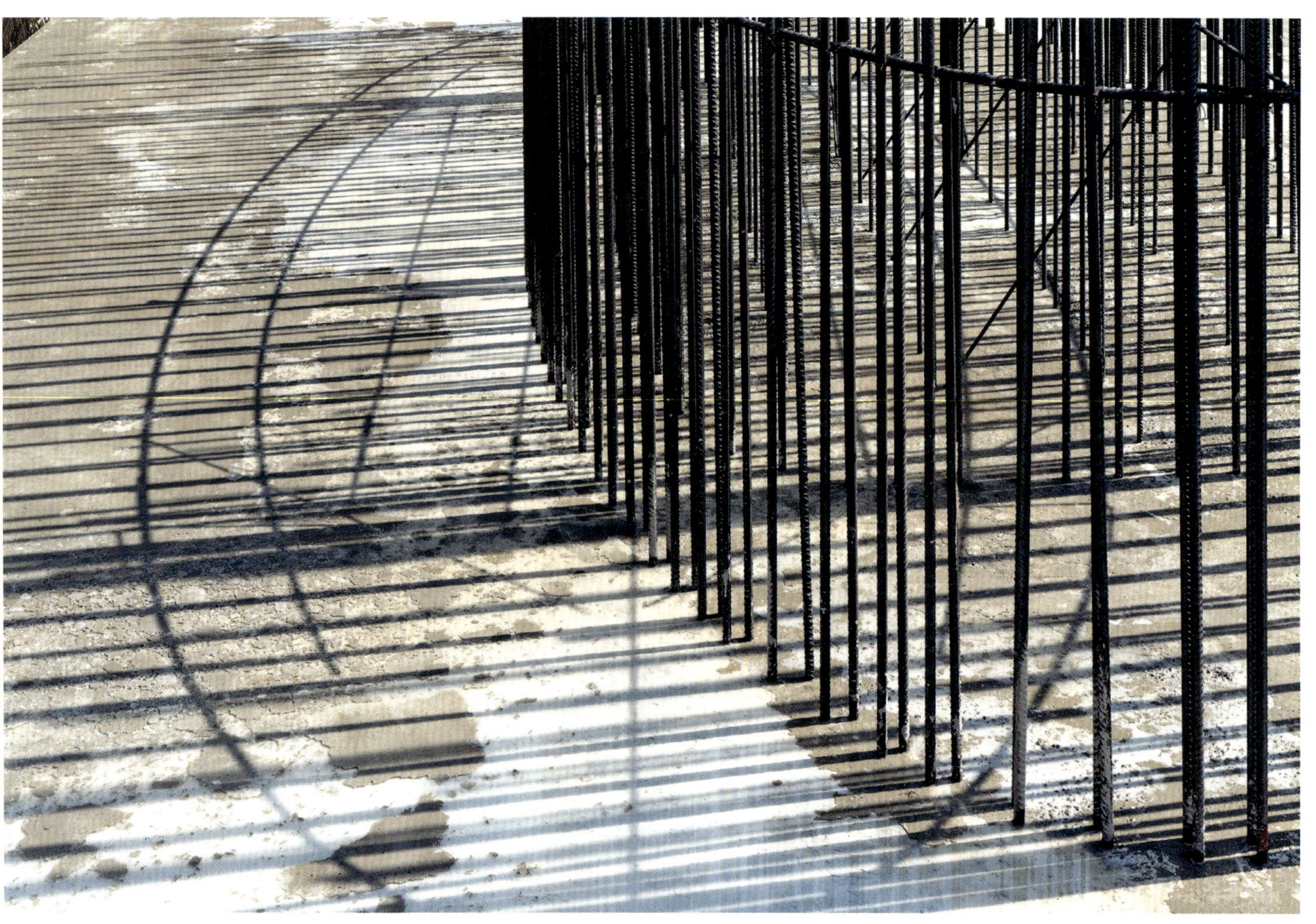

Building
the New Bridge

The job of reconstructing the viaduct over the Polcevera was given to a Company Consortium, PerGenova, controlled equally by Salini Impregilo (now called Webuild) and Fincantieri Infrastructure. The artistic management of the project was undertaken by Renzo Piano Building Workshop, while the planning of the infrastructure was assigned to Italferr.

The demolition and reconstruction phases partially overlapped, as the work of excavation and piling of the new work had already begun on April 15, 2019, when the demolition was still underway. The infrastructure, based on the architectural project developed by Renzo Piano Building Workshop, consisted of 18 elliptical-section reinforced concrete piers (9.5 meters by 4 meters), almost all of which placed with a constant gauge of 50 meters, with some exceptions, such as that of the crossing of the Polcevera torrent and the two adjacent ones, for which the interaxis distance rose to 100 meters, as well as of a principal deck made up of a continuous steel girder of 1,067.17 meters in length, consisting of 19 spans altogether.

The piers are an average of 40 meters tall and are founded on piles that can be up to 50 meters deep, for an overall length of about 8 kilometers of large-diameter piles.

The assembly of the metallic deck (weighing about 20,000 tons) was carried out by crane (single or in pairs) for the 50-meter portions, and by strand jacks for the 100-meter portions. Additionally, the portions of deck for the shoulders were raised in sections.

The new bridge also features robotic and sensor automation systems for infrastructural control and maintenance, and a special dehumidification system to avoid saline condensation and corrosion from occurring. It includes continuous monitoring systems that make it possible, thanks to big data and artificial intelligence algorithms, to implement predictive maintenance logic. Furthermore, it provides a solid basis for the future design of similar infrastructures.

The bridge has a contained environmental impact thanks to solar panels, which produce the energy required for the functioning of its systems (lighting, sensors, installations).

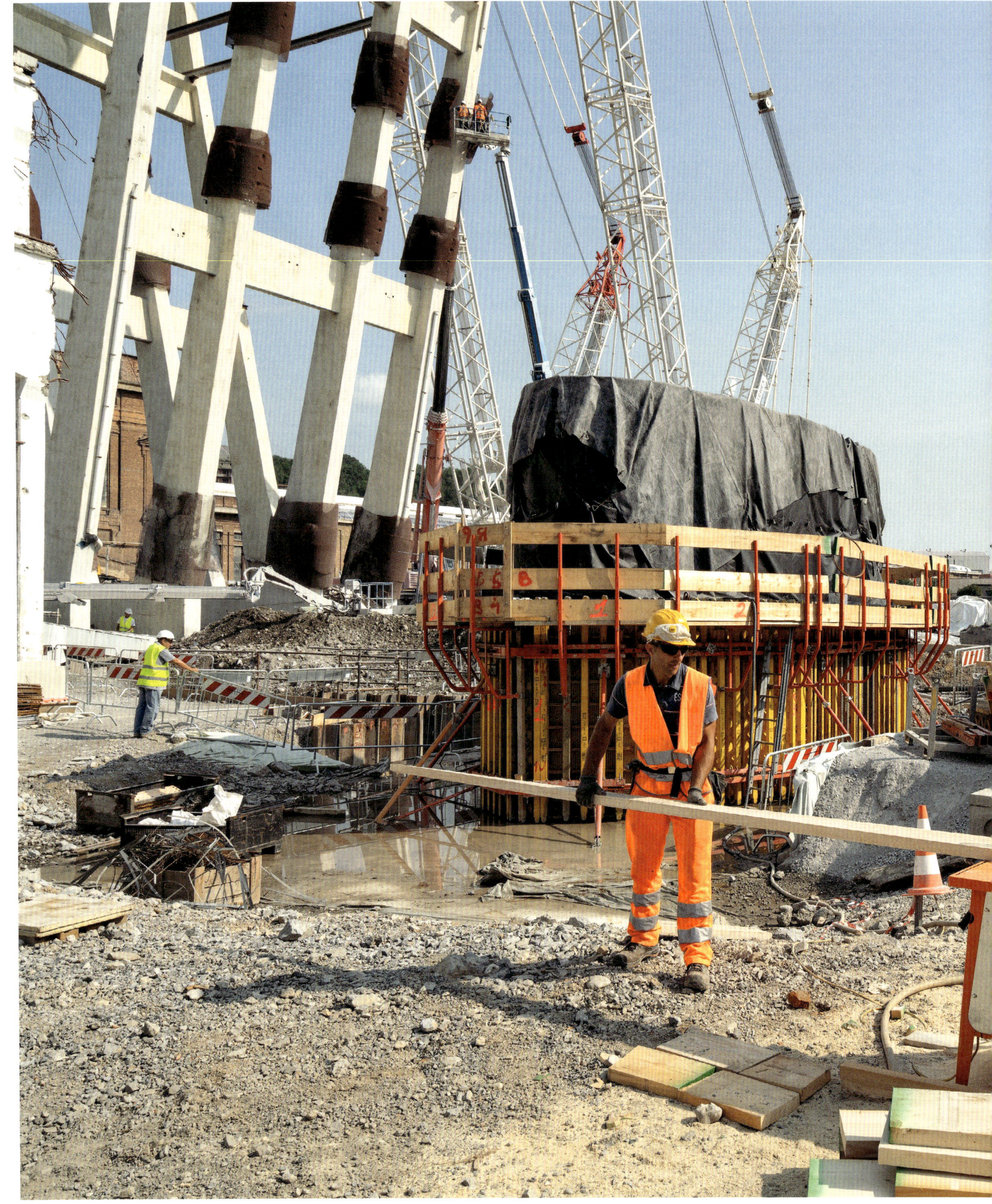

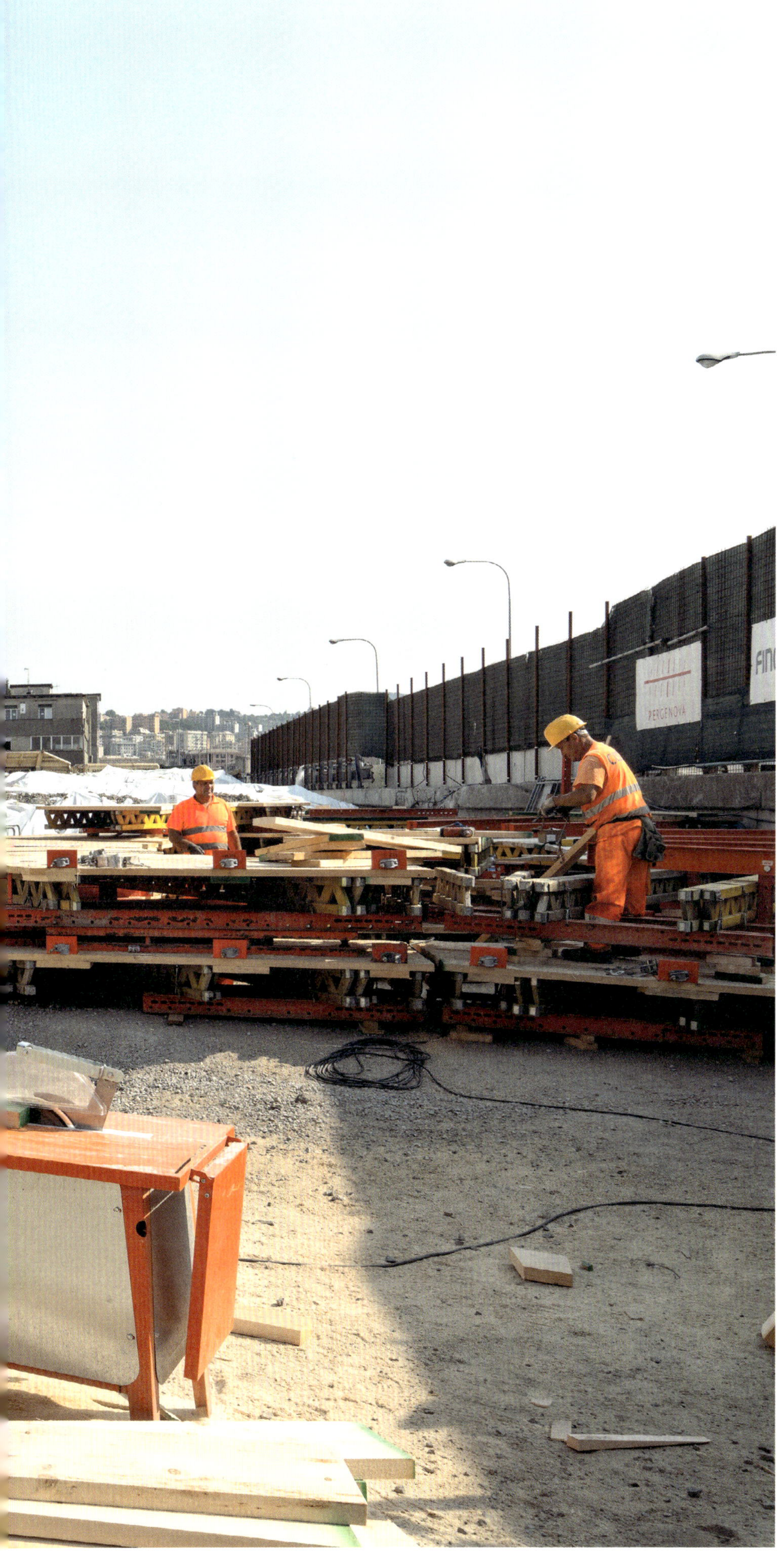

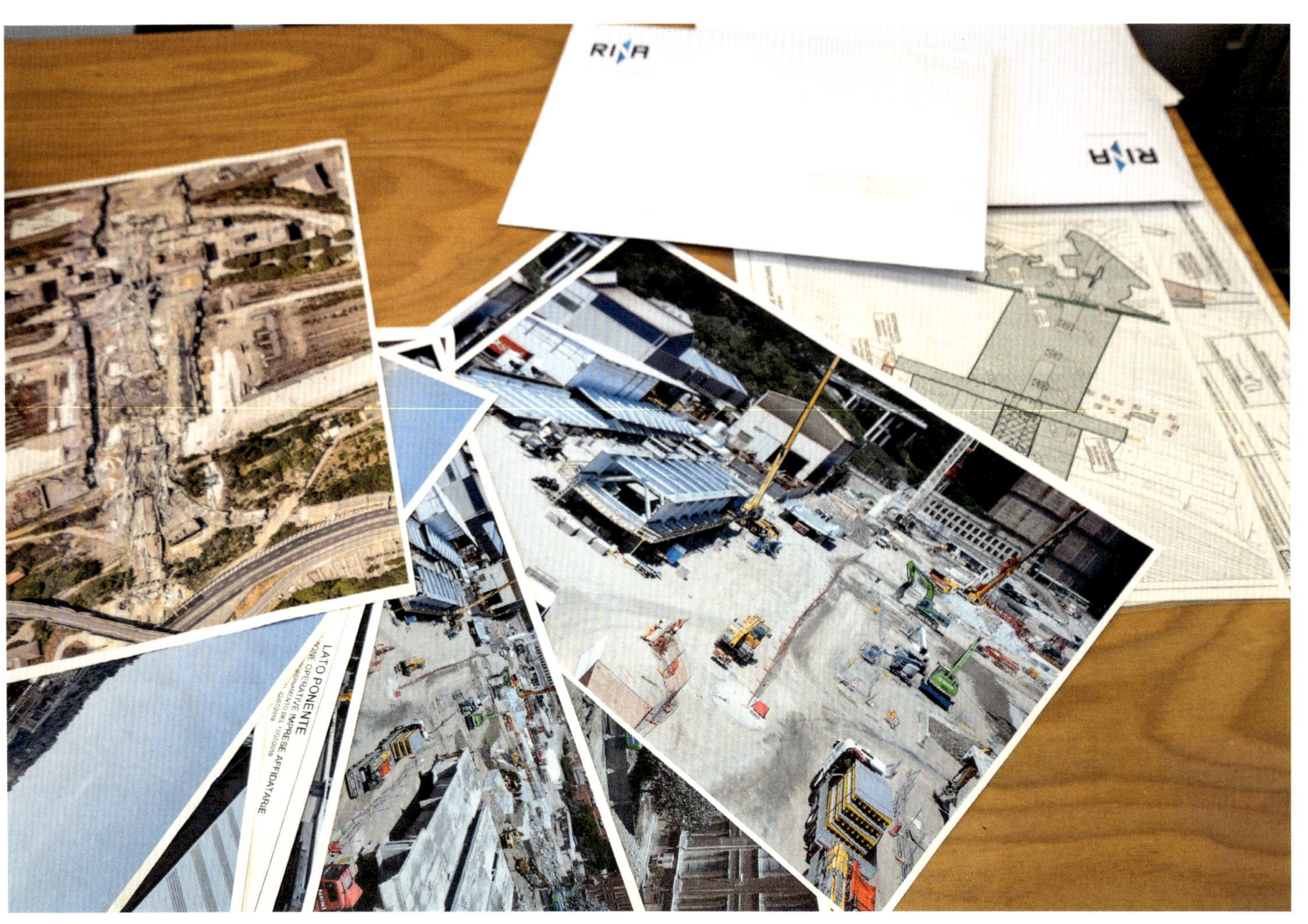
LATO PONENTE

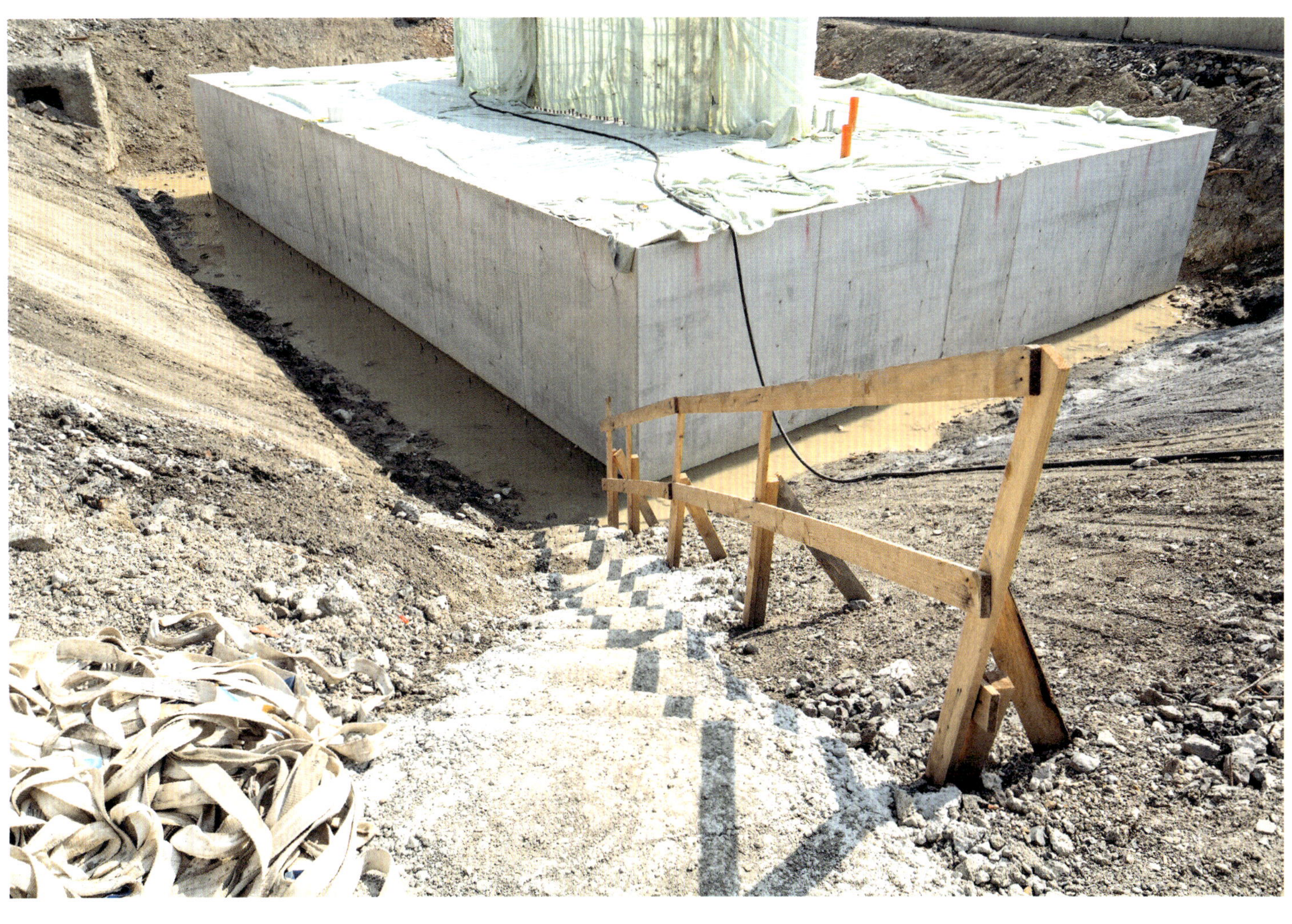

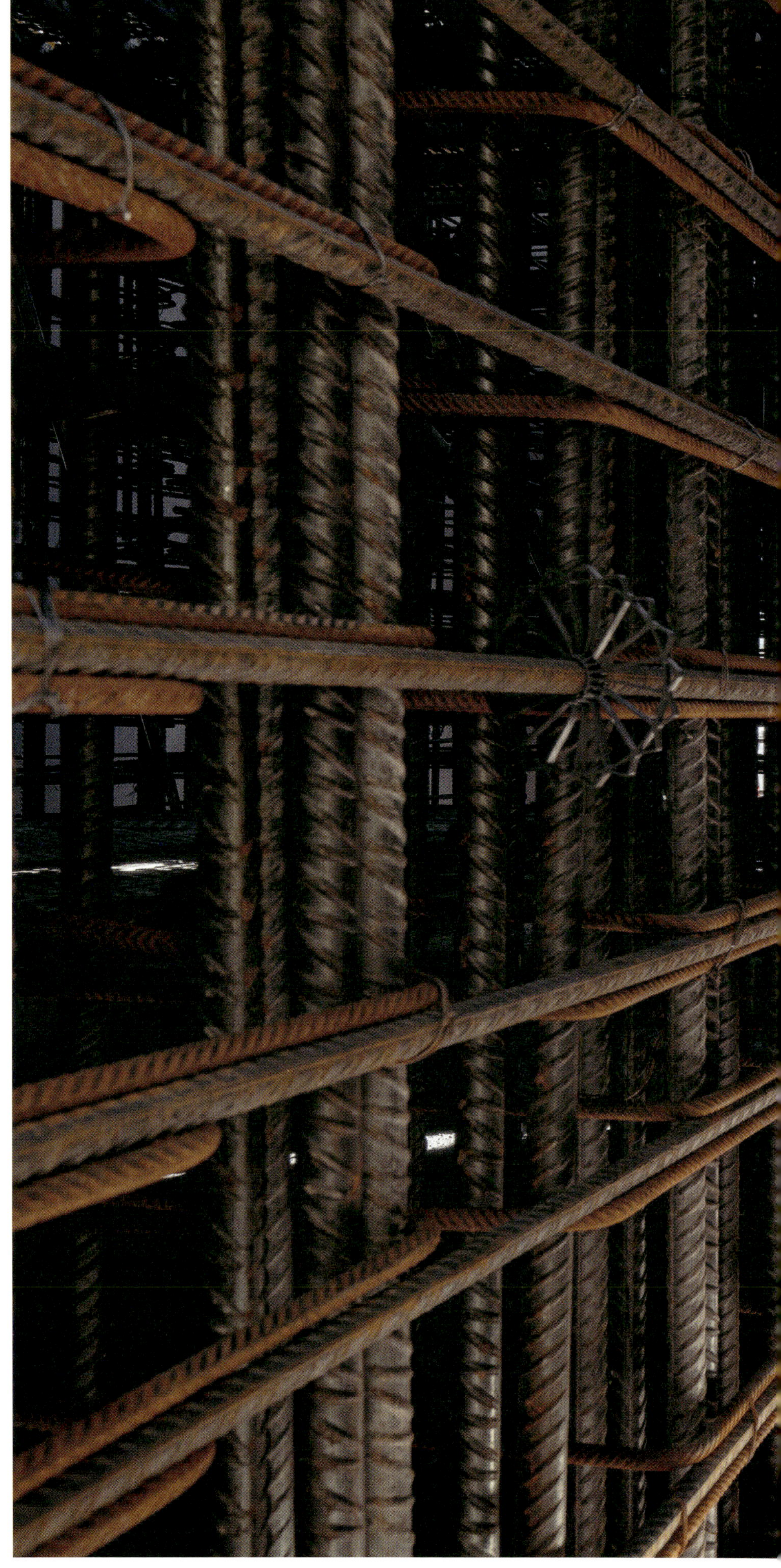

RINA's Work Supervision team was responsible
for inspections aimed at verifying compliance
with the specifics of the project, during both
demolition and construction.

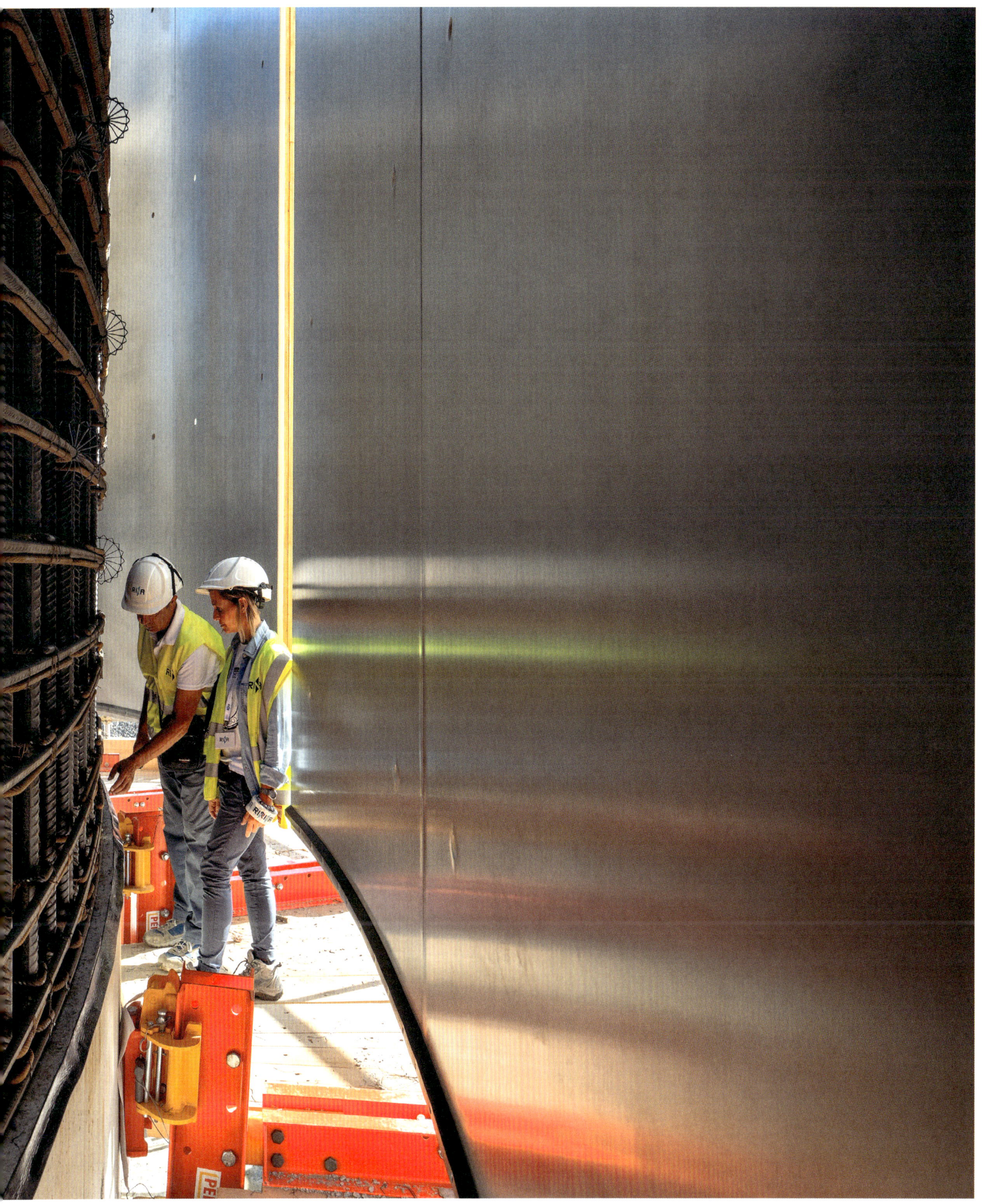

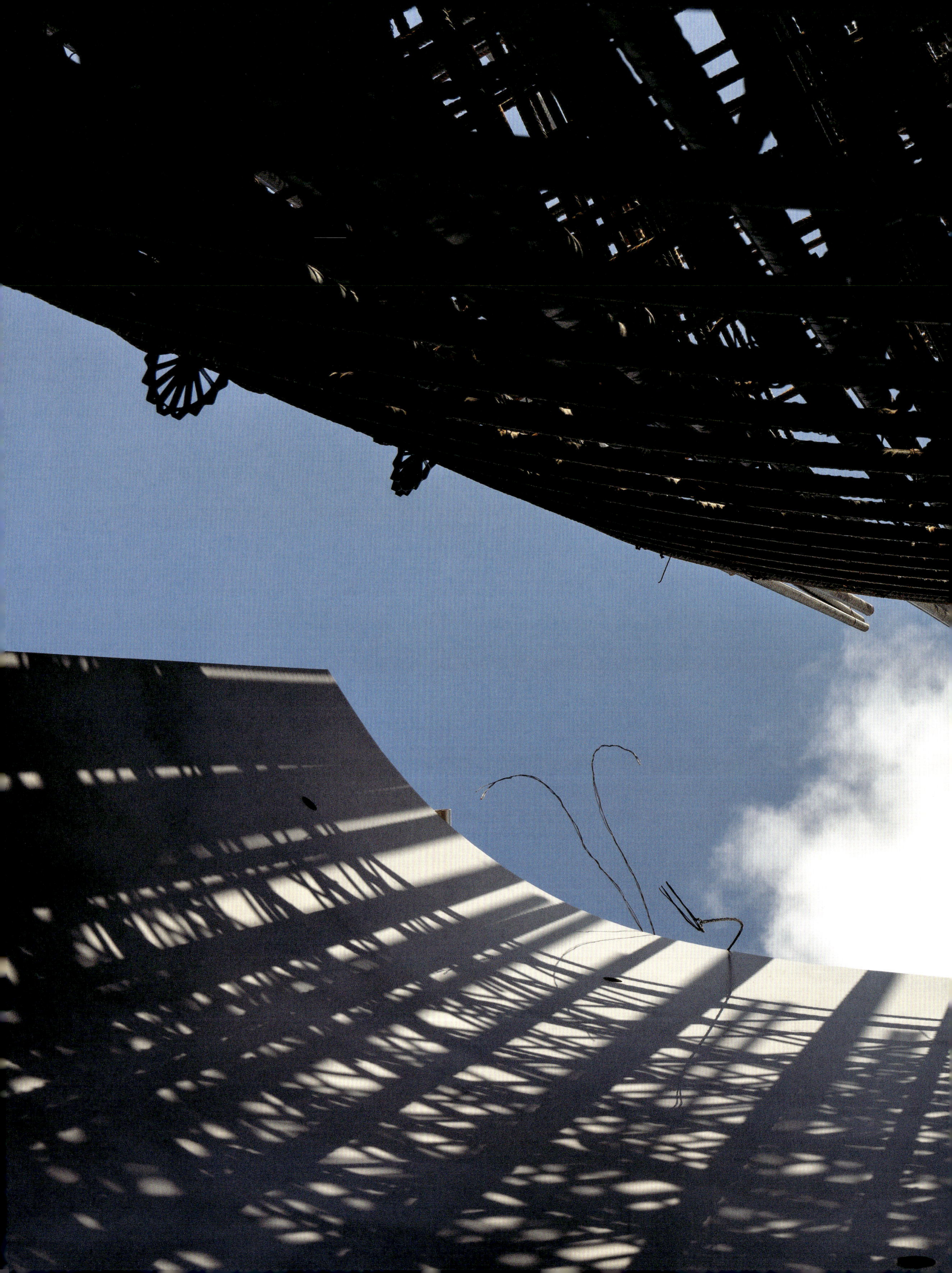

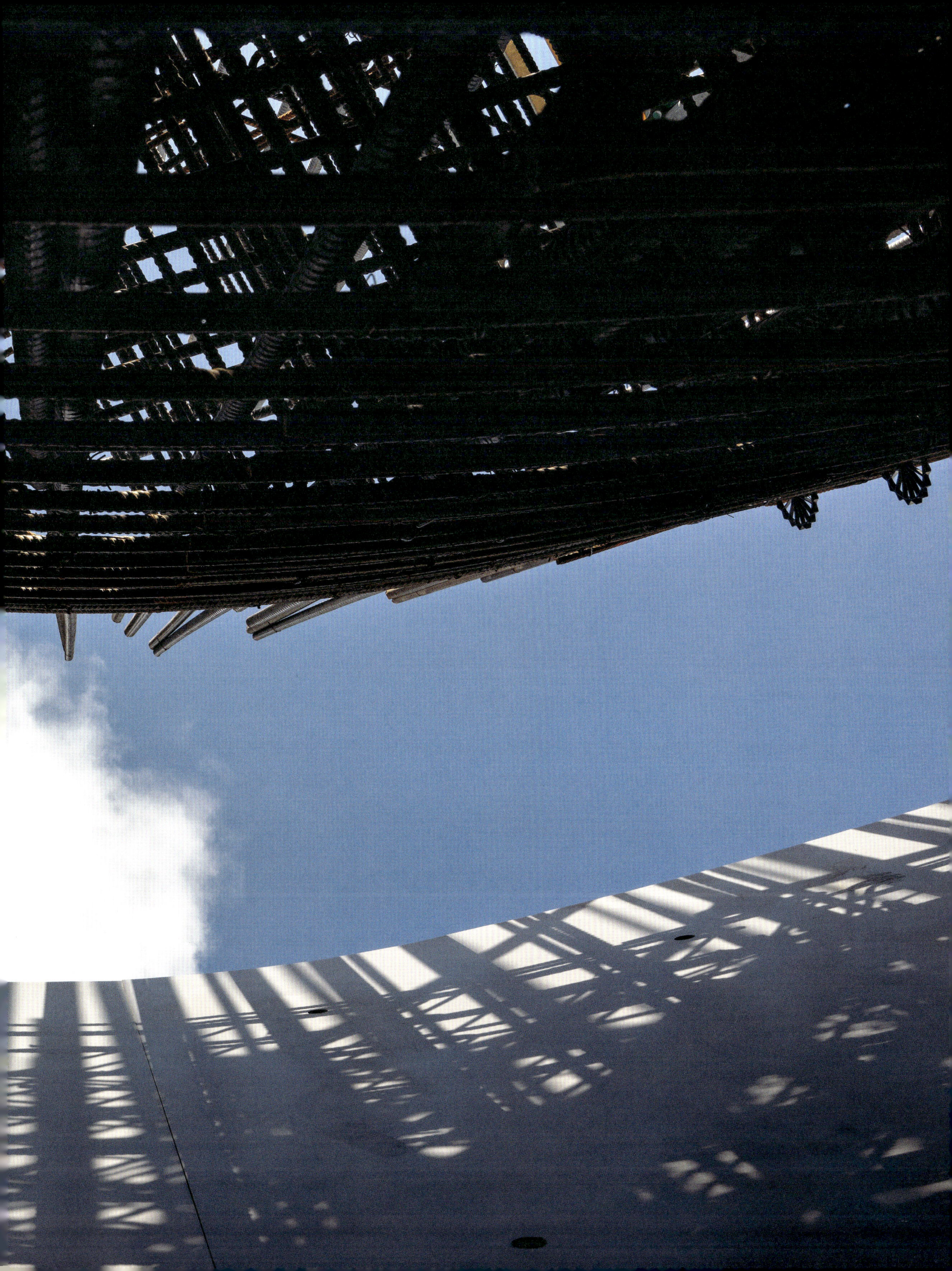

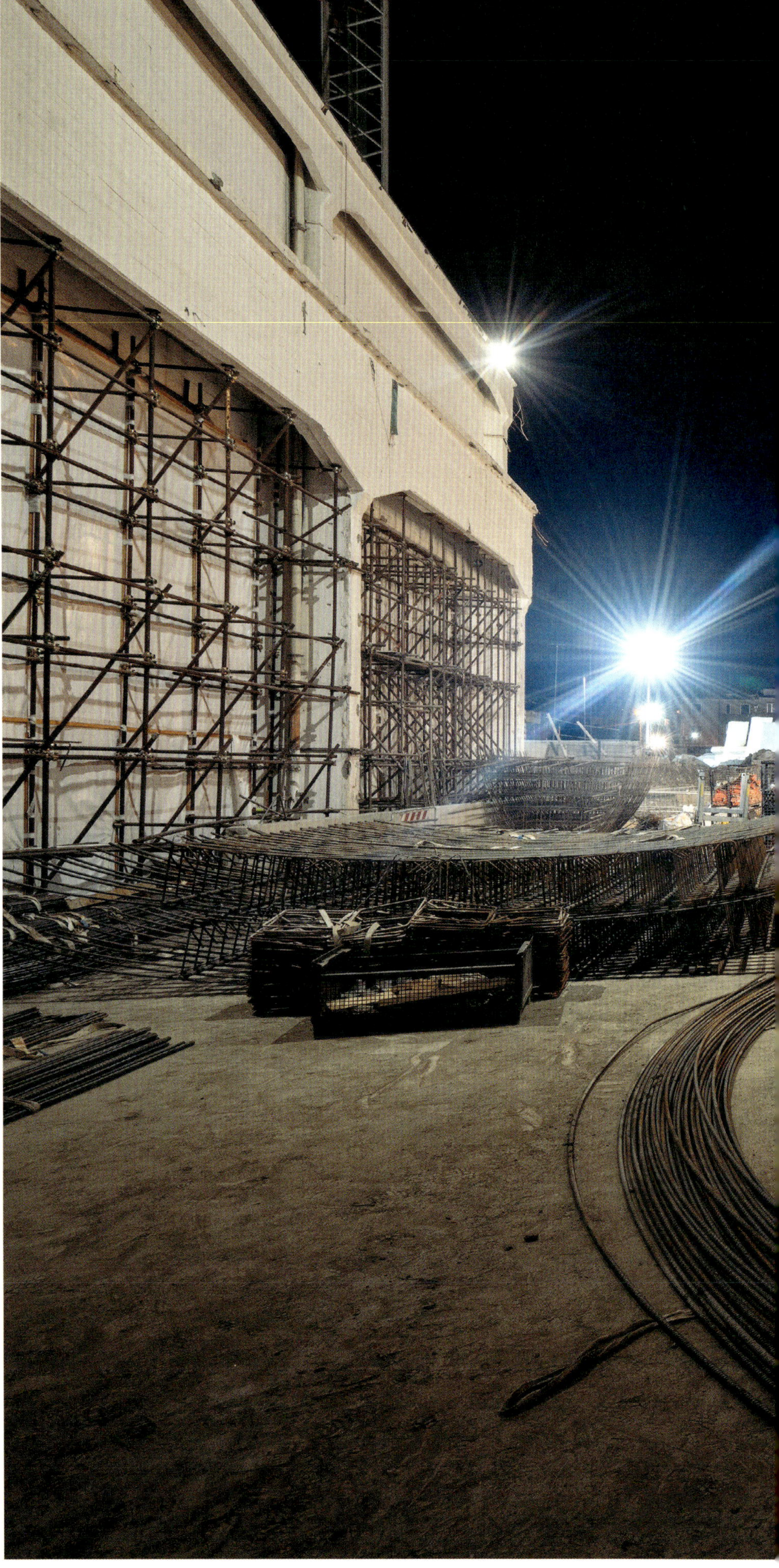

As occurred for the demolition of Ponte Morandi,
the construction phase also followed an "accelerated"
schedule, with shifts to cover nighttime work.
This resulted in the name "the building site that never
sleeps." This was further supported by the fact that
it continued to work even during the Covid-19
health emergency.

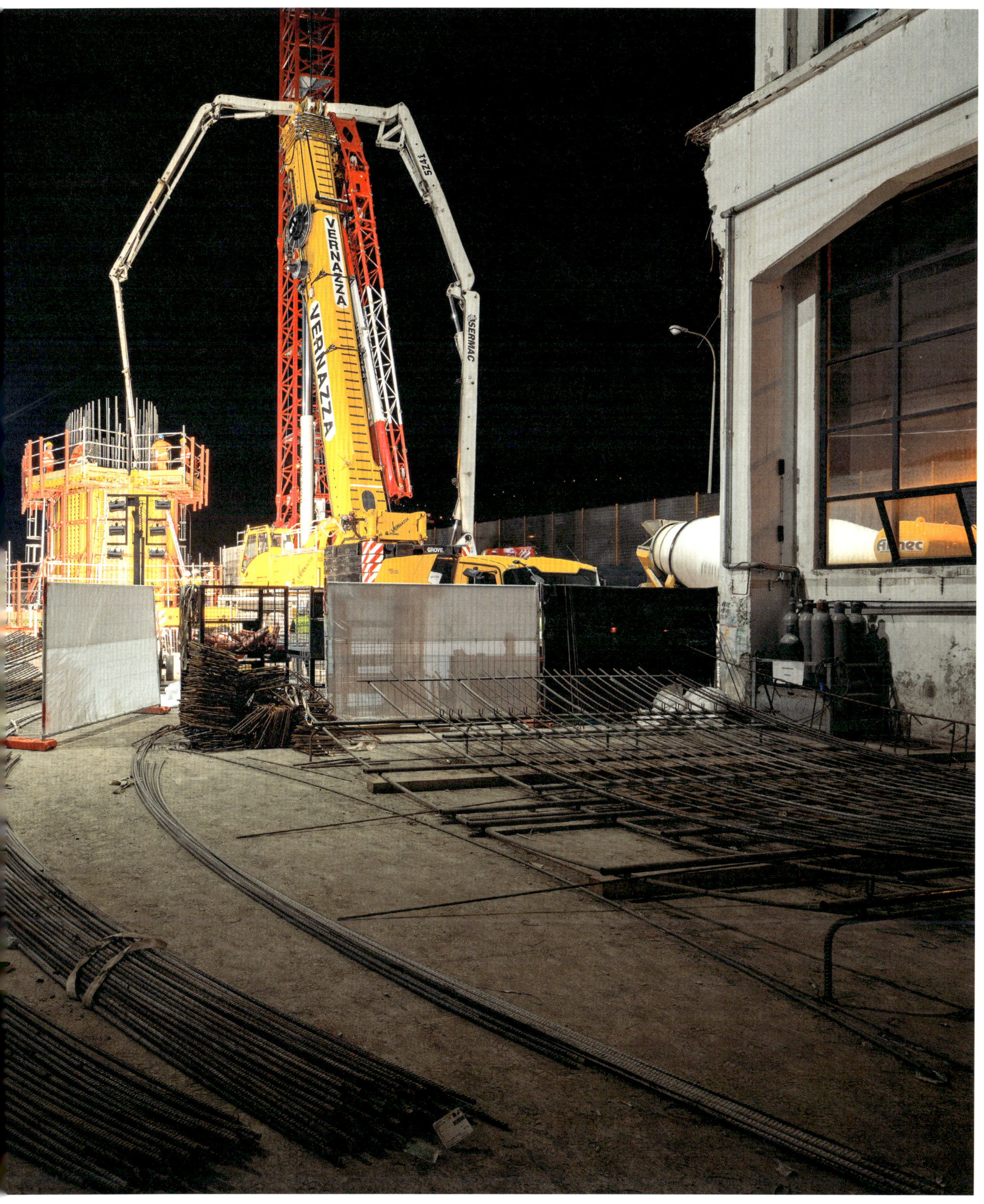

VERNAZZA
VERNAZZA
SERMAC
S24L
GROVE

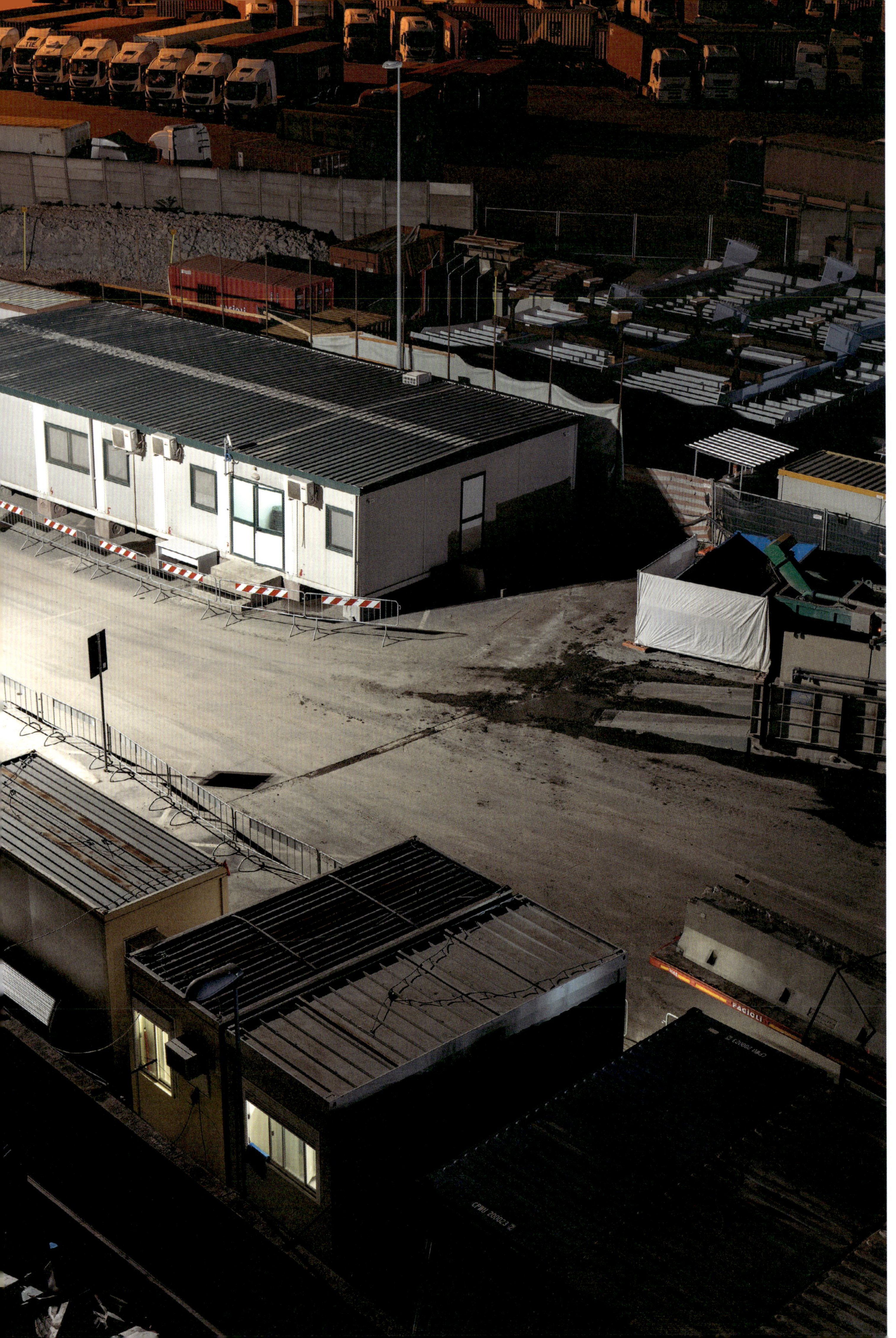

JULY 31, 2019

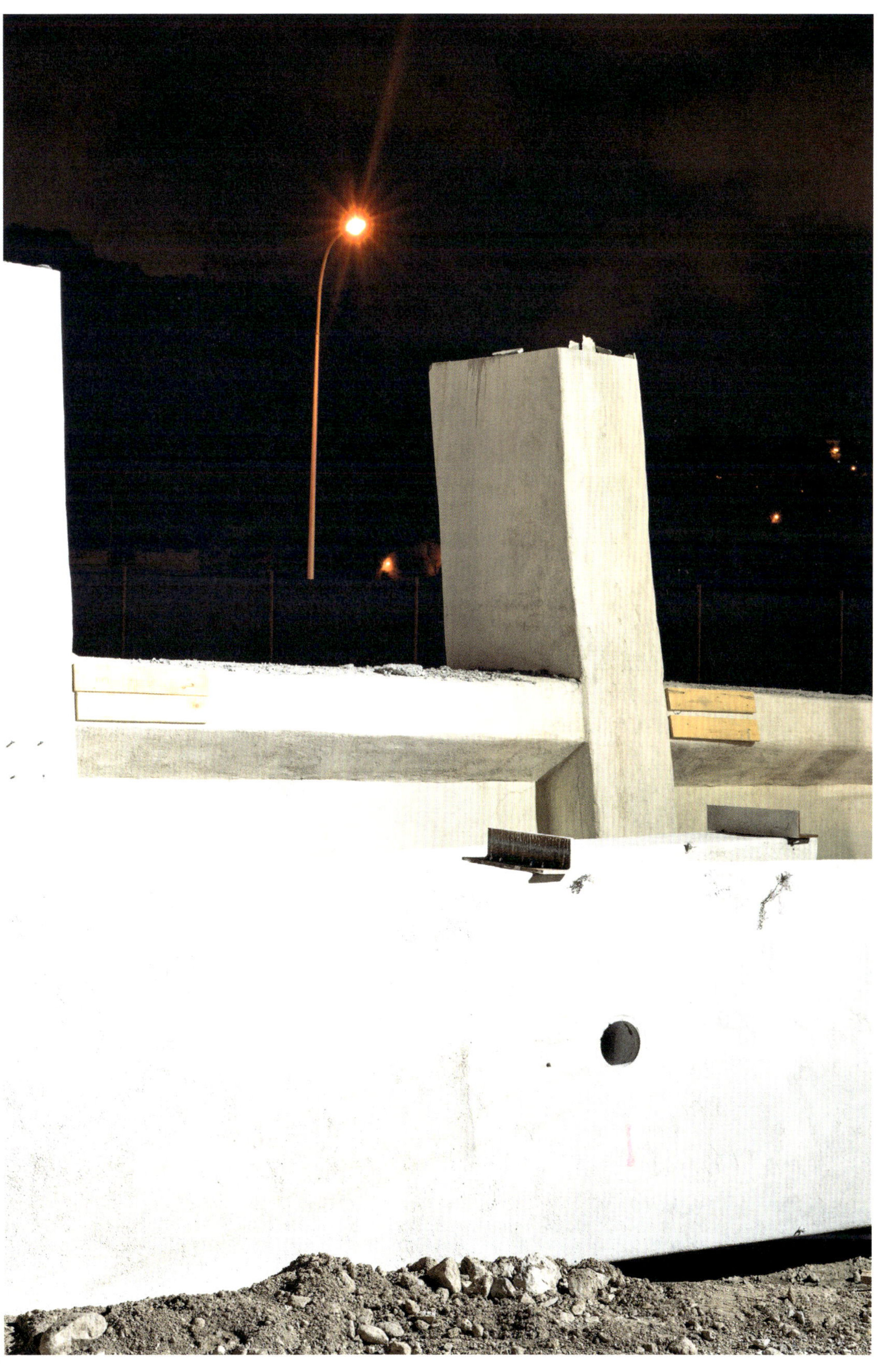

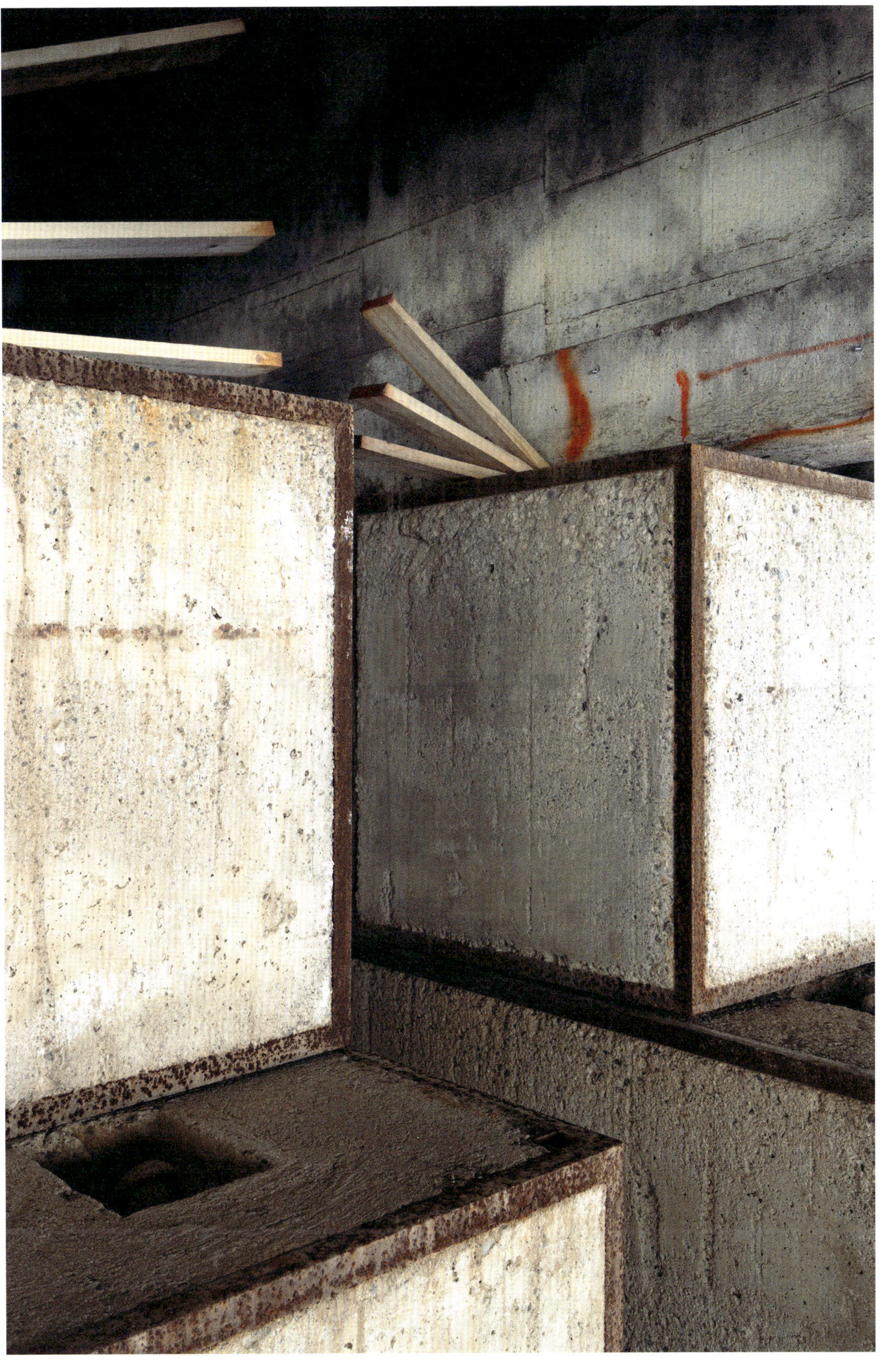

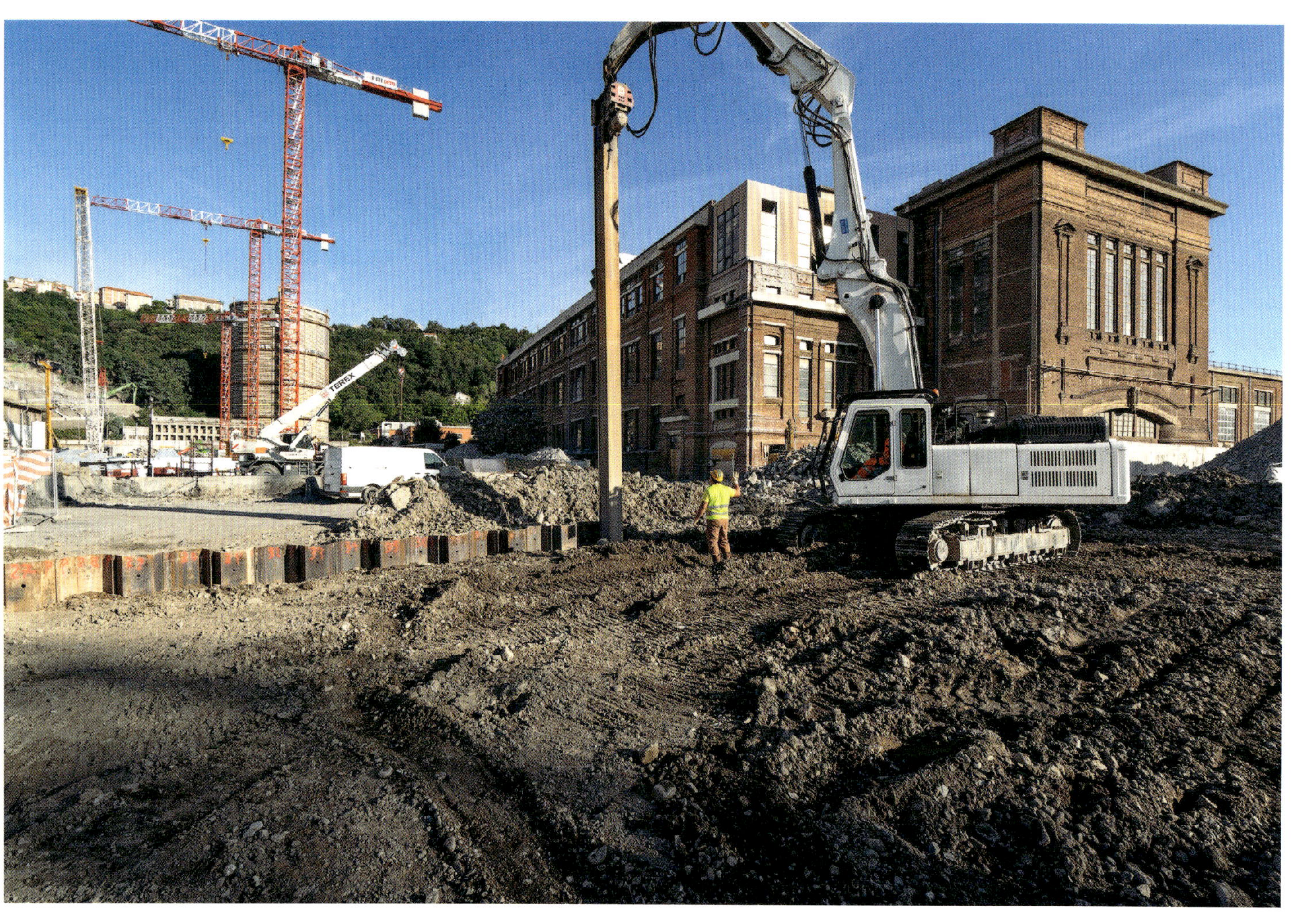

AUGUST 14, 2019

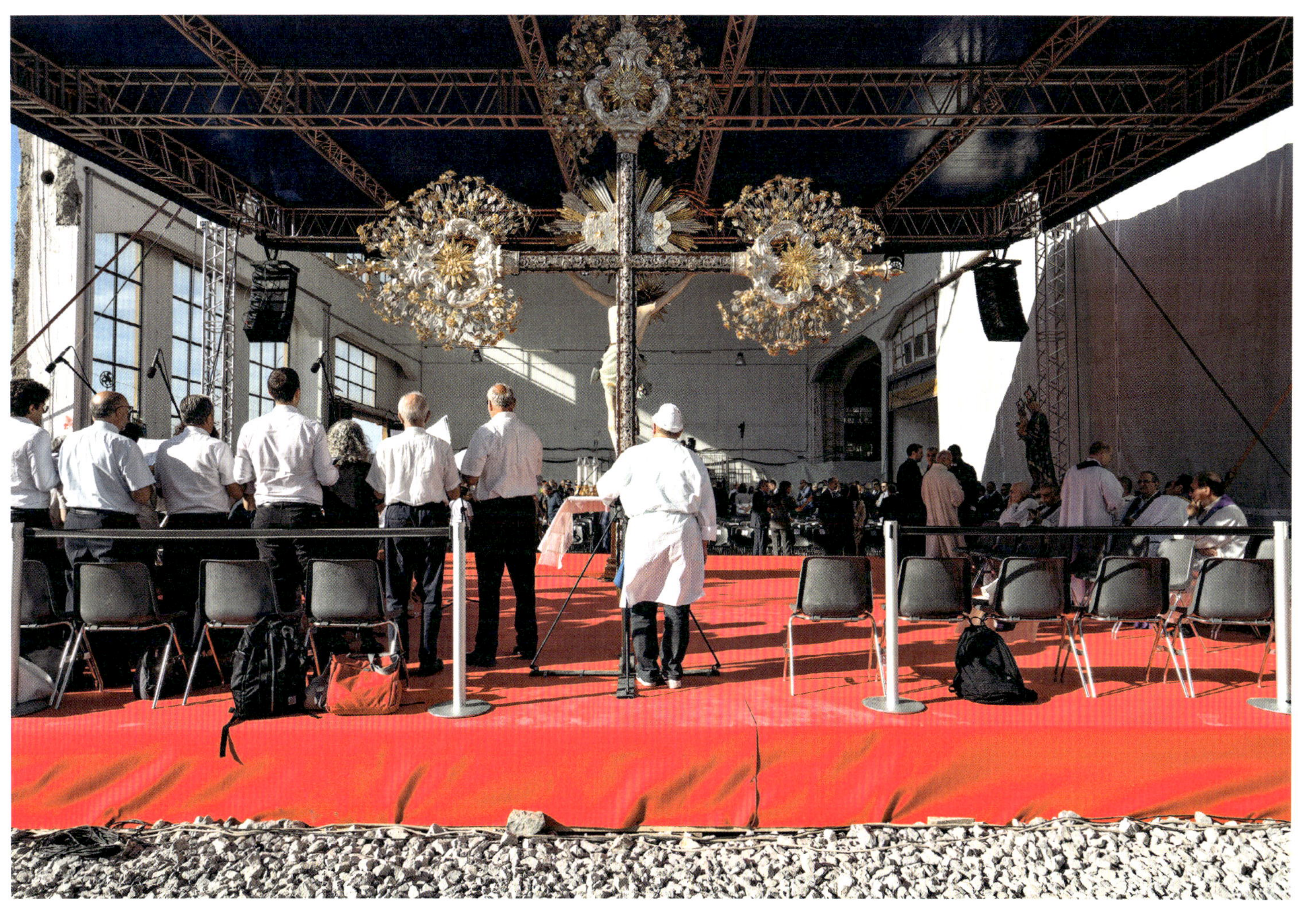

On August 14, 2019, at the building site, close to the new pier 9 that could already be seen rising up, a religious ceremony was held in memory of the 43 victims, with the State's most senior officials in attendance.

Visible behind the altar is the "Christ," the artistic processional crucifix typical of Genoese brotherhoods, transported to the building site from the local parish of Campasso for the celebration of the ceremony.

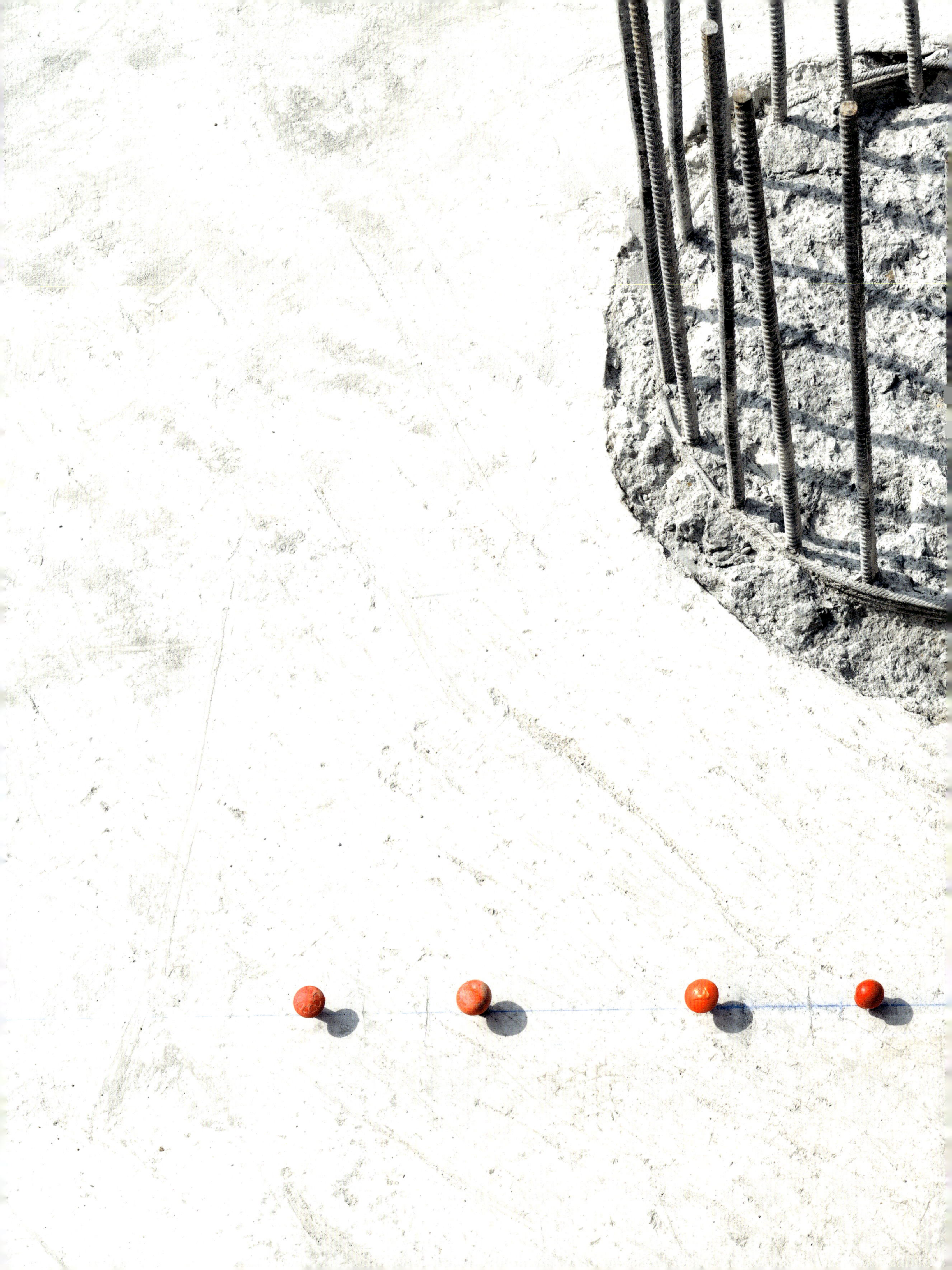

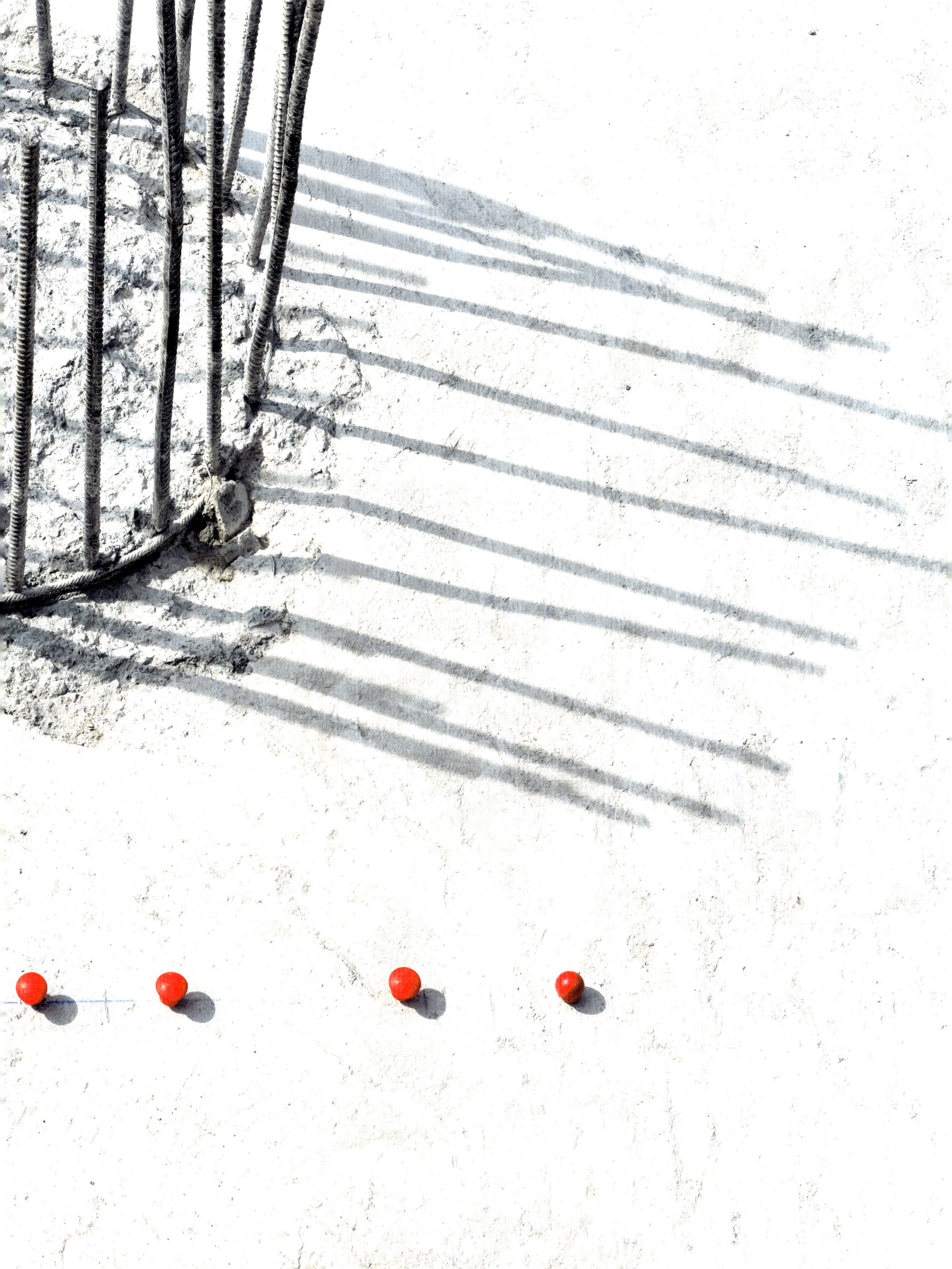

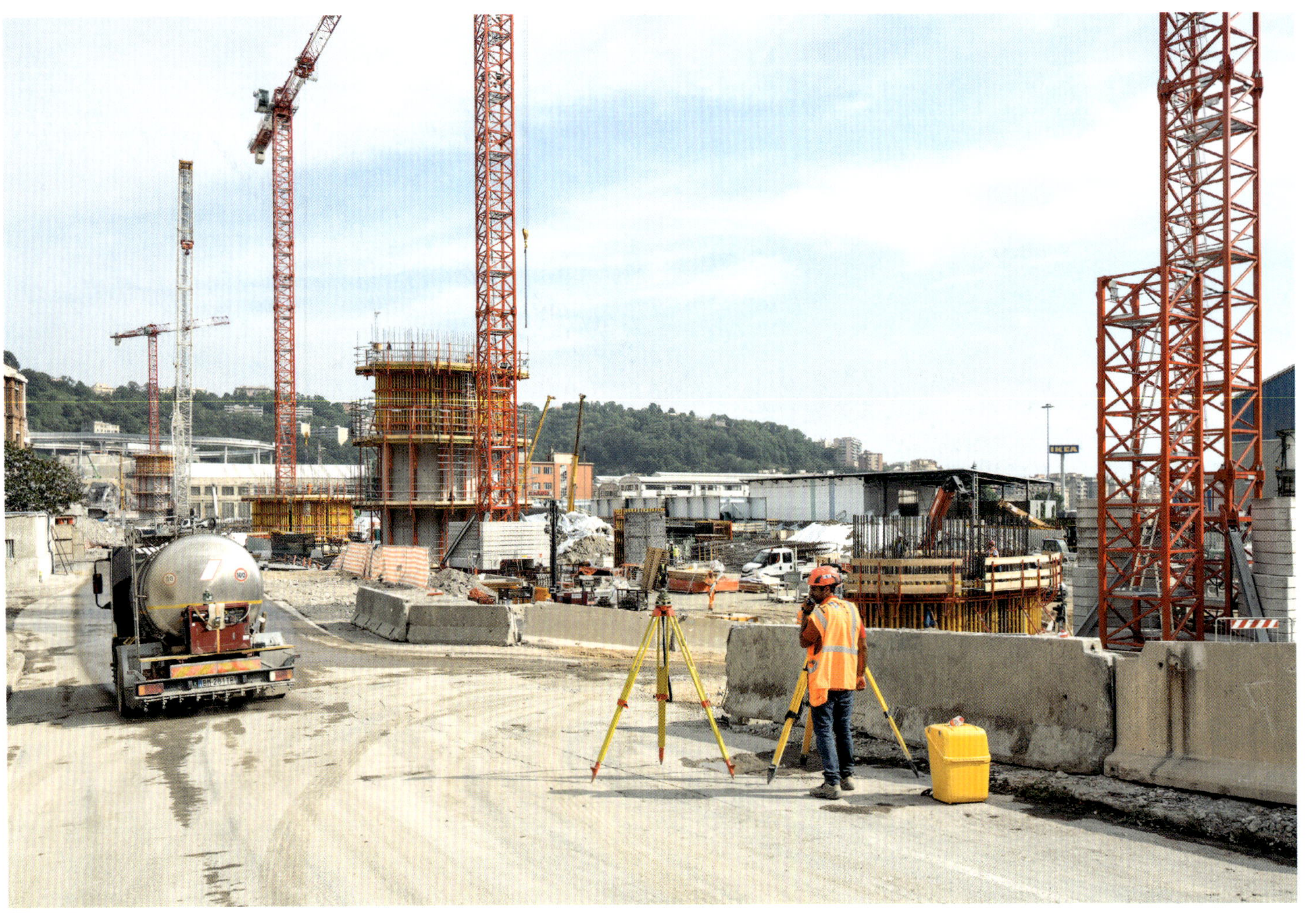

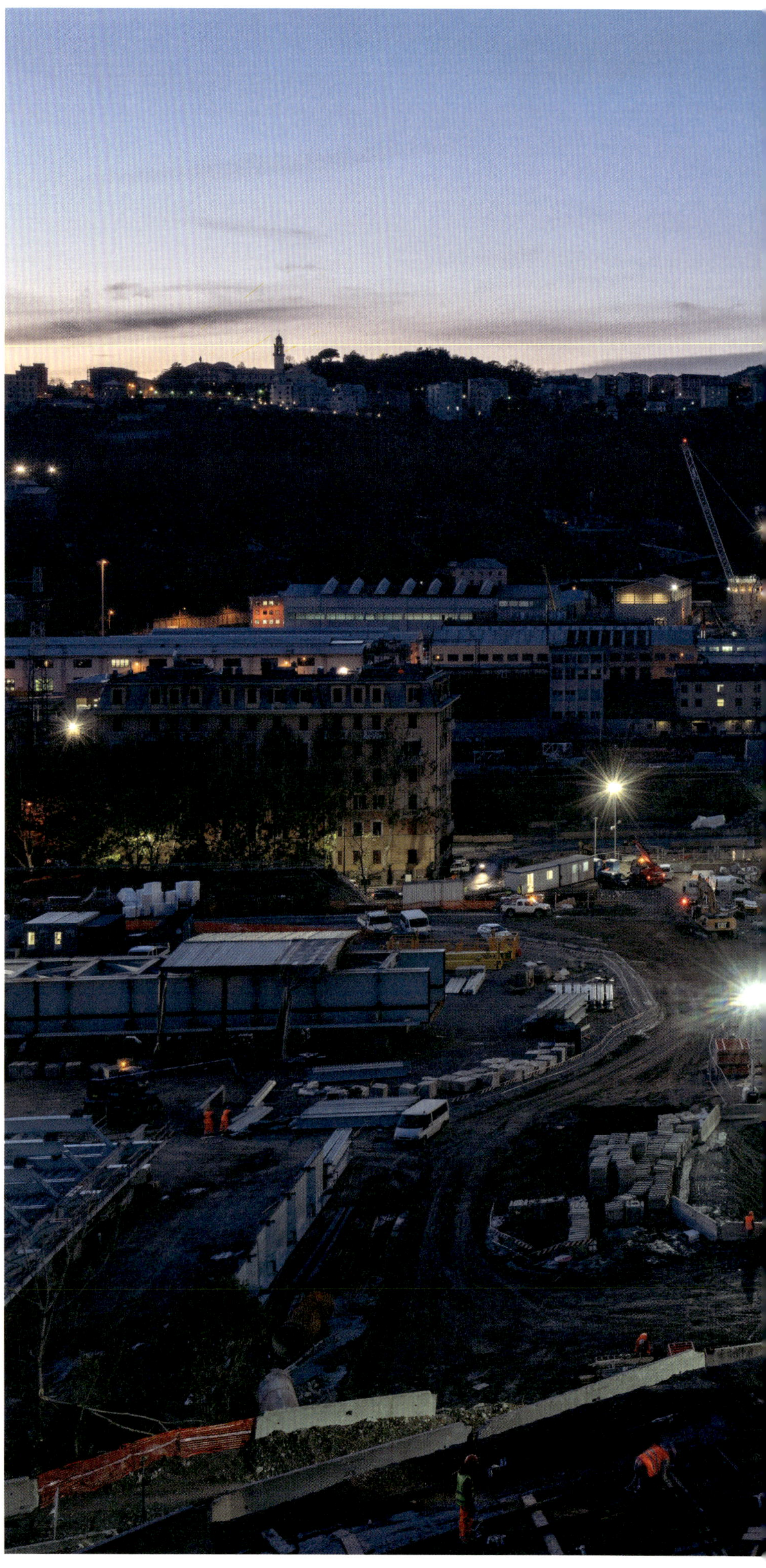

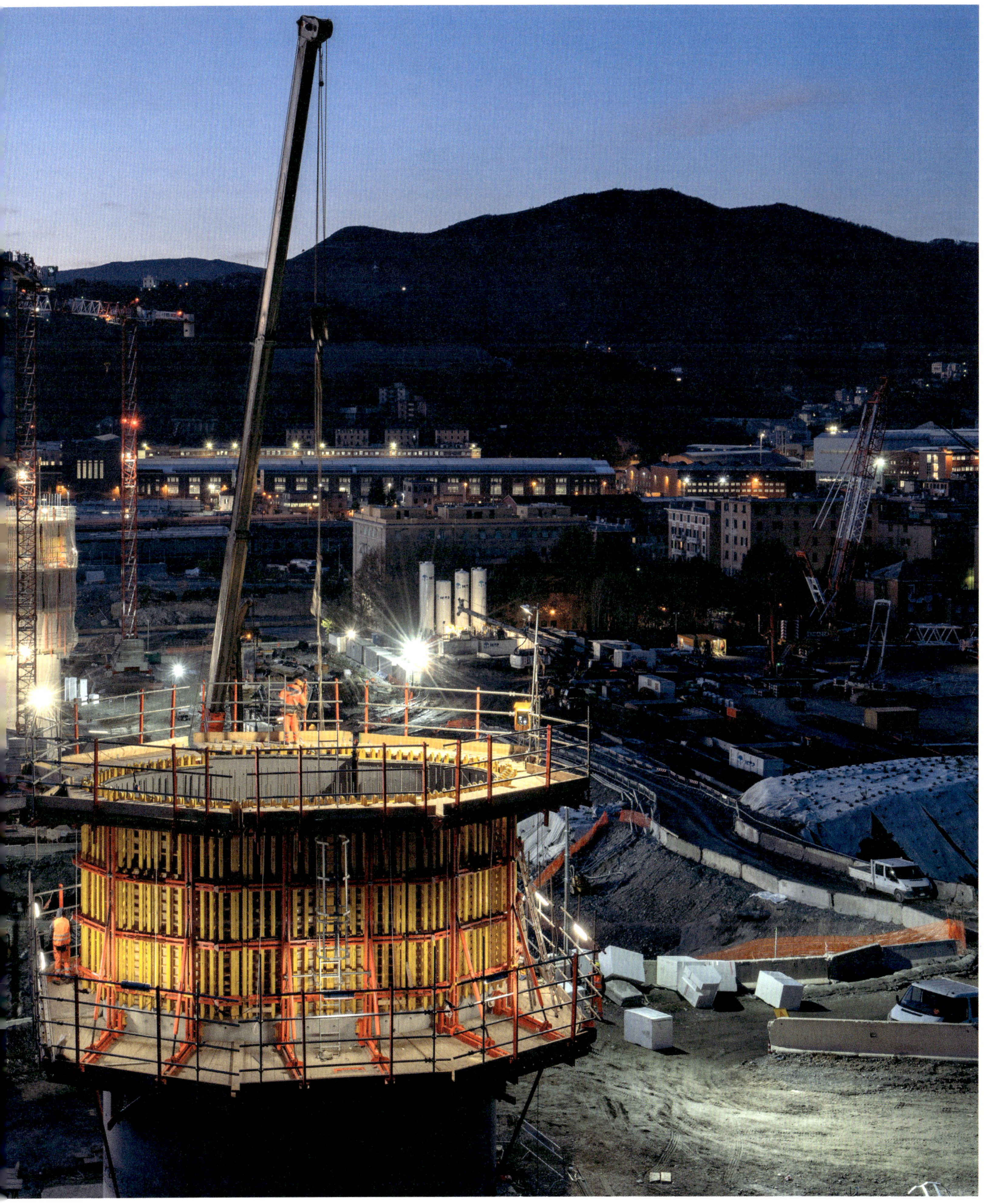

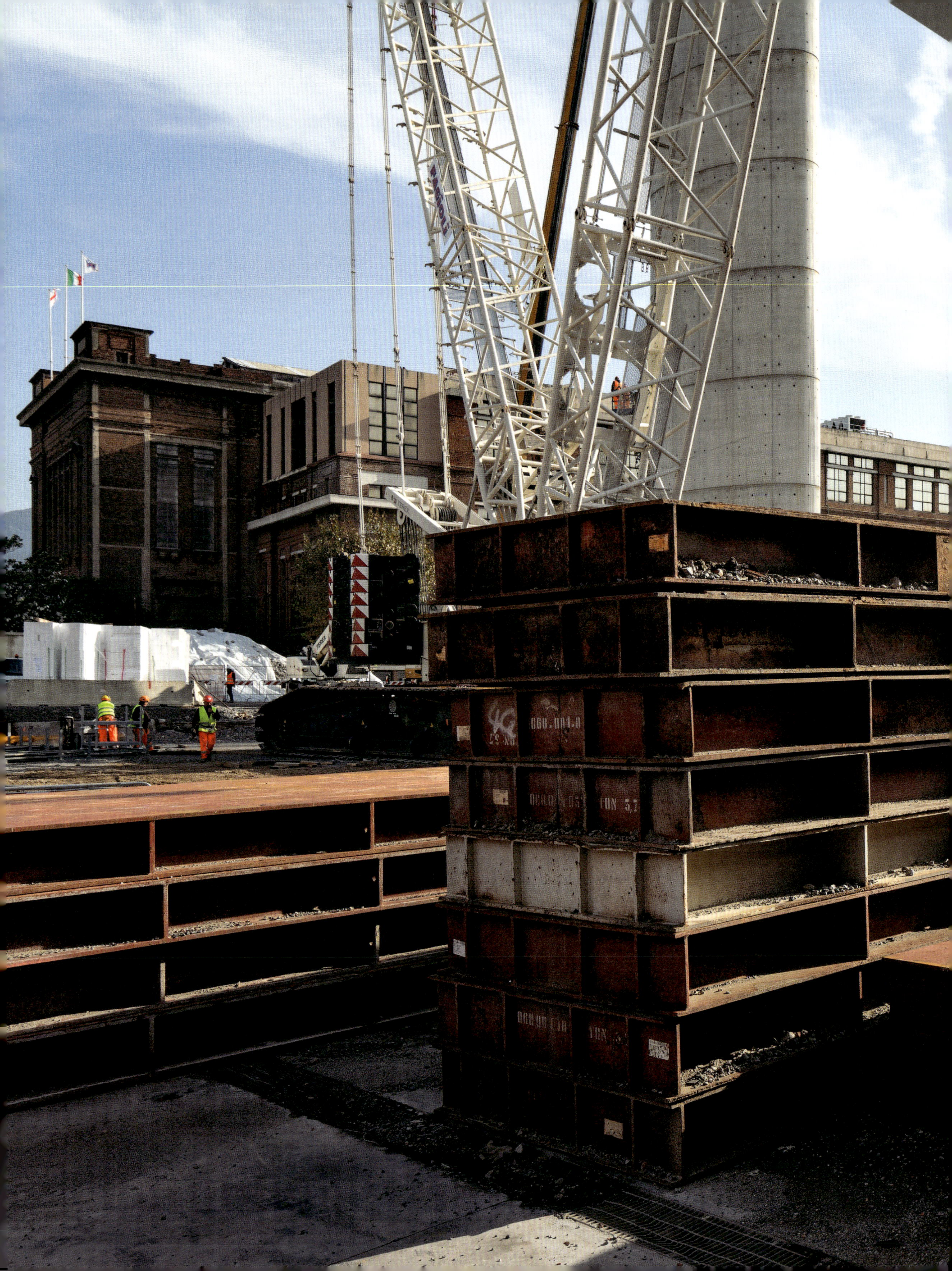

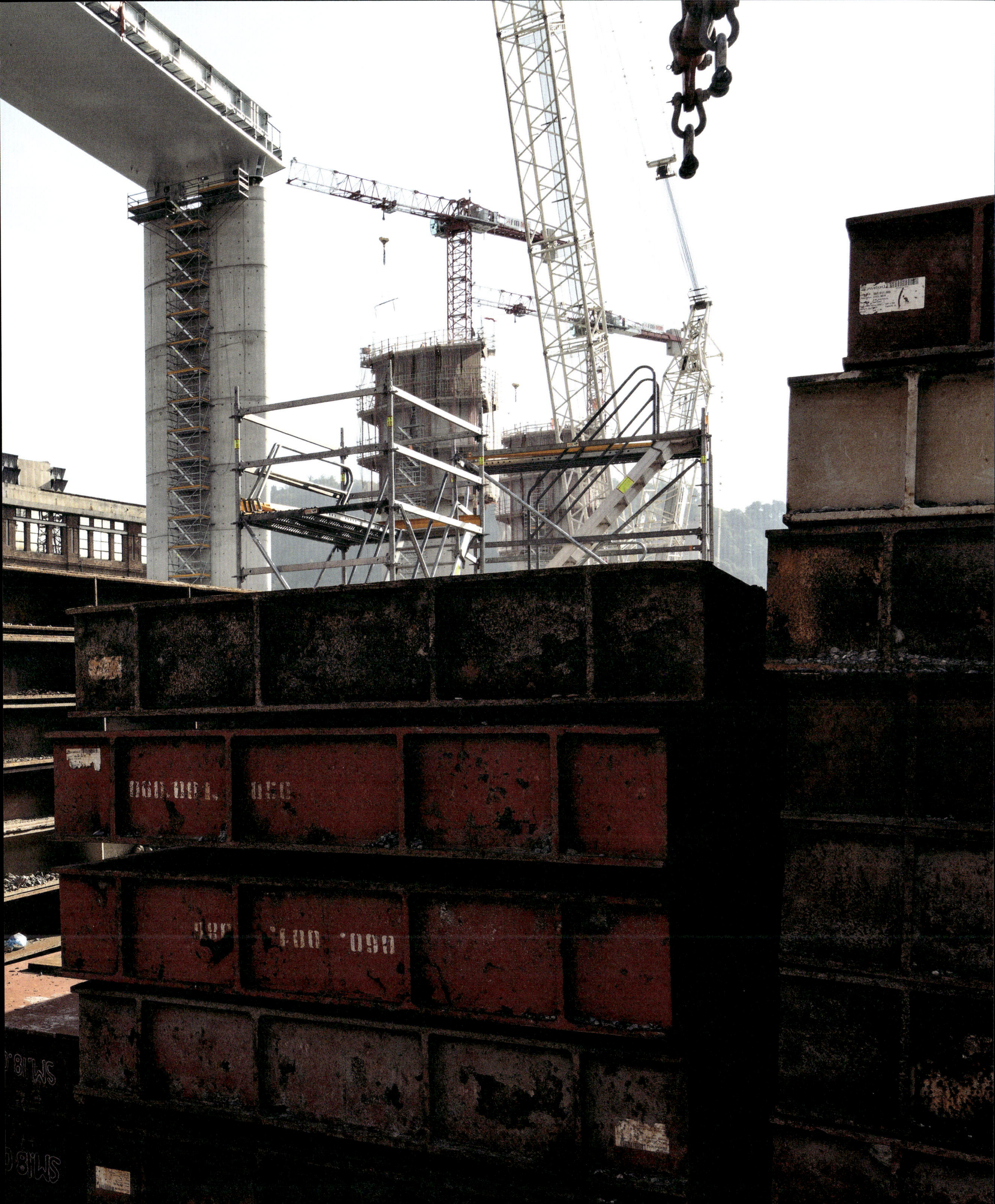

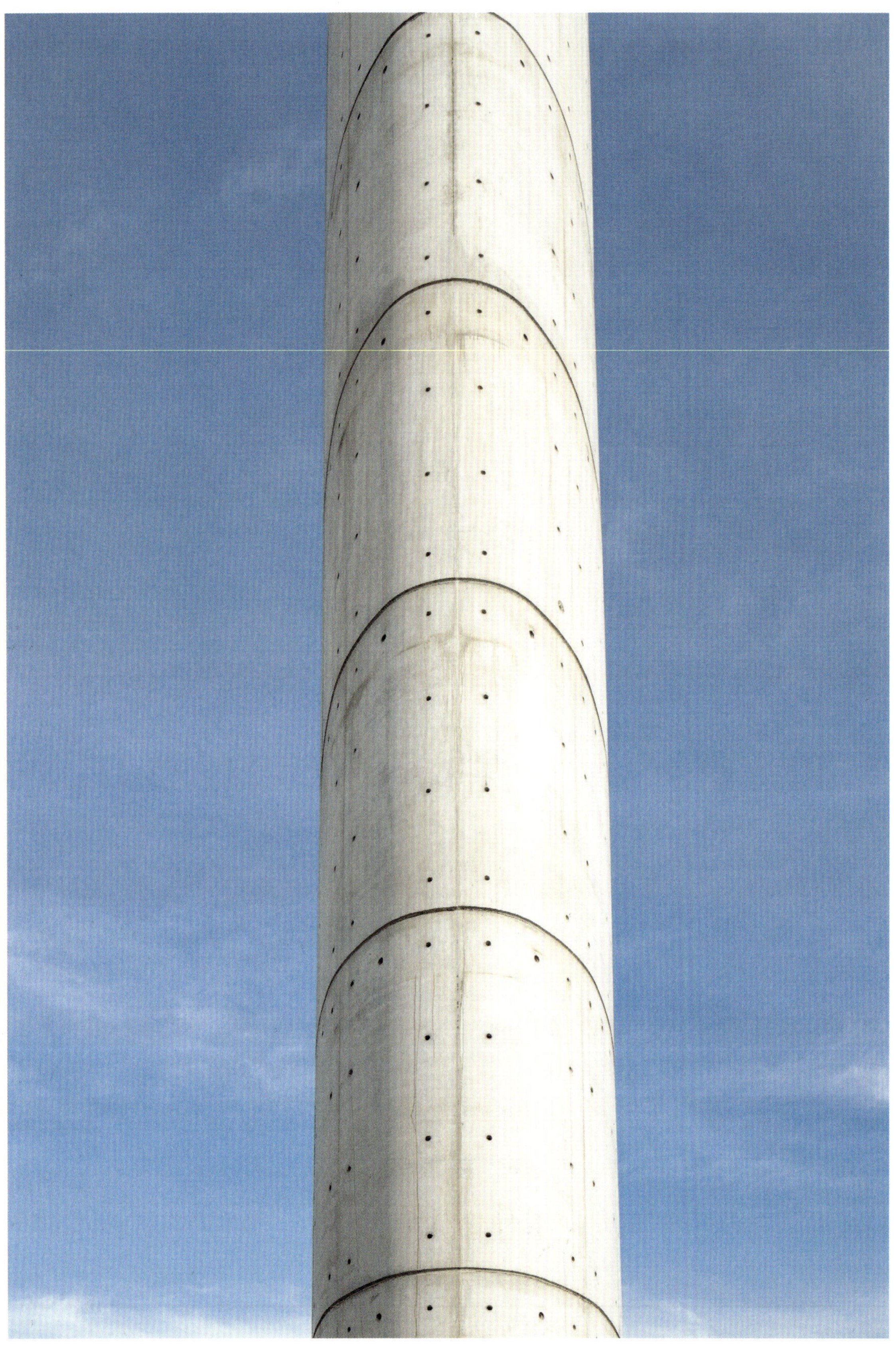

THE HIGH NUMBER OF TECHNICAL AND LOGISTIC DIFFICULTIES IN THIS PROJECT WERE ACCOMPANIED BY A STRONG EMOTIONAL COMPONENT THAT WAS DUE TO WHAT HAD OCCURRED DURING THE COLLAPSE ON AUGUST 14, BUT ALSO TO THE STRONG FEELING OF A REVIVAL OF ONE'S CITY THAT DROVE ME ON FROM DAY ONE.

EMILIO PUPPO
RINA

WHAT MATERIALIZED IN THIS
EXPERIENCE WAS THE DREAM
OF BEING ABLE TO OPERATE
BASED ON COMMON SENSE
AND THE BEST INTERNATIONAL
PRACTICES, ADOPTING
TELOCRATIC AND DYNAMIC
PROCEDURES IN PROGRESSIVE
AND PARALLEL PHASES, ENOUGH
TO OVERCOME THE RED TAPE
AND THE CONTRADICTIONS
OF OUR LEGAL SYSTEM.

MAURIZIO MICHELINI
COMMISSIONER'S OFFICE

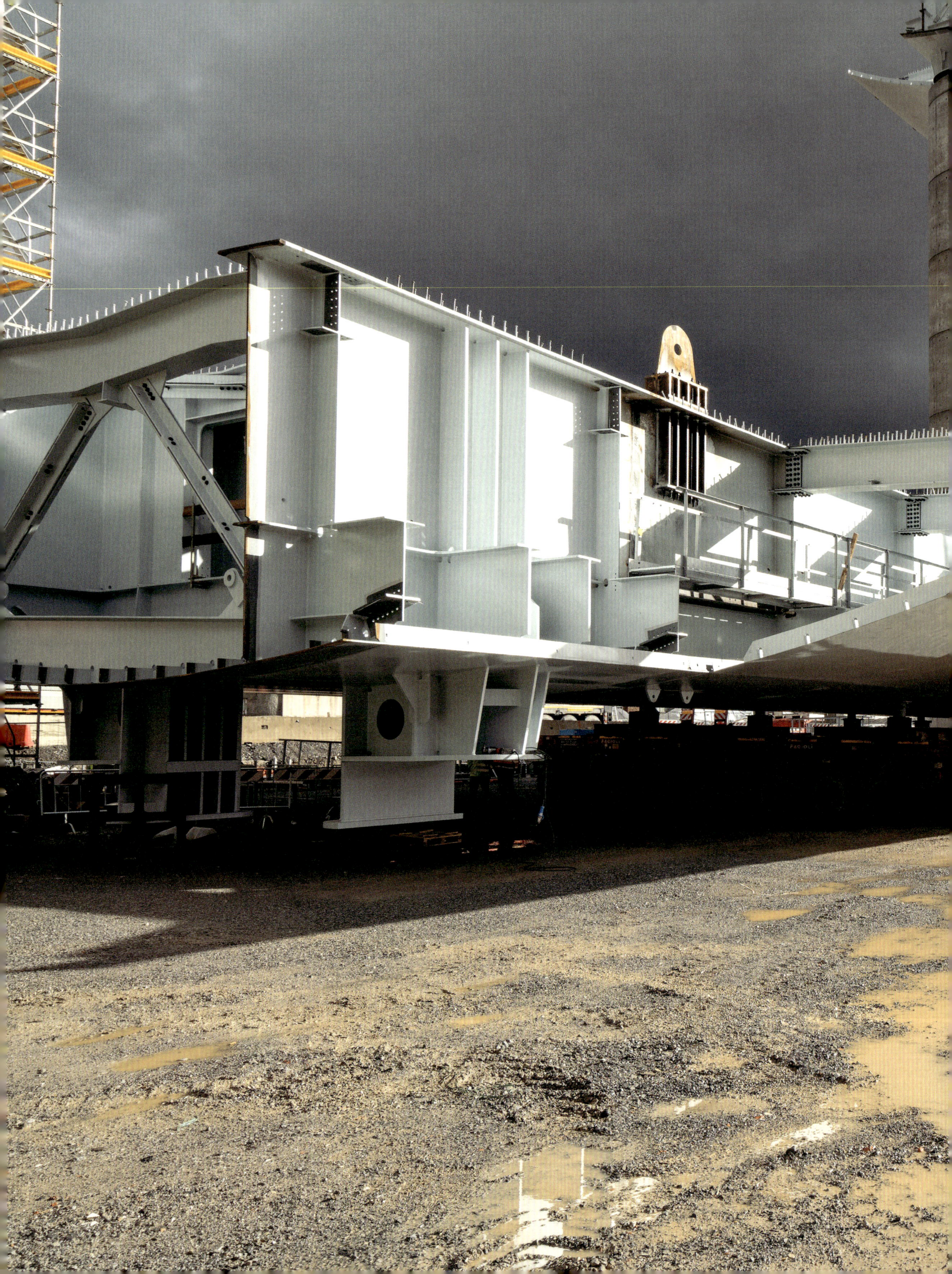

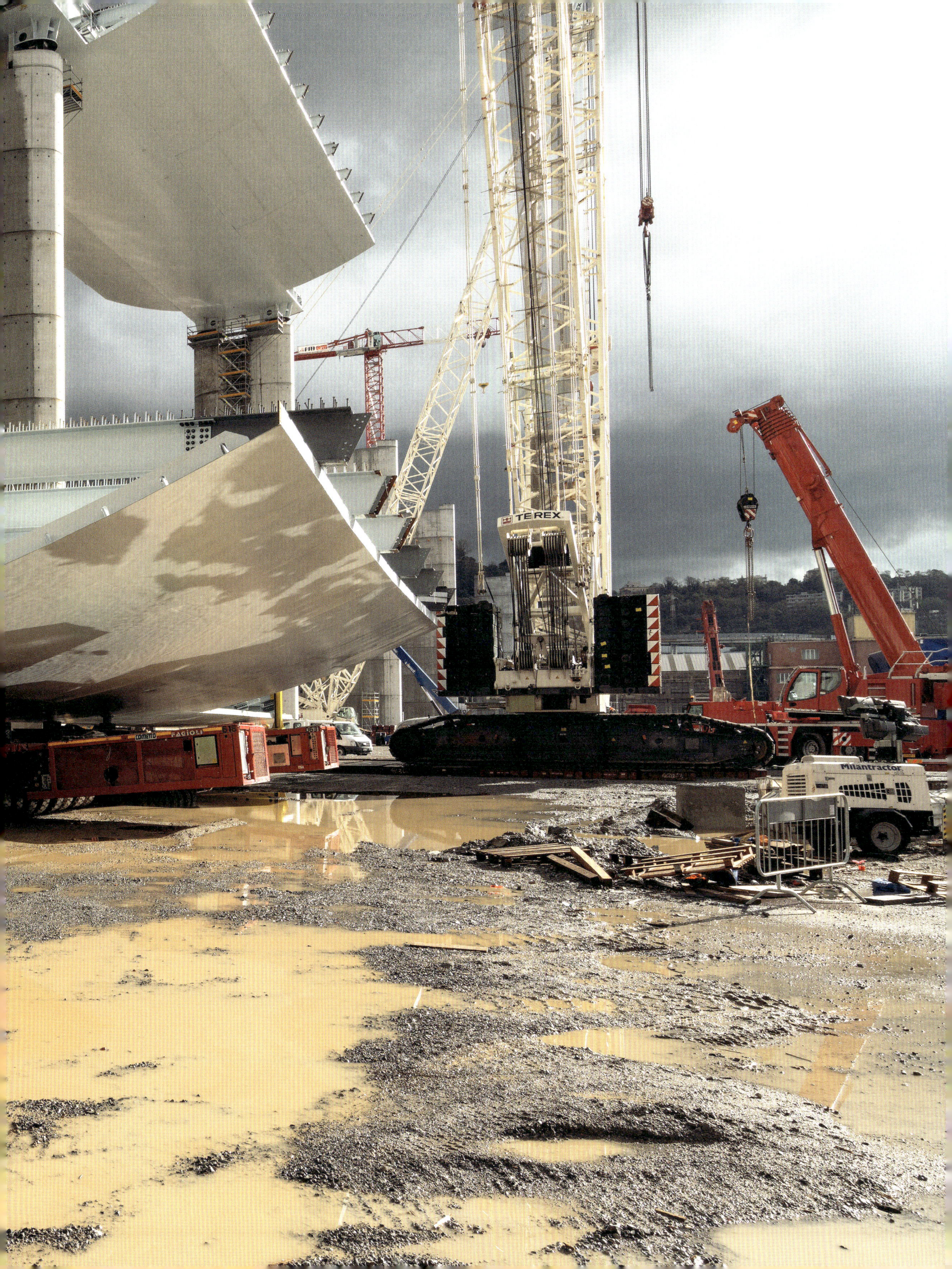

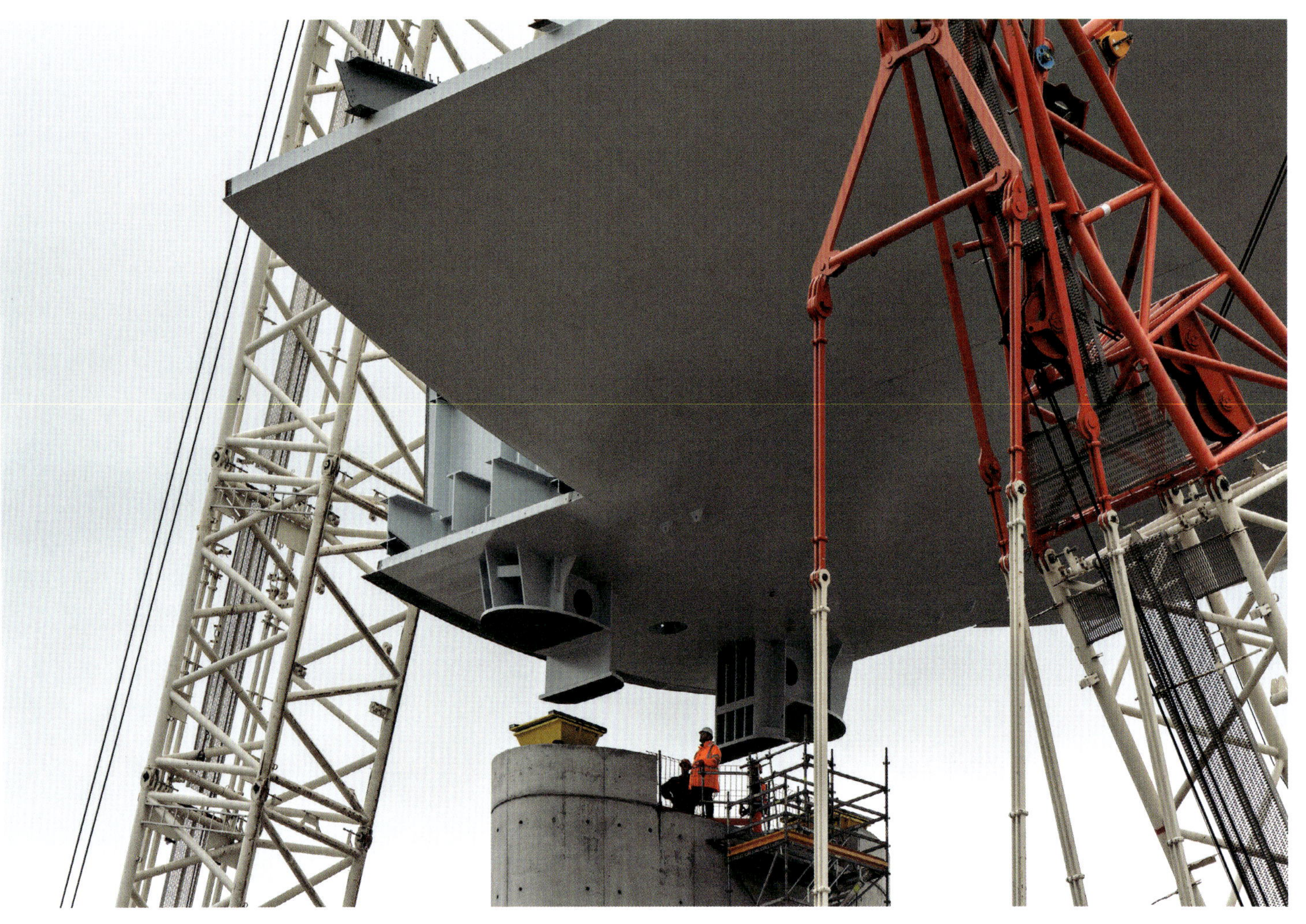

NOVEMBER 7, 2019

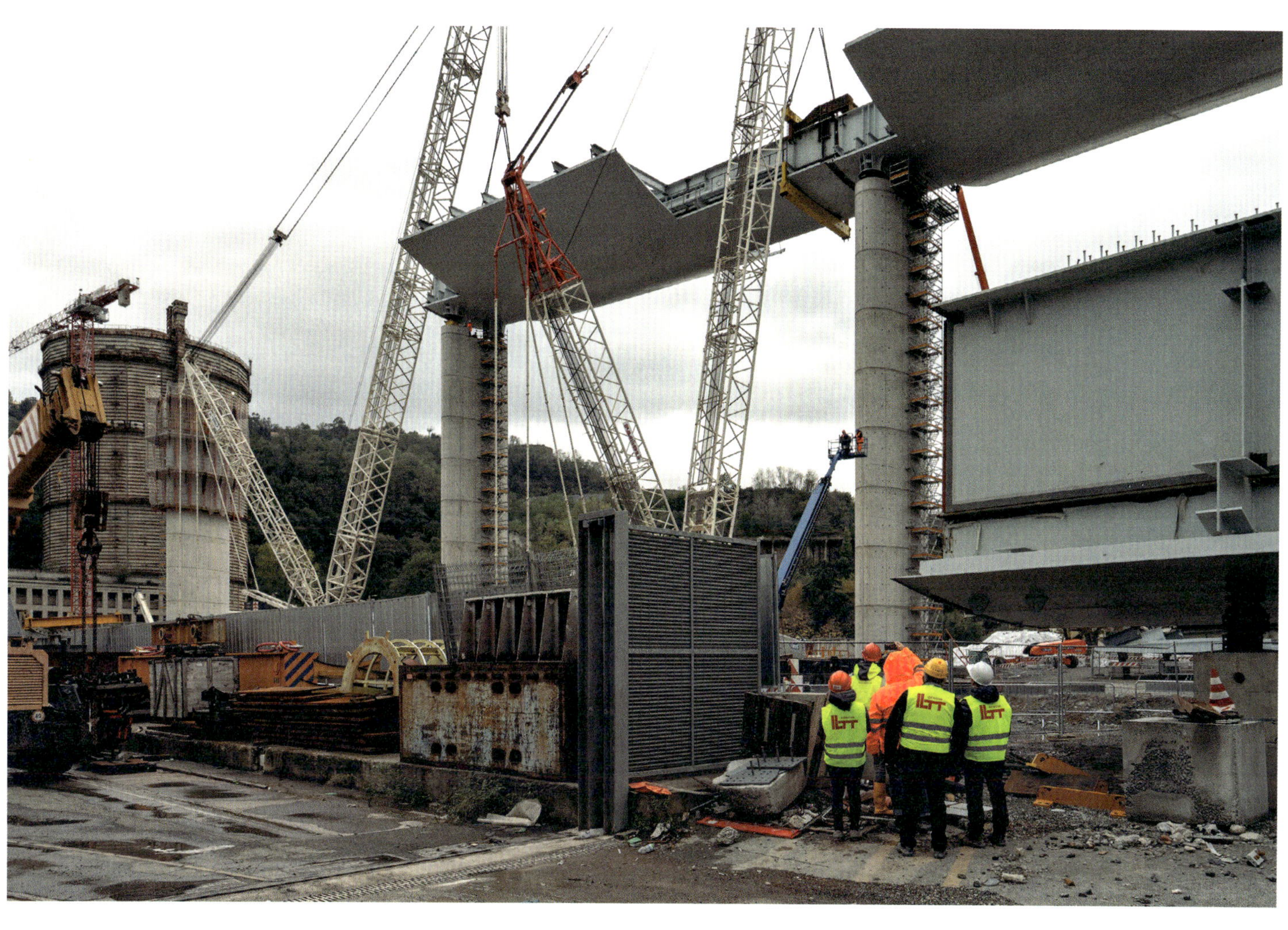

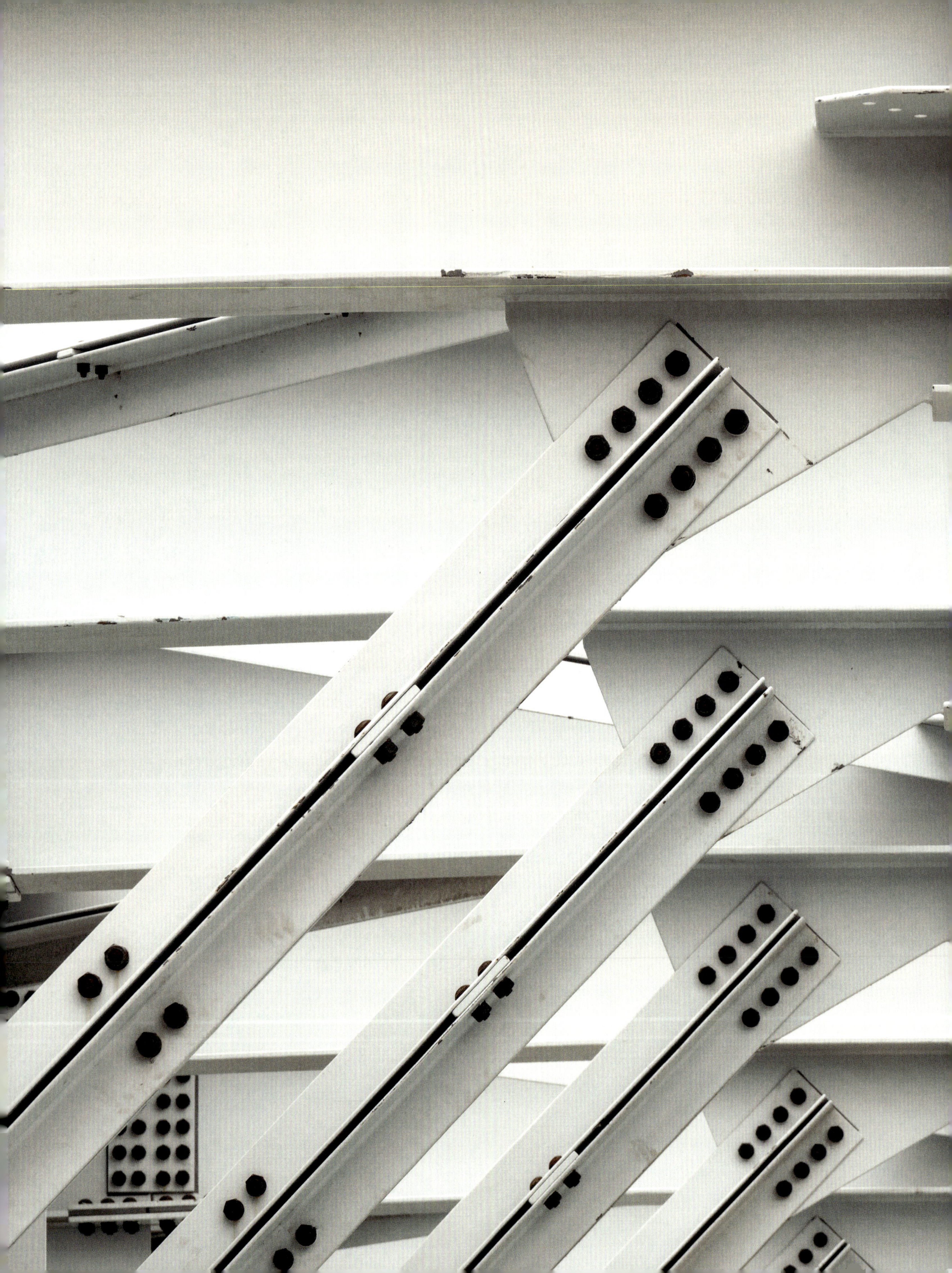

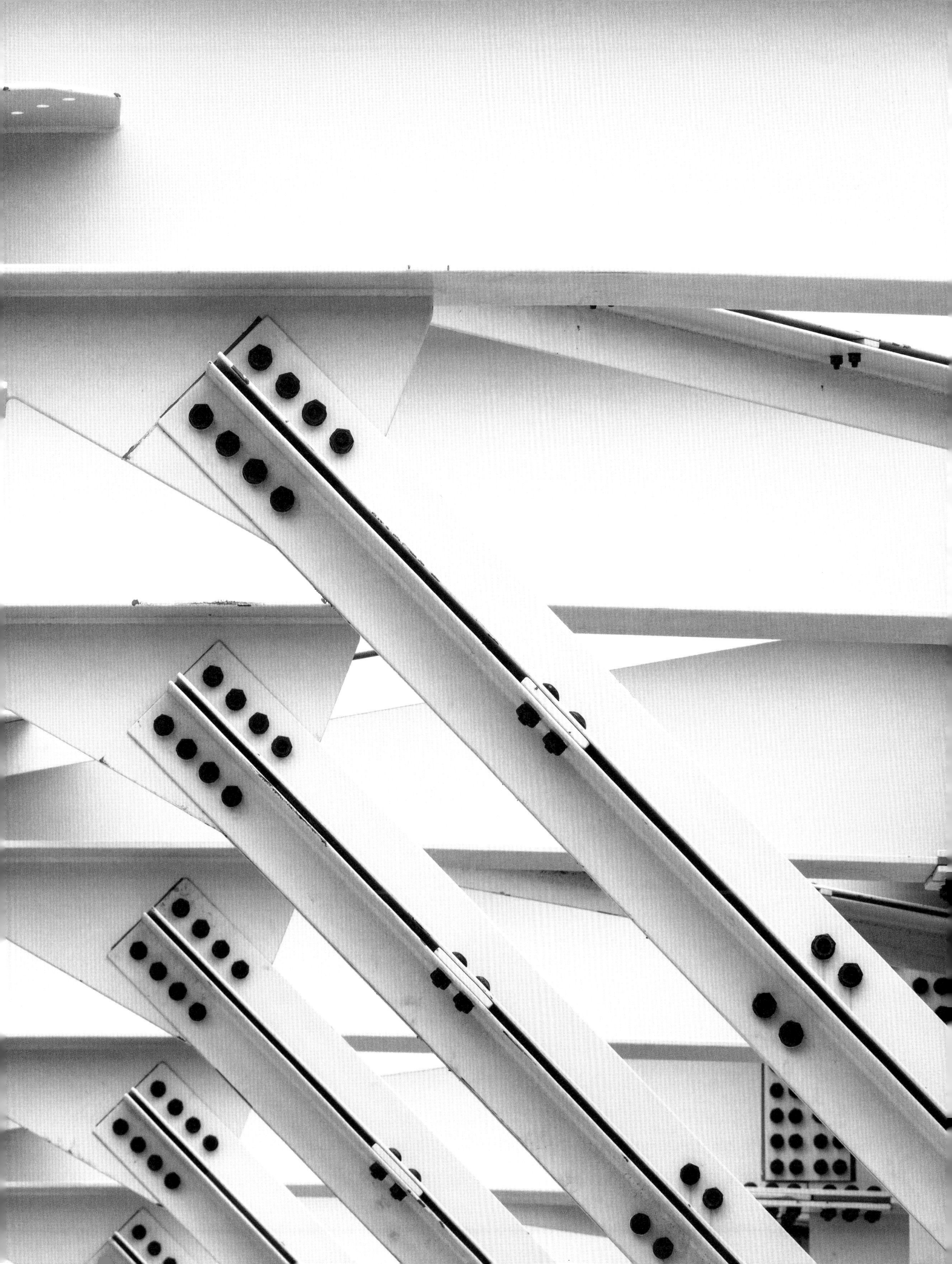

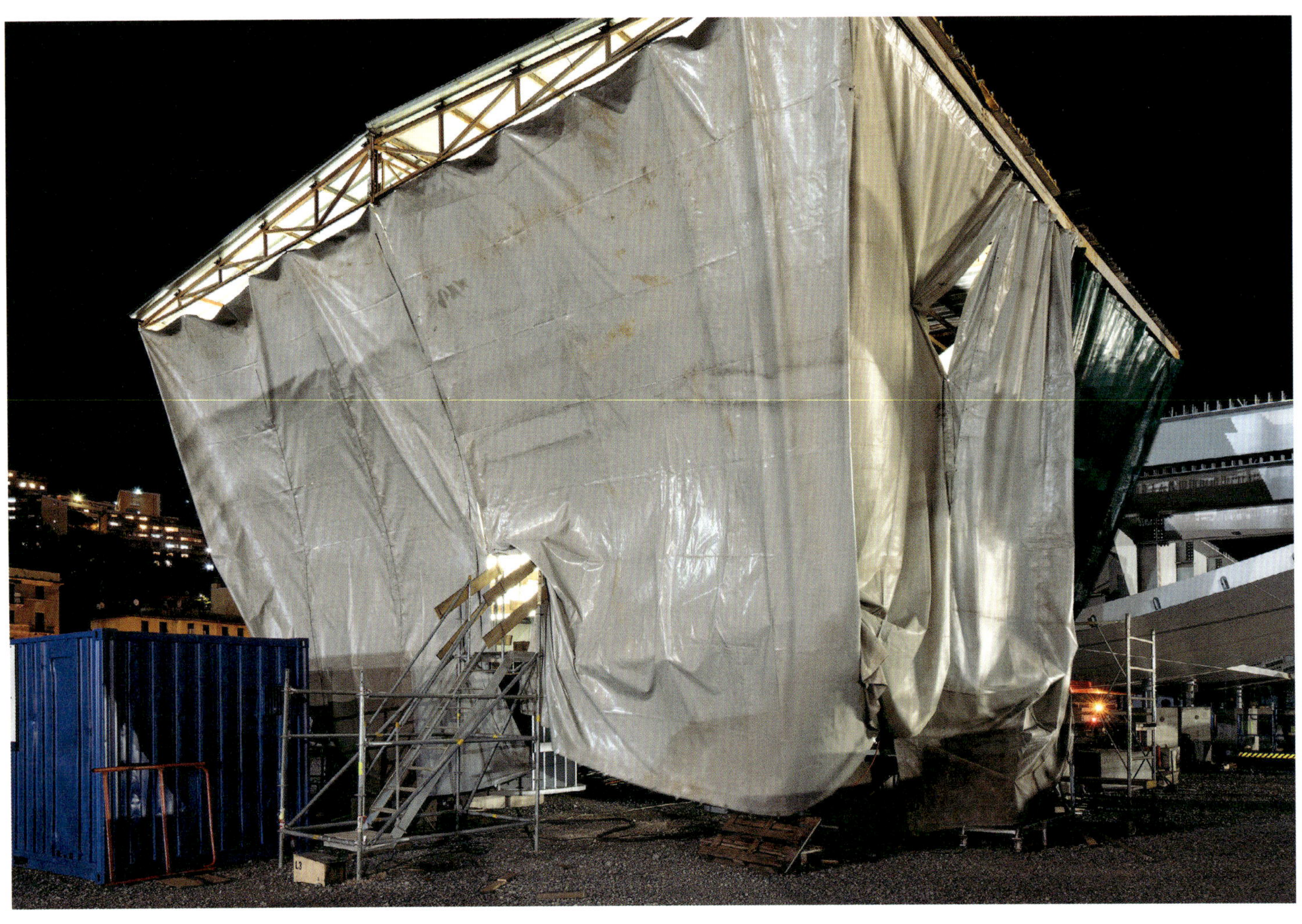

The portions of metallic deck that were transported
to the building site on special vehicles required
further assembly operations before the site could be
"launched" high up. For this reason, the building site
also included small "huts" set up for welding operations.

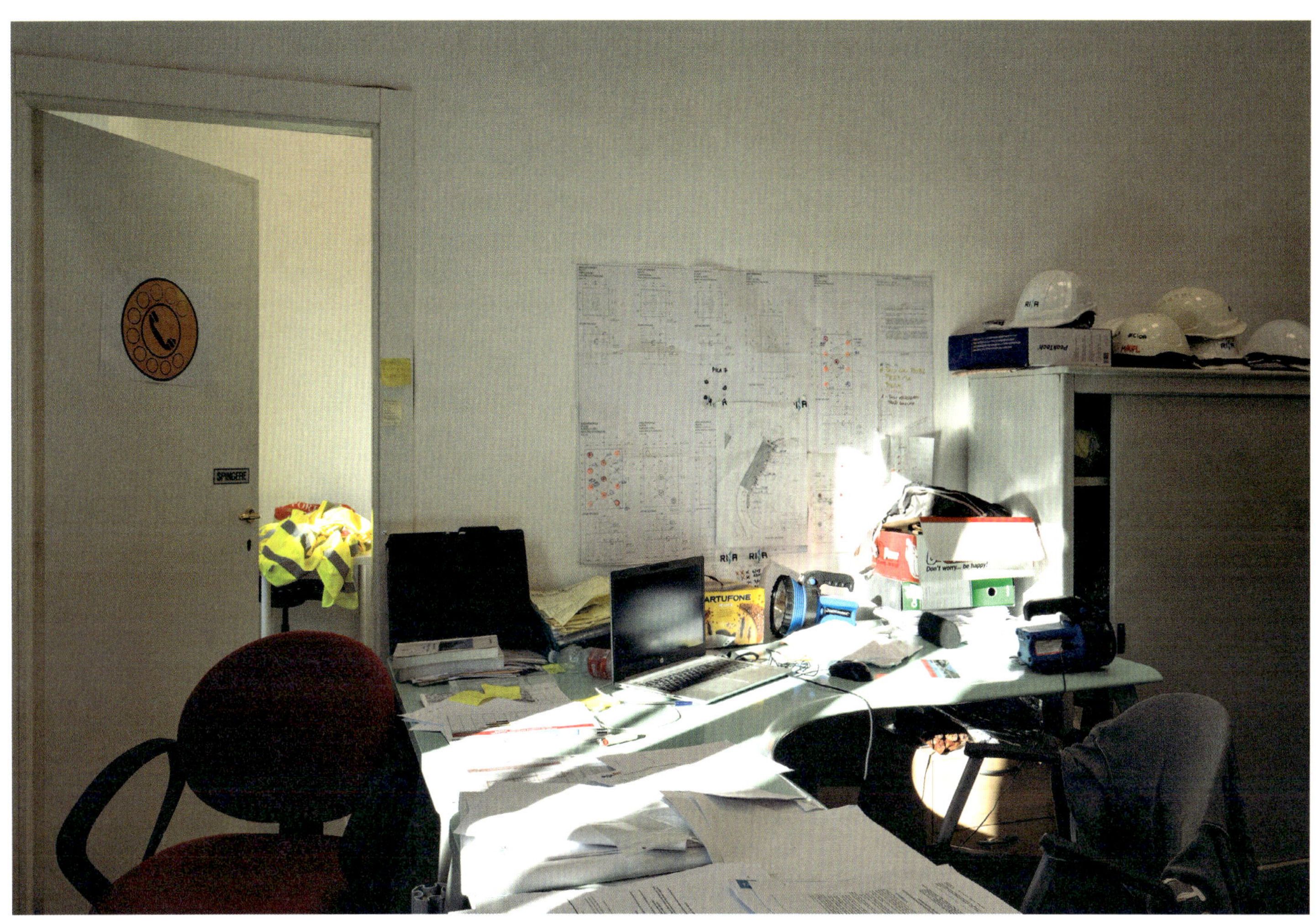

The RINA team dedicated to the project mainly worked
using as its base the building site office, located
at the northern entrance to the western building site.
Located in this area were the offices of Work
Supervision and Safety Coordination. This was also
where meetings were held to coordinate the companies
working together. The management of the project
instead met also at Palazzo Tursi every Friday,
with the Commissioner always in attendance.

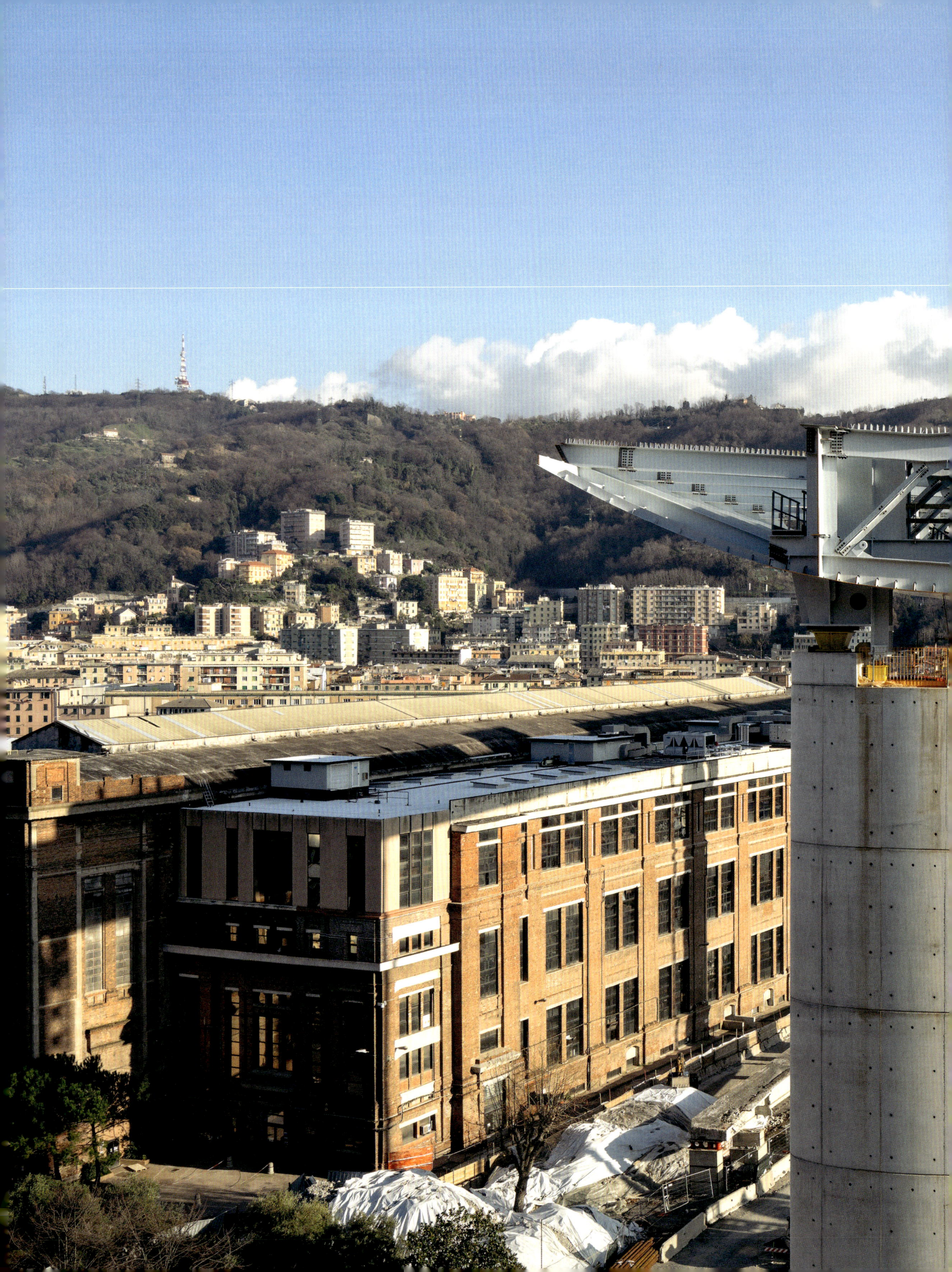

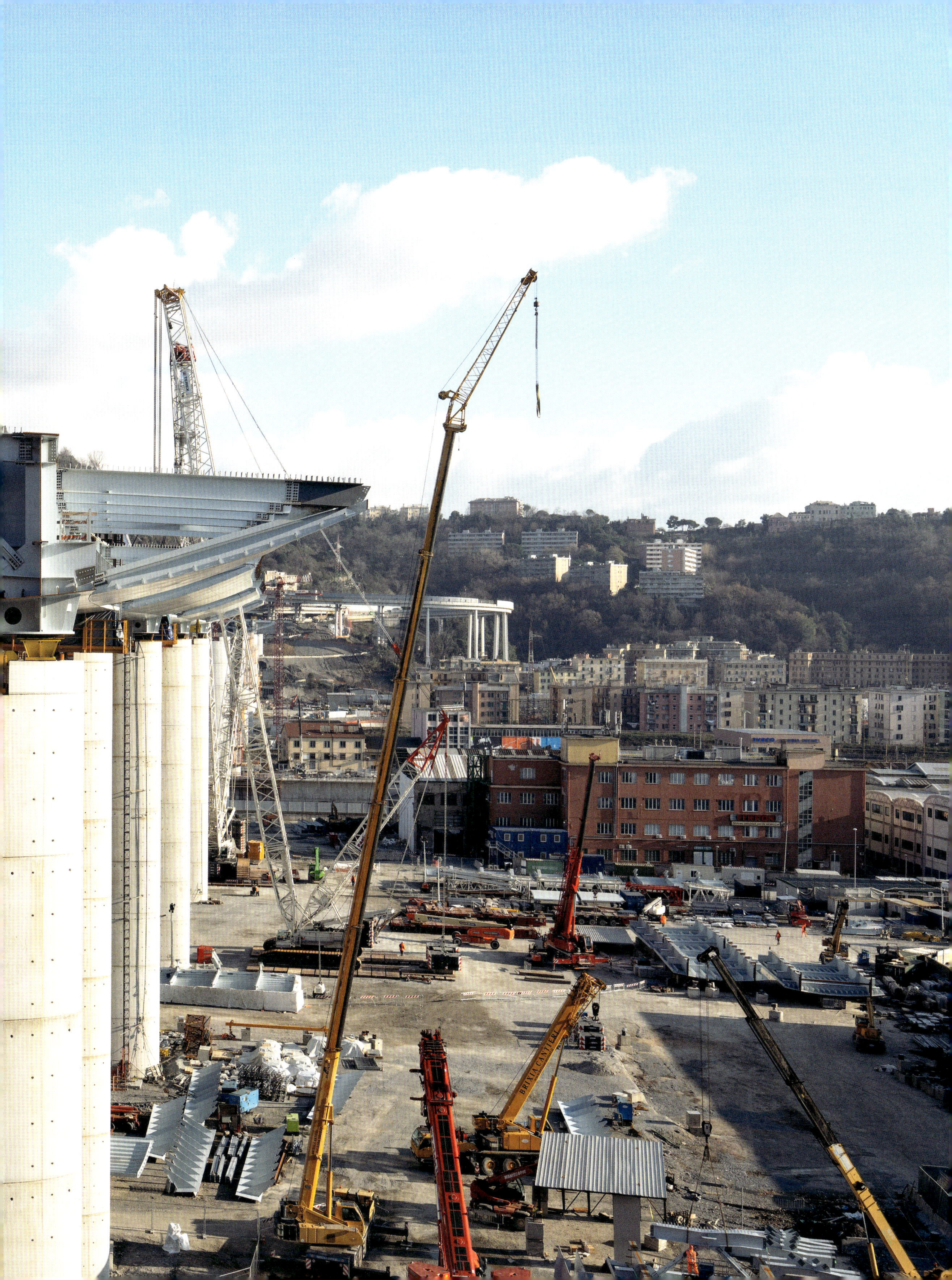

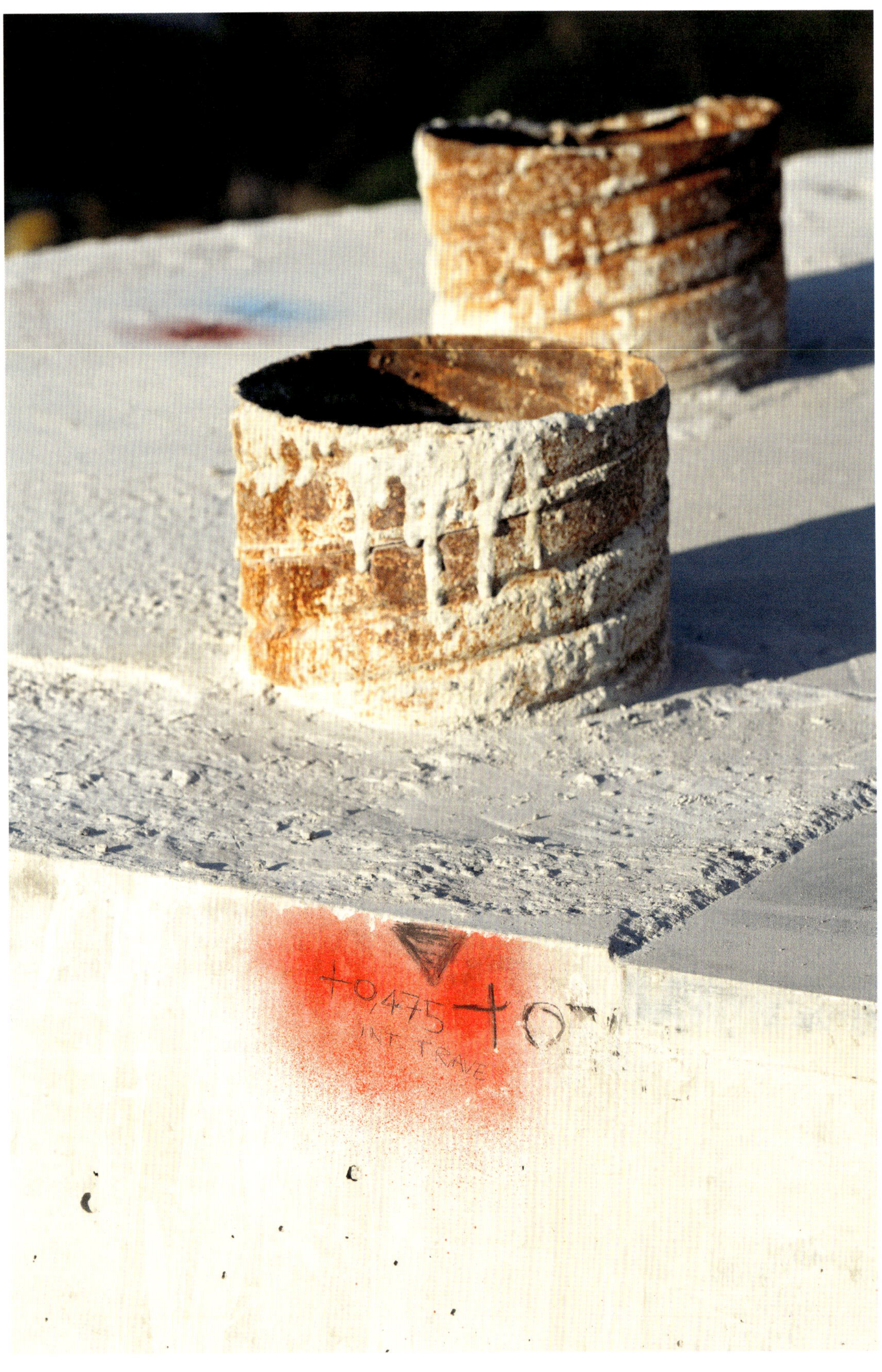

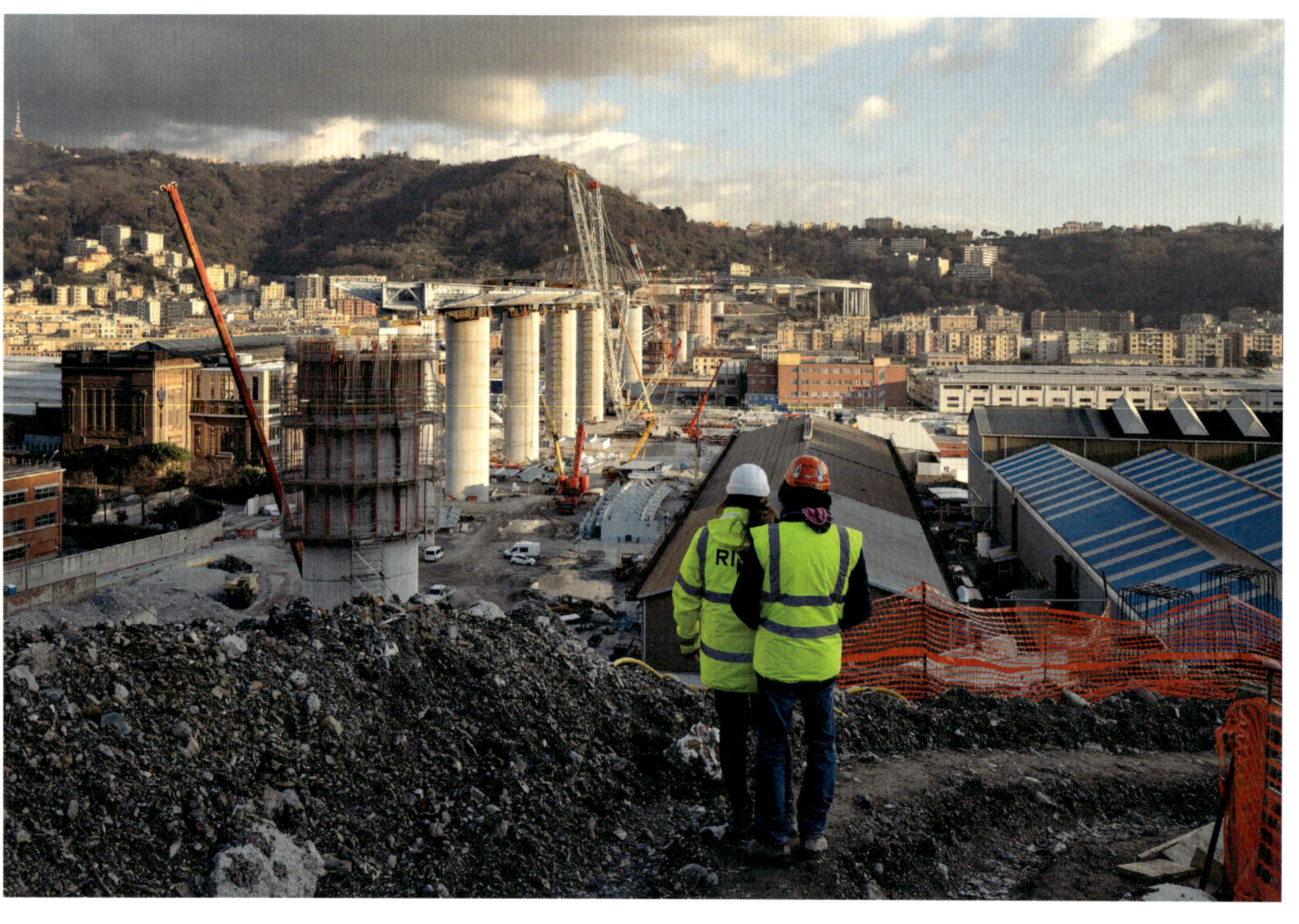

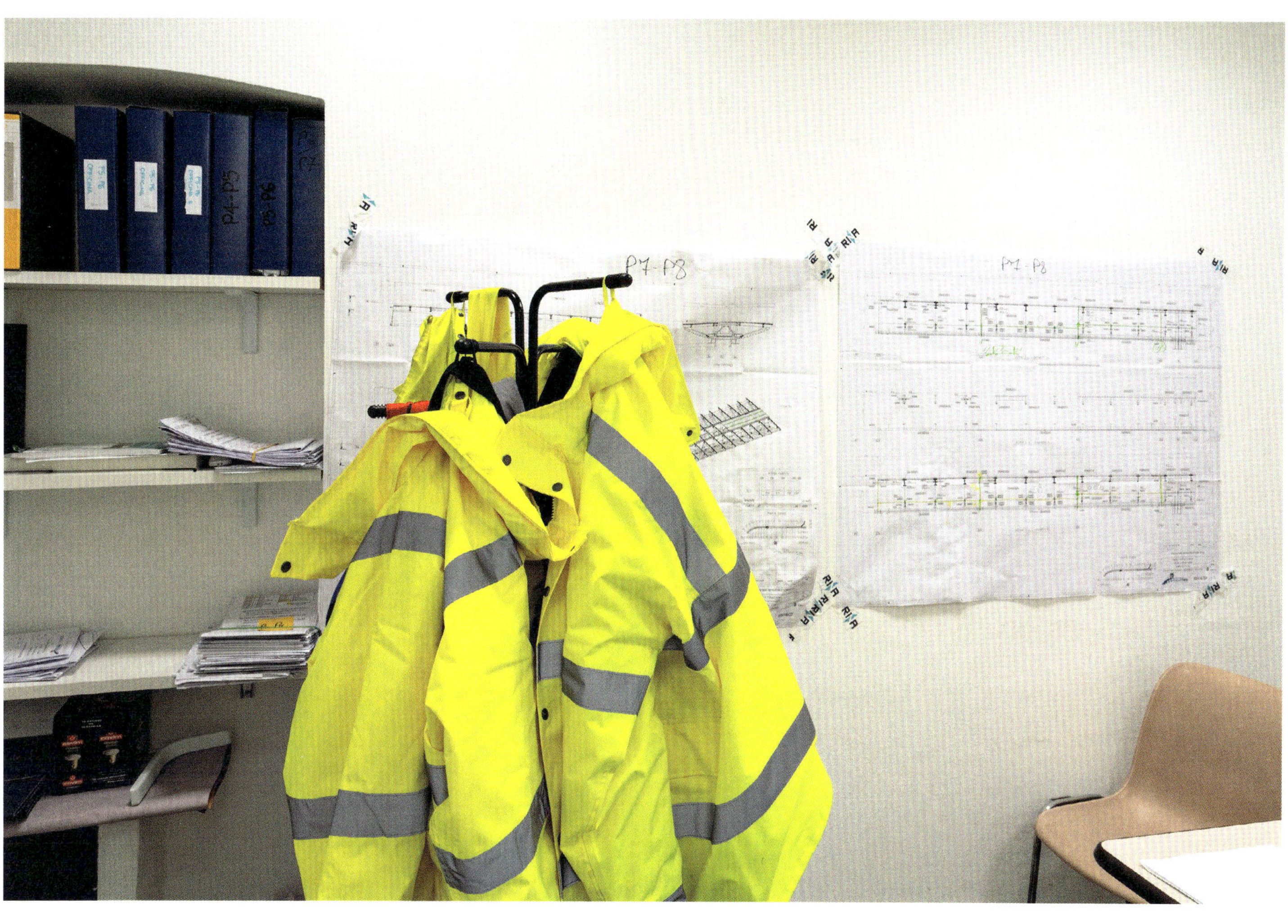

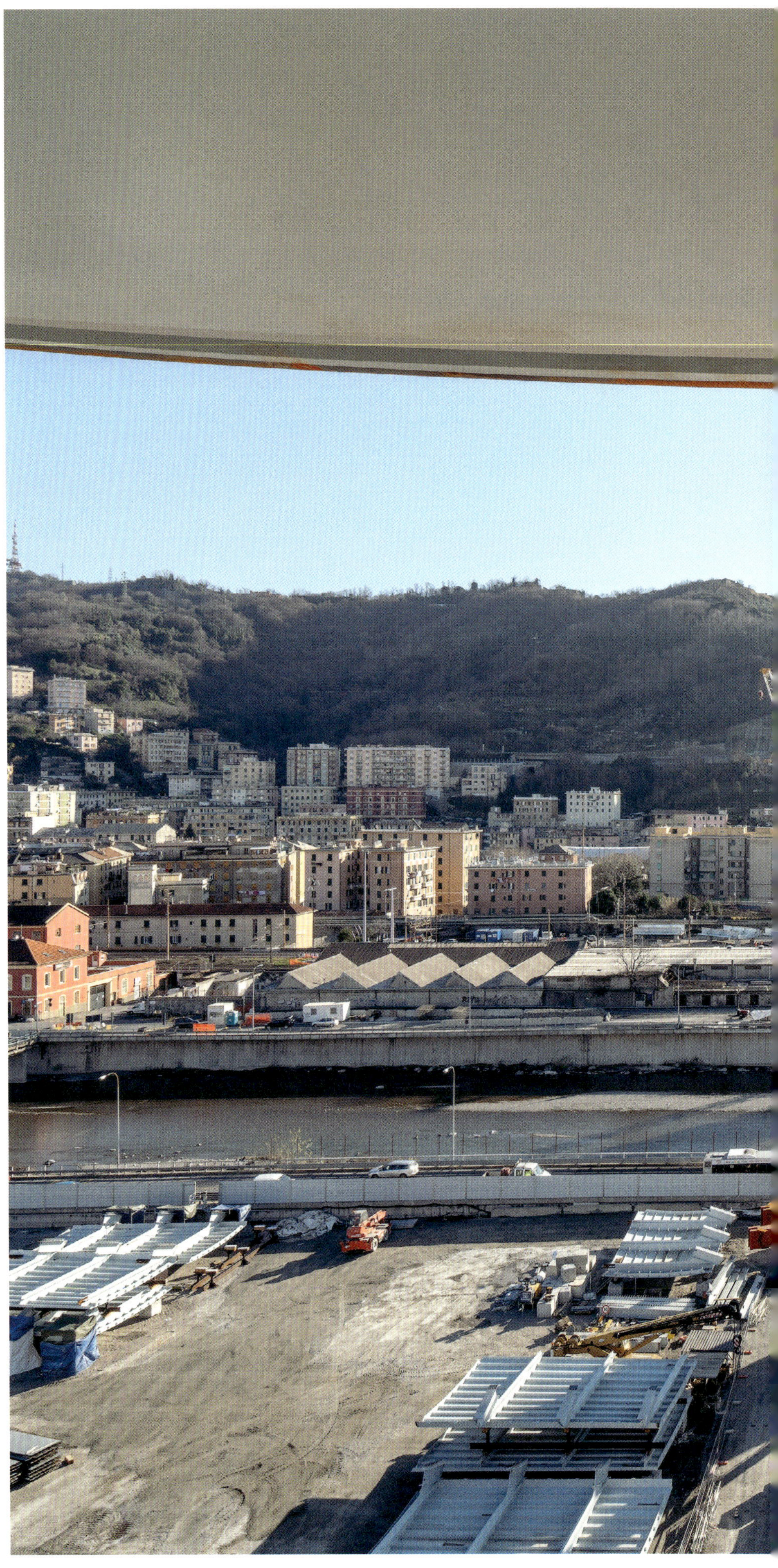

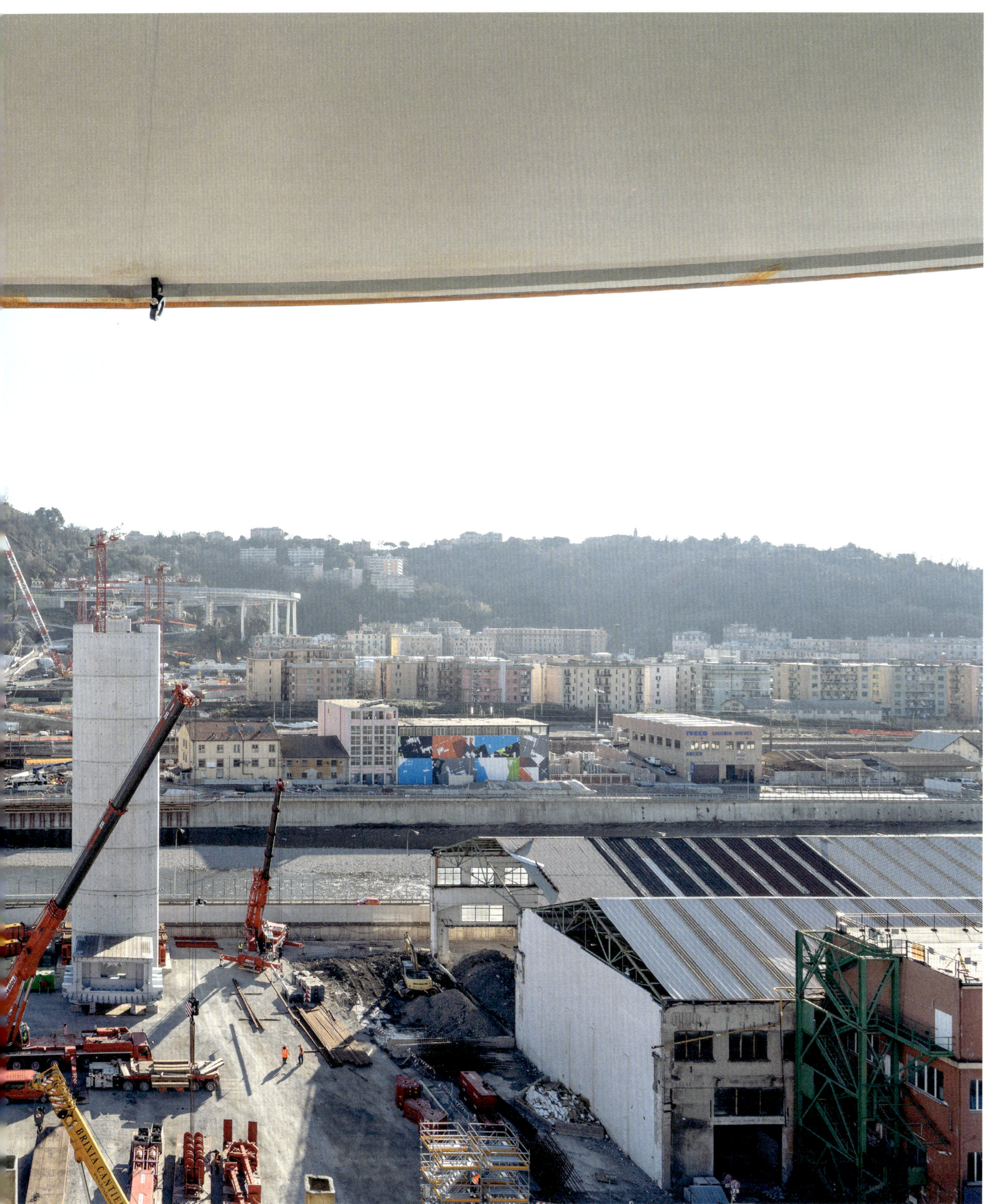

BRAXIA CANTIE
IVECO LIGURIA DIESEL

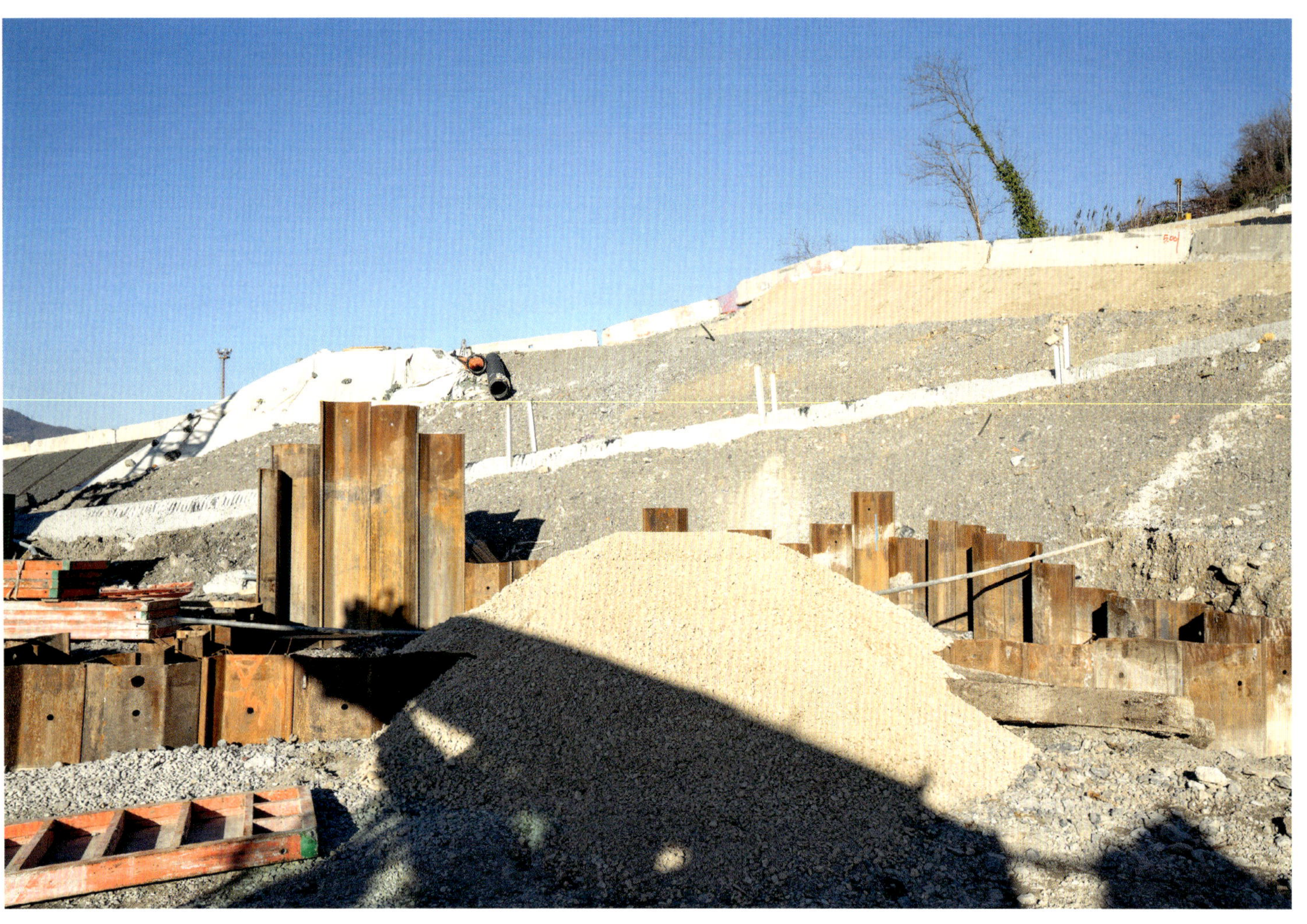

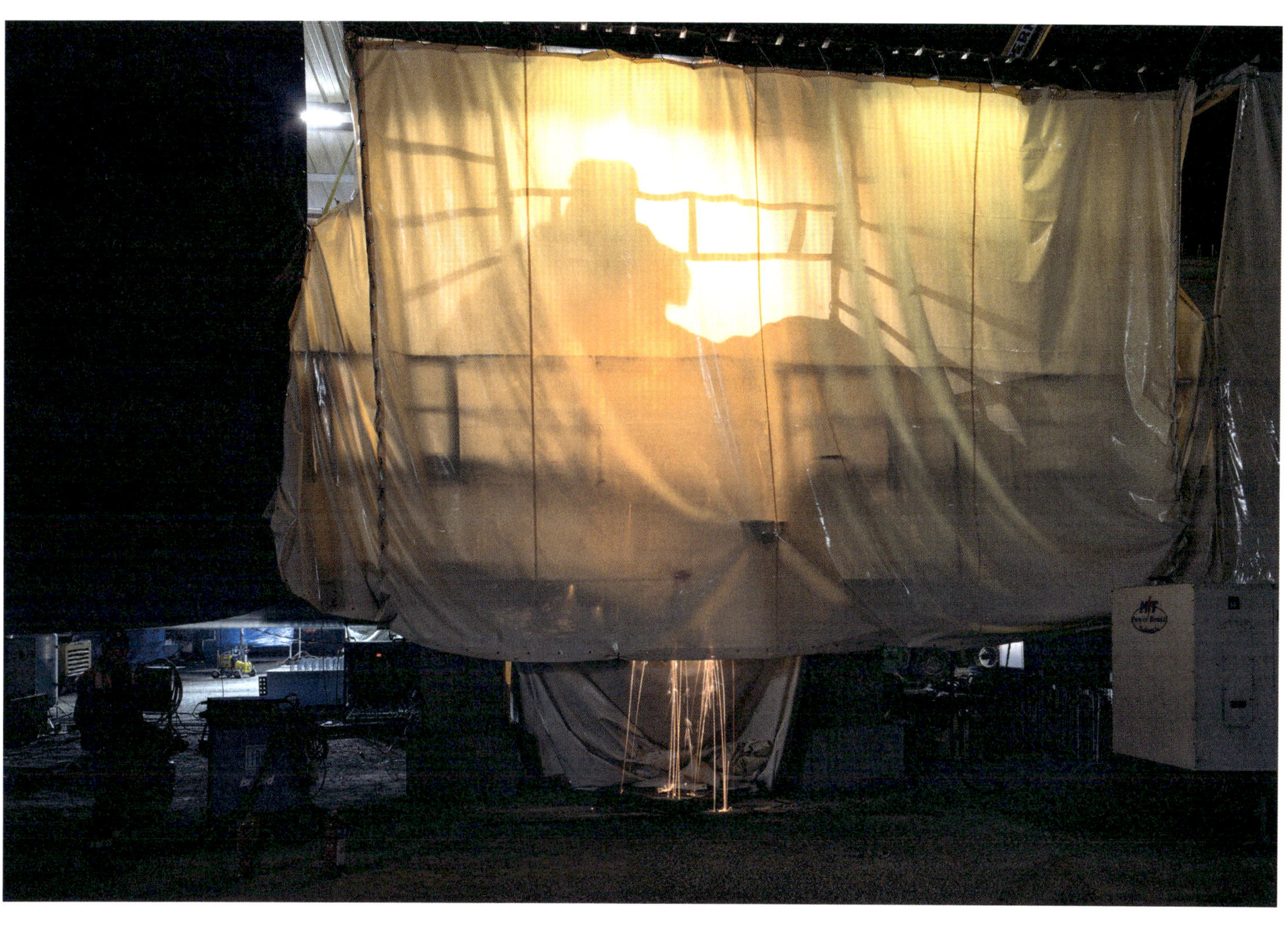

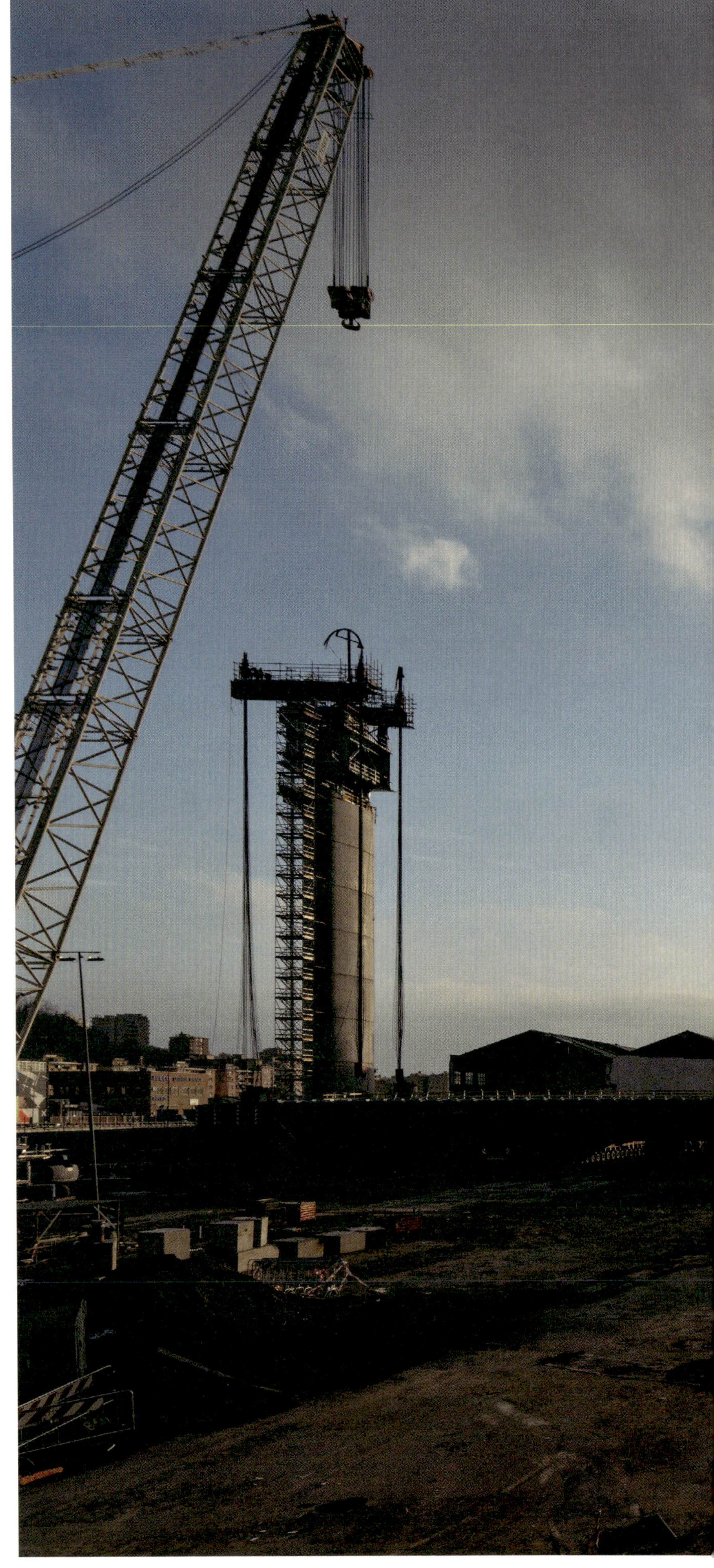

Strand jacks were again used to launch the 100-meter
spans. These spans were elevated practically complete
in all their parts, and weighed almost 2000 tons each.

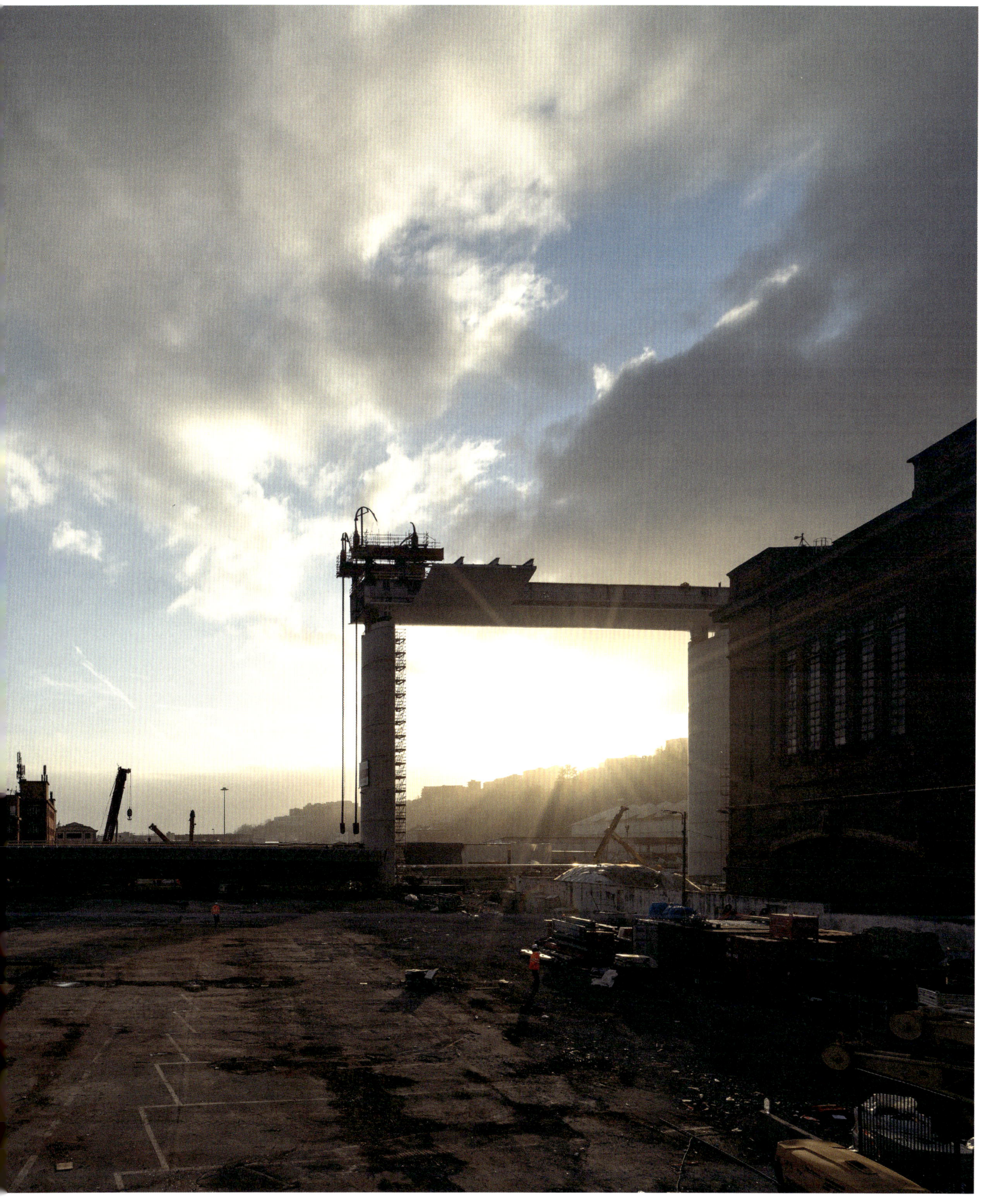

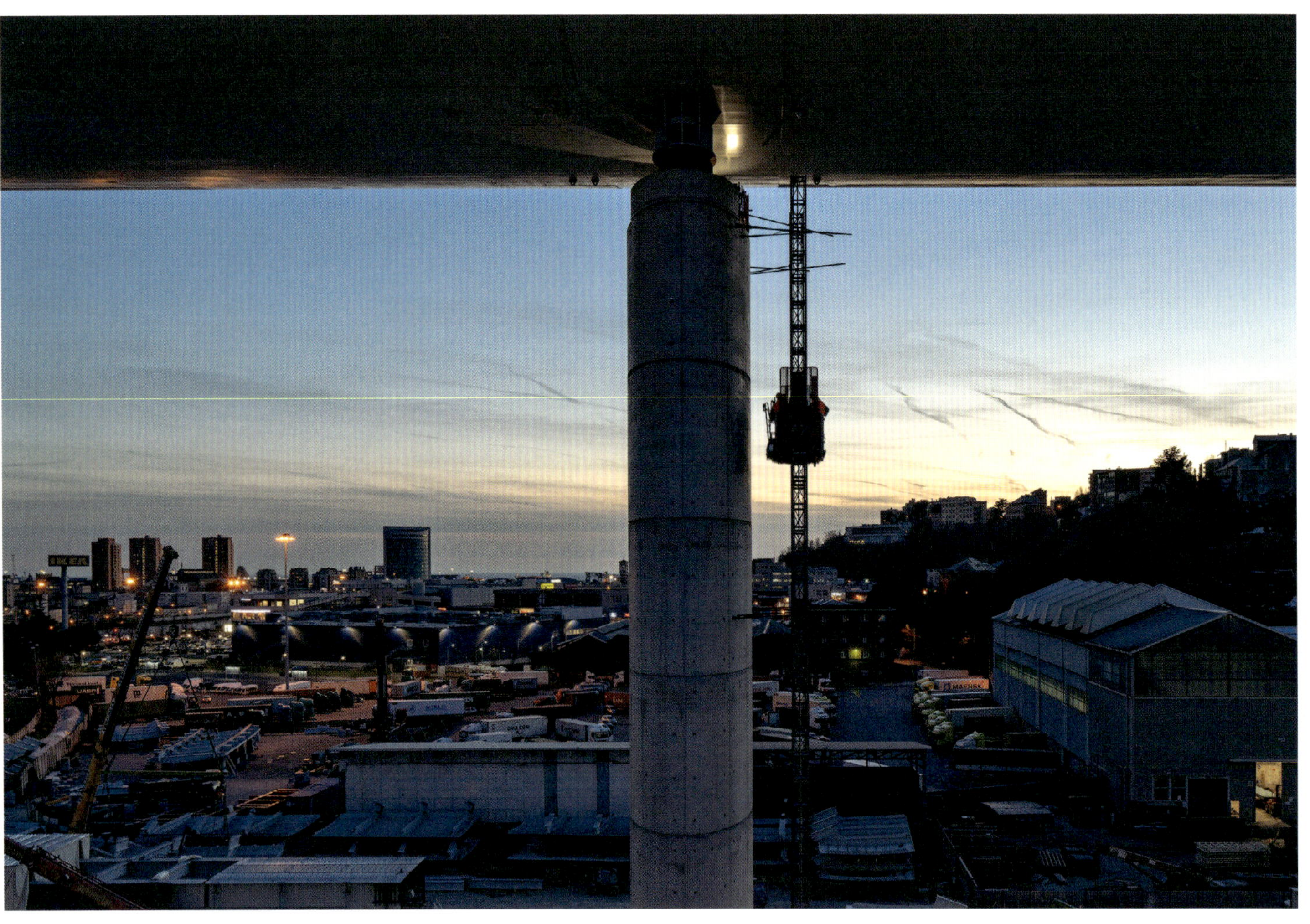

The strong desire of the group of companies at work over the Polcevera and the centralization of coordination around a single actor allowed for the continuation of the works even during the Covid-19 emergency.

As Safety Coordinator RINA, together with PerGenova, enforced the necessary protocols to mitigate the risk of infection as soon as the virus made its appearance on the Italian scene. (This was earlier than the limitations imposed by the Government's decrees, which were instead implemented at a later date.)

The main actions undertaken included informing the personnel on the state of emergency, and ongoing training as concerned the compulsory measures of self-protection that were needed and provided, the daily and systematic checking of body temperature, the daily tracking of "close contacts" between people (enforced for the first time ever in this building site), group shifts to be able to carry out isolation promptly should the need arise, a review of all the operative procedures and the Operative Safety Plans (OSP).

There was only one case of Covid-19 on the building site. It was promptly identified, and twenty-three workers were isolated. Their test results were negative and when their quarantine ended they returned to the building site.

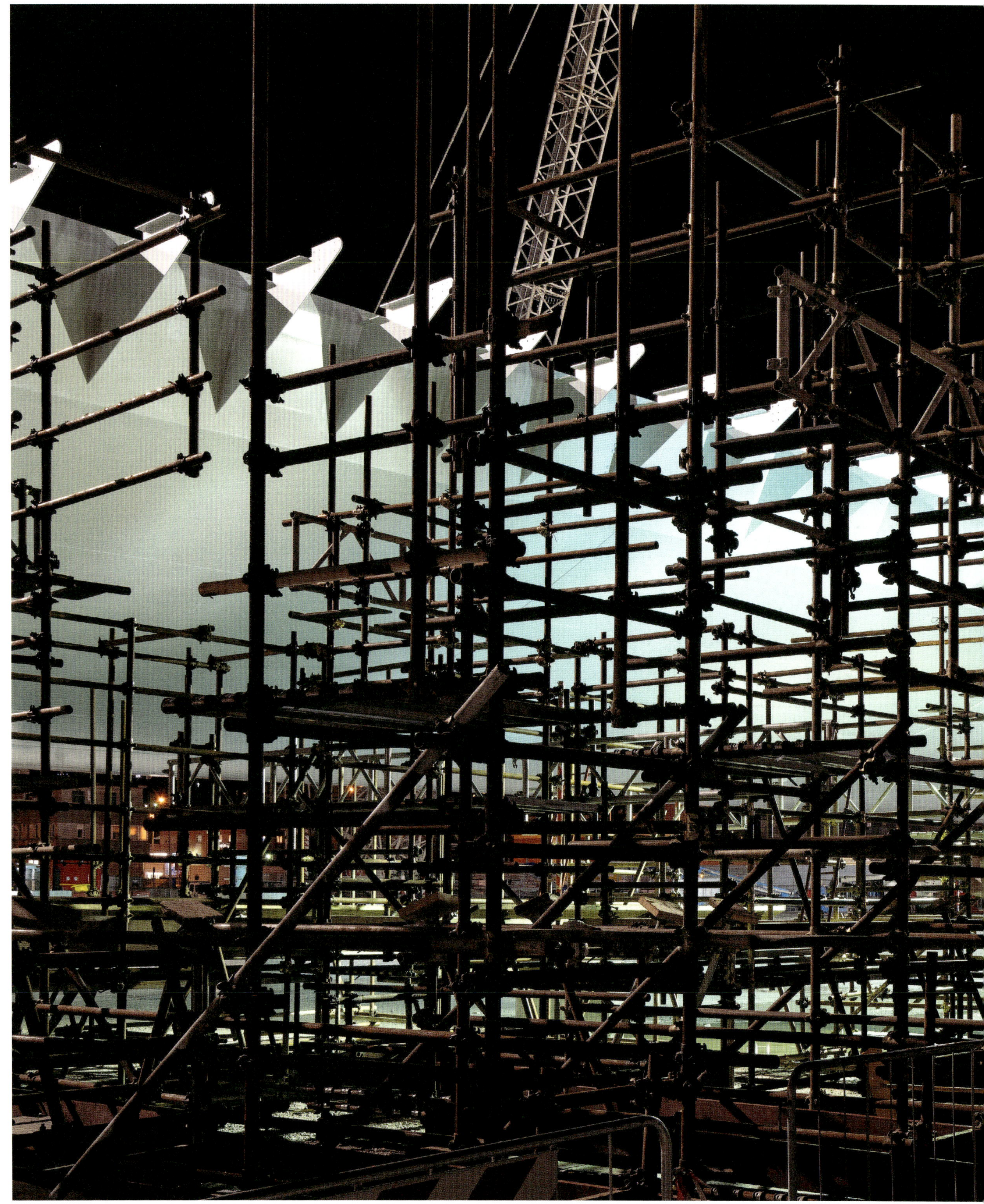

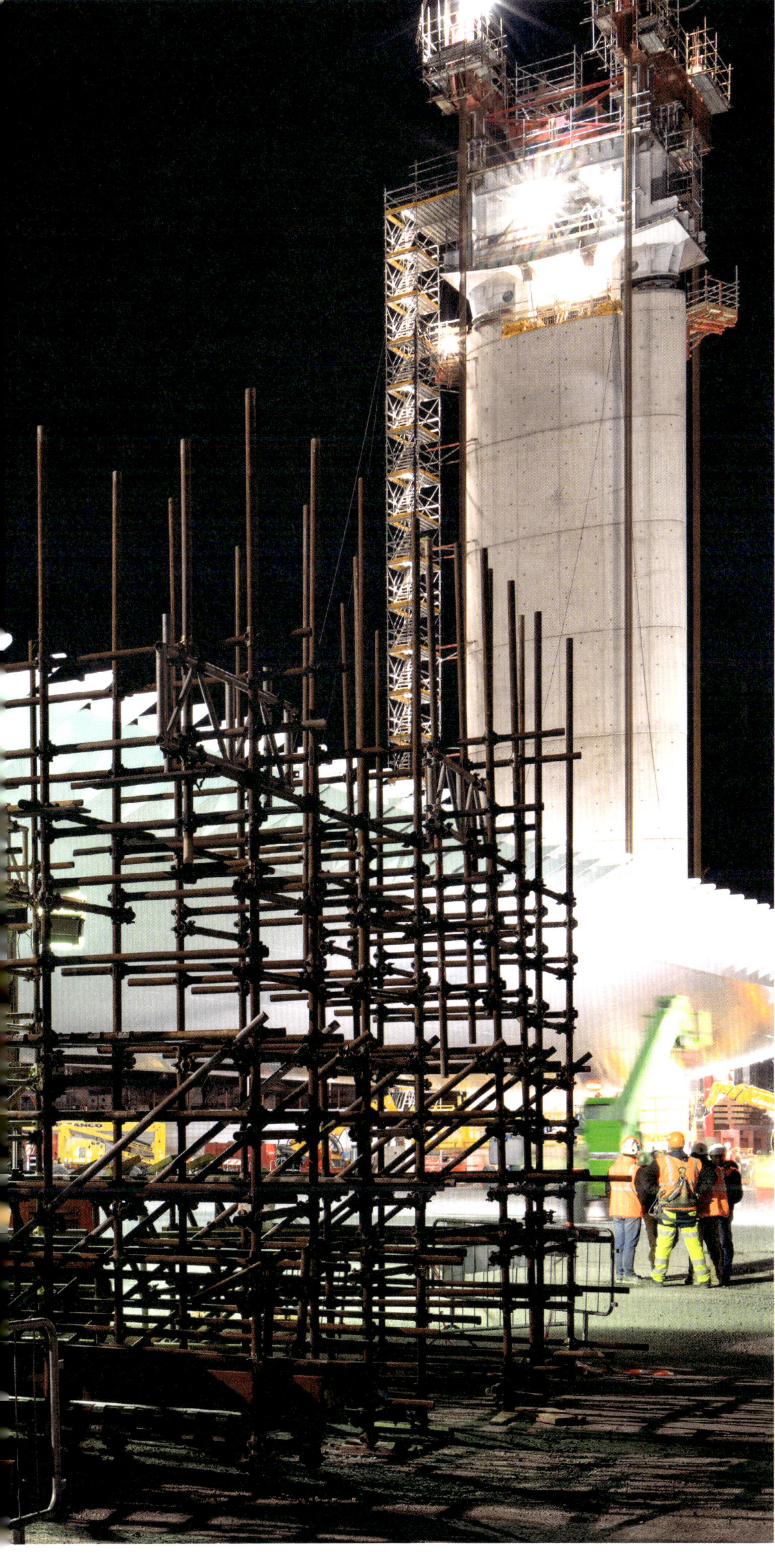

FEBRUARY 12, 2020

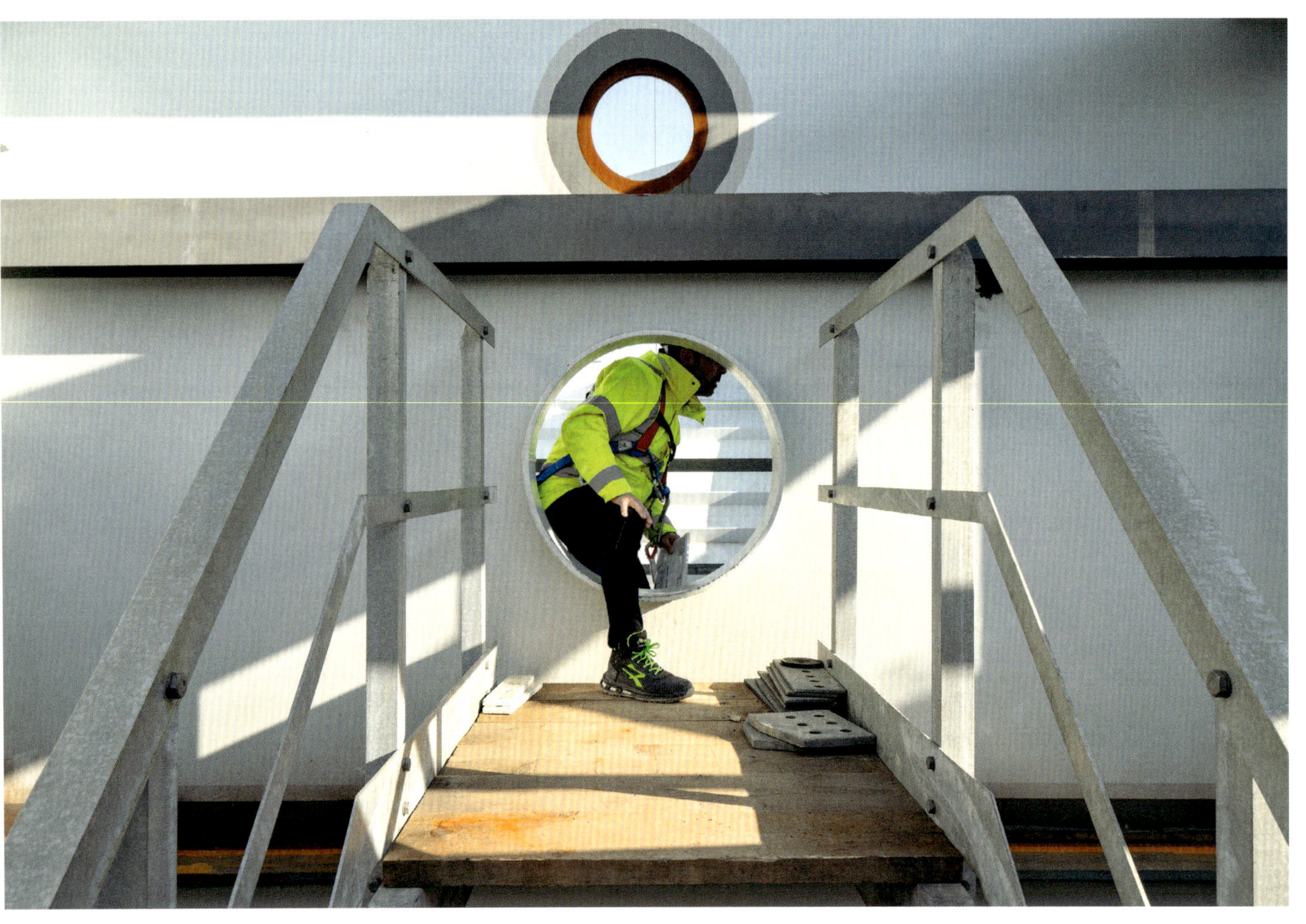

FEBRUARY 19, 2020

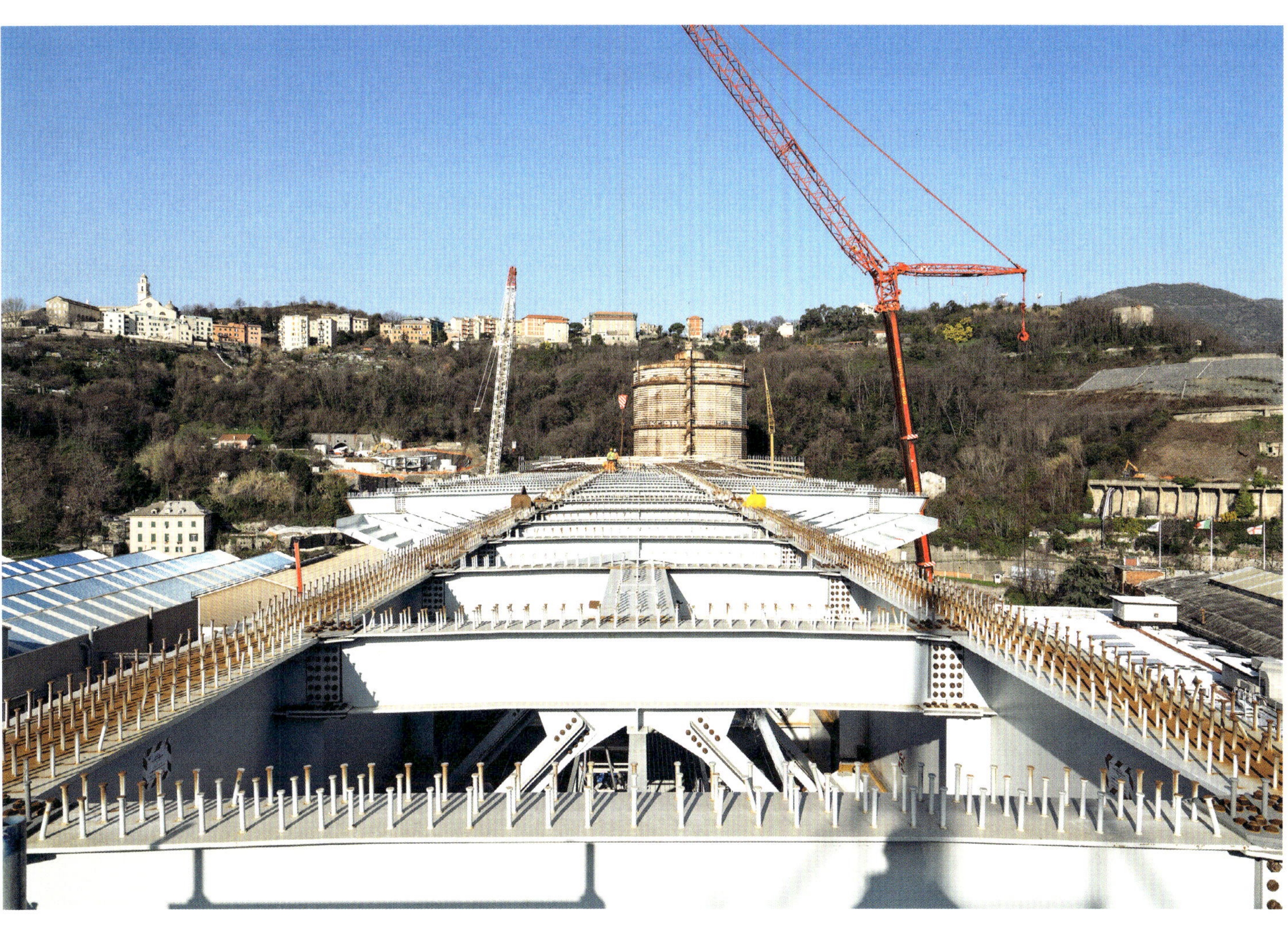

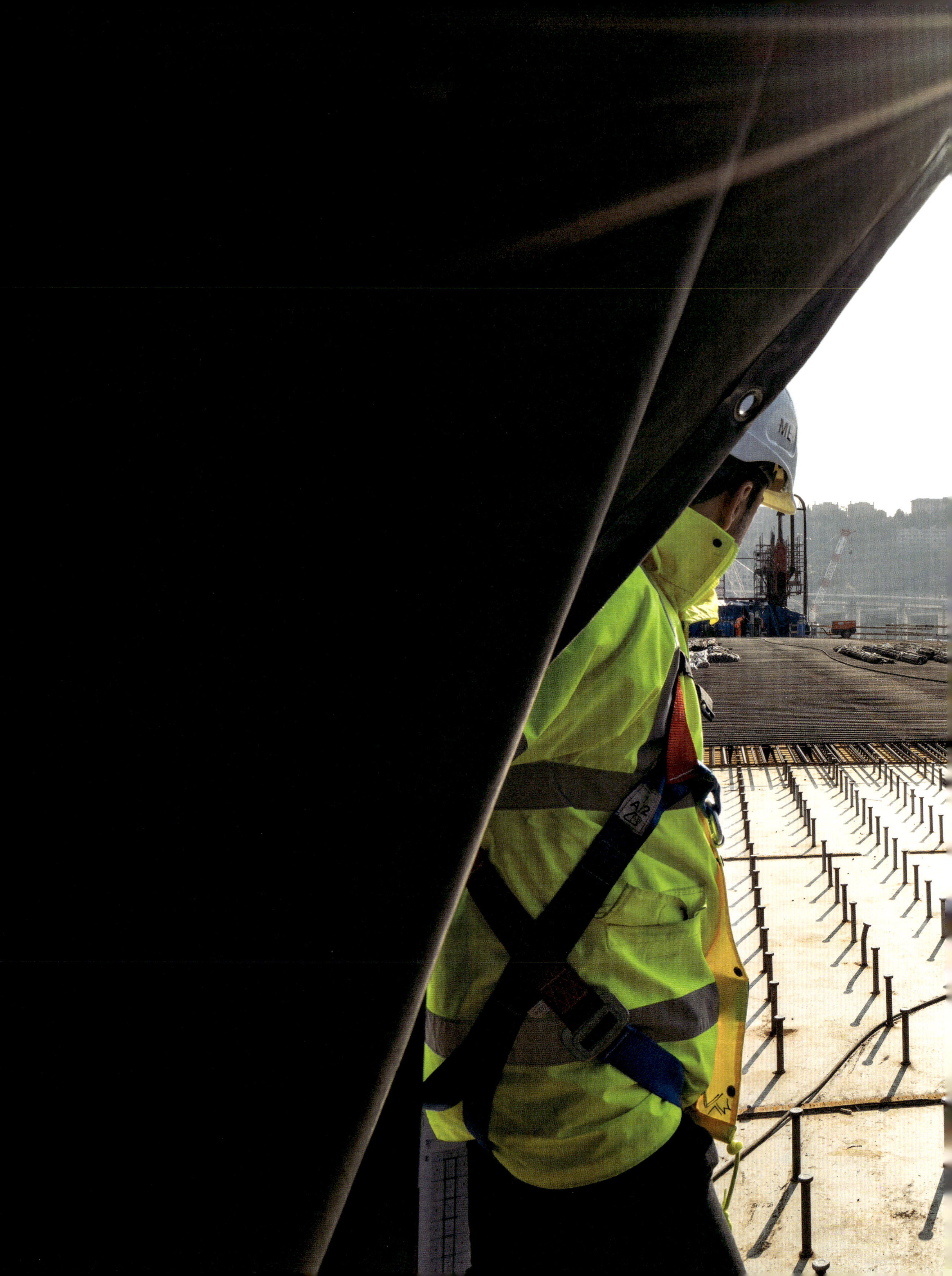

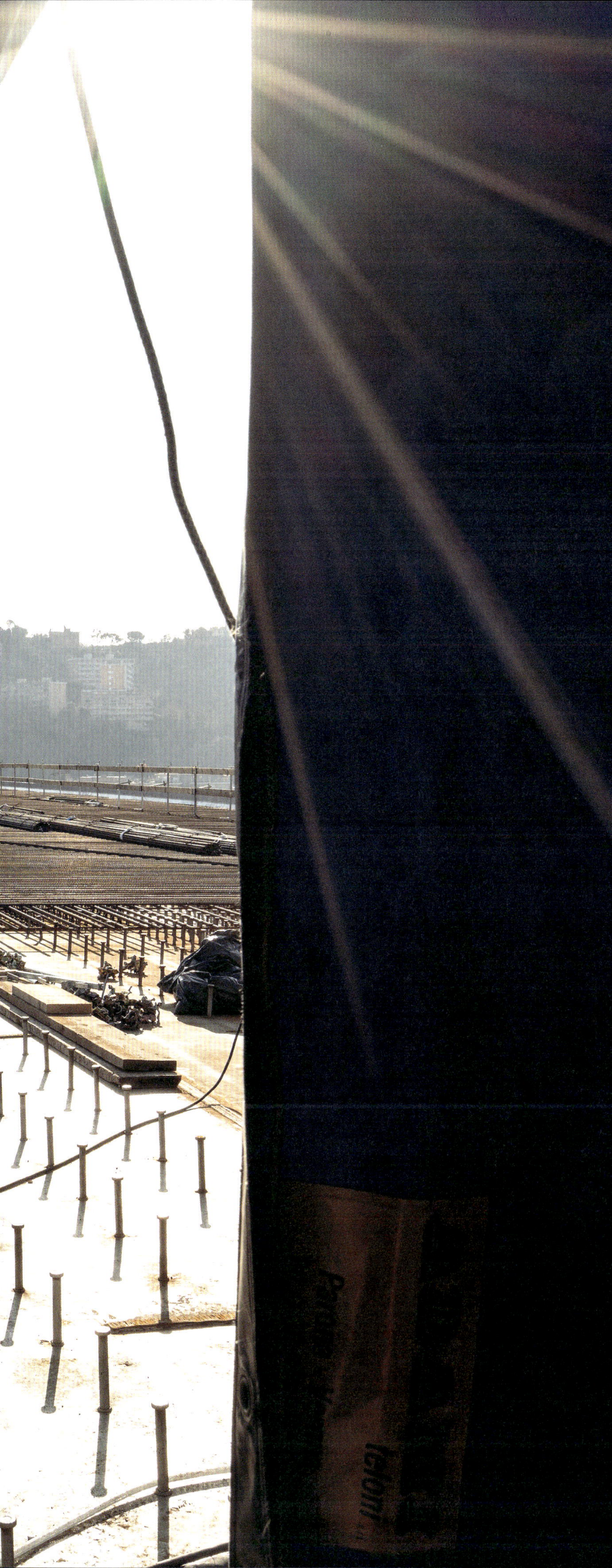

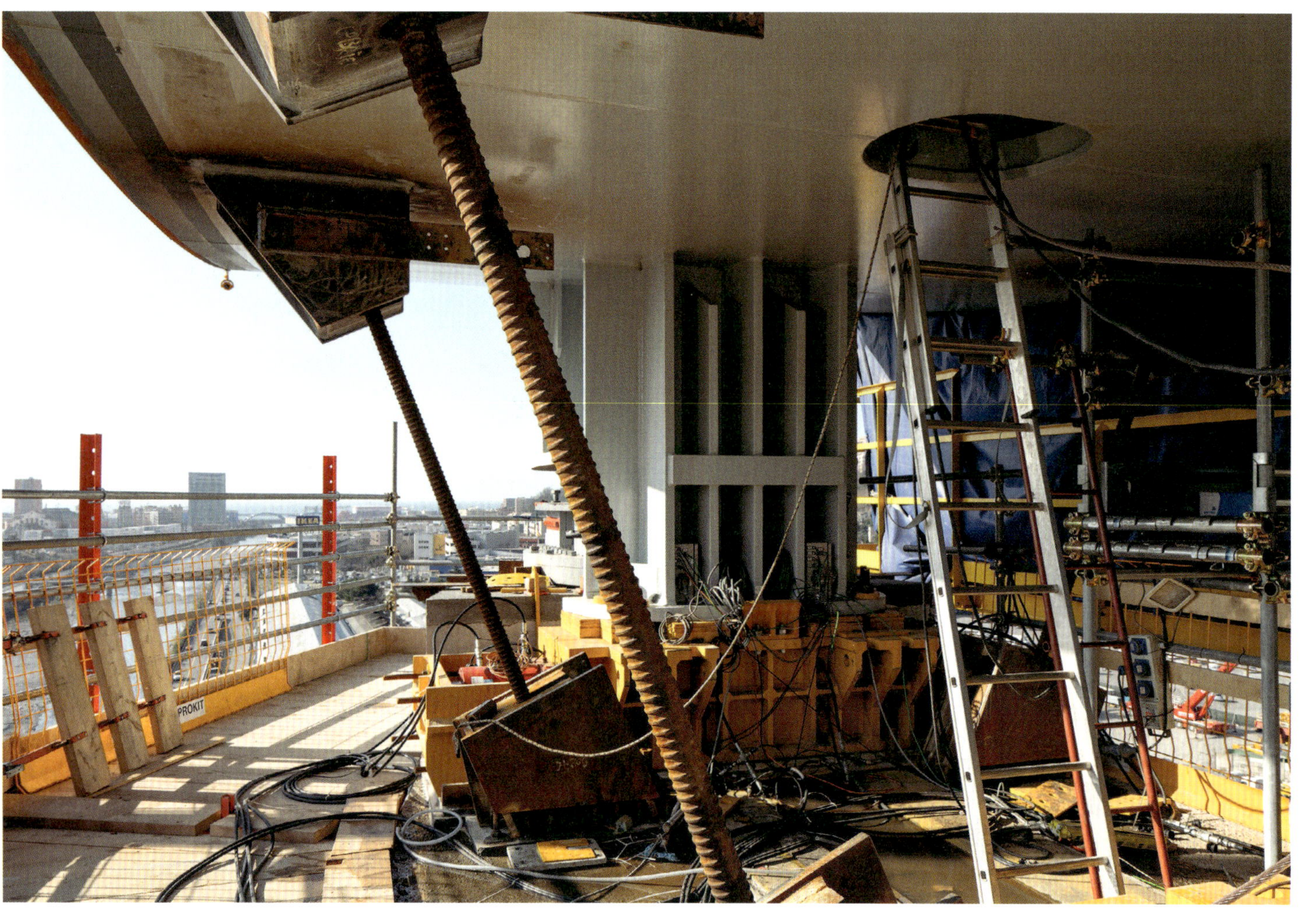

FEBRUARY 19, 2020

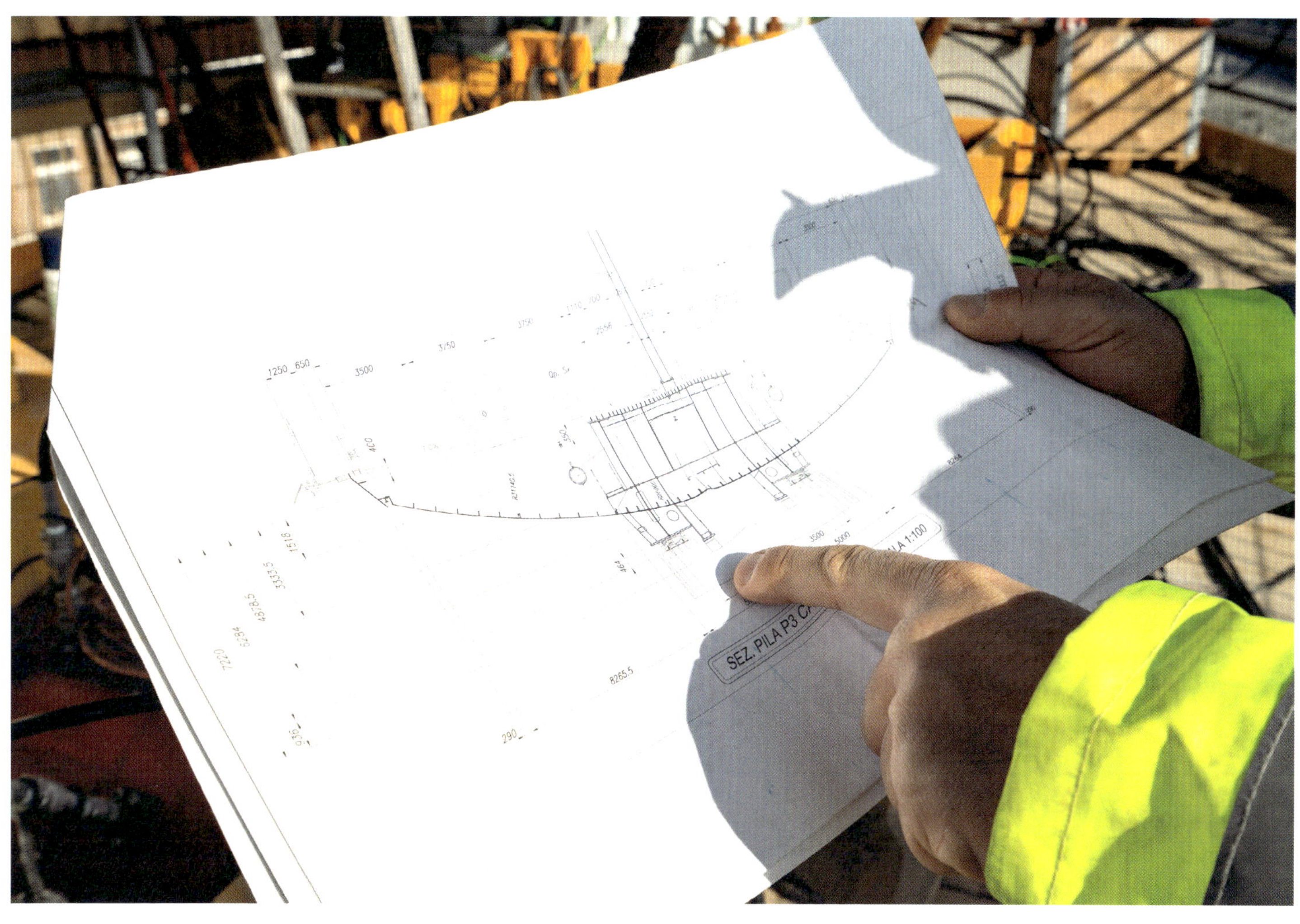
SEZ. PILA P3 C

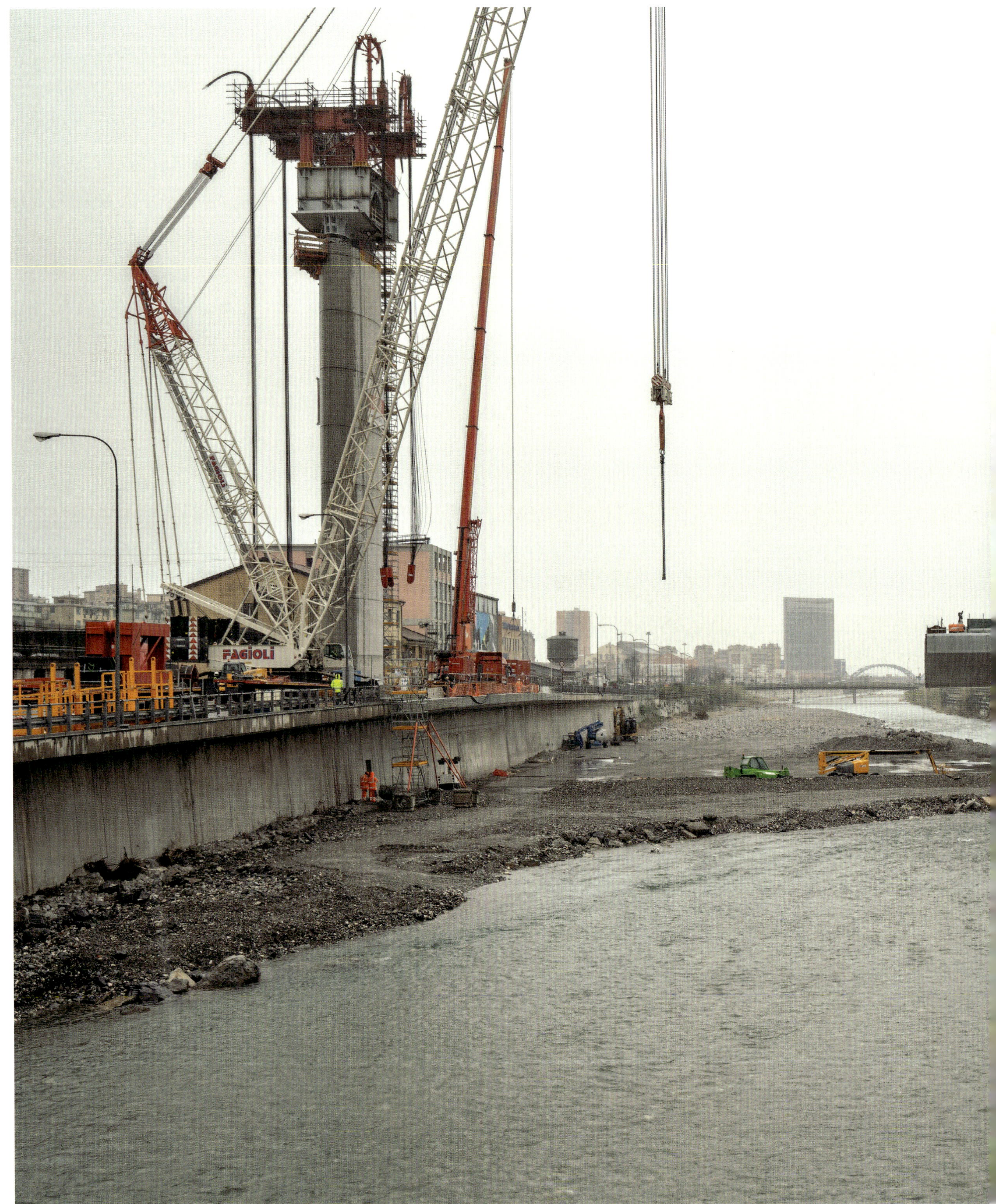

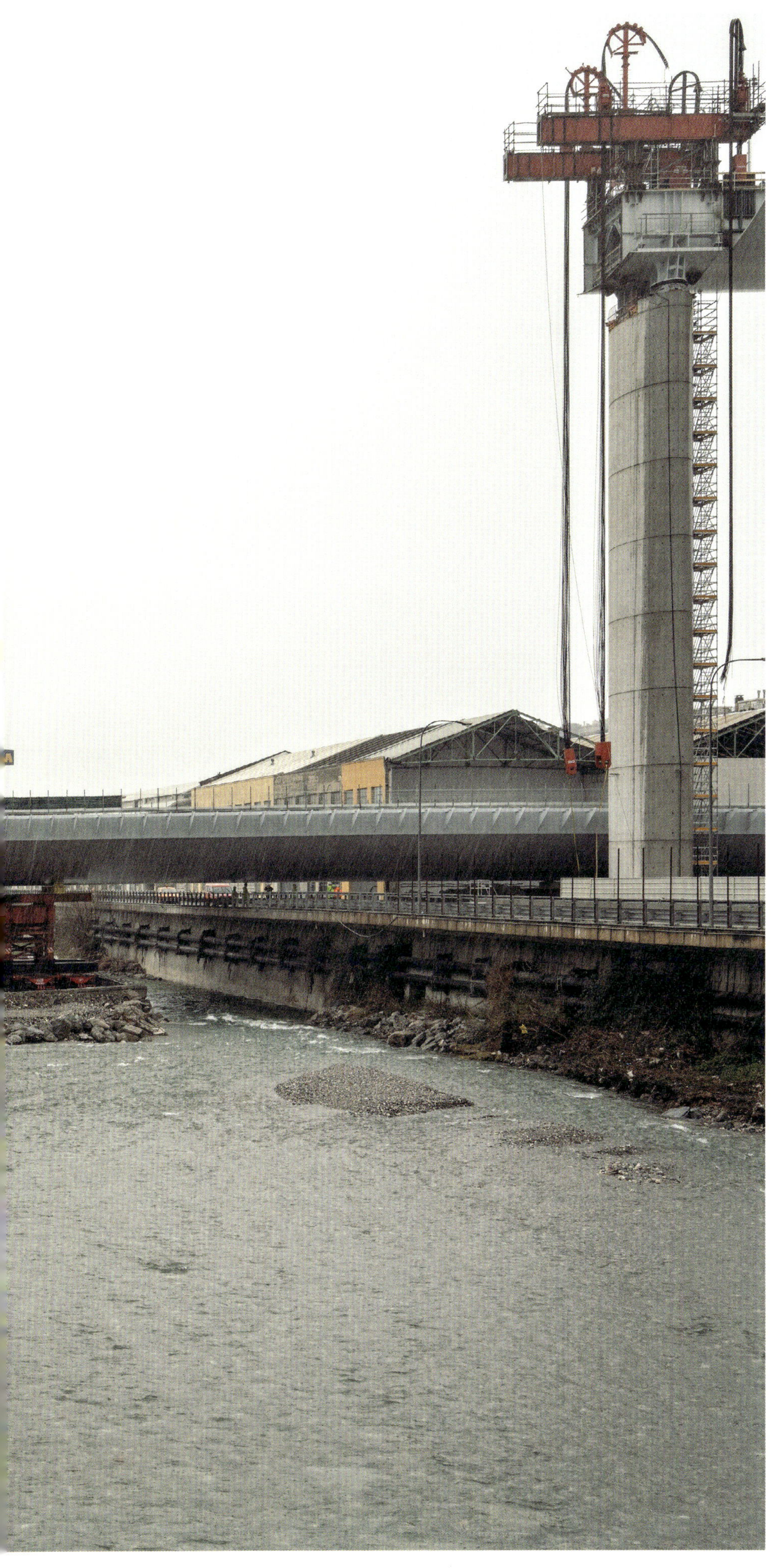

The movement of the span between pier 9 and pier 10 over the Polcevera riverbed, to allow for its installation high up, required hydraulic works to alter the course of the torrent. A first intervention in the riverbed was destroyed by the bad weather, and the deviation had to be reconstructed.
The use of an SPMT (Self-Propelled Modular Transporter, special remote-controlled machinery used to transport exceptional cargo) took place on the day when the Ministerial Decree was issued, officially sanctioning the lockdown phase in response to the Covid-19 emergency.

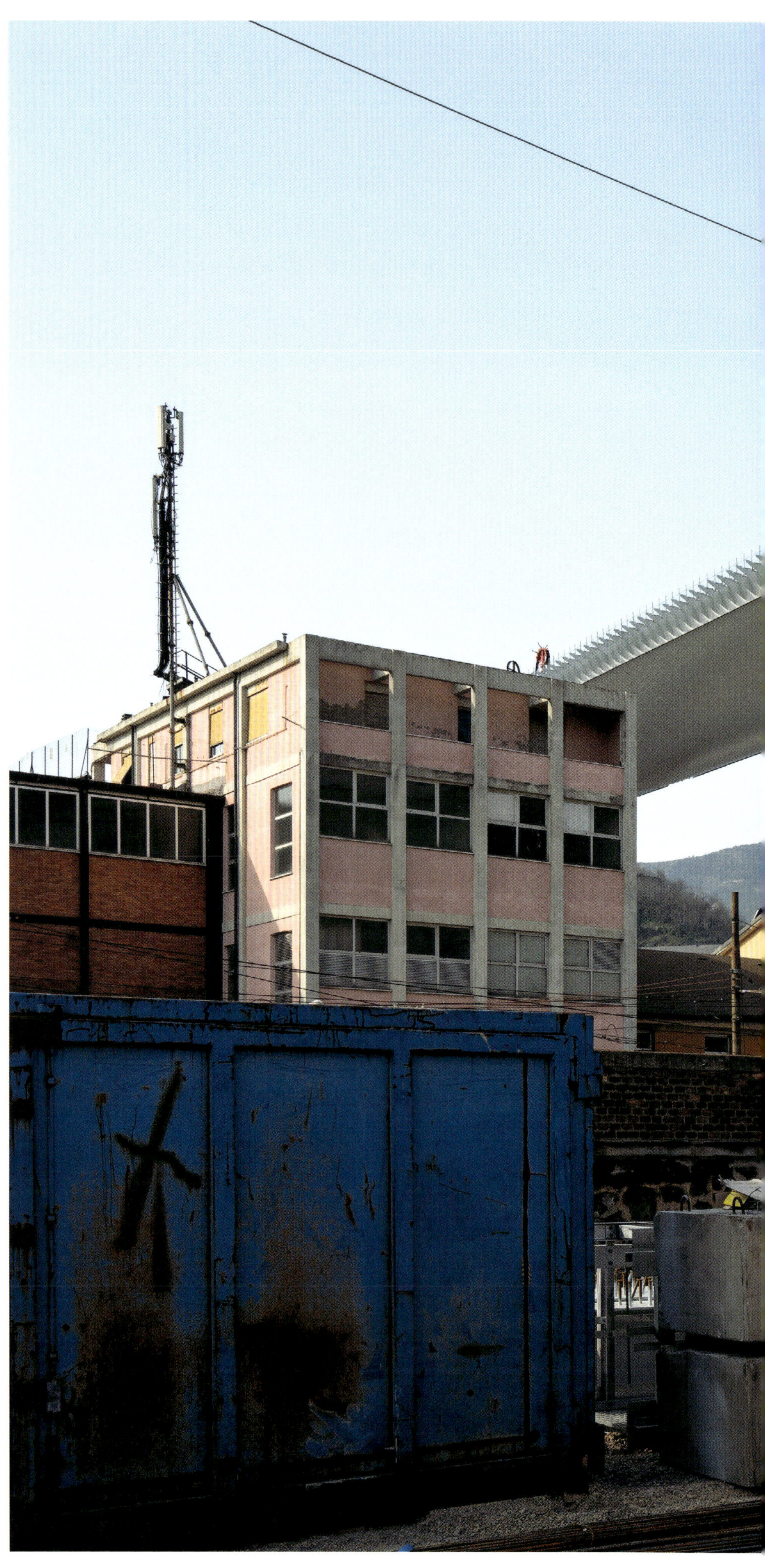

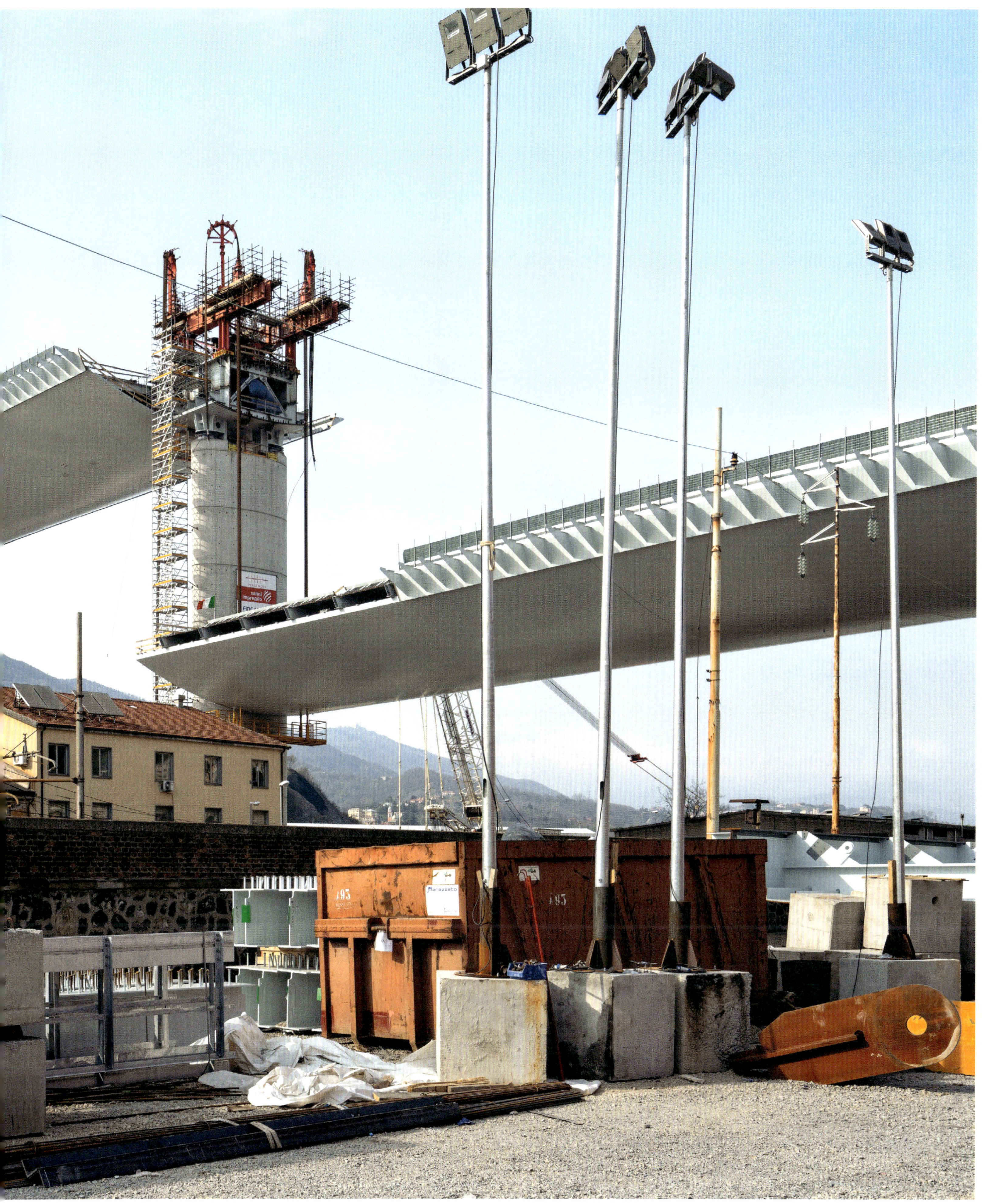

IT WAS NOT JUST
A WORK-RELATED CHALLENGE
LIKE THE MANY OTHERS
I HAVE HAD TO FACE.
OF COURSE, THIS OFTEN
MEANT HARD WORK, TENSION,
TIREDNESS, BUT THE AIM
WAS ALWAYS CLEAR: TO DO
THINGS WELL, ACCORDING
TO SCHEDULE AND IN
TOTAL SAFETY, FIRST THE
DEMOLITION, AND THEN
THE RECONSTRUCTION.

ALESSANDRO ALIOTTA
RINA

NEVER BEFORE HAD WE
EXPERIENCED JUST HOW
IMPORTANT IT IS IN THE
ACHIEVEMENT OF A COMMON
GOAL TO GUARANTEE THE
COMPLETE INTEGRATION
BETWEEN DIFFERENT
BUT COMPLEMENTARY
PROFESSIONAL SKILLS AND
A MUTUAL AND AUTHENTIC
UNDERSTANDING.

SABRINA CARTA
RINA

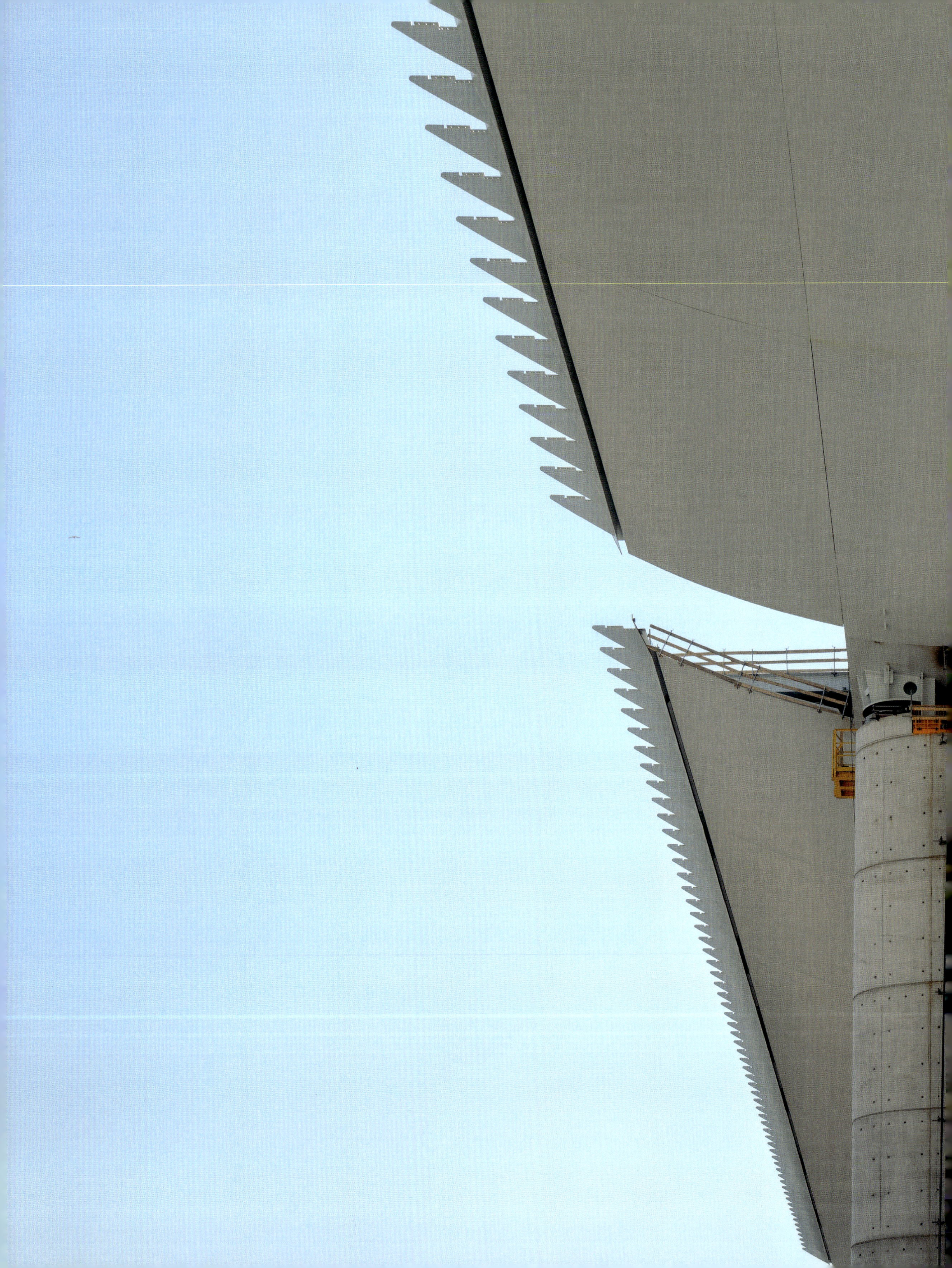

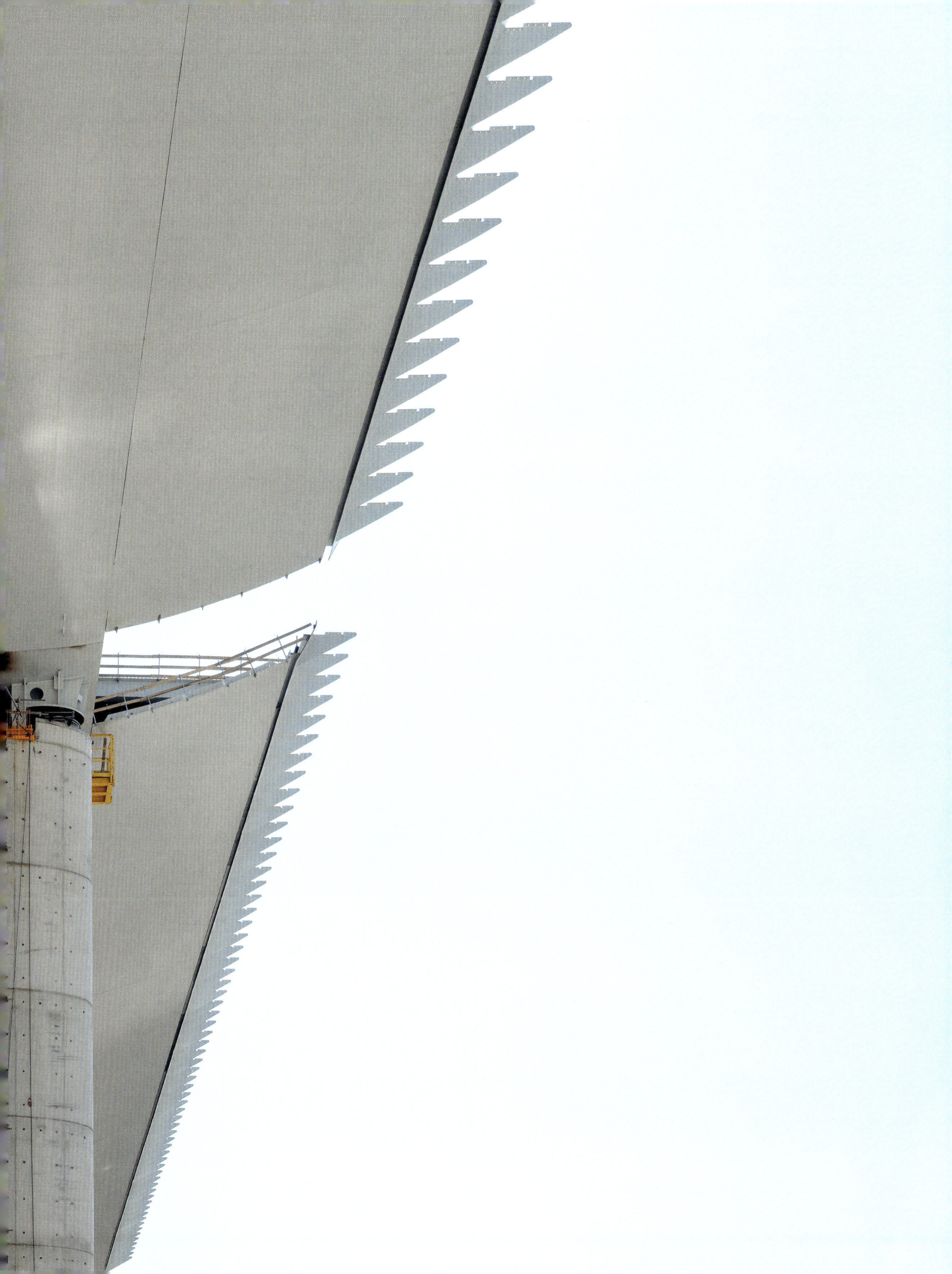

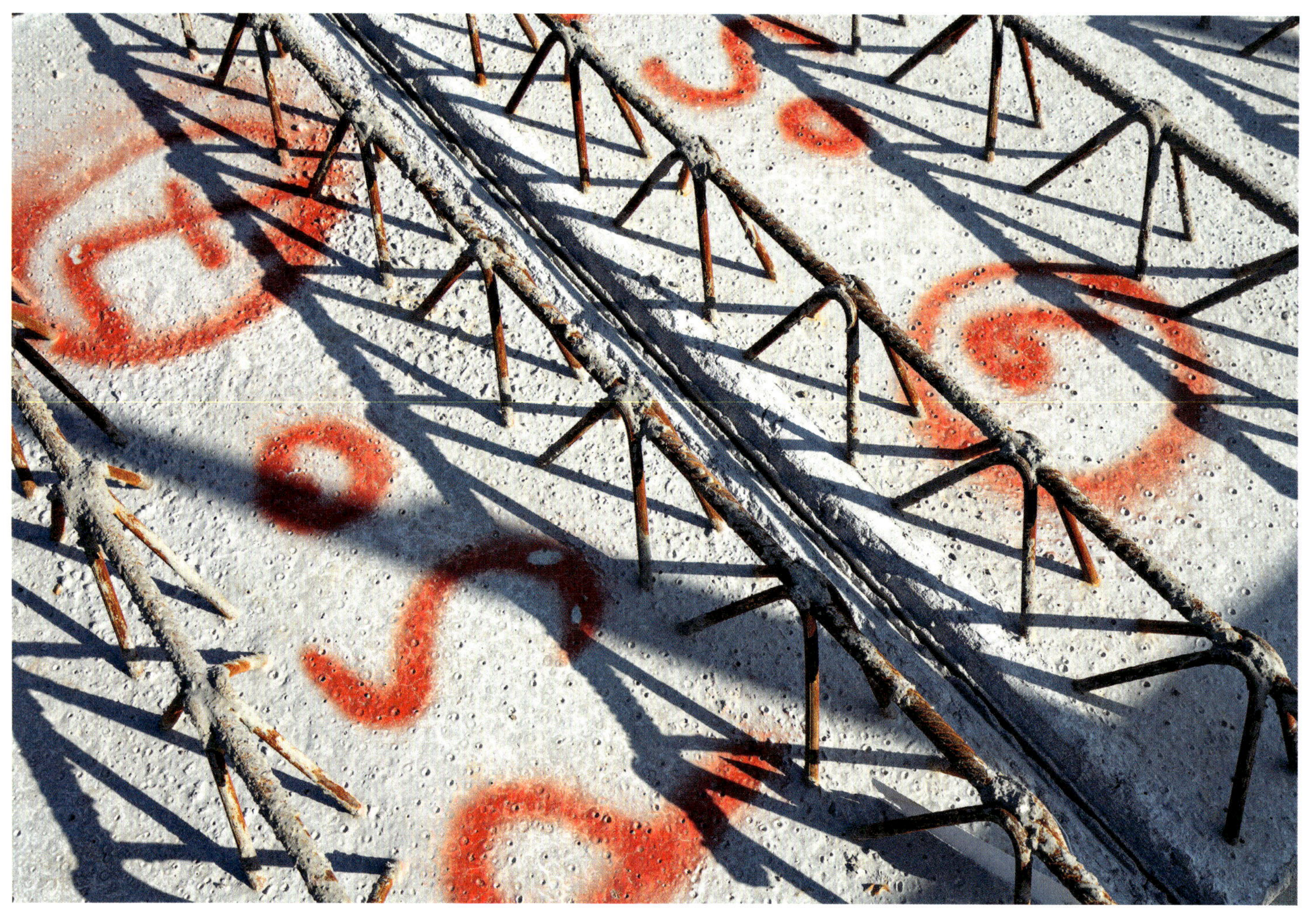

MAY 7, 2020

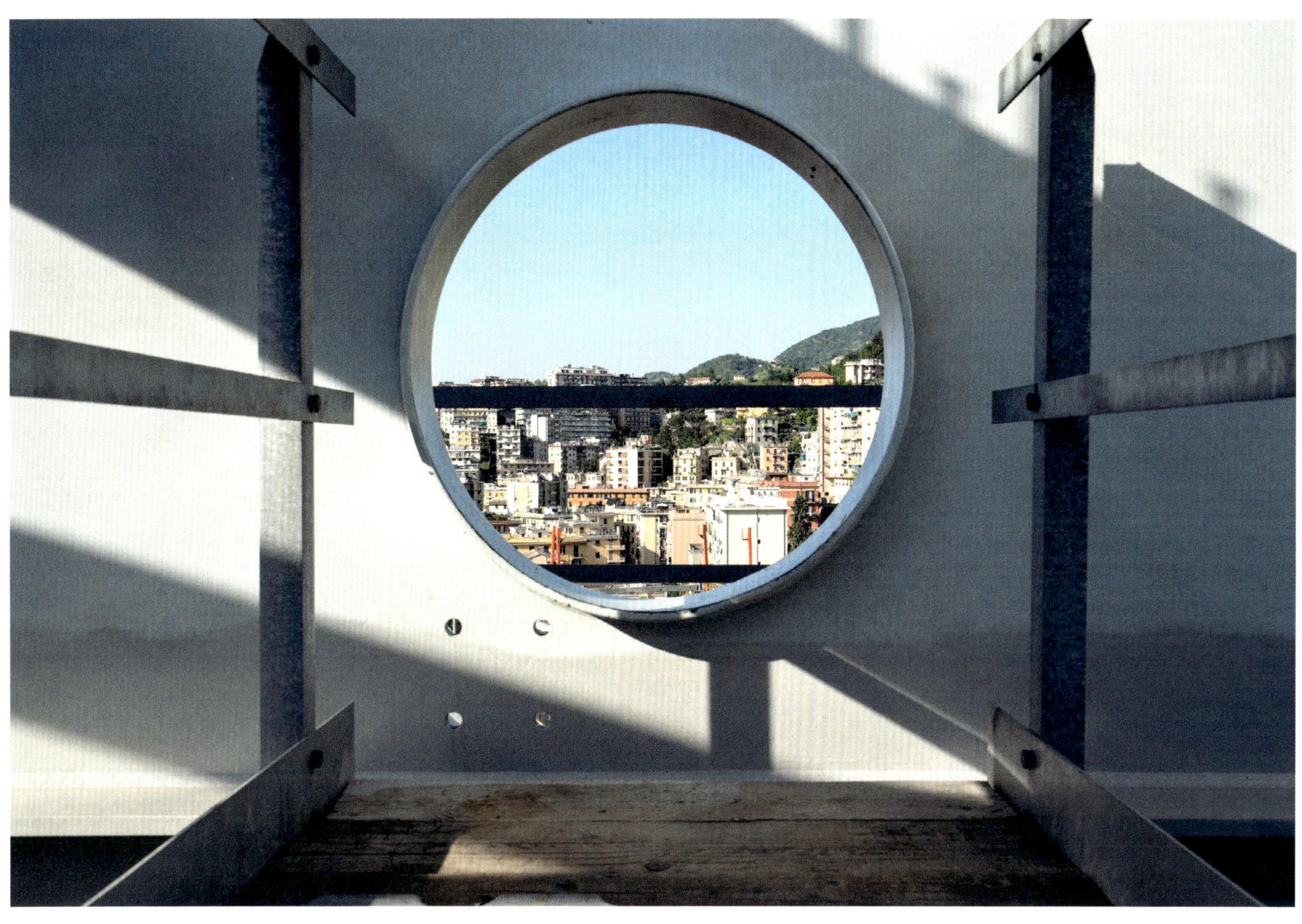

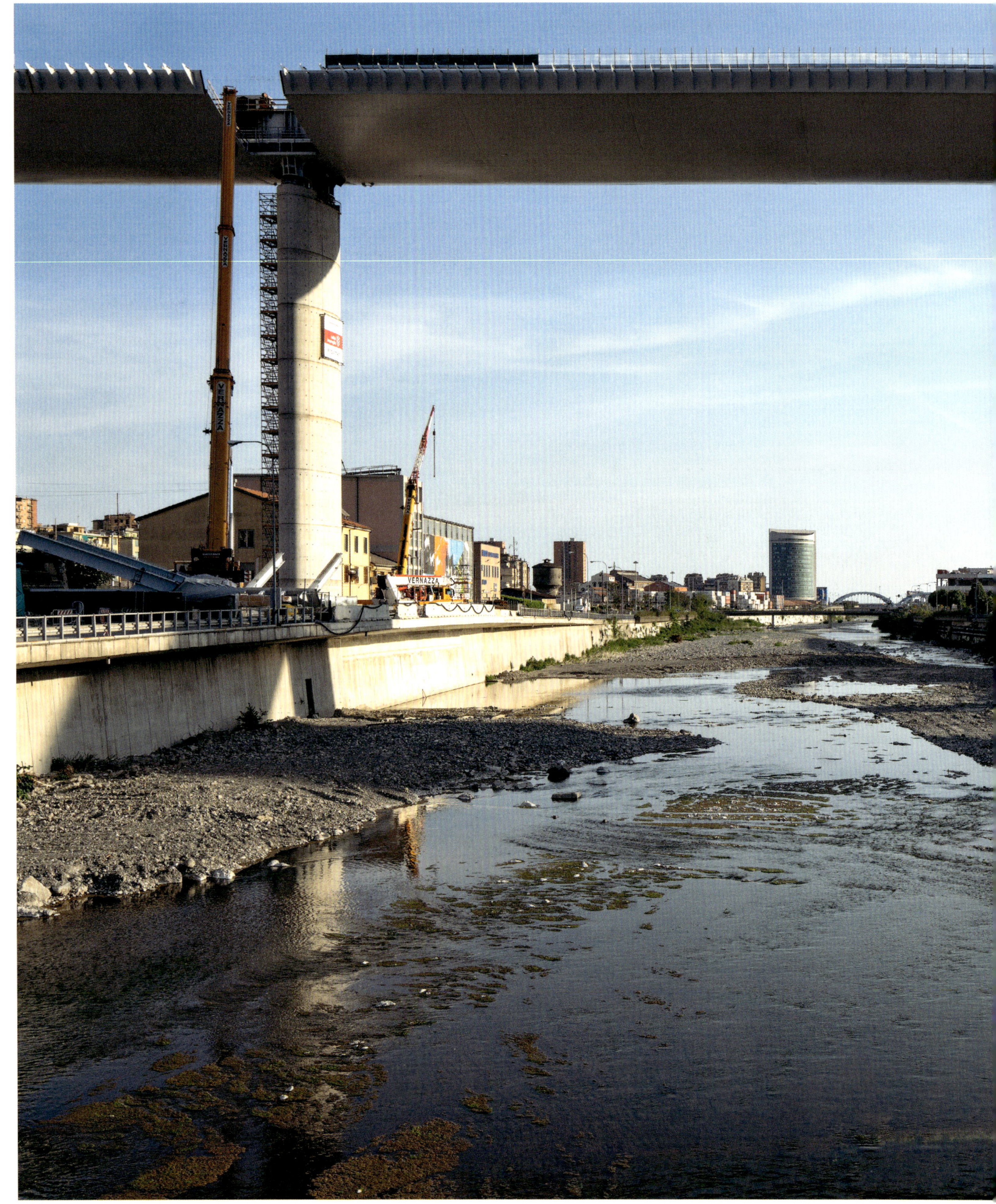
VERNAZZA

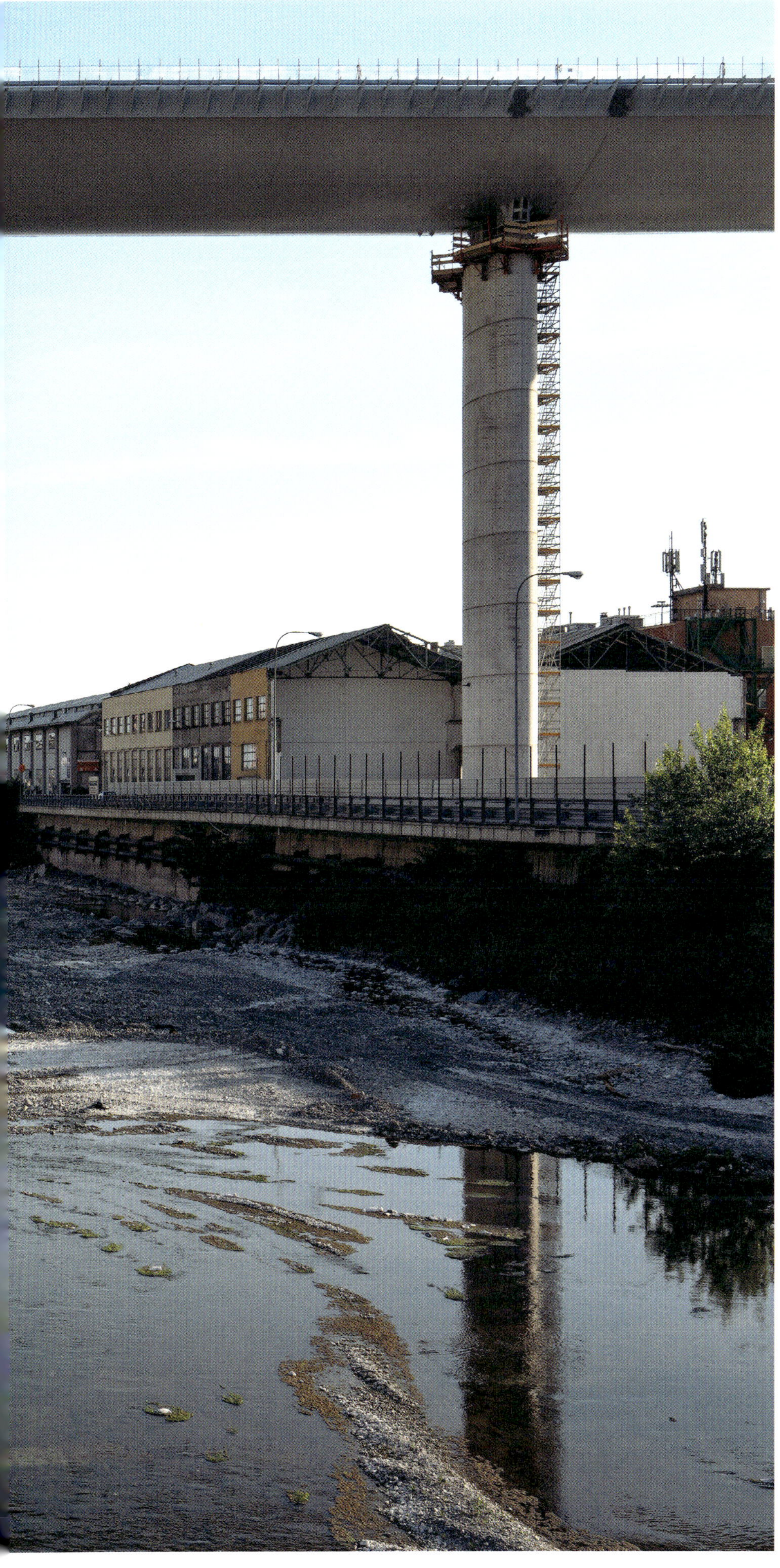

MAY 7, 2020

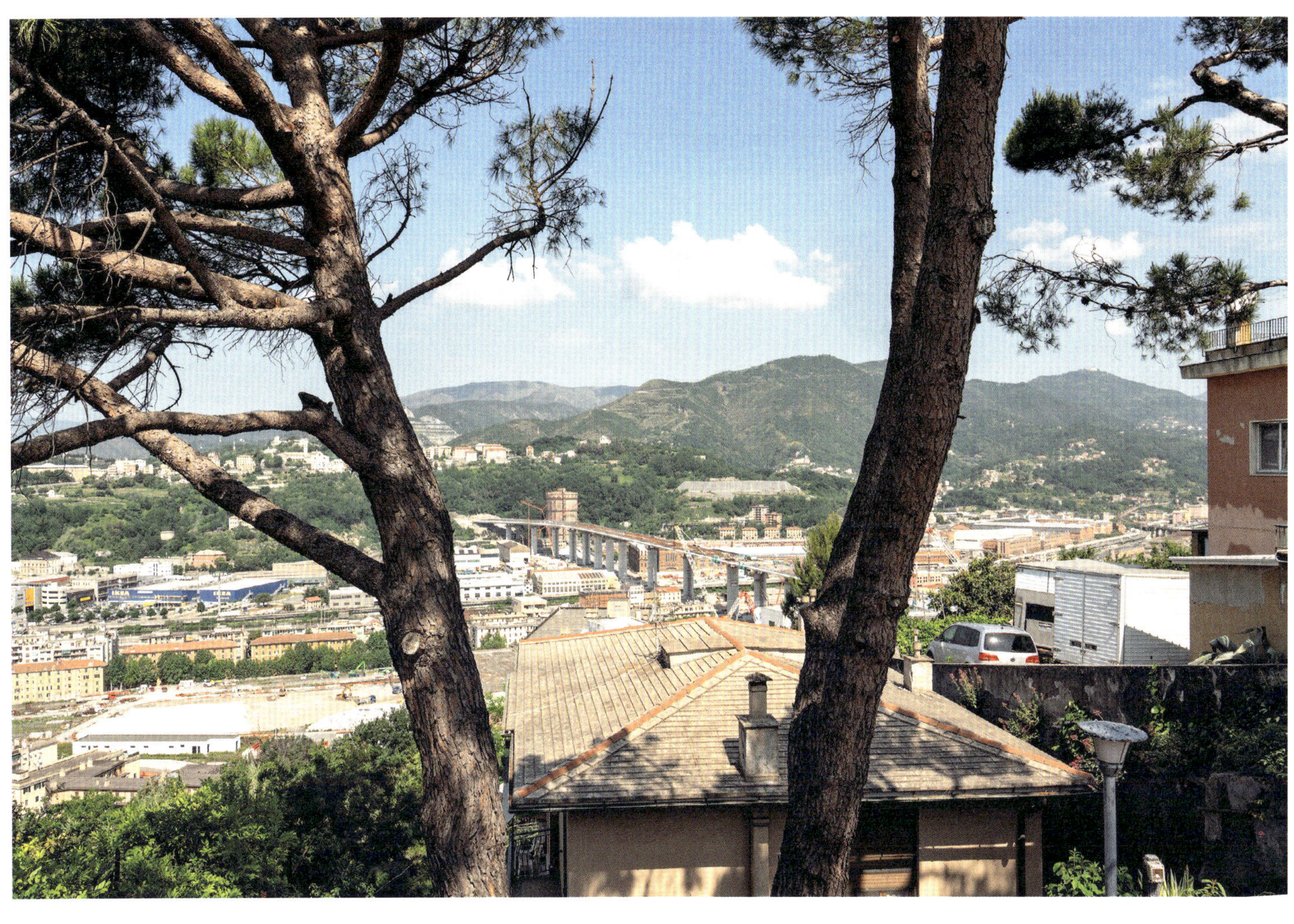
MAY 21, 2020

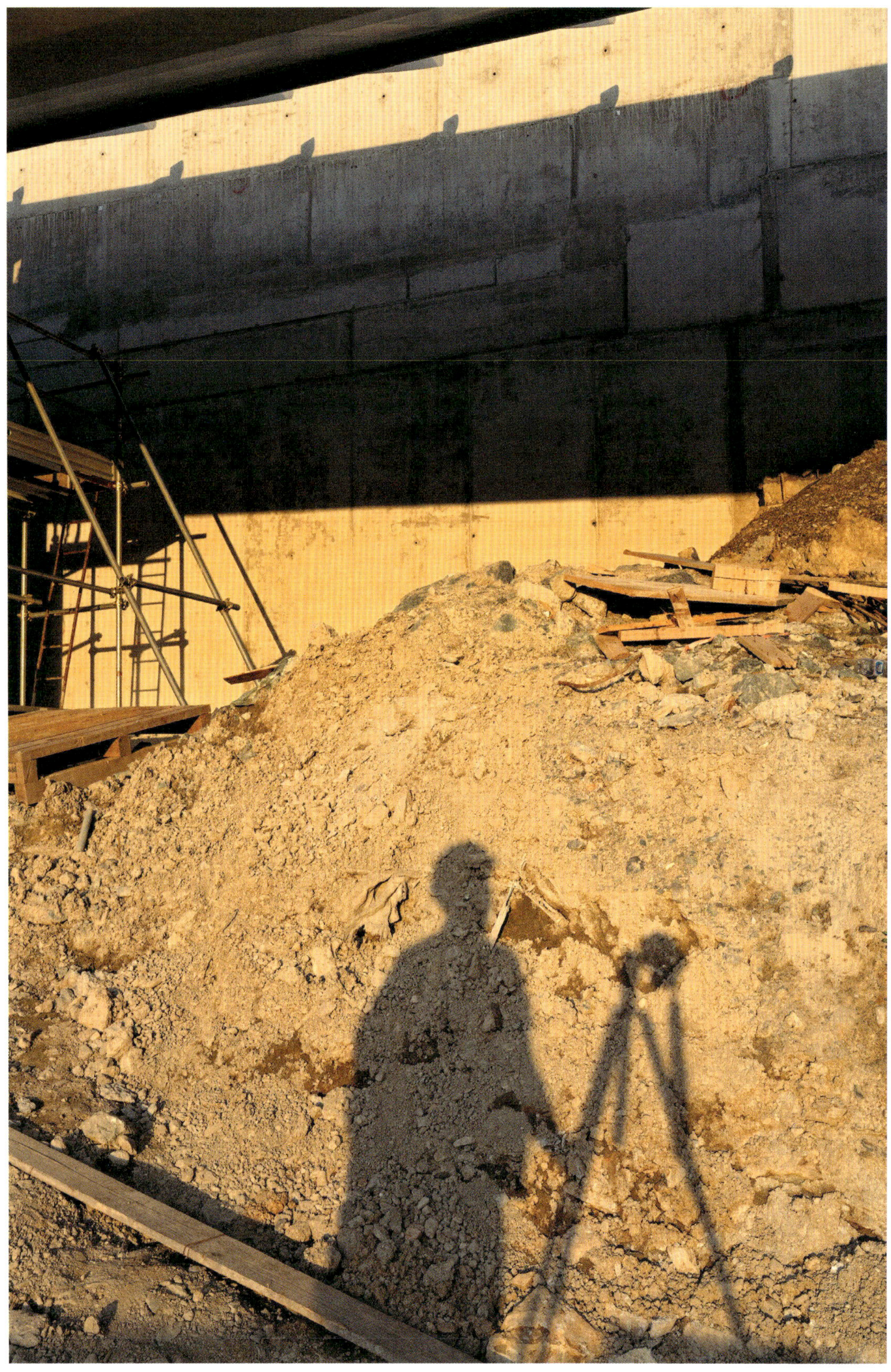

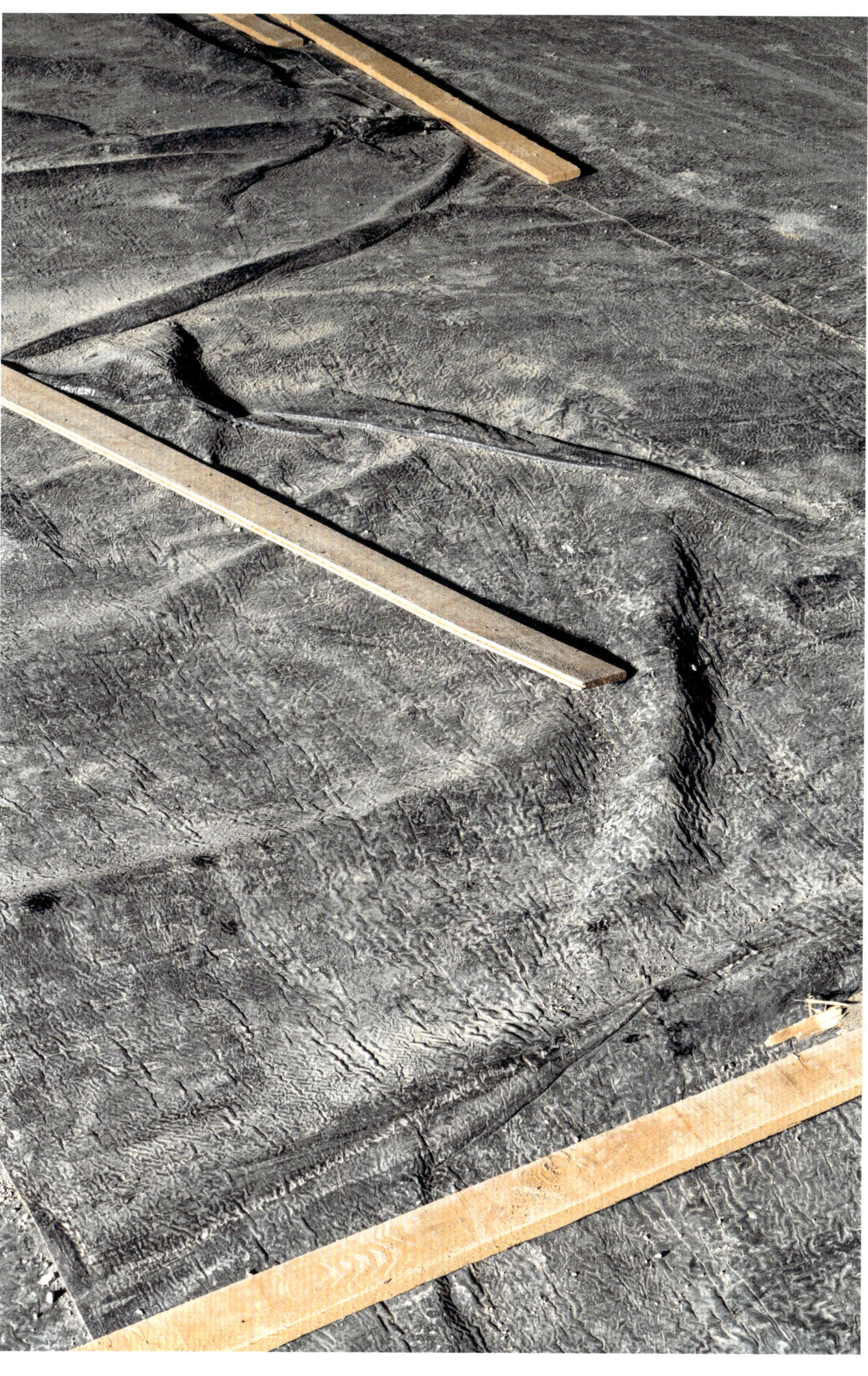

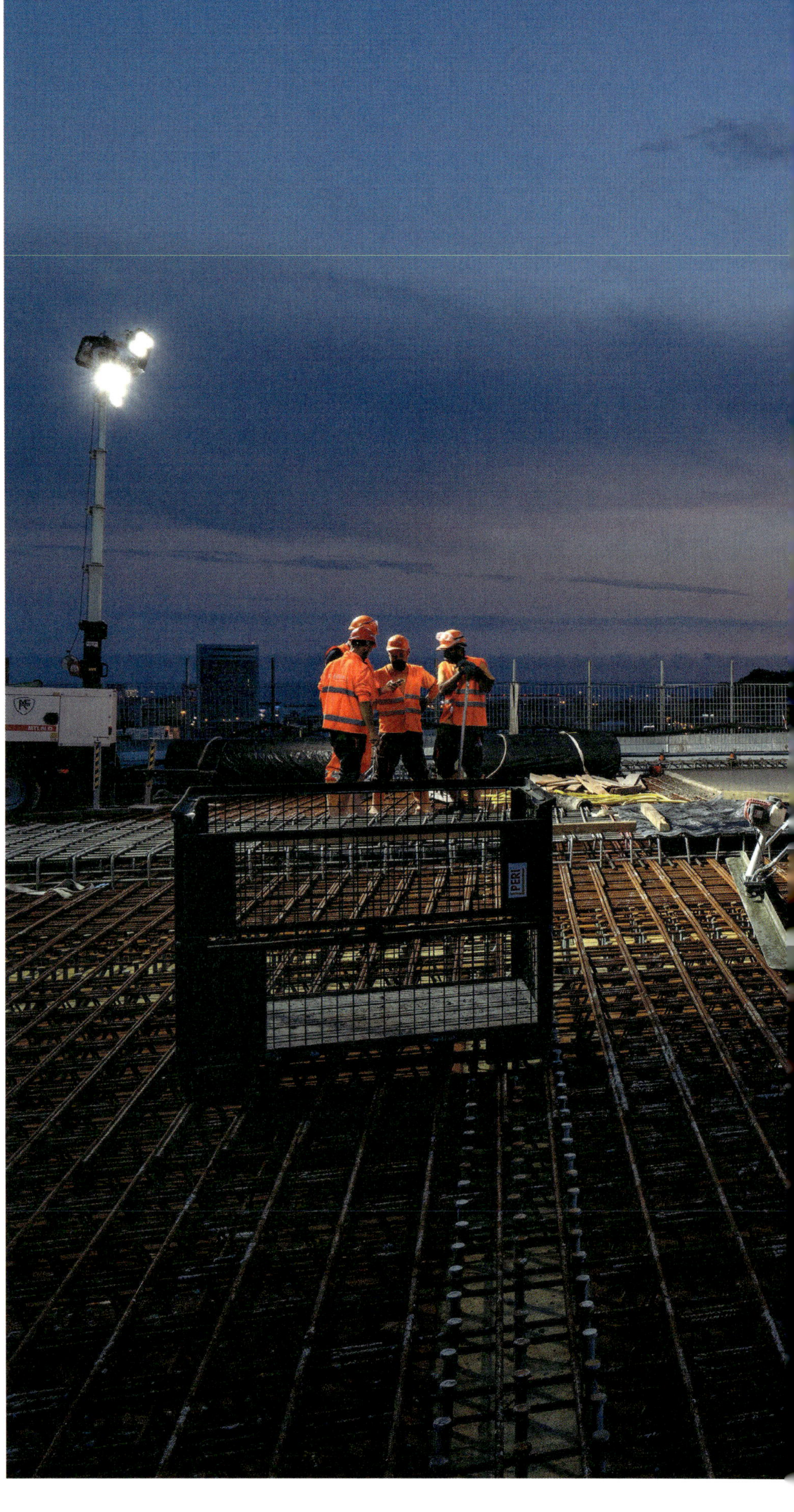

The completion of the elevation phase of all the parts
of the bridge was following by the "calaggio" (lowering)
phase, which was required to install the bridge to its
definitive position. The following phase was referred
to as "solettatura" (casting the concrete slab).
Casting the concrete slab began during the night,
starting from the two "shoulders," first from
the west, then from the east. It then proceeded
toward the center of the bridge, following a precise
pattern that would allow for its completion in as
little time as possible.

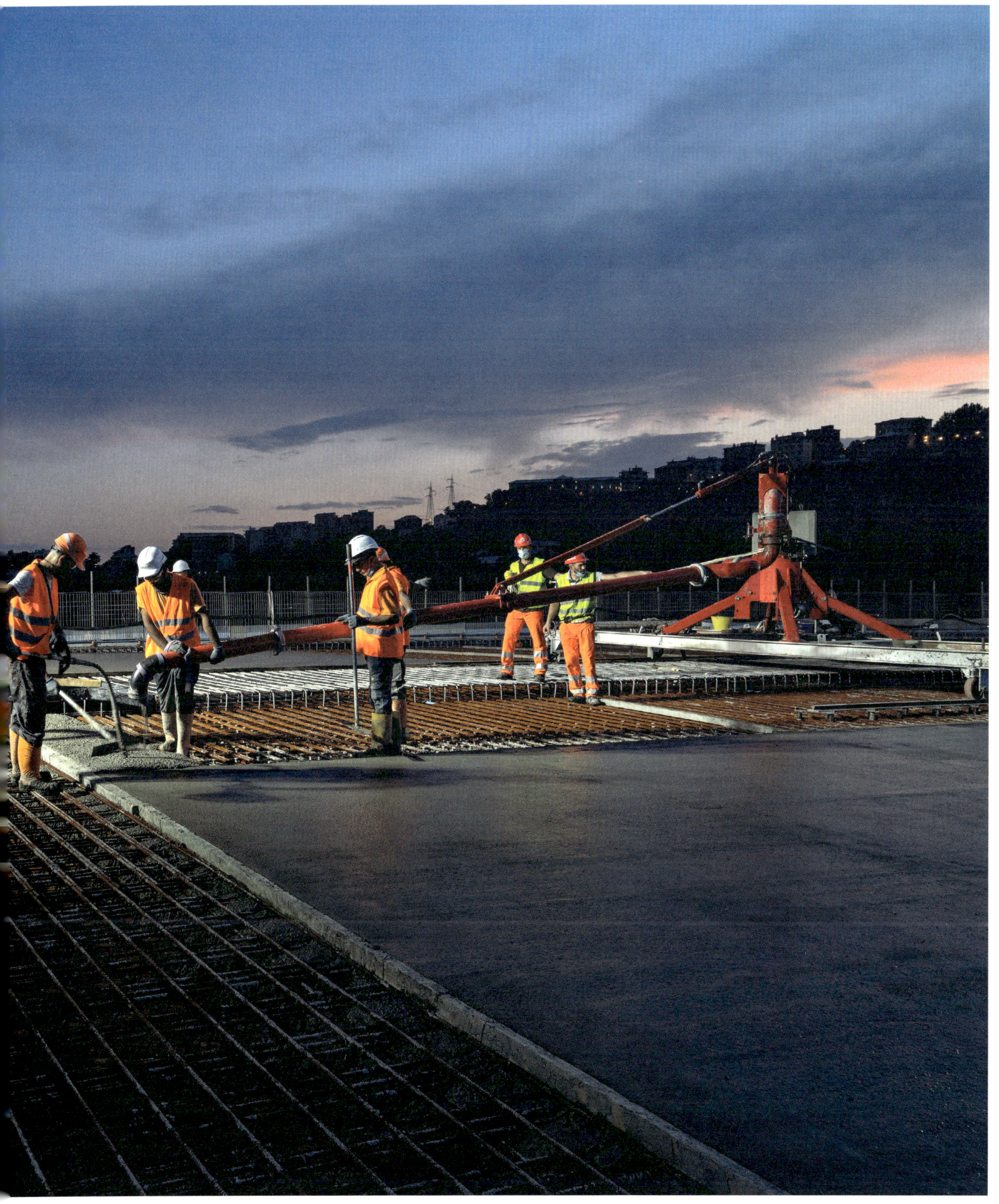

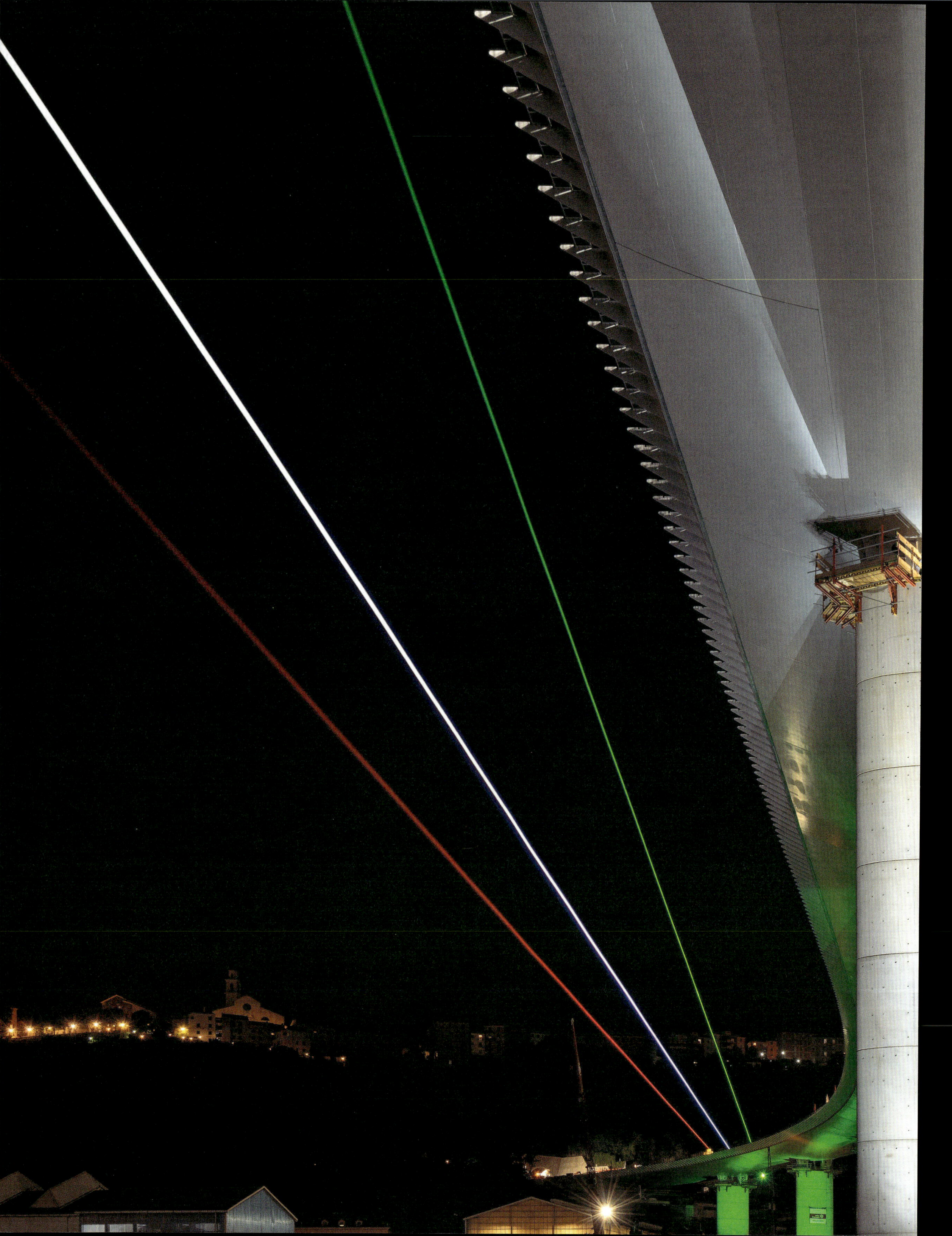

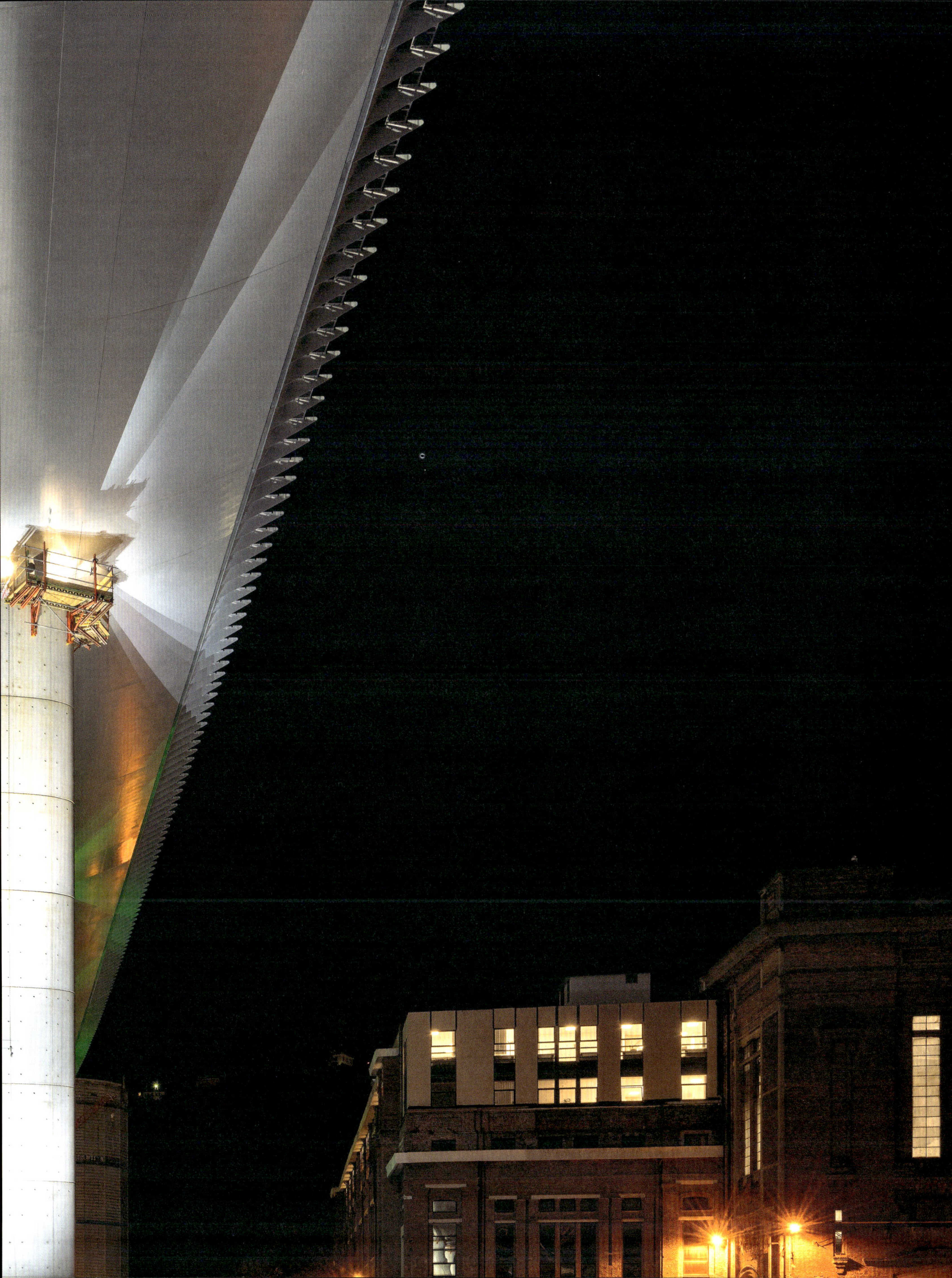

JUNE 18, 2020

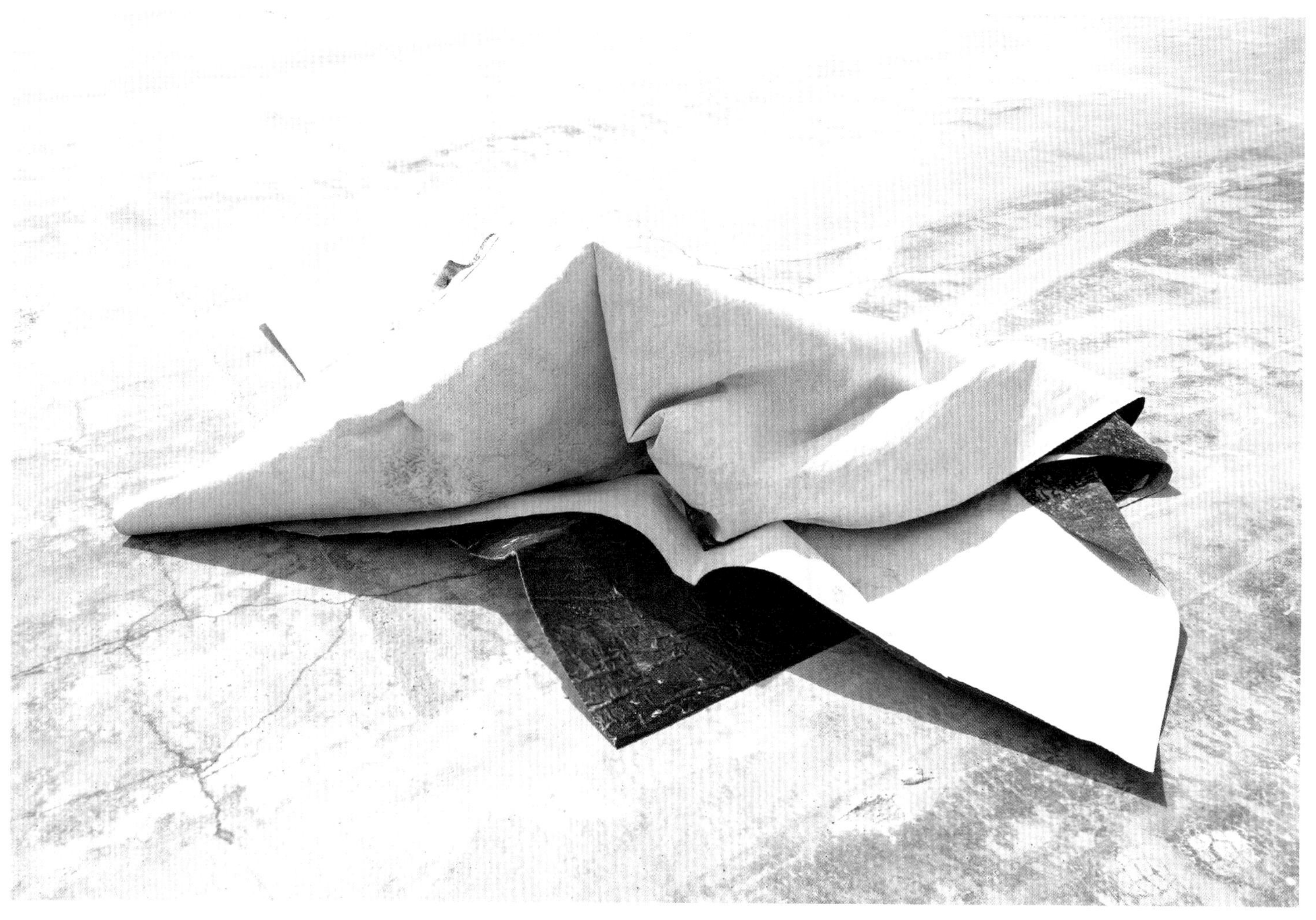

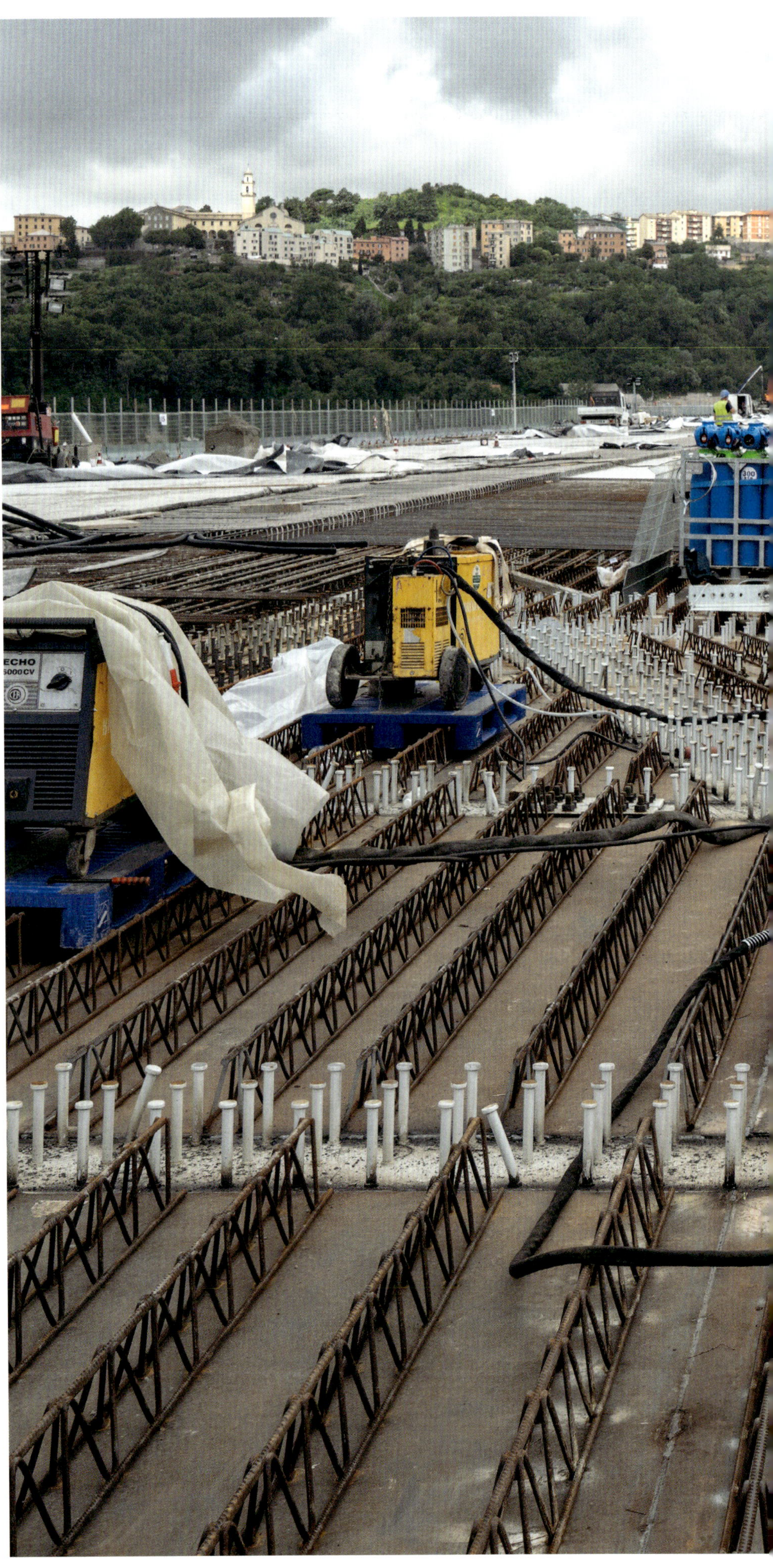

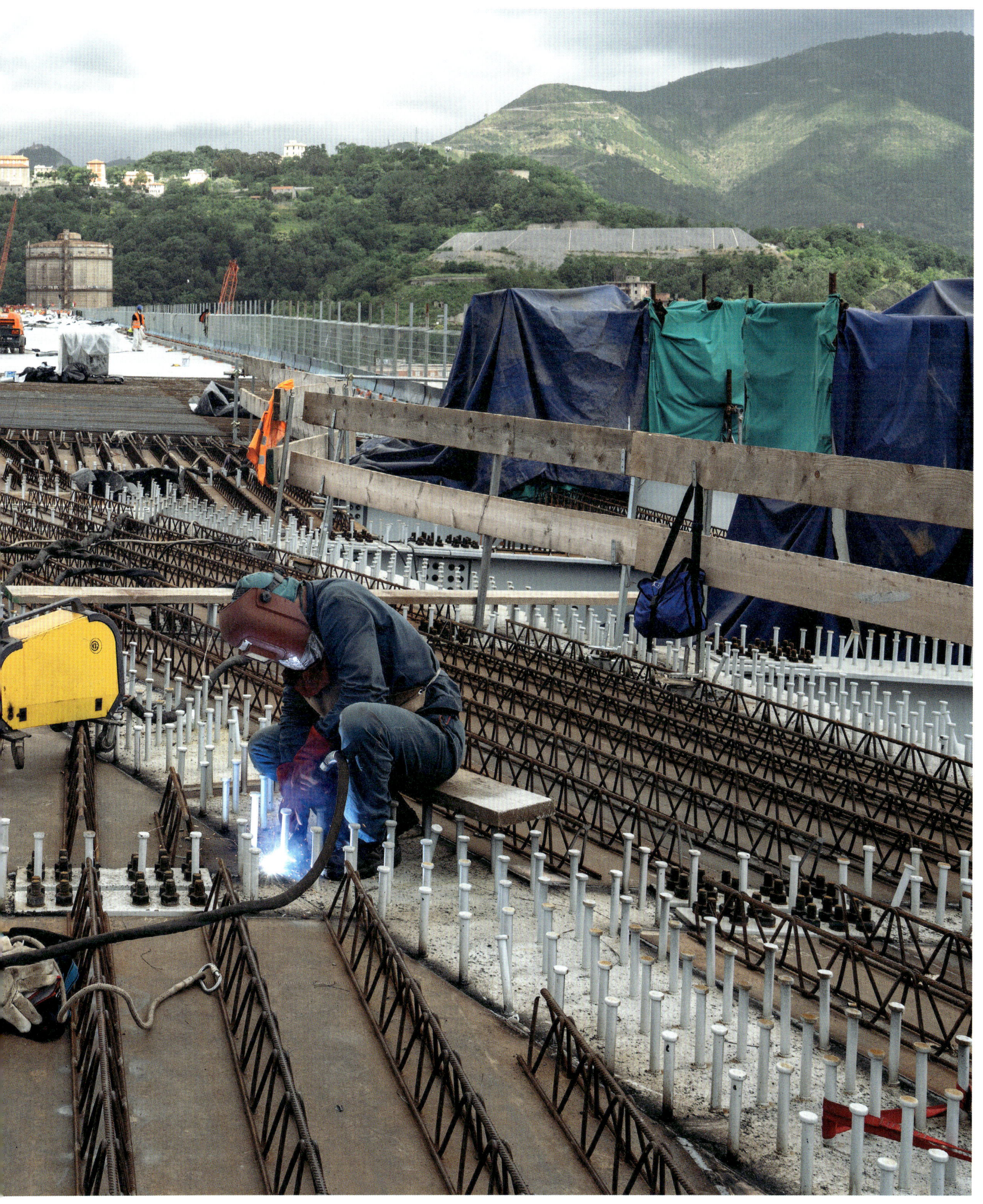

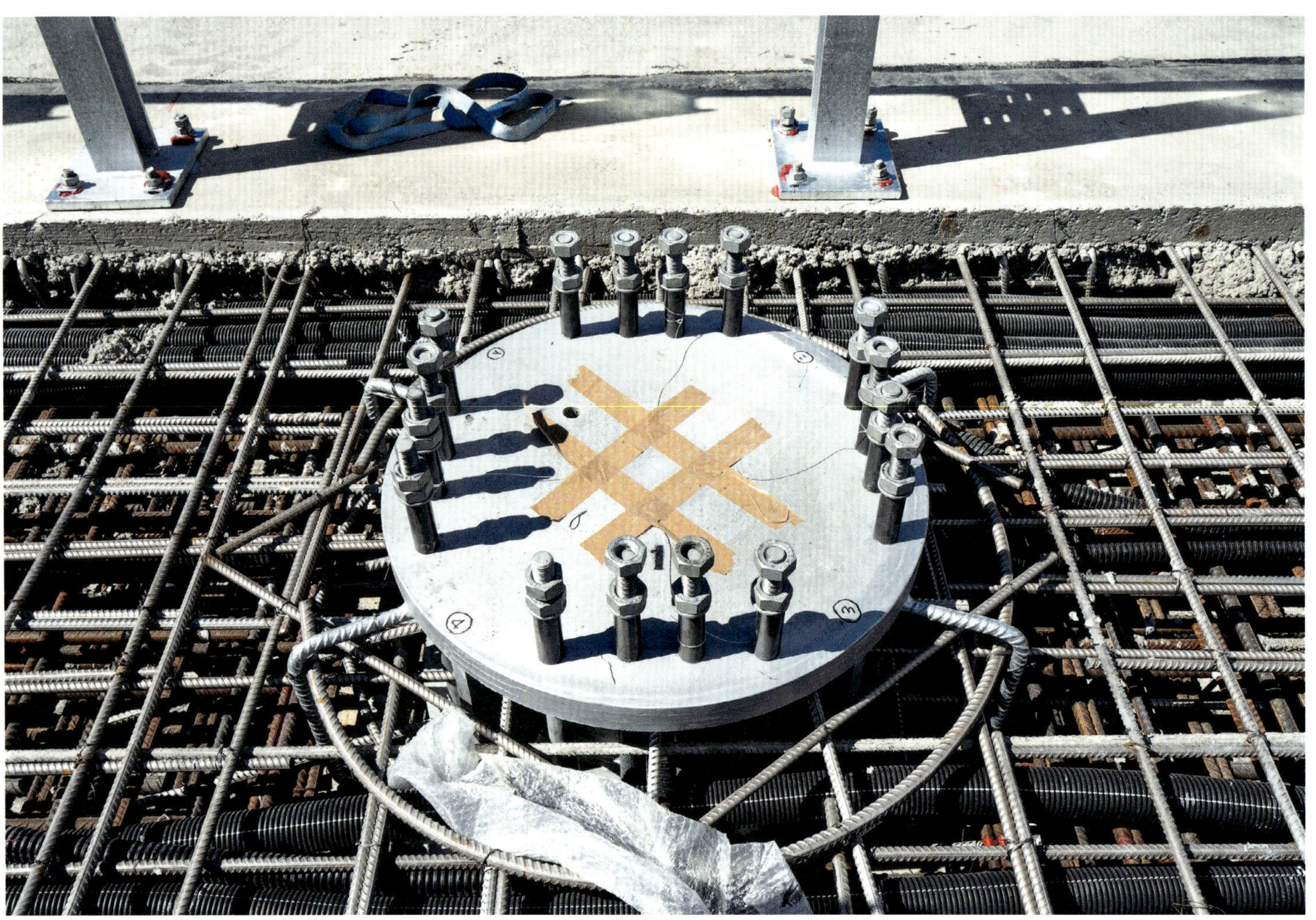

JULY 7, 2020

JULY 7, 2020

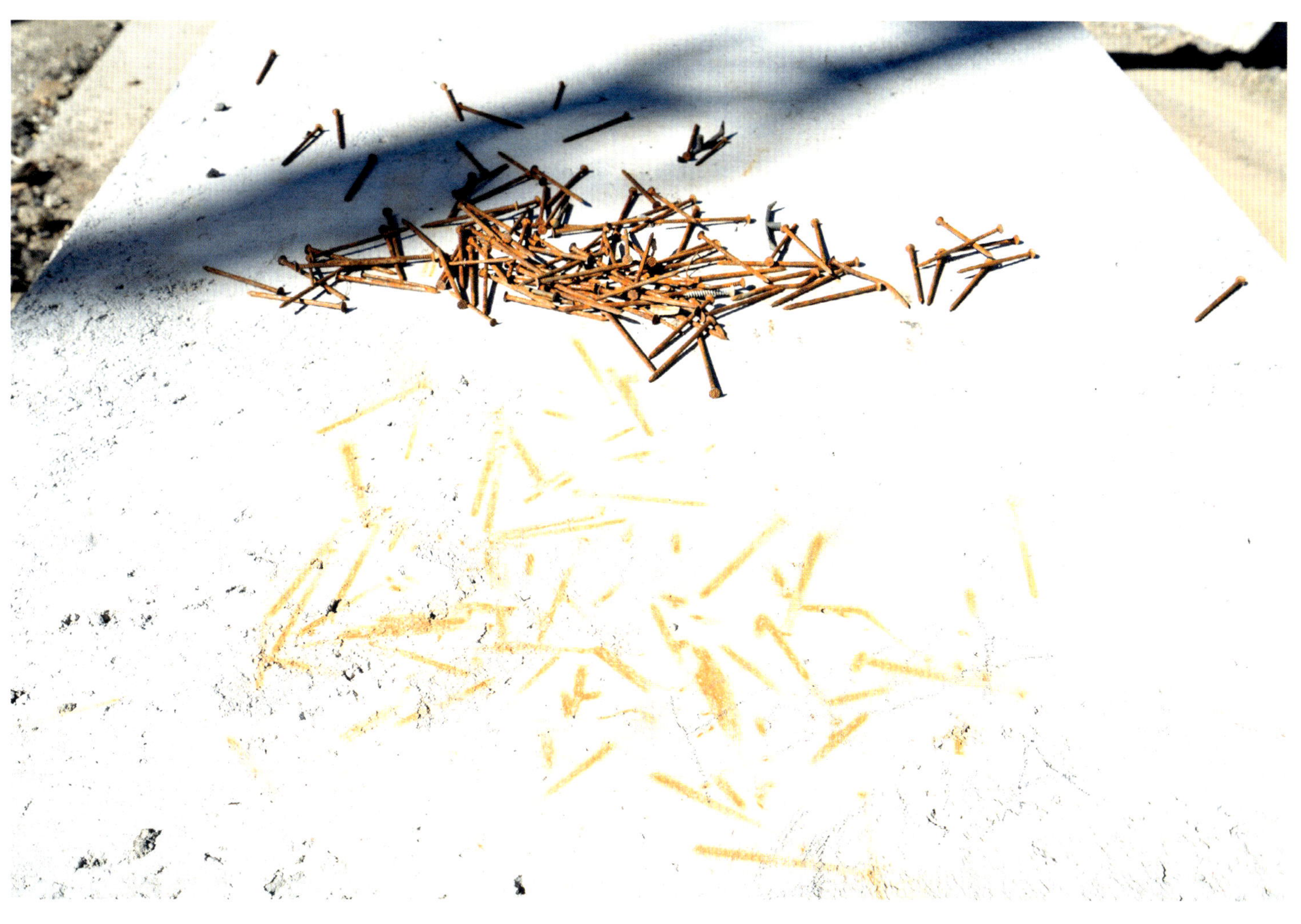

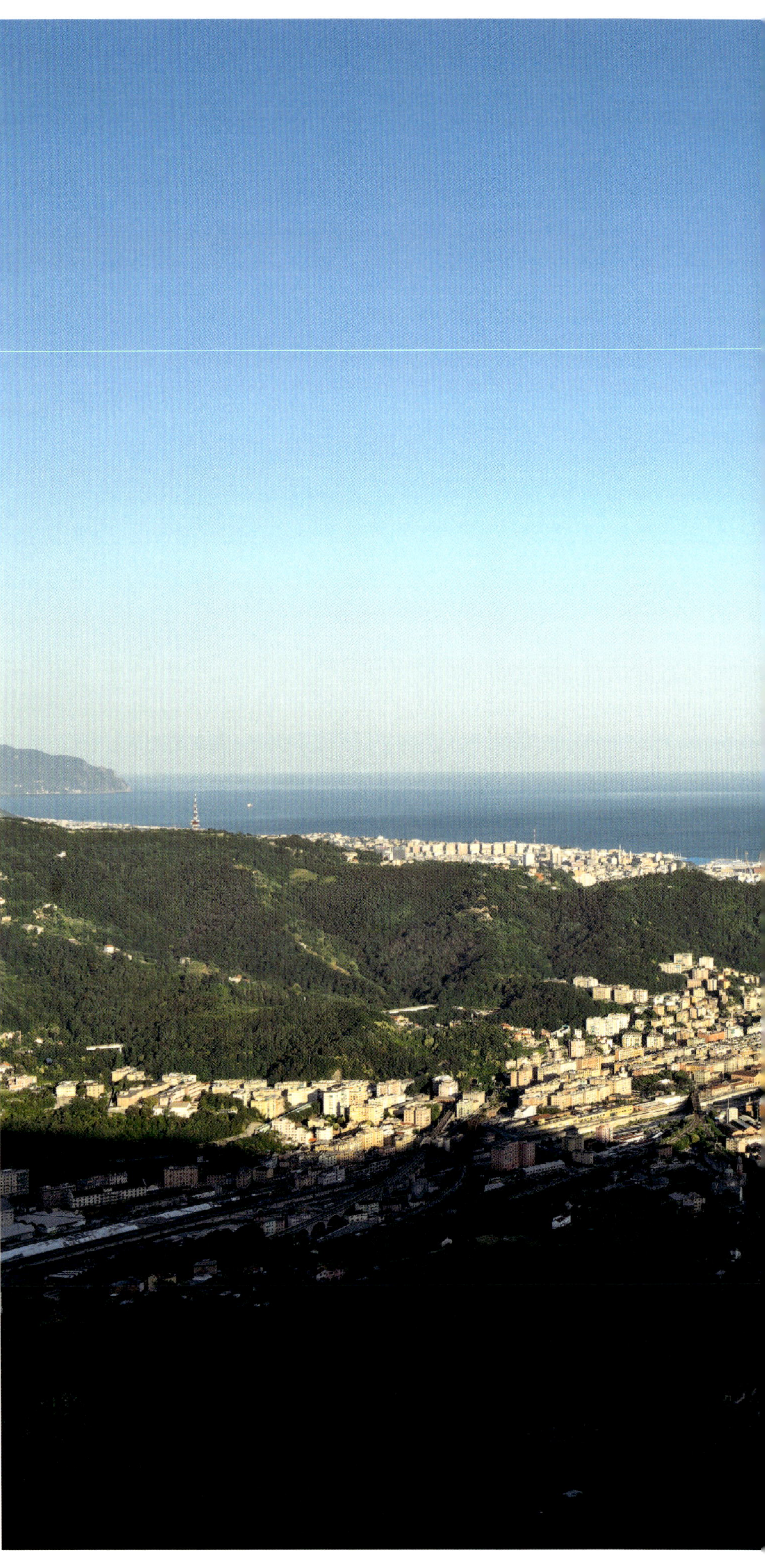

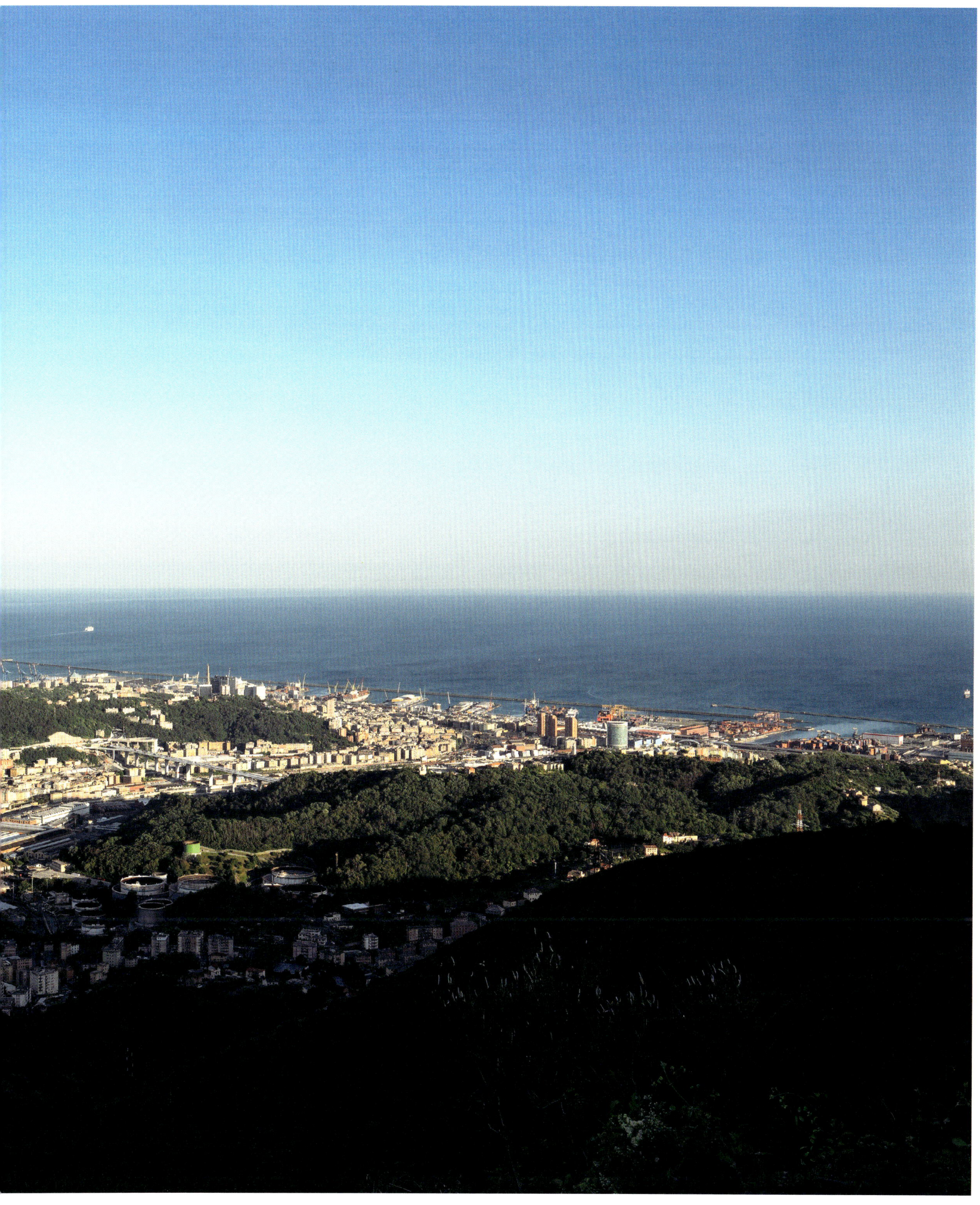

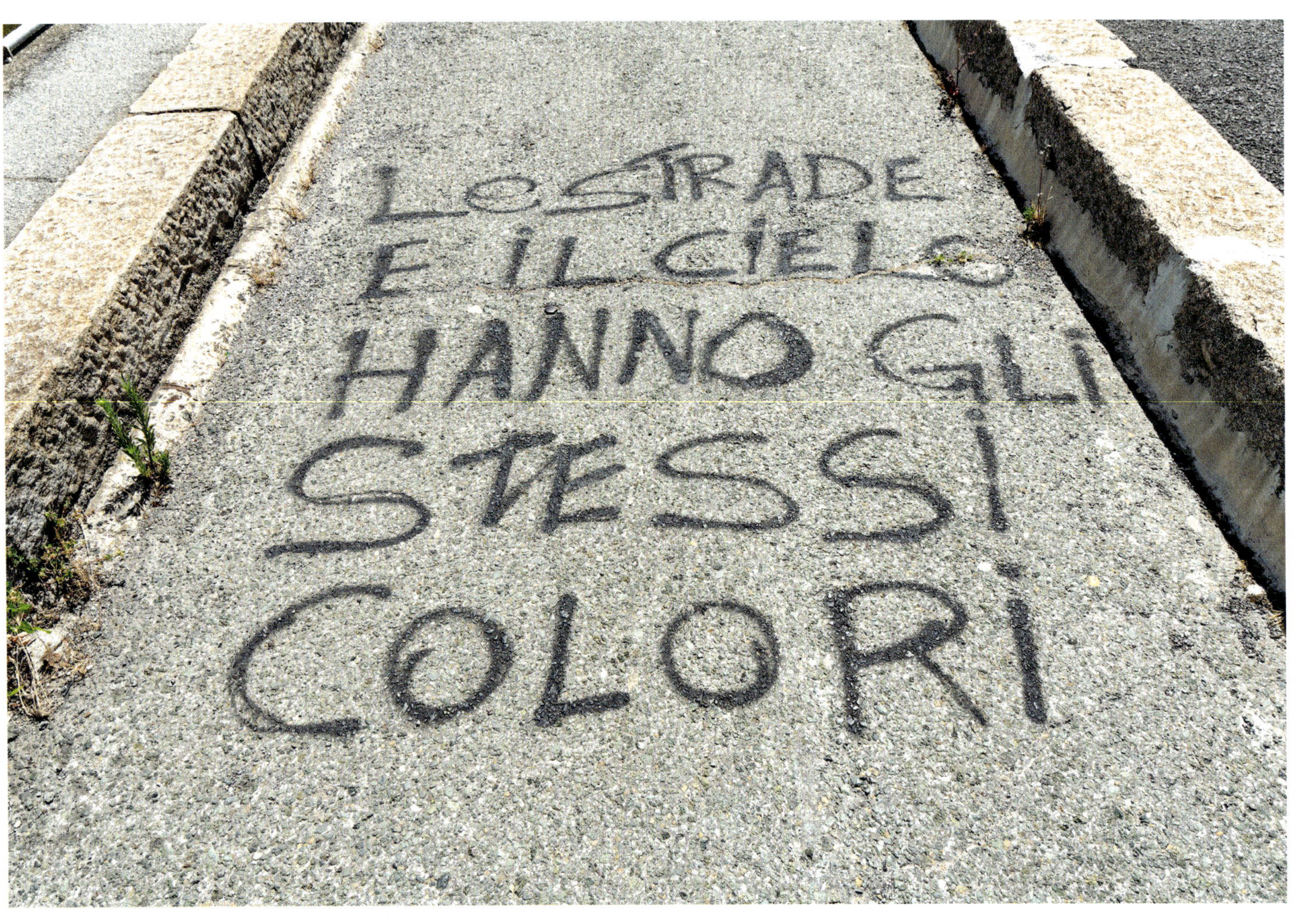

LO STRADE
E IL CIELO
HANNO GLI
STESSI
COLORI

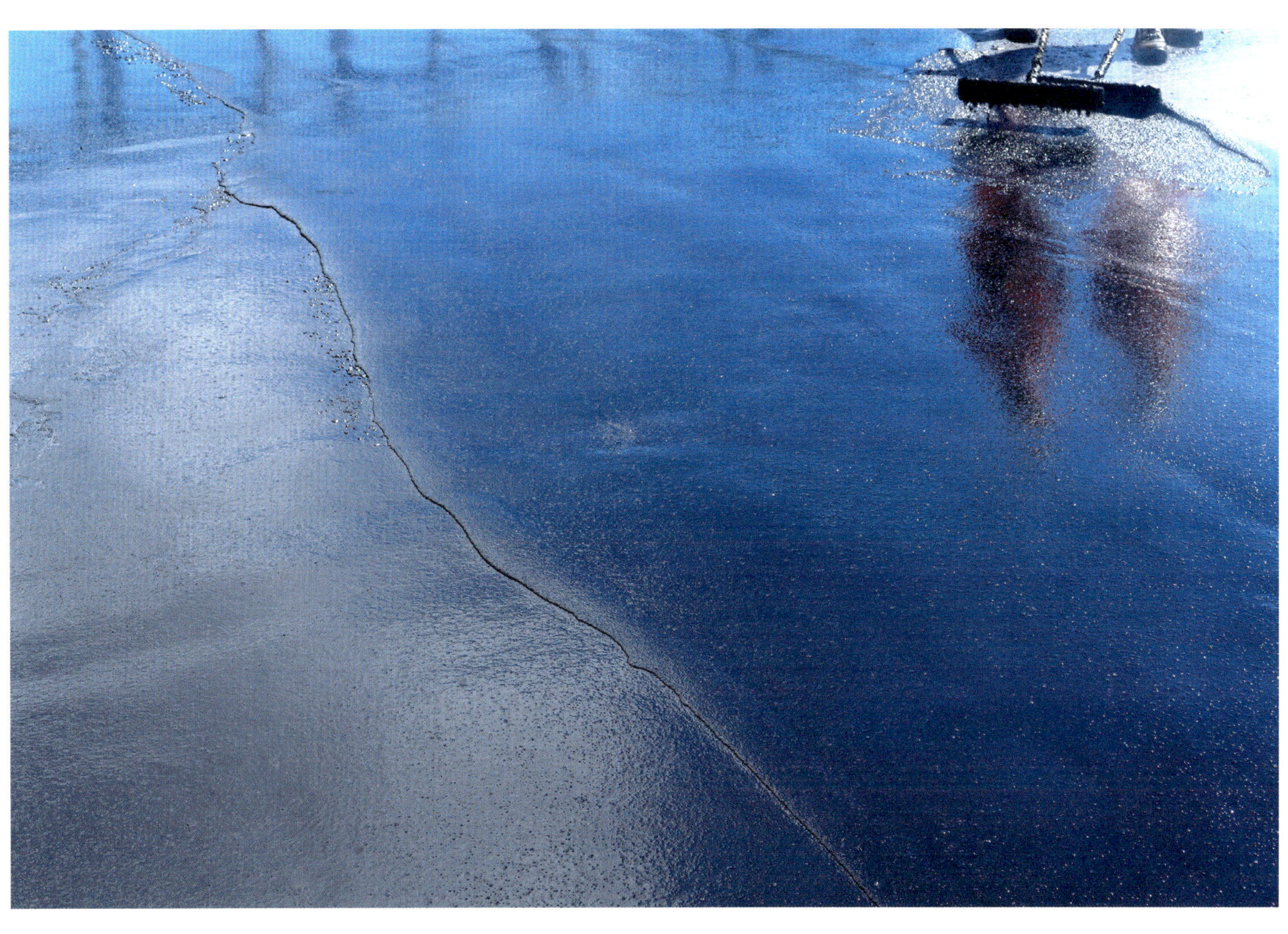

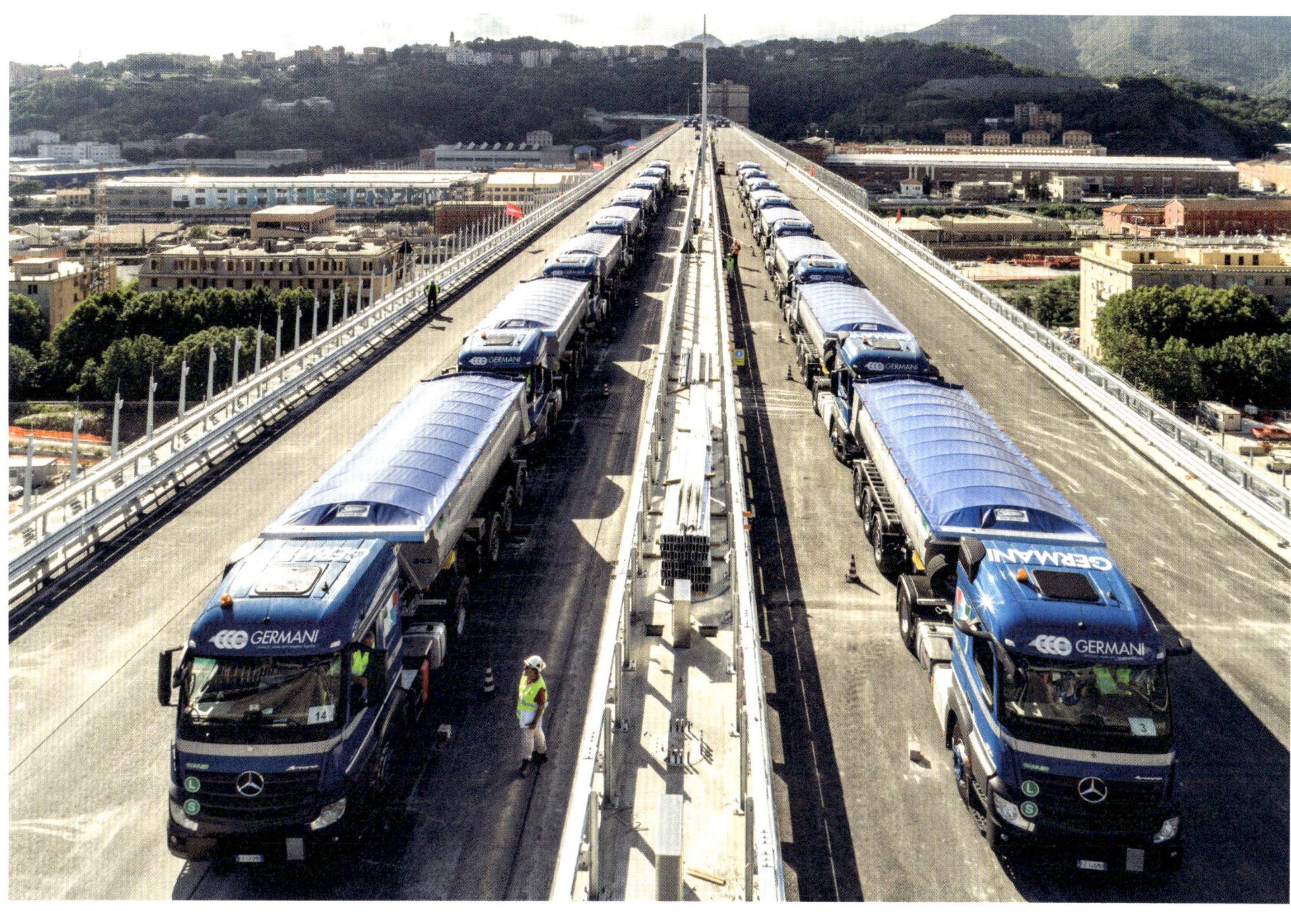

The static testing of the bridge lasted three days. It involved a total of 56 articulated trucks, with a cab and transporter for testing over the viaduct, while four SPMTs were used to test the highway A7 junction ramp.

Afterwards, the vehicles were positioned on preset portions of the deck and in such a way as to determine stress tests in the structure superior to the ones that the viaduct is expected to withstand routinely.

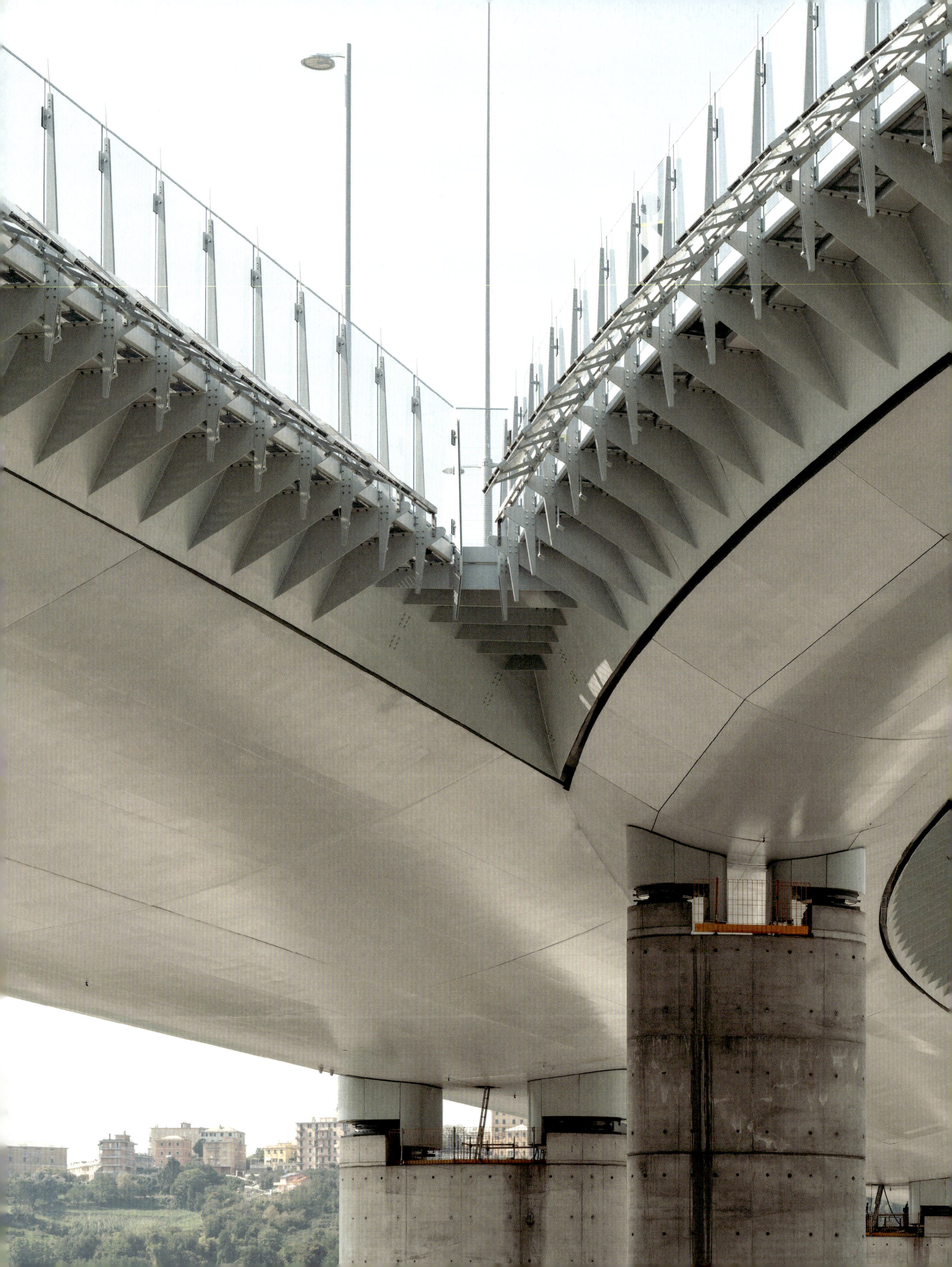

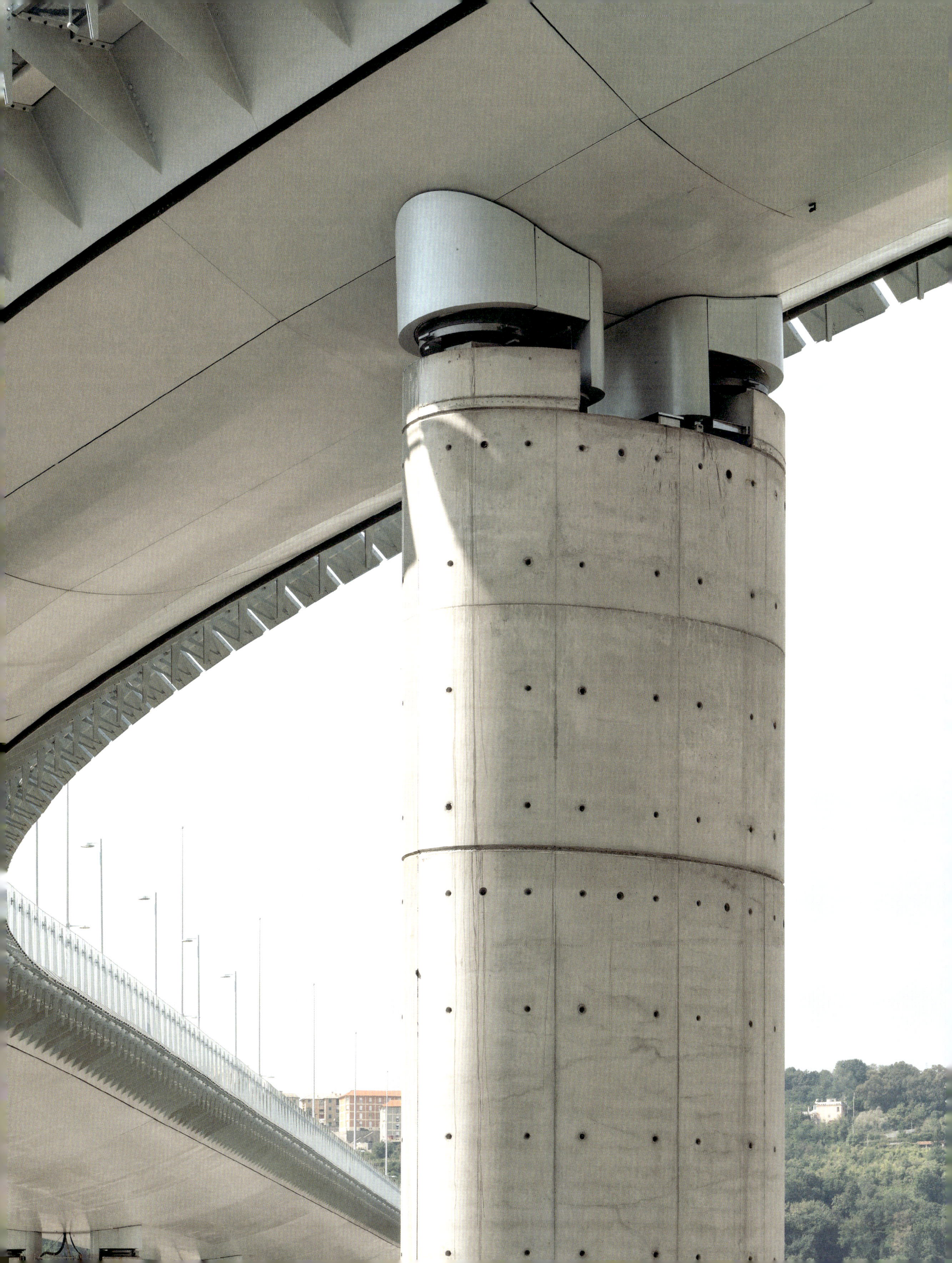

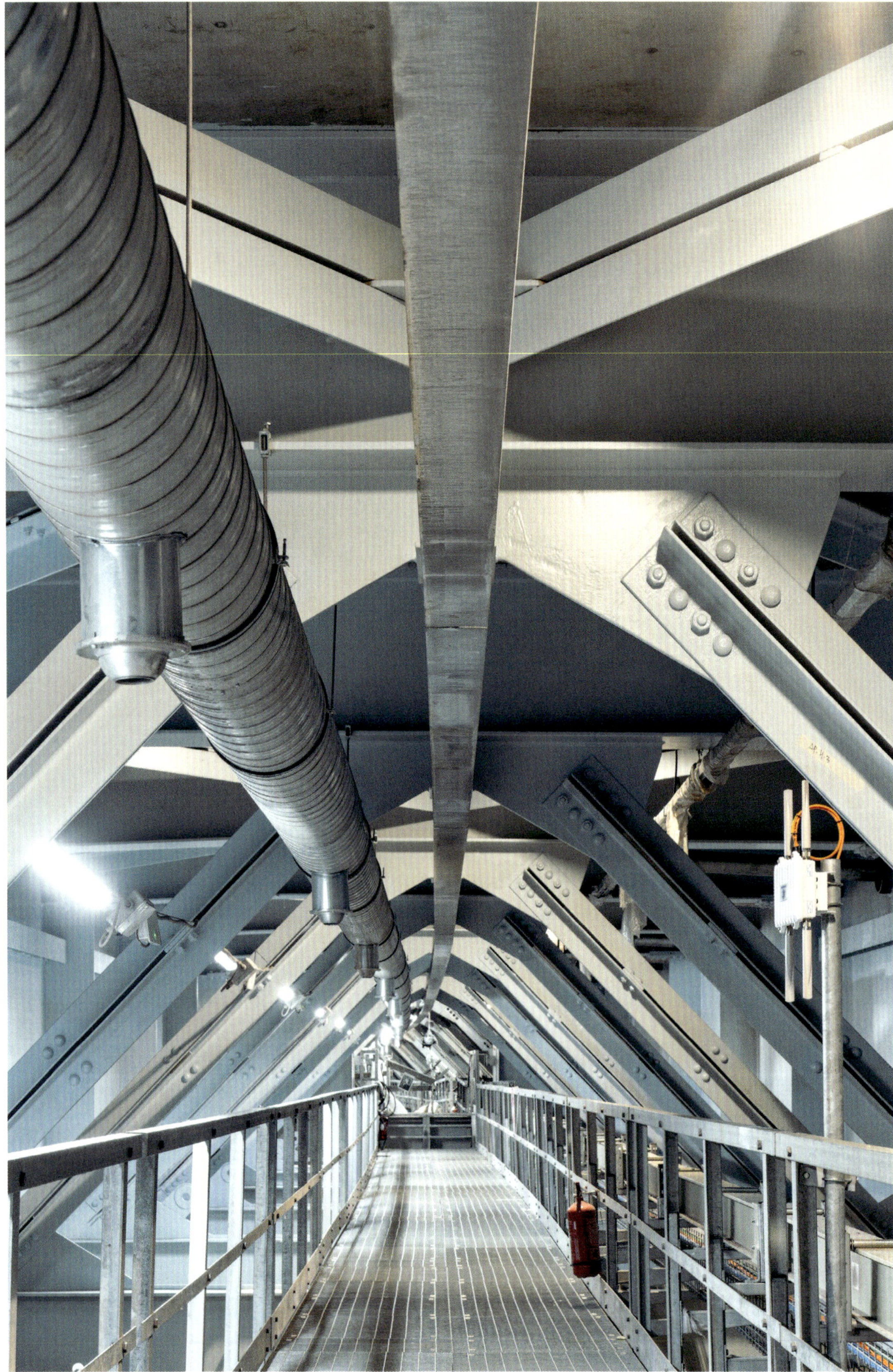

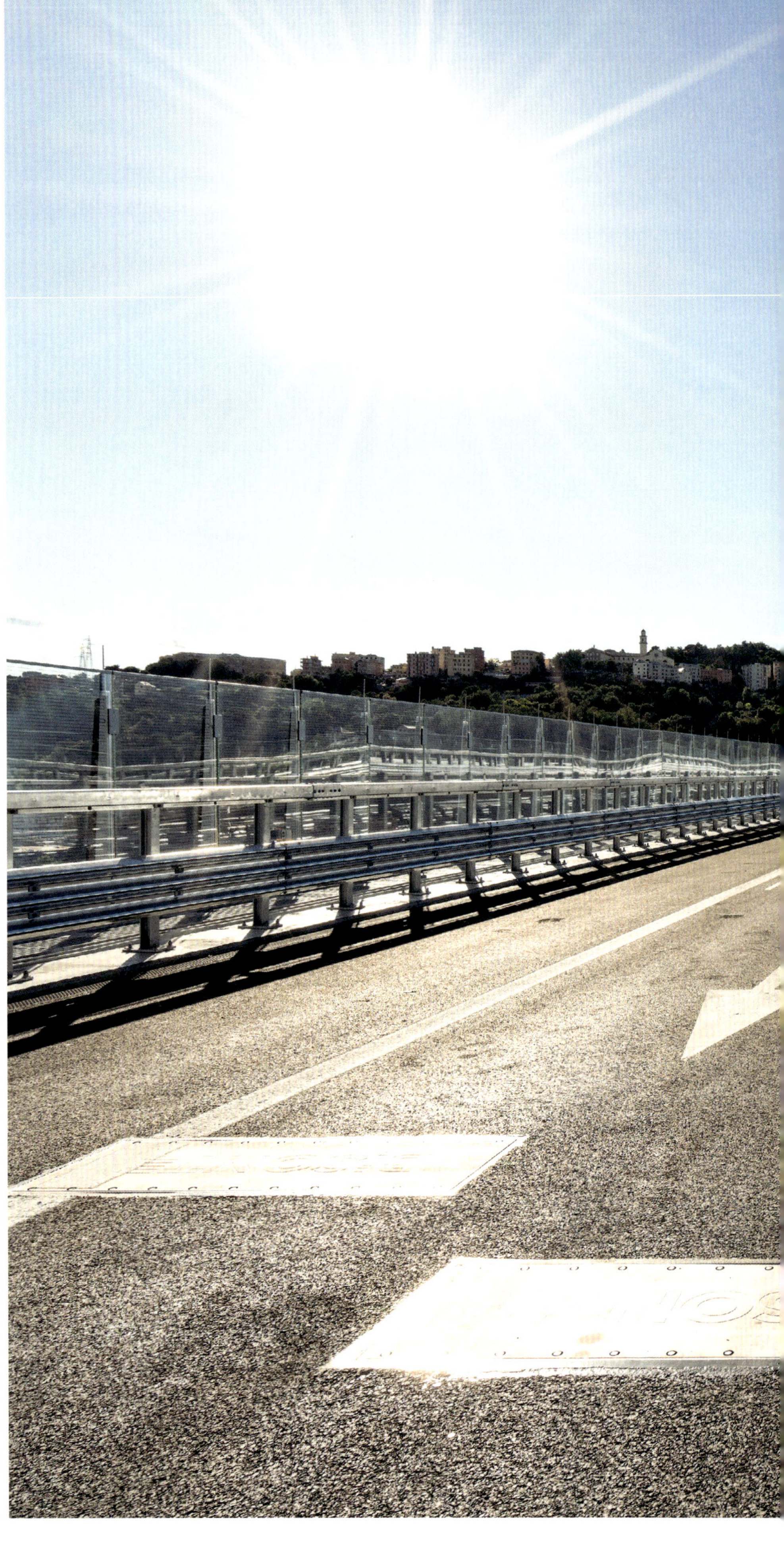

In the late afternoon of a sunny day in August, the bridge, which had already been inaugurated, was cleared of the last of the machinery and equipment—and inspected by the relevant authorities so that it could be opened to traffic. This took place at 8 p.m. The traffic once again flowed along this major artery, less than two years after the tragedy of the collapse, and one and a half years after the opening of the demolition site.

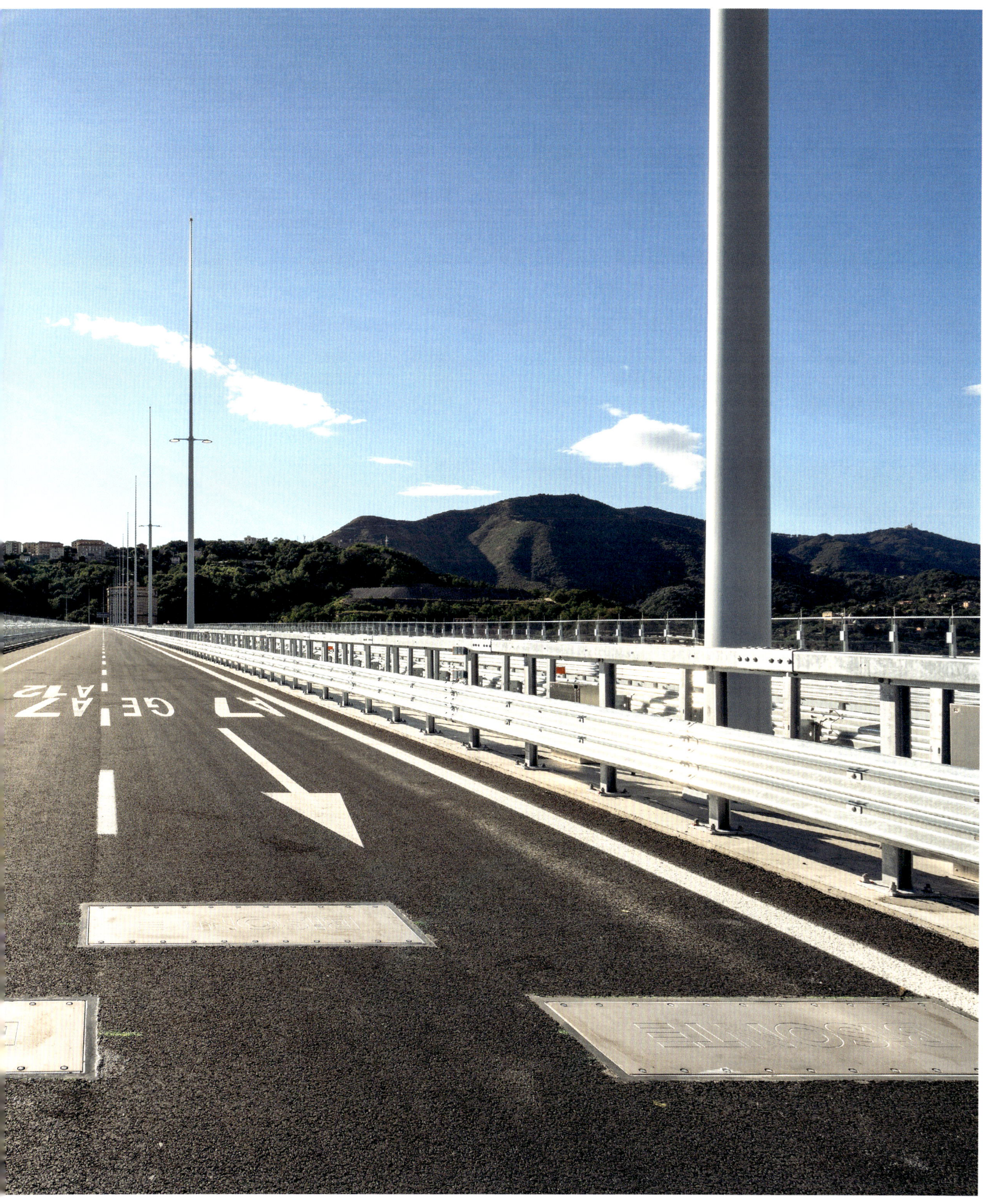
GE A7
A12
17

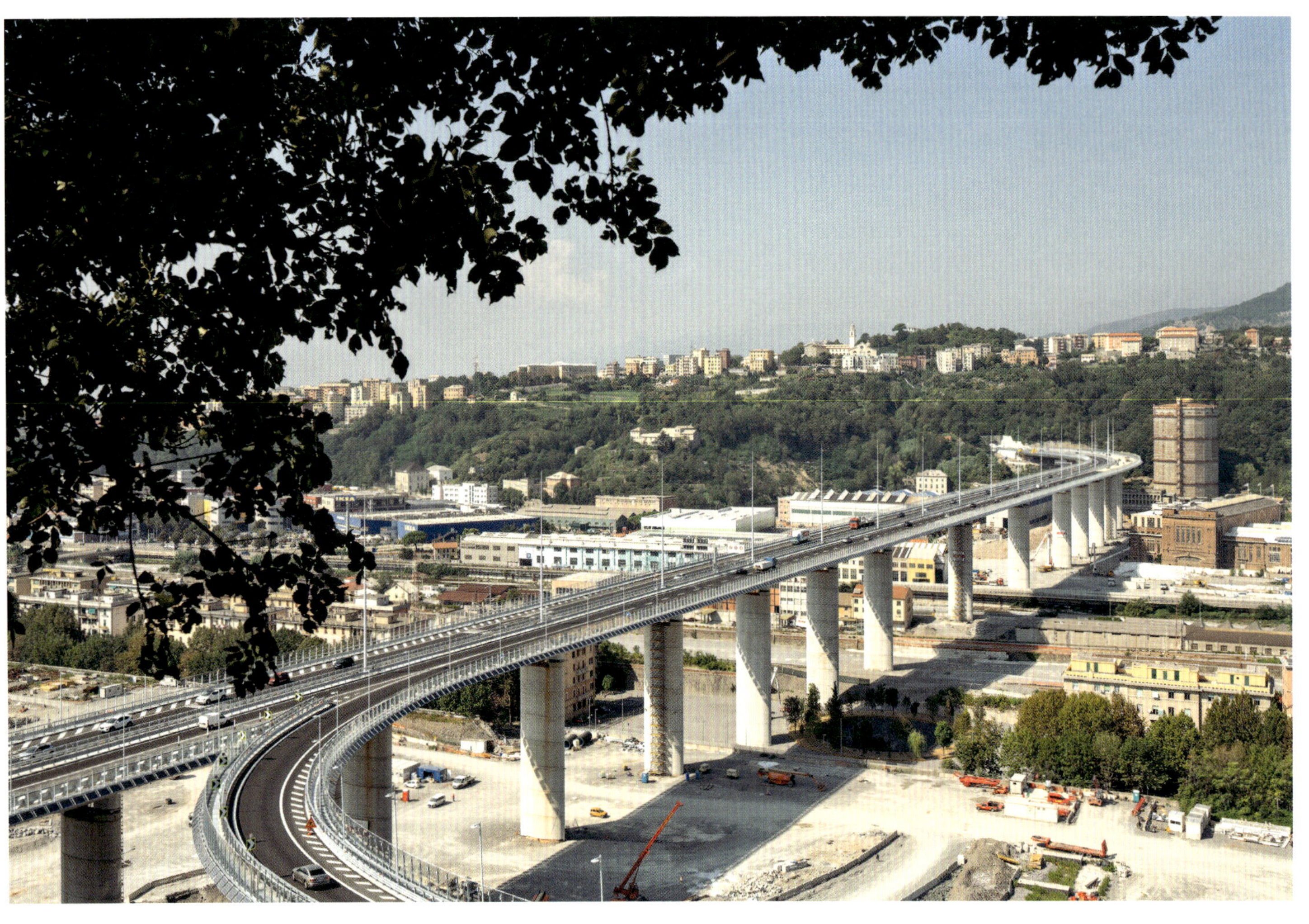

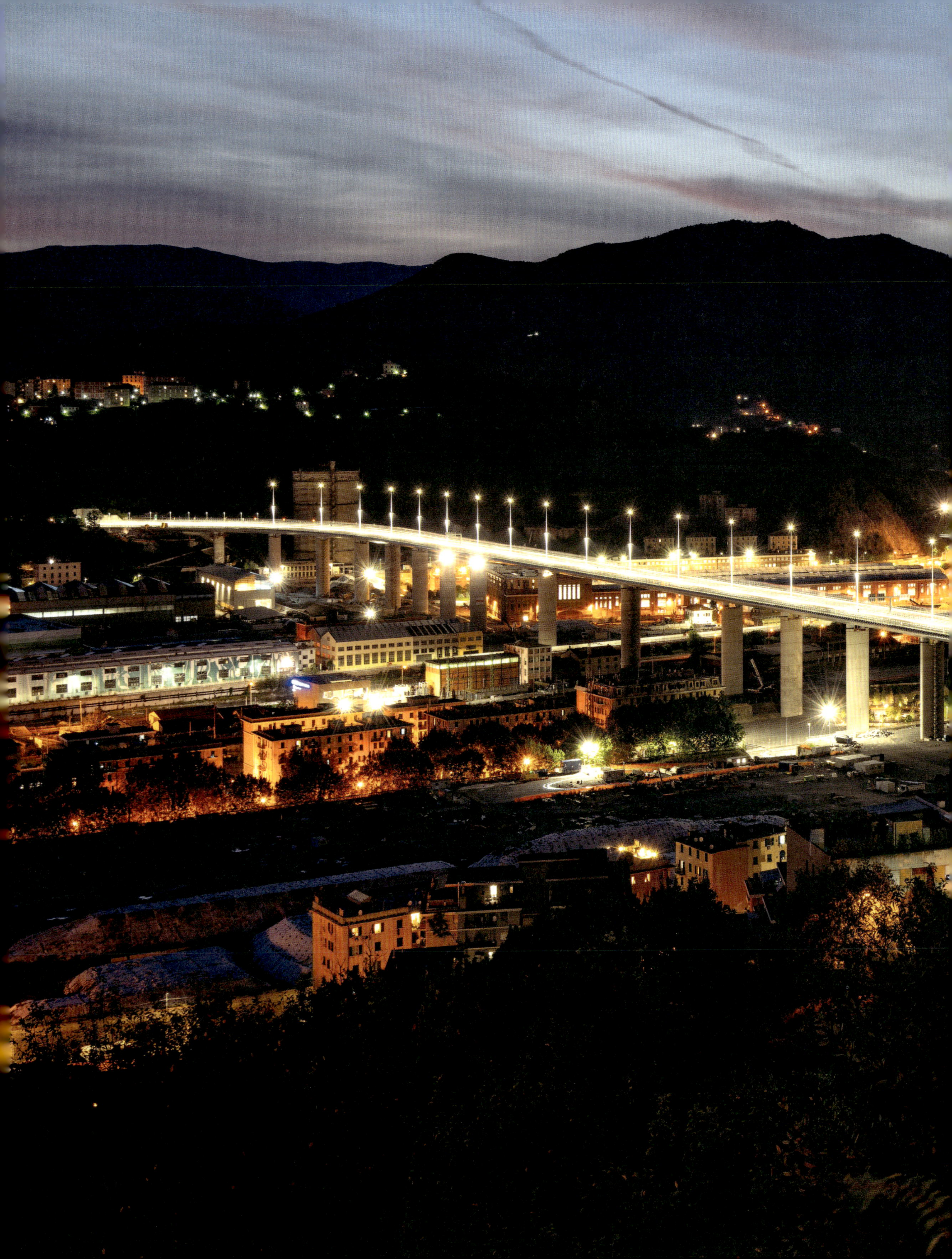

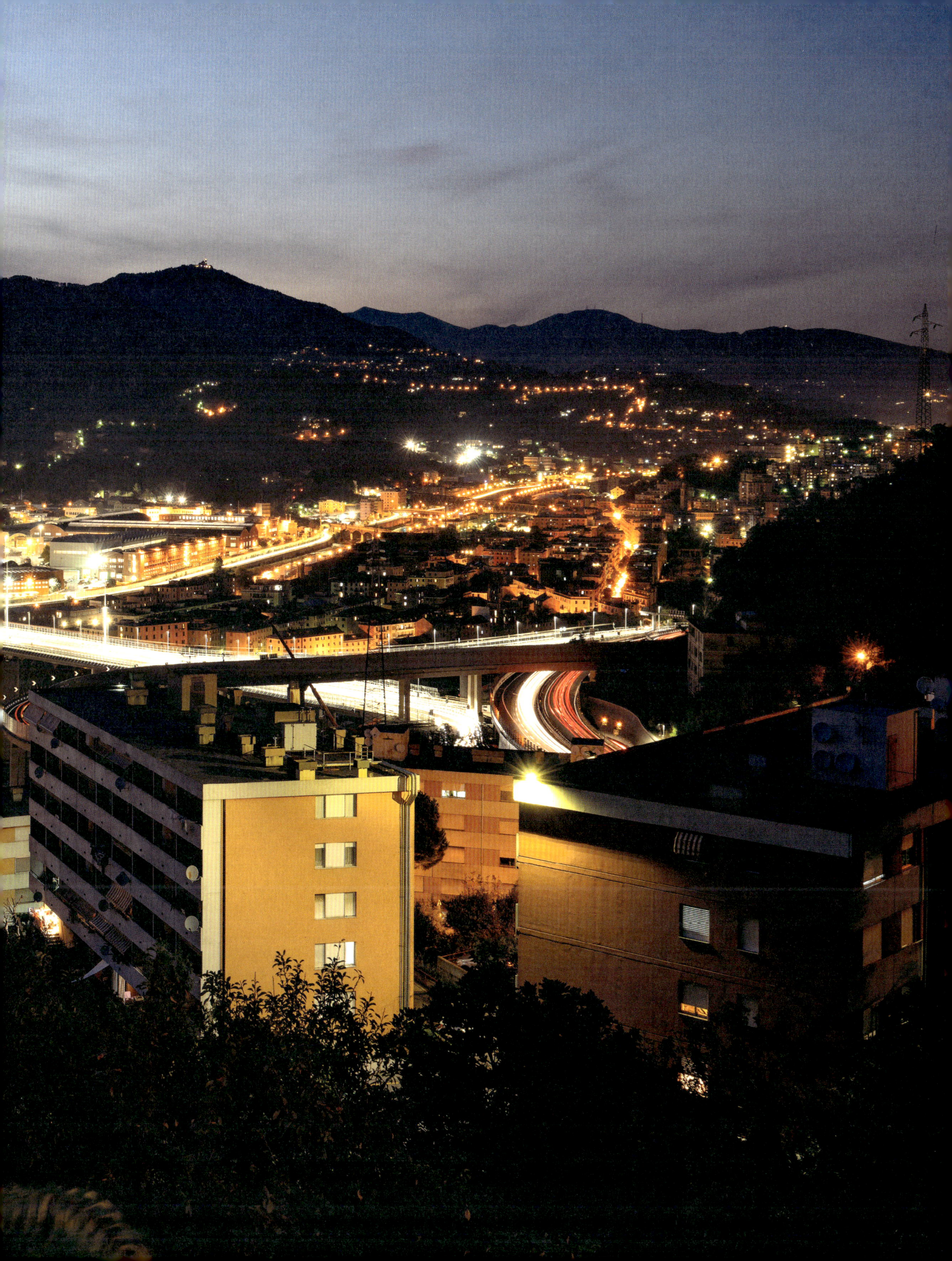

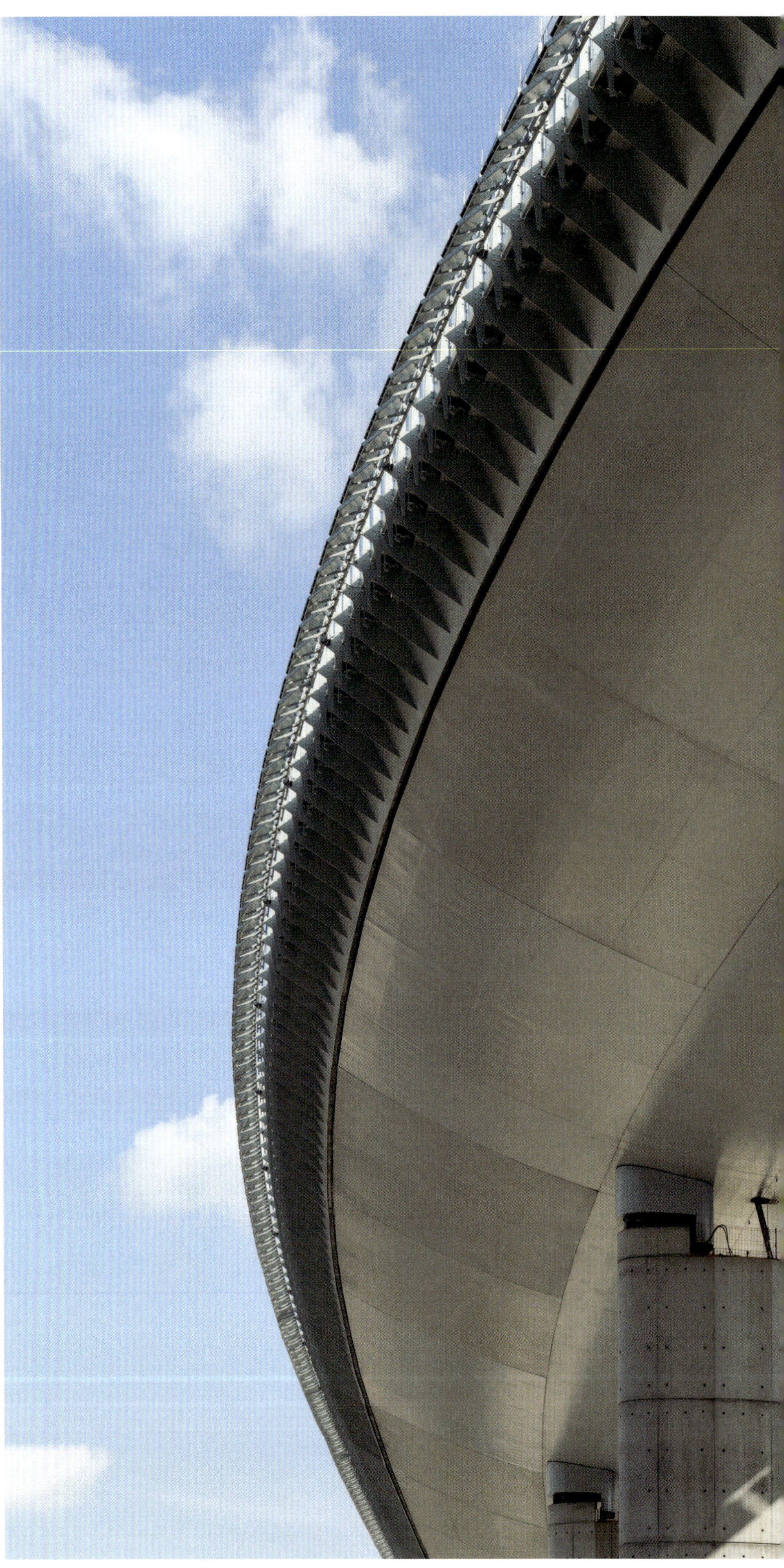

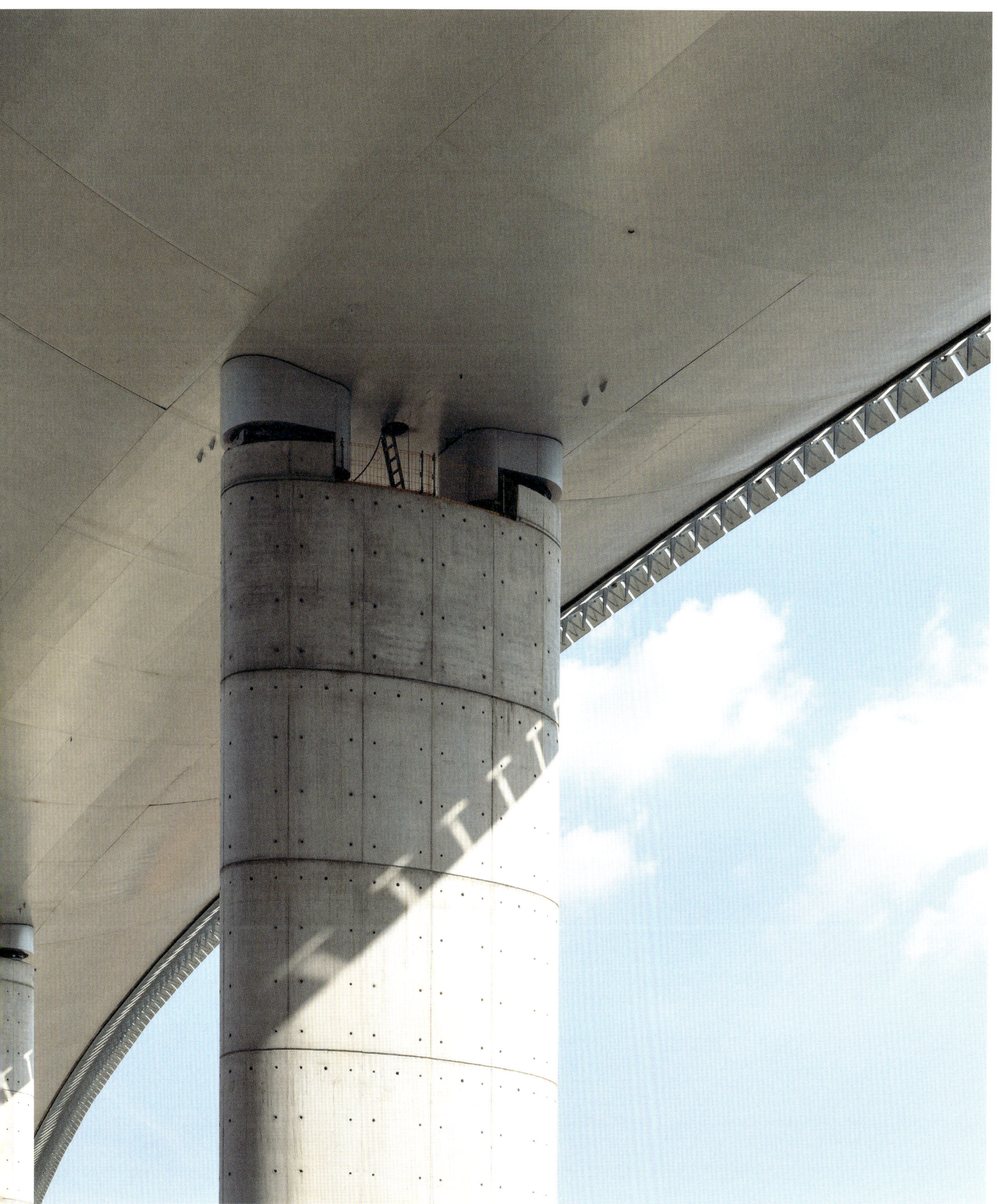

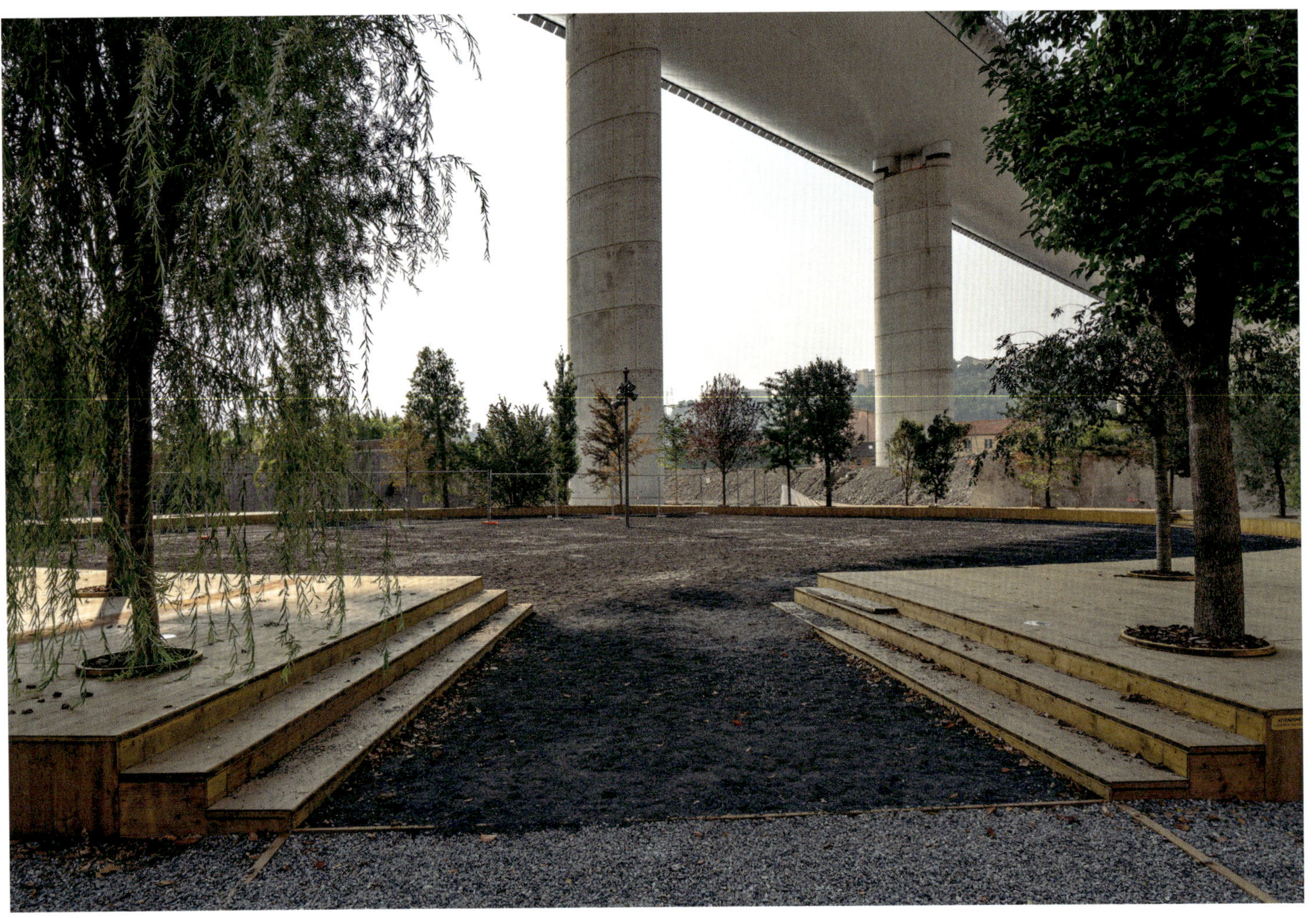

Rising up on the eastern shore of the Polcevera torrent,
beyond the railway line, is the "garden of memory."
Forty-three different trees arranged in a circle,
located close to the site where Ponte Morandi's pier
9 collapsed, to commemorate the forty-three victims
of the tragedy.

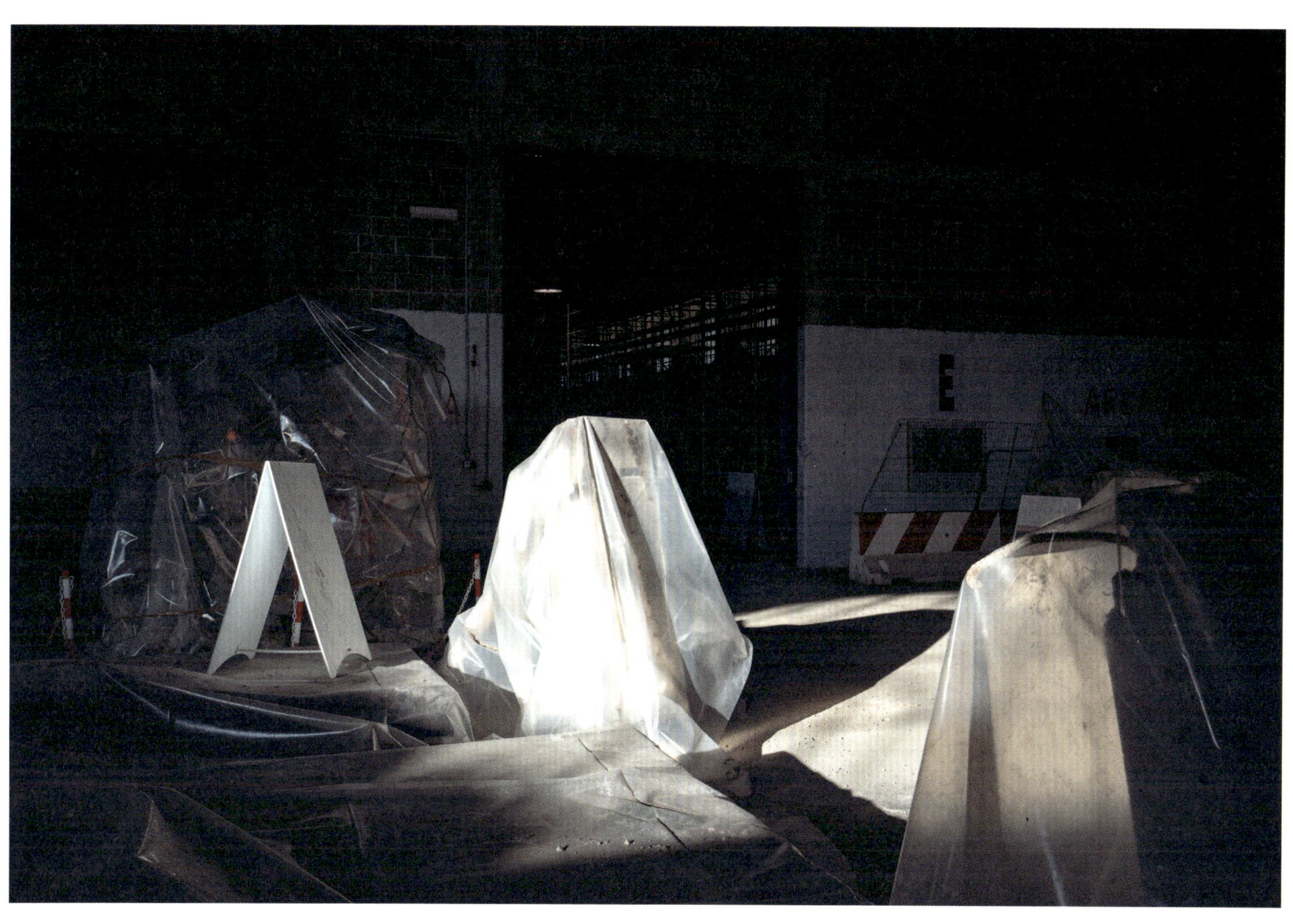

Along Via Perlasca, inside a hangar that is still
under seizure due to the ongoing investigation,
is the debris from pier 9 and its tall piles, which
collapsed on August 14, 2018.
The great effort made by all those who worked to
reconstruct the bridge will never erase the sense
of injustice for this loss of lives.

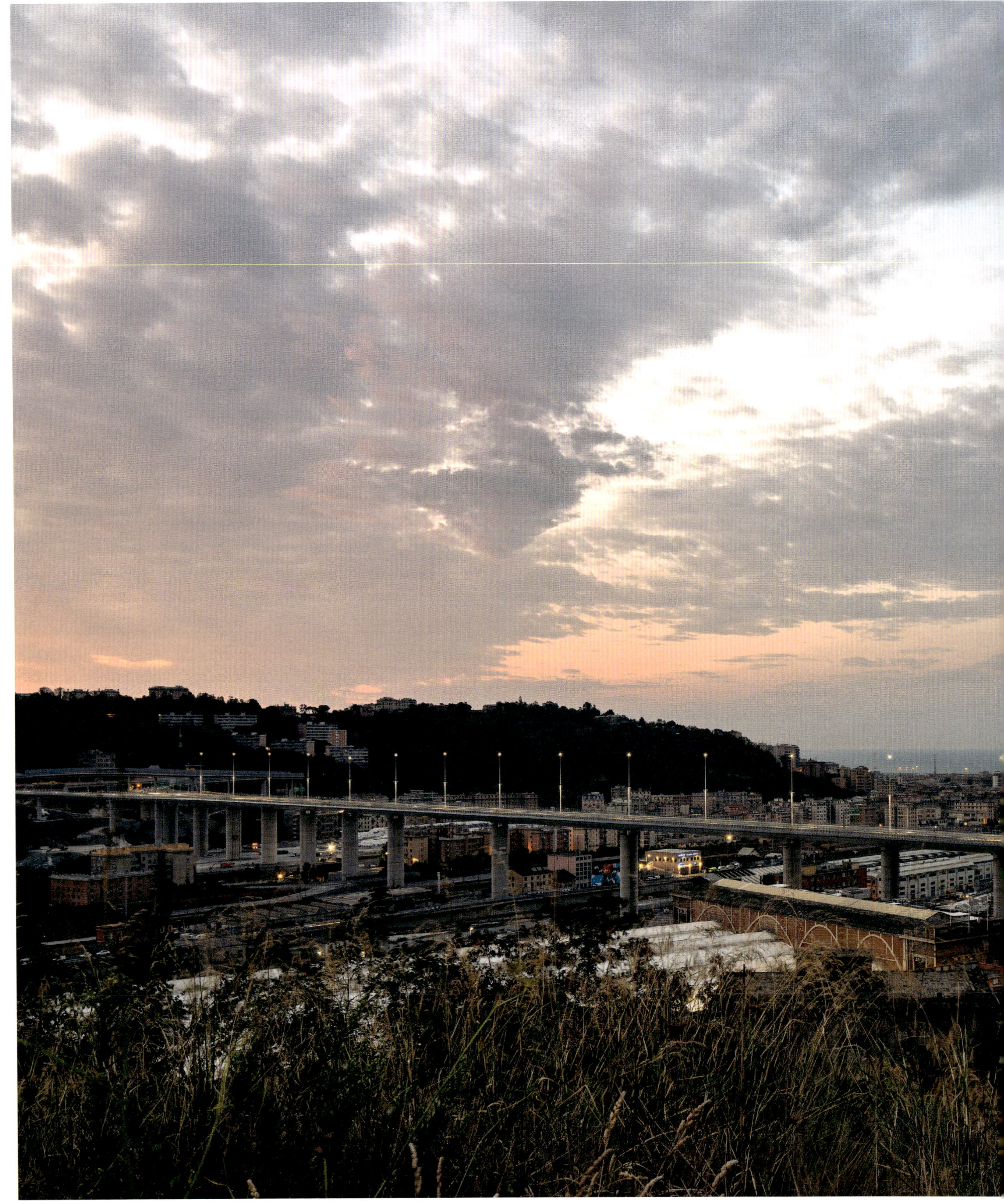

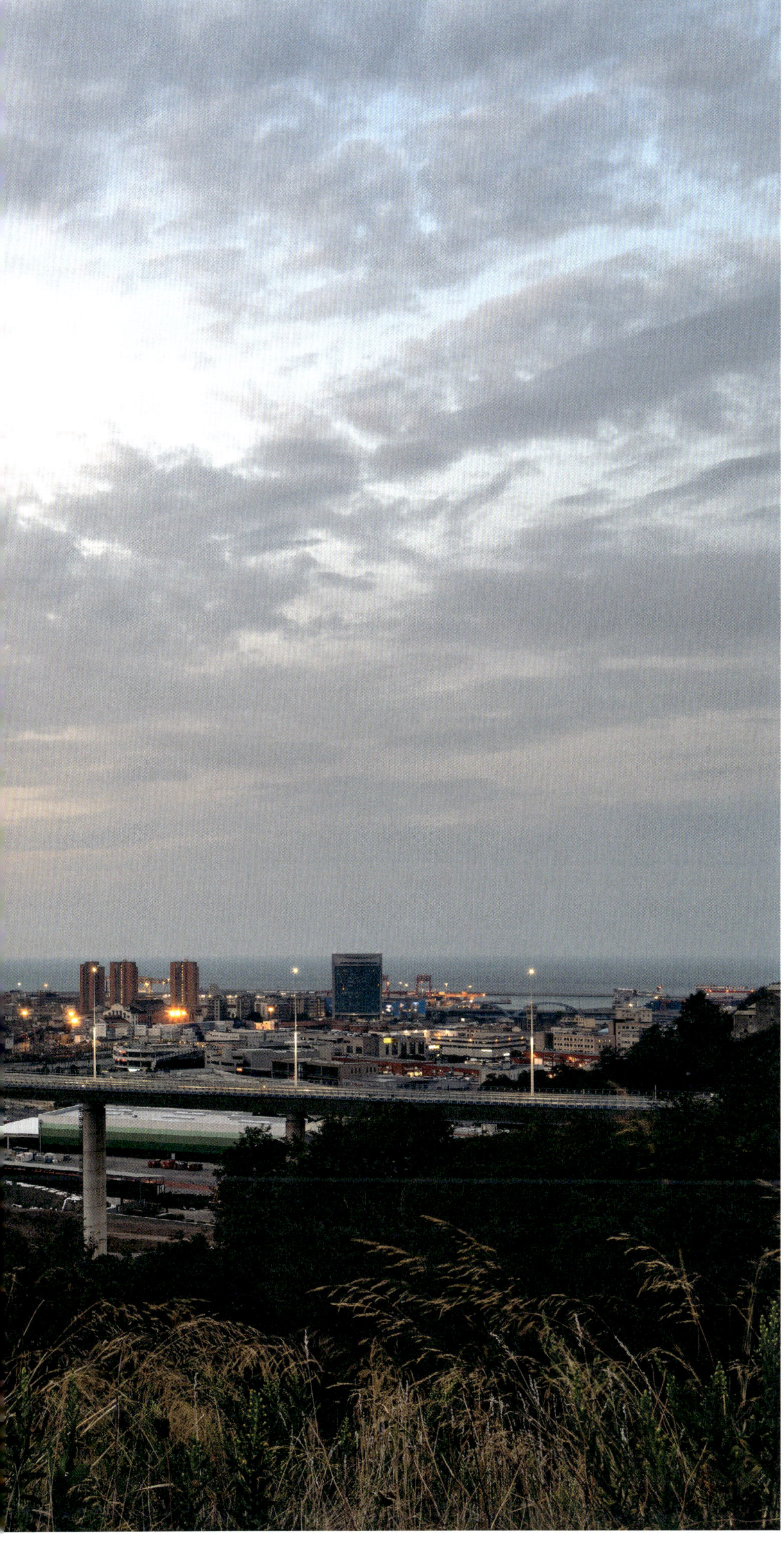

RINA

With almost 160 years of experience in a vast range of industrial sectors, RINA is a multinational that helps its clients to build resilient and successful businesses. Through a global network of 3,900 talented professionals who operate in 200 offices spread out across 70 countries, RINA supports the market operators throughout the life-cycle of their projects, assisting them in renewing their products, technologies and services.

Thanks to the operative company RINA Consulting, it filled the role of PMC for the whole project for the demolition of Ponte Morandi and the construction of the new Ponte Genova San Giorgio. The RINA teamworked alongside the Commissioner in the management of all the technical/engineering, procedural, administrative, and legal aspects, and in the quality control and the coordination of safety in the execution phase.

Special Commissioner for the Reconstruction of the Polcevera Viaduct of the A10 Highway Pursuant to Government Decree Law 4/10/2018

The Special Commissioner was supported by two sub-commissioners and the technical skills of a staff of about twenty people (architects, engineers from various sectors, legal experts, technical/administrative personnel) for the control of the proper execution of the projects.

Attorney General's Office

The Attorney General's office, set up with a Royal Decree dated October 30, 1933, no. 1611, is the legal body of the State tasked with providing legal consulting and defending the State Administrations in all the civil, criminal, administrative, arbitration, community and international disputes. Art. 10, section 3 of decree law 109/2018 tasked the Attorney's Office with the advocacy of the Special Commissioner.

This role was expedited not only with a view to representation and defense in the judicial processes brought against the Commissioner, but also through a constant consulting activity in the complex and multiple administrative and contractual activities that the Commissioner has been called upon to carry out.

The integration between these components created a strong synergy that confirmed the exent to which the PMC was a fundamental element in guaranteeing the project's success, especially as concerned meeting the deadlines for the different phases of the project.

The Witnesses

Giovanni Librici
COMMISSIONER'S OFFICE

"The most beautiful feeling was when I could read in the eyes of the people I worked with, whether during the most difficult or the least significant times, my own state of mind: the awareness of a person who had the privilege to bring to life and to see the growth, day after day a unique and indelible thing for one's city, one's fellow citizens."

Laura Zanoner
RINA

"If I think of how the presence of a woman in a work environment with a predominance of men is usually perceived, I can safely say that I found myself in a different world this time. The esteem, the collaboration, and the respect at every level made me feel like I was part of one big family, unified and ready to deal each and every day with problems both big and small ones that were in any case always resolved. Perhaps this is also why the bridge can be thought of as 'a miracle'"!

Caterina Traverso
RINA

"As I worked on this project I always thought about both the past and the present. No one will ever be able to forget what happened. Nevertheless, seeing the new bridge being built, day after day, was both a moving and unforgettable experience."

Domenico Napoli
COMMISSIONER'S OFFICE

"The tragedy of the bridge collapse proved once more that life is short. For those who built the bridge, this distressing thought will be mitigated by the marvelous feeling of having lived a part of one's life guaranteeing other people's safety."

Luciano Grasso
COMMISSIONER'S OFFICE

"I was constantly filled with emotion during these months of work. Powerful and engaging like the blowing up of the old bridge."

Michele Di Lecce
COMMISSIONER'S OFFICE

"I get emotional thinking back to the first time we were all together as a team, each of us with our different skills, as we began a project that was so relevant and vital to the city I live in."

Michele Iasoni
RINA

"Night, day, wind, snow, storms, but there was still just one goal for all of us: to build the bridge."

Angelo Massimo Figundio
RINA

"I had just moved to Genoa, and the Morandi viaduct was one of the things I admired about the city. Its collapse made me feel distraught. For me, rebuilding it was a matter of honor and pride, and it made me feel more 'Genoese.' Each time I crossed the walkway overlooking the viaduct, looked at the flowers that had been placed there in memory of the victims, I promised myself that the new bridge would be even better."

Erika Falone
COMMISSIONER'S OFFICE

"I had the honor of putting all my energies, my sense of commitment, and my skills at the service of my city. I believe there is no greater privilege."

Paolo Arvigo
COMMISSIONER'S OFFICE

"Succeeding in acquiring over 400 real estate units in a months' time was a huge professional challenge. But it was from a human point of view that it proved to be an absolutely unique and involving experience."

Franco Risso
RINA

"For me the project has been a concrete way to try to make sense of the tragic death of the victims of the collapse, honoring them with facts, and not just with hollow words. At the same time it has been an opportunity, as a Genoese citizen, to put my experience at the disposal of my hometown and my fellow citizens with a view to getting back to normal."

Fabrizio Mansueto
RINA

"Three years in one: condensing all of life in one year. Of the many things that this experience taught me, the management of time was the most meaningful. Anything can be done in the proper way, in the right amount of time, and it can be done well. All you need is the will to do it."

Alessandra Figliomeni
COMMISSIONER'S OFFICE

"Working on the reconstruction of Genoa's bridge was like playing for the national soccer team: you feel the weight of the privilege, but also the pride in contributing to a work that will represent our city in the world and that did not just connect two valleys, but the people who worked on it as well."

Claudia Gallone
COMMISSIONER'S OFFICE

"Commitment, a sense of belonging, involvement. Feelings that are unique."

Irene Marras
COMMISSIONER'S OFFICE

"For me this bridge is an alliance between our utopian idea of the world, and the promise made for a better reality."

Simone Gambula
RINA

"My experience in this project is not summed up with a sentence, but with a single word: 'challenge.' Challenges that make you deeply explore the ability you have at hand and in some cases you did not know you had. This project represented a great challenge and a unique moment of growth for all of us."

Gianluca Roggerone
COMMISSIONER'S OFFICE

"The horror of August 14, the city wounded and isolated. The silence. Then the immediate restart, the emotion and the commitment of the first days and the teamwork conducted without wasting a minute, at the service of the building site 'that never sleeps.' Genoa is a door open onto the Mediterranean and all of Europe. Its new bridge symbolizes peace and hope."

Paolo Corradeghini
RINA

"If I look at my own work on the Ponte San Giorgio building site, I imagine a very small brick in a huge project. But I also believe that it is only with the many contributions and all the elements of a large team that great things like this can ever get done. The evacuation operations during the controlled explosion of piers 10 and 11 of the old Ponte Morandi are definitely the ones with the highest level of tension and stress I have ever experienced professionally!"

Chiara Tartaglia
COMMISSIONER'S OFFICE

"This bridge will always be ours. It belongs to all those who, like us, experienced it firsthand, in their minds, and in their hearts.... from the first day to the last."

Katia Chiappori
COMMISSIONER'S OFFICE

"While working I came across a child who was on the viaduct with his grandparents the day Ponte Morandi collapsed. I saw fear, despair, and incredulity in his eyes because of what had happened. In our offices I introduced him to my colleagues, and I showed him a model of the new bridge. His smile, projected into the future, became our hope."

Marcello Cademartori
RINA

"When I first began working, I never would have thought I would one day take part in such a stimulating project, an emotional involving and technically challenging one. It was a journey made up of photo stills that will forever be etched in my mind and that will always be an unrepeatable experience. What will instead be repeatable is the teamwork that characterized this period."

Andrea de Napoli
COMMISSIONER'S OFFICE

"Having contributed to restoring Genoa's bridge and reconnecting Italy once more: a professional and human experience that cannot be erased."

Matteo Loggia
RINA

"For me personally it is a source of pride to have taken part in this project that is so unique from every point of view, both in human and professional terms, and which I shared with a competent team that worked well together."

Emanuela Marighella
COMMISSIONER'S OFFICE

"The direct contact with the many people who have suffered dire consequences allowed me to get to know many different realities. Being able, along with the entire team, to offer them concrete help in a very short time filled me with great satisfaction and a feeling of strong solidarity."

Sergio Abbondanza
COMMISSIONER'S OFFICE

"'I build the bridge.' For the whole duration of the building site the words on my yellow helmet were the motivation, the motto, and the emblem of what this task meant to me. Knowing that I played an active part in the process that helped us to get back our bridge in the Polcevera Valley, in our city, for the Genoese people is a great source of pride."

Simone Novaro
RINA

"Very few breaks, skipped meals, sleepless nights, unending days, but also the confirmation of certain things and the discovery of other unexpected ones. The affection of my family that was always close to me and that never complained, the unexpected trust I received from my fellow workers from day one and that I hope I never betrayed."

Ginevra Beverini
COMMISSIONER'S OFFICE

"Days, nights, and months devoted to our greatest duty to give the city its bridge again. That is how this 'special' adventure all began. So much willingness and determination accompanied me along the way, as rapid as it was intense. The emotions ebbed and flowed and in the end the challenge was won, with pride in the heart of all those who were a part of the team."

Eriselda Lirza
RINA

"Besides the pride of a Genoese native for having made my contribution to the reconstruction, there are two emotions that will forever be etched in my mind: the feeling of emptiness when I saw the demolition of the old deck, and the excitement I experienced the first time I walked across the new bridge."

Maria Rosa Cosenza
COMMISSIONER'S OFFICE

"I was summoned to make my small contribution to a great team that had the difficult task of giving Genoa its bridge again. Each of us gave the best of themselves with no reservations, as well as they could. The miracle has come true, Genoa now has its bridge, beautiful and majestic. Everyone talks about the 'Genoa model' as an example of the utmost efficiency and efficacy."

Michele Mililli
RINA

"My feeling was that in this period of time my entire life was put aside so that I could make room for something more important. It was a mixture of satisfaction, fatigue, and frustration. Today, what prevails is the pride in having participated."

Federico Barabino
RINA

"In this late summer season, the building site is undergoing its final phase: many of the companies have left, and others are about to. It's sad, like when the people who run an amusement park leave the city. I too, in the office, have begun putting my papers and my thoughts in order: unexpected occurrences, emergencies, the fear of not being able to manage, the viaduct taking shape... I still need to find a synthesis for all this. But yesterday, when I saw the bridge completely lit up, I thought to myself: it was definitely worth it."

Gabriele Carere
COMMISSIONER'S OFFICE

"The strongest emotion was the pride I felt for having contributed to the realization of a huge work, which can be seen from below, while looking upwards. A work that deserves respect, that harbors memories, that conveys strength and equilibrium. And that will outlive us."

Francesca Rubino
RINA

"If someone were to ask me to use three adjectives to describe this experience, they would be: educational, complex, and unforgettable. This project asked each one of us to understand how far our consistency in and dedication to work could go. And to raise the bar still more."

Paola Silva
RINA

"This project, which was born out of an event that, when I think back to it, still brings tears to my eyes, made me appreciate even more the professional and human value of the colleagues with whom I had the pleasure and honor to work, and to experience firsthand the strength that joins people to overcome difficulties."

Matteo Brandani
RINA

"When I was asked to be part of the team working on the bridge, I accepted the task right away. The project was one of a kind, based on a different method for dealing with issues and conducted by a united team, all of which strongly aimed at a common goal. It was a challenge that was personally marked by devotion, commitment, proactivity, 'positive' tension, sacrifice, and a strong emotional charge—which derived from the memory of what had happened—and by the pride for having taken part in such an important and successful experience."

Simona Bonanno
RINA

"This beautiful, moving, touching project truly taught me a great deal. A project in which there have been beautiful times, hard ones, and sometimes sad ones too. All of this will be a 'moment' in my life that I will never forget, just as I will never forget all the people I worked with directly and that I met along the way."

Simone Dellacasagrande
RINA

"The experience of the project for the bridge meant calling into play my entire sense of civic responsibility, my professionalism, and my attention to detail. The objective has always been to guarantee the realization of a safe and reliable project."

Maurizio Florio
RINA

"This project has taught me to look behind the professional and find the person.
To look behind the sacrifice and see the devotion and the passion. It has taught me that hidden behind the tiredness is an inexhaustible reserve of energies. Ultimately, this project has taught me that there is no greater act of realism than to ask (and ask oneself) for the impossible and see it come to life."

Cinzia Pica
RINA

"Walking on the debris left over from piers 10 and 11 the day after the explosion was the most surprising, painful, and at the same time instructive experience of my entire career. Crossing under protective tarps we found ourselves before a landscape that looked like something out of the movies: the giant had collapsed upon itself just as it was planned according to the demolition project. At that moment I understood that I too, in my own small way, was doing my bit for the recovery of my city."

Antonia Vallarino
RINA

"Like everyone else, I lost hours of sleep, I worked hard, I unfortunately had to neglect my partner, my family, and my friends, because work on the bridge never stopped, like a running train until the bridge was opened up to traffic and even for some time after that... But when I crossed that bridge for the first time I experienced such a great emotion."

Fabio Nazzaro
RINA

"When they tell you that you're going to work on the building of an infrastructure that was part of a tragedy you are overwhelmed by very discordant feelings. Inevitably one's thoughts go to those who lost their lives and to those who feared they wouldn't make it. Out of respect for this, we worked quickly, with great professionalism, with attention and regard towards the people of that place, so that we could give them a new and safe bridge."

Antonio De Lorenzo
RINA

"...Being a part of this wonderful family that worked so hard to rebuild the bridge left me with a sense of pride and the memory of wonderful people, very special colleagues, which allowed me to deeply experience the relationship with a city that knew how to embrace me in spite of its wounds. These were important days, lived in the memory of those who, like me, first used their heart and then everything they knew and could have done."

Luigi De Prisco
RINA

"When I was a child, I would cross Ponte Morandi with my father, and the bridge always fascinated me. The immense concrete arches reminded me of America. Who knows why, but I imagined that somehow when I was older I would be involved with that bridge.
A year and a half ago the opportunity arose to participate in this project and my premonition came true!"

Federico Cisi
RINA

"Seeing the bridge grow, monitoring it, measuring it every day was a source of pride that I will cherish for the rest of my life."

Photographs
Andrea Botto

Graphic Design
Martina Toccafondi

English Translation
Sylvia Adrian Notini

© 2020 Mondadori Libri S.p.A.
Distributed in English throughout the World
by Rizzoli International Publications Inc.
300 Park Avenue South
New York, NY 10010, USA

ISBN: 978-88-918303-0-2
2021 2022 2023 2024 / 10 9 8 7 6 5 4 3 2 1

First edition: March 2021

This volume was printed at Errestampa. S.r.l., Bergamo
Printed in Italy

Acknowledgments

Andrea Botto wishes to express thanks
to all those who made this book possible

Ugo Salerno
Roberto Carpaneto
Cinzia Pica
Sabrina Carta
for having followed, supported, and promoted
the photographic project.

All the workers at Rina who were at the building
site, especially
Federico Barabino
Emilio Puppo
Antonia Vallarino
Laura Zanoner
Matteo Loggia
Paolo Corradeghini (for the photograph on p. 185)
Federico Cisi

Genoa Court Attorney General's Office
(for having authorized the publication
of the photograph on p. 199)
Ansaldo Energia S.p.A.
Leonardo S.p.A.
Circolo Angeli delle Mura
Municipio II Centro Ovest
Associazione La Piuma Onlus
Federico Casabella (for the photograph on p. 74)
Luca Pezzoni
Ilaria Poggi
Marco Balostro
Simone Noziglia
Emanuele Piccardo
Alessandro Cimmino
Angelo Zammarrelli

And very special thanks to the Rizzoli
editorial staff.